18257539

# West Goes East

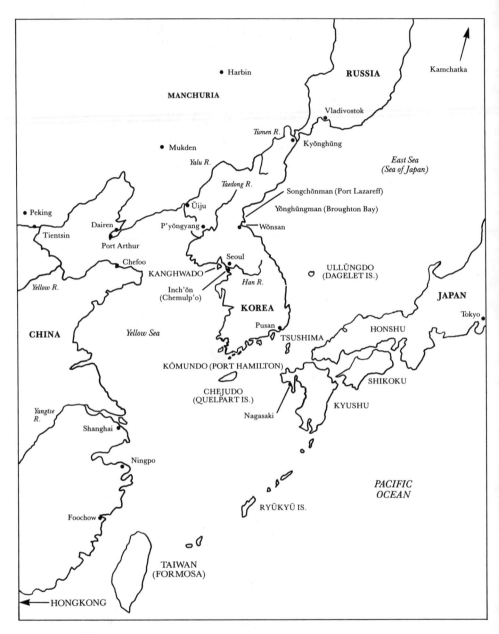

*Korea in the Late Nineteenth Century*

# West Goes East

## PAUL GEORG VON MÖLLENDORFF AND GREAT POWER IMPERIALISM IN LATE YI KOREA

Yur-Bok Lee

University of Hawaii Press • Honolulu

Photographs, with the exception of that of King Kojong, reproduced with permission of the publisher from Rosalie von Möllendorff, *P. G. von Möllendorff: Ein Lebensbild.* © 1930, Otto Harrassowitz Publishers, Leipzig.

**Library of Congress Cataloging-in-Publication Data**

Lee, Yur-Bok, 1934–
    West goes East.

    Bibliography: p.
    Includes index.
    1.  Korea—Foreign relations—1864–1910.
    2.  Möllendorff, Paul Georg von, 1847–1901.    I.    Title.
    DS915.37.L43      1988          951.9'02          88–20640
    ISBN 0–8248–1150–X

*The paper used in this publication meets the minimum requirements of American National Standard for Information Sciences—Permanence of Paper for Printed Library Materials*

ANSI Z39.48–1984

*To Grace, Edward, and their Friends, who live in a world increasingly less divergent between East and West*

I must confess von M [Möllendorff] has gone ahead very cleverly: perhaps he'll end by being King of Corea [Korea].

In 1883, Sir Robert Hart in Peking,
The Inspector General of The Maritime Customs Service of China (1863–1911)

Korea could maintain its independence and secure respect among its neighbors only through the development of modern education and industry. Although the country itself is small, its people are intelligent and its resources are rich; therefore, the peninsular kingdom can earn its rightful and due respect from its neighbors. The Korean people are more intelligent than the Japanese, who are likely to have difficulties in learning and adopting Western science. The Koreans do not have this particular problem; however, they will do well not to push forward too rapidly when changing from the old to the new.

In 1884, Paul Georg von Möllendorff in Seoul,
The Inspector General of the Customs Service and Vice Minister of the Office of Foreign Affairs of Korea (1882–1885)

# CONTENTS

# PREFACE

Although I did not begin the active research for this book until the academic year of 1975–1976, when I was on leave in Korea, I had started preparations for it by gathering the necessary materials and reading pertinent sources during a period of several years preceding my leave. In fact, I have worked on this study, off and on, for about fifteen years. During that time I made research trips to the libraries of Korea University and of Seoul National University, Seoul, Korea; the Institute of Modern History, Academia Sinica, Taipei, Taiwan; the National Archives and the Library of Congress, Washington, D.C.; the New York Public Library and the libraries of Columbia University, New York City; the libraries of the University of California, Berkeley; the libraries of Stanford University and of the Hoover Institution, Stanford, California; the library of the University of Oregon, Eugene; and the Yenching and Houghton libraries of Harvard University, Cambridge, Massachusetts.

My research in Seoul and Taipei was made possible by a leave of absence from my teaching duties at North Dakota State University, Fargo. Other research trips to different libraries in the United States were supported by a National Science Foundation fellowship and by a number of research grants that were made available to me by Archer Jones, now dean emeritus, of the College of Humanities and Social Sciences, North Dakota State University. In addition, the staff of the Interlibrary Loan Department of North Dakota State University, and especially Mrs. Deb Sayler, obviated further research trips by diligently acquiring masses of materials vital to the study.

For transliteration systems employed throughout the book, I used McCune-Reischauer for the Korean, Hepburn for the Japanese, and Wade-Giles for the Chinese. Some exceptions have been made for well-known place names (such as Seoul and Tokyo). My sincere appreciation is due to Curtis A. Amlund, Fred Harvey Harrington, Wayne Patterson, Lawrence H. Starkey, Robert R. Swartout, Jr., and others, who read portions of this manuscript at different stages of its preparation and made editorial, stylistic, or other helpful suggestions for its improvement. I am especially gratified to four readers, two of whom were in-house and the other two anonymous referees for the University of Hawaii Press, for their expression of extremely constructive comments for the betterment and publication of this book. Professor Emeritus Stephan A. Popel of North Dakota State University generously helped me in translating some Russian-language sources used in this book. To Damaris A. Kirchhofer of the University of Hawaii Press, who edited this manuscript in its final form, I owe my gratitude. I am also thankful to Mrs. Gail Hokenson and Mrs. Cathy Heiraas, who ably typed the entire manuscript, and to Kathy Franchuk, Paul Kelly, Thomas E. Himmelberger, and Robert C. Ferguson, four graduate assistants in the History Department at North Dakota State University, for serving as bridge between my office and our library and for generally helping me with the many routine but time-consuming tasks involved in the preparation of this book. My two children, Grace and Edward, to whom and to whose friends this book is dedicated, endured magnanimously the frequent neglect of fatherly duties while the material was researched and written both here in the United States and abroad. For the preparation of an index, as well as for other assistance with the book's publication, I would like to express my affection to my wife, Ae-Hyung. Though a number of people have made varying contributions, I alone assume ultimate responsibility for the whole work.

# West Goes East

# Introduction

Paul Georg von Möllendorff (1847–1901), a German diplomat, proved to be of significance to the history of late Yi Korea for several reasons: he served as the first "official" Western adviser to the Korean government from 1882 to 1885; he advised and guided the Korean government in foreign as well as in domestic affairs; he won from King Kojong and some of his adherents an unusually high level of trust; he attempted a radical reorientation of Korean foreign policy in cooperation with Russia, thereby involving the Chinese, Japanese, British, and Americans and irking them all; and he was a uniquely talented scholar-diplomat reminiscent of modern-day Peace Corp volunteers serving peoples of different backgrounds by learning and practicing their cultures and languages. For these reasons, the study of von Möllendorff's goals and accomplishments in Korea is an extremely fascinating pursuit.

As interesting as he and his career were, this is not a biographical study. Rather it is a study of Korea's response to foreign encroachment and its search for a new world order in place of the shattered East Asian world order that existed when von Möllendorff served as King Kojong's only "official" Western adviser. Since the main emphasis of this study is on Korean foreign policy during von Möllendorff's tenure, the international incidents and events that happened in and to Korea prior to his arrival are reinterpreted from the perspective of the 1980s or reanalyzed in hindsight rather than being recounted in full detail: the breakdown of the East Asian world order; the French attack on Korea in 1866; the American attack on

Korea in 1871; Japan's challenge to sinocentrism in the 1870s; the conclusion of the Korean-Japanese (Kanghwa) Treaty of 1876; the signing of the Korean-American (Shufeldt or Chemulp'o) Treaty of 1882; Sino-Japanese involvement in Korea during and after the *Imo* Revolt of 1882; the beginning of China's new imperialism toward Korea; and Kojong's futile faith in the United States. Even so, because of the great influence these events exercised upon the minds of von Möllendorff and Kojong in formulating a new foreign policy for Korea, they are briefly but properly examined in this study.

It should be noted herewith that although von Möllendorff worked for the German foreign service in China for several years before becoming an adviser to Kojong, his diplomatic services in China from the standpoint of modern German and European diplomatic history were negligible. Even his services in the Chinese Imperial Maritime Customs and on the staff of Viceroy Li Hung-chang were not appreciably important from the viewpoint of modern Chinese and East Asian history. However, his services in and to the Korean government turned out to be controversial and significant not only for the modern history of Korea but also for the diplomatic histories of China, Japan, Great Britain, Russia, and, to a lesser extent, the United States.

Although the focus of this study is on von Möllendorff's influence on Korean foreign policy, there is also an evaluation of his accomplishments and goals in domestic modernization projects, the object being to determine his general importance to modern Korean history. Moreover, since the Korean Customs Service he organized and operated had both domestic and international ramifications, special attention is given to the subject.

The main problem in studying von Möllendorff's contributions in Korea is the loss of his manuscripts. Paul Georg von Möllendorff's papers contained, among other items, his diary, his diplomatic documents (comprising his correspondences with the king of Korea, with Viceroy Li Hung-chang of China, and with other foreign diplomats), and personal letters exchanged with members of his family and friends. Although the papers had been in the possession of his wife, Rosalie von Möllendorff, they were unfortunately lost in the eastern part of Germany during World War II.[1] Even if the von Möllendorff papers had been preserved, it would still have been necessary to employ Korean, Chinese, and Japanese sources. In view of the loss of his papers, however, it becomes even more vital that sources in these languages be utilized because of his contacts with Korean, Chinese, and Japanese officials and also because of the keen and close attention that the governments of China and Japan paid to his role in Korean affairs and to his activities in the area.

To be sure, there are a number of studies touching on or covering some aspect or another of von Möllendorff's activities in Korea.[2] However, none of them presents any comprehensive or detailed analysis of the crucial diplomatic role that von Möllendorff played.[3] It is for this reason that this study is concerned with von Möllendorff's goals and accomplishments in foreign affairs in general and in particular with his search for a new world order for Korea in place of the decayed suzerain-dependency system. In seeking a new direction and a new course of foreign policy for Korea, he had to take several factors into serious consideration. First, he had to consider fully Korea's geopolitical situation. The policies he was to advocate for newly independent Korea had to make sense from the standpoint of geopolitics if they were to have any chance of being adopted and implemented by Korea and the other nations concerned. Second, as a talented Orientalist and scholar, he realized that Korea's political heritage (suzerain-dependency relations) would inevitably influence the concept and conduct of its new foreign policy.

Third, whatever innovative solutions he conceived for Korea, he fully understood that they must appeal to King Kojong and be supported by him. Otherwise, no effort would be made to implement his ideas; they would never be put into practice. Finally, he was convinced that, in view of the fact that the peninsula had been repeatedly subjugated by foreign military attacks or occupations before and during his tenure in Korea, whatever proposals he put forward must be designed to make Korea safe from further aggression. The impact that those foreign incursions into Korea made upon von Möllendorff and Kojong tremendously influenced the formulation and implementation of the new foreign policy.

Chapter 1 is devoted to an explanation of these factors. All of them make it imperative to provide a perceptive and concise account of Korea's traditional international system, of its historical relations with neighboring countries, especially with China, and of Kojong's rising faith in the United States (and subsequent loss of it). In addition, the reasons for and pertinent aspects of the repeated occupations of Korea, or of portions of its territories, by foreign troops, especially during von Möllendorff's tenure, must be explained. After all, if von Möllendorff had been appointed to serve the governments of Thailand or Japan, two countries with geopolitical, historical, and international factors different from those of Korea, then his advice to either of them would have been quite different from what he proposed to the Korean government.

Beginning, therefore, with an account of the importance of Korea's tributary relations with China, this study examines how Kojong came to seek a new world order whereby his kingdom would have a new "elder brother" (protective ally) even before the arrival of von Möllendorff in Korea. Kojong's first choice was the United States—a supposedly benevolent rising power. Von Möllendorff, correctly believing that a country of the New World thousands of miles away would have no interest in becoming Korea's senior partner, did not support Kojong's pro-American posture. Kojong himself, sensing a lukewarm attitude on the part of the U.S. government, decided to try his luck with the Japanese by unofficially supporting the pro-Japanese Progressives' coup attempt of 1884. Von Möllendorff, however, worried about Japanese ambition in Korea and mistrustful of the islanders, remained neutral (malevolently, to be sure) both before and during the coup. Loathing what he perceived to be Japanese "duplicity" before and during the coup and disgusted with Japan's imposition of harsh terms upon Korea after the incident, von Möllendorff secretly approached Kojong with the idea of making Russia, the largest neighbor of Korea and, in fact, the largest country in the world, the senior ally of Korea. Thereupon Kojong, deeply resentful of China's unprecedented interference in his country, clearly disappointed with the Japanese behavior toward his country during and after the coup, and grossly misinformed about Russia's capability and willingness to become involved in Korean affairs, gave tacit but strong support to von Möllendorff's pro-Russian policy.

In two extremely important incidents that occurred in Korea during von Möllendorff's tenure—the *Kapsin* Coup of 1884 and the British occupation of Port Hamilton in 1885—he did not play a dominant role, mainly because he was not the major actor in the events as a whole. The main players in the first incident were the Korean Progressive leaders and Japanese minister Takezoe Shinichirō in Seoul;

those in the second were the British diplomats and naval forces in East Asia. Nevertheless, the incidents and the personalities involved in them are here analyzed in detail and interpreted carefully, because both strongly influenced von Möllendorff as well as King Kojong, leading them to believe that Korea should seek a protective senior ally or partner that could stand up against the Japanese or the British, or any others for that matter.

Of all the cloudy and controversial issues surrounding von Möllendorff's services in Korea, one of the most thorny is whether he sought a Russian protectorship over Korea with or without Kojong's approval. Not only many Western diplomatic historians but also some of the most distinguished Korean diplomatic historians insist that von Möllendorff did so without Kojong's support or knowledge.[4] This study places due emphasis on the subject as well as on other important issues, such as (1) how von Möllendorff attempted to adopt a policy of "rejecting China and allying Korea with Russia"; (2) how the Imperial Russian government responded to such a radically new policy; (3) how their attempted realignment troubled the Japanese and Chinese governments and worried the American diplomats in Korea; (4) how this policy alarmed the British and provided an excellent excuse for their occupation of Port Hamilton (Kŏmundo), which they had earlier seized on account of the Afghan crisis; and (5) why this new foreign policy failed and caused von Möllendorff's downfall but ultimately made an impact upon Korea and left it with some significant legacies. Special attention is given to the question of whether Korea's (Kojong's and von Möllendorff's) search for a new protective senior ally, even after it had supposedly become independent, was influenced entirely by the traditional elder brother-younger brother concept or was predominantly dictated by geopolitical factors and by the reality of Korea's weakness.

Although King Kojong and his independent-minded advisers made another bid for a Russian protectorship in 1886 without von Möllendorff's direct participation, the incident is examined carefully here because (1) it was von Möllendorff who had been mainly responsible for causing King Kojong to become and remain pro-Russian; (2) the new Chinese resident in Korea, Yüan Shih-k'ai, attempted, in vain, to use the incident as a means of dethroning Kojong; and (3) von Möllendorff, who was in China while the incident took place in Korea, ironically and blindly defended Yüan's behavior after the crisis was over. Attention is also given to von Möllendorff's brief return to Korea in 1888 and his disputes with Owen N. Denny, his successor in Korea, on the Sino-Korean status and on the need for Korean regeneration and independence, a subject on which the German showed an almost radically shifted position by 1888.

The study also looks at how differently von Möllendorff and Kojong should have responded to the problems caused by new Oriental and old Western imperialism toward Korea. While nothing is wrong with a historical approach that searches only for "precisely what happened" (as Leopold von Ranke put it) and nothing more, it would probably be more desirable and relevant to the real world if more history books and essays were concerned also with "what should have been."

Moreover, good books of history or political science will on occasion attempt to convey a message or lesson as, for example, John K. Fairbank's *United States and China* and Edwin O. Reischauer's *Wanted: An Asian Policy* do so efficiently. In prefacing the fourth edition of this now-classic work, Fairbank flatly states that "like any sincere professor I aimed in writing this book to explain China to Americans so we could live in peace and friendship."[5] Likewise, Reischauer, in his provocative study, extends a wise message to American leaders and public for formulating a farsighted and intelligent policy toward Asia.[6] Surprisingly, none of the studies examining the diplomatic history of the late Yi dynasty attempts to convey any message or lesson, except for Hilary Conroy's *Japanese Seizure of Korea*.[7] In my own study, I deliberately strive to convey a message to the Koreans and others who, because of initial failure, started late and thus have yet to catch up with Japan and many of the Western nations in coping with modern-day problems in political, economic, and technological fields. After all, if George Santayana's statement, "Those who cannot remember the past are condemned to repeat it," makes sense to Westerners, then it should also make equally good sense to Easterners.

All in all, therefore, I concern myself not only with how and why Kojong and his foreign policy adviser von Möllendorff acted the way they did in coping with newly created international problems but also with how differently they should have acted to meet the new challenge. In addition, I place emphasis not only on how Western and Chinese expansionists approached the Korean leaders before and after 1882 but also on how differently they should have approached them. Another focus I give in this study pertains to what historians describe as "might-have-been" or "counter-factual" propositions regarding historical figures and events. Such approach makes the study of history not only interesting but meaningful and therefore obligatory.

This study has been researched and written in the spirit of human progress and with the idea that man's advance toward a more enlightened society and higher levels of modernization (in terms of minimizing ignorance and disease and of improving agricultural production and general living conditions) has been and still is not only desirable but ultimately inevitable, and that the sooner the leaders of the developing nations realized this, the better the results were for themselves and their peoples.

If my study seems Sinophobic in tone, that is not because of an anti-Chinese philosophy, which in fact I do not hold, but because of my belief that it would be bad enough for a highly advanced and prosperous country to impose its will on a technologically and politically weak nation without any regard whatsoever to the welfare and interest of that nation; and that it would be even worse for a degenerated country such as nineteenth-century China, unable even to take care of itself, to try to impose its will on a tiny neighbor (Korea) striving to improve itself. Furthermore, as weakened and decayed as the Ch'ing dynasty became by the 1880s, there still would be reason to defend the virtues of this new imperialism, but only if the Chinese policy of interventionism in Korea had done something good for the betterment and salvation of the Chinese as well as the Koreans. In view of the fact that the Chinese policy of interference in Korea eventually brought nothing but disaster to the Koreans and to the Chinese themselves, China's new imperialism in the peninsula kingdom after 1882 can hardly be praised. If I were to inquire into the Russian policy toward Korea around the turn of this century, I would sound equally Russophobic for the same reasons. On the other hand, if I were to write about T'ang China–Silla Korea–Heian Japan, or about Ming China–Yi Korea–Ashikaga Japan during a period when China's influence on Korea and Japan were tremendously beneficial to them, I would then sound like a strong Sinophile.

While in general a thematic approach is used in each chapter to give emphasis and crystallization to the main theses of this study, the chronological approach is also applied throughout the work in a conscious effort to present and interpret in an orderly and clarifying fashion many of the much-complicated diplomatic events that took place in Korea during and following von Möllendorff's tenure. Kojong changed his title from king to emperor in 1897; I have therefore used the latter title in reference to him for the period following this date.

Although my message is meant to be directed toward the Koreans and other East Asians still in the developing stage of their modern history, the study is written for a larger audience of students in East-West relations as well as for the public at large unversed but interested in international relations, in both Western and Asian countries. Inasmuch as this study purports to explain, clarify, analyze, and interpret the foreign policies and behavior of the Korean government under the influence of von Möllendorff rather than to mystify them in the name of the adage "East is East, and West is West; and never the twain shall meet," the book should have an appeal not only to those who believe that East shall never become like West but also to those who believe that East (Japan, South Korea, Taiwan, and others) is destined to become more and more like West.

# CHAPTER 1

# Korea's Entrance into the International Community

## Korea and the East Asian World Order

According to the traditional East Asian world order, Korea was a dependency (tributary) of China. From the perspective of China and of its dependencies, their suzerain-dependency relations had been ordained by *li* (the right principles), deeply rooted in the teachings of Confucianism.[1] Although the origin of Korea's tributary ties with China dates back to the fourth century A.D., the relationship reached its consummate stage between Ming China (1368–1644) and Yi Korea (1392–1910), following the termination of Korea's unhappy relations with the Yüan dynasty (1279–1368) in China. The Yi dynasty, based on neo-Confucianism, thoroughly embraced the sinocentric view of the world order and became the most important and closest dependency of Ming China.[2]

While Korea's tributary relations with the Ming were harmonious, its relations with the Manchus started out on a stormy basis. After establishing the new state of Ch'ing in southern Manchuria in the 1620s, the Manchus demanded the submission of Korea. Korea refused, considering them to be illegitimate rebels. Twice, in 1627 and 1637, the Manchus sent troops to force Korea to accept their demands. Thereafter, Korea again became a tributary—this time to the Ch'ing state—by signing the Treaty of Samjŏndo of 1637.[3] After conquering China and establishing the Ch'ing dynasty (1644–1911) at Peking in 1644, the Manchus restored the traditional system of suzerain-dependency relations with Korea.

9

The most important features of the tributary relations between China and Korea were the exchange of envoys, symbolic and ceremonial observations, and barter trade. In addition to dispatching one regular tributary mission annually, Korea sent several embassies to China on such special occasions as the accession or death of a Chinese emperor and that of a Korean king and queen.[4] Whenever a new ruler took over the Korean throne, he would request an investiture from the Chinese emperor, who in response would send edict-bearing envoys to confer upon the new king an imperial patent of appointment. The Chinese emperor would send a command each year for the admonition and instruction of the Korean king. As a symbolic act of submission, Korea would also receive a Chinese calendar arranged in terms of the reigning dynasty of China. In communicating with the Chinese government, the Korean king was required to correspond with the Board of Rites, not with the Chinese emperor directly. In addition, there were barter trades, arranged by both governments.[5]

It should be noted that because of the importunate experiences Koreans had had with the Mongol rule of Korea (1231–1356), with the Japanese invasion and destruction of Korea (1592–1598), with the Manchus in the 1620s and 1630s, and with the Catholics who preached, among other things, against the doctrine of ancestor worship (since the end of the eighteenth century), the Confucian-oriented Korean authority became xenophobic. Even after normalizing its relations with Tokugawa Japan in 1609 and with Ch'ing China in the 1640s, Korea desired and maintained only minimum contact with these neighboring nations. The Korean reservation toward the Ch'ing dynasty was partly because of the latter's non-Han origin and partly a result of the forcible way Korea had been made to become a tributary to it.

Even so, as long as Korea's relations were confined mainly to China and also to Japan, another state within the sphere of the East Asian world order, the suzerain-dependency system between China and Korea had worked fairly well. After the Opium War (1839–1842), however, a new factor was introduced. Western powers began to disturb the East Asian world order by successfully imposing unequal treaties first on China (1840s) and then on Japan (1850s) and by conducting diplomatic relations with these Eastern nations on the basis of the Western system of international laws and rules.

From their tributary missions to China, the Korean leaders had learned of the consequences of the Opium War and of the "humiliation" that the Chinese had suffered at the hands of the Western "barbarians." In the 1850s and 1860s they were especially shocked to learn of the Anglo-French occupation of Tientsin and even of Peking itself, of the flight of the emperor, and of the burning of the Summer Palace.[6] In general, however, Korean knowledge about Sino-Western relations and about the nature of Western expansionism was rather one-sided and limited. With only a half-truthful understanding about China's foreign policy problems and with a distorted view of the rest of the world, the Korean leaders, and especially the Taewŏn'gun (r. 1864–1873),[7] came to believe strongly that not only Japan but even China had too easily yielded to Western demands and that Korea could and should keep the Western "barbarians" out of their country forever. As the de facto regent to the young Kojong and as de facto ruler, the Taewŏn'gun and his adherents were determined to keep Korea away from the influence of Western "barbarians" and even from that of the Japanese, whom they considered as "traitors" for their quick adoption of Western ways.[8]

Yet it was inevitable that sooner or later not only the Westerners but the Japanese would make serious attempts to open Korea for trade, in order to guarantee the humane treatment of shipwrecked mariners or for religious purposes. It should be noted that according to traditional Korean laws, Western mariners shipwrecked off the Korean coast were to be humanely treated and sent to China to be released to their homelands.[9] As for willfull violators of Korean law, they were to be put to death. So far as any formal diplomatic and trade relations with the West were concerned, the Koreans considered them illegal and undesirable. Whenever Westerners would request such relations, the Korean government would reject them and refer the subject to the Board of Rites in China. Thus, the West appealed to China either to assume responsibility over Korea or to urge its tributary to negotiate with Western countries directly. China, in fact, did neither.

Uncertain of China's responsibility over Korea, the British asked the Board of Rites in 1832 to clarify its relations with Korea. The Board of Rites replied that Korea was a tributary of China and that a tributary state could not engage in foreign commerce.[10] In 1845, in response to a British request for a clarification of Korea's status in relation to China, the Chinese government advised the British, in a confusing dictum, that China was not in a position to open a tributary state for international trade, inasmuch as it was not a part of China.[11] The contradiction was that a tributary state could not open itself to foreign trade because it was not independent.

After Korea came to share a common border with Russia in 1860, a number of Korean peasants and laborers emigrated into an agriculturally more fertile area of Siberia with the encouragement of the local Russian officials. The Korean government, however, repeatedly asked the Board of Rites to persuade the Russian authorities to discourage Korean immigration. Although the Board of Rites then asked the Tsungli Yamen (the Foreign Office) to negotiate with Russia on behalf of the Korean government, the Tsungli Yamen rejected the request on the grounds that such negotiations should be undertaken by the Korean government itself.[12] Thus already in the 1860s, the Board of Rites and the Tsungli Yamen were unable to establish a uniform and clearly defined policy on advising Korea in dealing with Western powers. In the 1860s and the early 1870s China finally declared to the French and Americans that Korea was sovereign and independent enough to make its own decisions on matters of trade and religion.

To the Westerners attempting to pry open the closed door of Korea, there seemed to be much contradiction, confusion, and inconsistency in the Chinese position vis-à-vis Korea, and the question as to why this was the case (as Westerners saw it) was an interesting and important one. To begin with, the international rules that governed the relations between China on the one hand and its dependencies on the other were radically different in their premises from those that governed Western international relations, particularly as regards their profoundly different assumptions on the concept of sovereignty. In the Western international system each independent nation possesses complete and equal sovereignty in dealing with other independent nations. In the modern world, moreover, Western nations accept the premise that each sovereign and independent nation has not only the right but the obligation to enter into treaty relations with other independent and sovereign nations.

In the Confucian East Asian world order, however, only the Chinese emperor, answerable only to Heaven, has absolute and complete sovereignty; the sovereignty of China's dependent kings is theoretically subordinate to the ruler of the Celestial Empire. It is true that, in general, the king of Korea was regarded as de facto sovereign and as independent in both internal and external affairs, so long as his relations were confined to China and other members of the East Asian world order. In theory, however, the king of dependent Korea was not "officially" a king unless and until an investiture was conferred upon him by the Chinese emperor. Thus, the sovereignty of the king of Korea was not as absolute as that of the Chinese emperor; it was certainly limited, at least in theory, in a way that the sovereignty of the Chinese emperor was not. Consequently, neither the Chinese nor the Westerners had any clear idea as to whether Korea in fact possessed the full sovereignty required for it to enter into treaty relations with other sovereign countries. Furthermore, in accordance with the Confucian teaching of *li*, the Korean leaders strongly believed and claimed that they were morally obliged not to come to terms with the Western "barbarians," even after China and Japan had been compelled to do so. Westerners who went to Korea during the mid-nineteenth century, as their predecessors had gone to China earlier, did not comprehend the philosophy and system of the East Asian world order. Nor did the Koreans understand Western international rules.

Another factor contributing to the confusion was that the treaties China had been forced to conclude with the Western powers following the Opium War dealt only with the ways in which China should conduct its diplomatic, trade, and other relations with the Western treaty powers; they said nothing about how its tributaries should deal with them. Thus, China naturally assumed that, although it might have to subscribe to Western international rules in its dealings with Western powers, in its dealing with its dependencies, on the other hand, nothing had changed and it could continue its age-old traditional practices. Partly because China opposed the Western concept of international relations that regarded the sovereignty of other nations as equal to that of China and partly because it was forced to accept the modern treaties, China had been as evasive and obstructive as possible in subscribing to the provisions of the treaties, yielding only if and when necessary. In the absence of any provisions relating to tributaries, the Chinese leaders felt fully justified in applying and maintaining the traditional practices in dealing with them. They believed that, while it may be granted that the Middle Kingdom was no longer the center of the universe vis-à-vis the Western powers, it still occupied that central position as far as its tributaries were concerned.

Finally, the Chinese government, rather than asserting and taking a uniformly consistent, steady, and constant position on the issue, invariably shifted and drifted in its stand on relations with Korea, thereby making a confusing subject even more confusing, illogical, and contradictory in the minds of the Westerners. The illogic and contradictions of China's posture with regard to the opening of Korea became even more evident when compared with the stubborn and consistent position taken by Korea evincing absolutely no desire or interest in entering into modern treaty relations with the West.

## French and American Attacks on Korea (1866–1871)

Because of the philosophical incompatibility between Confucianism and Catholicism, the Christian rejection of ancestor-worship, and the illegal entry and proselytizing of French priests in Korea (since the 1830s), the Korean authority embarked on a long history of persecuting French missionaries and native converts.[13] In the early 1860s, the French legation at Peking pressured the Chinese government for mediation in order to inquire into Korean persecution of French missionaries in Korea. As before, the Tsungli Yamen rejected the French request on the grounds that China was not in a position to advise Korea on religious matters, although it was a tributary of China.[14] Nonetheless, realizing that this time the French would take drastic military action against Korea, the Board of Rites secretly sent the Korean government a notice of the impending French invasion.[15] Contrary to what Mary C. Wright claims, the Board of Rites did not advise the Korean government to negotiate with the French.[16] If China had strongly advised Korea to come to terms with the French, as it in fact did between 1874 and 1876 with regard to Japan, then even the Taewŏn'gun's regime would have heeded the advice, thereby avoiding unnecessary bloodshed. After all, China was then still the one and only elder brother of Korea.

Irked by China's "noncooperation" and angered by Korea's "act of savage barbarity" the fiery new French minister, Henri de Bellonet, declared that since China had refused to apply the Treaties of Tientsin (providing for the right to do missionary work) to Korea, he would punish the Korean government.[17] Without any authorization from the Paris government, Minister Bellonet dispatched Admiral Pierre-Gustave Roze's squadron of seven ships and six hundred men to Korea. After inflicting severe damage on the Korean defenders and their properties at Kanghwa Island, Admiral Roze withdrew from the Korean coast.[18] The Koreans, however, interpreted the French withdrawal as their own victory and became even more xenophobic than before.

Meanwhile, China missed another opportunity to advise or influence the Korean government to negotiate in a peaceful manner with the West—this time with the United States. In 1866, before the French attack, the *General Sherman,* an American ship consigned to a British firm (Meadows and Co.), had sailed to Korea, ostensibly for trade. Because of confusion and misunderstanding between its crew and the Koreans, the ship had been burned and the crew killed.[19] In response to American minister Anson Burlingame's request for mediation on the matter, the Tsungli Yamen stated that, although Korea was a tributary of China, the only actual connection between the two countries was "ceremonial."[20] At the emperor's order, however, the Board of Rites sent a note to Korea, informing it of imminent American action.[21] Again, quite contrary to Wright, the Board of Rites did not advise the Korean government to negotiate with the Americans in a conciliatory manner.[22]

Meadows and Co., reacting strongly, sought American and British aid in winning redress for the "wrongs" the company believed to have been committed against its ship and crew.[23] The American secretary of state, William H. Seward, without knowing that the earlier French expedition to Korea had been an unauthorized action and angered by the Korean destruction of the *General Sherman,* boldly proposed to French minister M. Berthemy in Washington that a joint expedition to Korea be mounted to obtain satisfaction for the murders of the French and Americans.[24] Even Russia was asked to join the proposed expedition.[25]

If any combination of the four governments (the United States, France, Russia, and Great Britain) had decided to punish Korea by sending a joint expeditionary force, the result would have changed the course of modern Korean history in a significant way. If, for instance, the combined Western forces had blockaded the sea and the Han River route (on which Seoul was dependent for its food supplies from other provinces) for a prolonged period of time, then even the Taewŏn'gun would have been forced to come to terms with them. In view of the uncompromising xenophobia of the Taewŏn'gun's regime, the only way that Korea could have been brought to terms with any Western powers would have been for those powers either to have mounted an expedition sufficient to invade Korea and inflict unacceptable damage and then to have forced treaties upon it, in the way that the Manchus had done in the 1620s and 1630s, or for China to have advised Korea in no unclear terms that it had better come to terms with the West, as it did later in the mid-1870s. Either eventuality would have made Korea a member of the international community and initiated its modernization just that much earlier. But Napoleon III of France, embarrassed by Admiral Roze's unauthorized action, which had been a fiasco, encumbered by the necessity of withdrawing his forces from Mexico, and preoccupied with the Annam crisis, declined Seward's proposal.[26] As for the British, they did not think that the destruction of the *General Sherman* and its crew was a serious enough infraction to justify involvement in the incident. The Russian government took the view that the whole incident was none of its business and let the American government handle the situation. As it turned out, two relatively small expeditions to Korea (French and American) spaced five years apart (and without any strong advice from China until 1874) stiffened Korea's resistance against the West.

In the meantime, the U.S. government decided once again to try its luck with Korea. In 1871, Washington directed Minister Frederick F. Low in Peking to proceed to Korea to inquire into the reasons for the destruction of the *General Sherman* and its crew in 1866 and, if feasible, to conclude a shipwreck and trade convention with the Hermit Kingdom as well.[27] Unable to obtain cooperation from the Chinese government, an American expeditionary force, consisting of five ships and 1,230 men and led by Minister Low and Admiral John Rodgers, proceeded to Korea. Failing to receive a satisfactory response and explanation from the Taewŏn'gun's regime, the Americans decided before their withdrawal to "punish" Korea by destroying the forts of Kanghwa Island, which involved the killing of at least 250 Korean defenders with the loss of only three American lives.[28] As with the French withdrawal earlier, the Koreans were convinced that they had won the battle, for the Americans did leave in the end. The Americans' eventual withdrawal "brought the Taewŏn'gun's anti-Westernism and seclusion policy to a climax."[29] No wonder that the American attack, as Minister Low complained to the Department of State, which "would have produced a profound impress upon any other government," had "no or little effect" on the Korean government.[30] Low's assessment of the Korean scene was essentially correct because, after the American withdrawal, such important leaders as Kim Pyŏng-hak and Yi Hang-no were still advising young Kojong that it was not only desirable but also quite possible for them to keep Westerners out of Korea forever.[31]

The year 1871 proved to be significant to East Asian countries in another way: Japan successfully pressured China to conclude a treaty on the basis of sovereign equality and of modern international law.[32] Now that Japan, once its tributary, had become equal in status to China, Chinese leaders should have realized that the age of sinocentricism was fast approaching an end. But apparently they did not. As far as Korea was concerned, the conclusion of a modern treaty between China and Japan on the basis of complete equality was not only shocking news but an amazing disclosure. First China had been humiliated by the Western "barbarians," and now Japan, whom Korea had at best regarded as its own equal among states theoretically subordinate to China, had become equal to China.

In the mid-1870s another important Sino-Japanese incident occurred that further damaged, if not destroyed totally, the sinocentric East Asian world order. Following the Ryūkyū-Taiwan incident of 1871–1874, in which the Japanese government successfully forced the Chinese government to indemnify families of the Ryūkyū Islanders who had been shipwrecked off the shores of Taiwan and killed by the Taiwanese, Japan compelled China to recognize implicitly its claim to suzerainty over the Ryūkyūs.[33] China "lost" the Ryūkyūs, one of its three most important tributaries, to Japan largely because it tried to retain them with the old argument of suzerain-dependency relations—claiming suzerainty over the tributary while disclaiming any responsibility for it. As for Japan, its daring venture turned out to be the second successful challenge to the traditional East Asian world order within five years.

After "losing" the Ryūkyūs to Japan, the Chinese leaders should have been able to see that, in the modern world, their ploy to keep their dependencies under control by appealing to the traditional argument would never be acceptable. Had the Chinese leaders been more far-sighted, realistic, and flexible in the late 1870s and early 1880s, they would have been able to utilize the lessons of the Ryūkyū-Taiwan incident in coping with the Korean problem, which was being caused by the assertion of Western and Japanese interests in the peninsula.

## The Japanese Move into Korea

Meanwhile, in Korea in 1873, the twenty-three-year-old Kojong had assumed full responsibility for the government of Korea. The reasons were twofold: (1) although the Taewŏn'gun's anti-Western and anti-Japanese policy had commanded popular and majority support, he made many enemies out of conservative literati and bureaucrats by depriving them of their power in favor of royal prerogatives and by 1872 they were pushing for his retirement; (2) in 1873 Kojong and his ambitious wife, Queen Min, who was anti-Taewŏn'gun, engaged in a power struggle against their father, the consequence of which was the semiretirement of the old regent.[34] Kojong was an alert, flexible, and pragmatic young man, willing and curious to learn about what had been happening in China, Japan, and the rest of the world. Since his main source of information about the world was largely members of the Korean tributary missions to China, Kojong often held long and inquisitive sessions with envoys who had returned from China.[35] Among them were Yi Yu-wŏn, Pak Kyu-su, and Chŏng Kŏn-jo.

In August of 1874, the Chinese government reversed its position toward Korea and changed from a policy of noninterference to one of extended advice in favor of Korean negotiations with the Western powers. Approving the memorial of the Tsungli Yamen,[36] the Chinese emperor, T'ung-chih, ordered the Board of Rites to send a secret communication to Korea, advising the king to concede to the French and American demands by negotiating treaties with them. The secret communication stated that the Japanese, after completing their expedition to Taiwan, might make an attack against Korea and that if the French and Americans were not appeased, they might join the Japanese in attacking Korea, which would be disastrous to the Koreans.[37] This secret communication turned out to be a significant turning point as far as Kojong's new outlook toward the world was concerned. After a great deal of debate with his advisers, Kojong became willing to make accommodations first to Japan and then to Western powers.

While King Kojong was becoming more flexible and realistic toward Japan in the mid-1870s, the moderate Ōkubo Toshimichi government in Japan was winning adherents to its "peaceful" way of handling the "Korean problem." What happened is this. Between 1869 and 1873, the newly organized Meiji government of Japan sent three different diplomatic missions to Korea in order to modernize its relations with Korea and to win Korea's official recognition.[38] But the Korean authorities under the Taewŏn'gun contemptuously refused to deal with the new Japanese government, not only because of the improper use of terminology in the Japanese correspondence but also (and probably more importantly) because of Japan's swift adoption of Westernization and modernization.[39] Korea's insulting and negative response to Japan's overture stimulated and intensified Sei-Kan ron (the "conquer Korea" argument) led by war minister Saigō Takamori.[40] In 1871, the Iwakura Mission, headed by Iwakura Tomomi, vice president of the Council and minister of the Foreign Office, had been sent to the United States and to the European treaty powers ostensibly to discuss the possibility of revising unequal treaties but actually to observe the West's technological, scientific, and industrial developments. After visiting only a few countries— including the United States, Great Britain, and Germany—the mission had to return to Tokyo in a hurry owing to the mounting crisis surrounding Sei-Kan ron. With the return of the Iwakura Mission in 1873 and the imperial edict against Sei-Kan ron, Ōkubo Toshimichi, imperial councillor Kido Kōin, and Iwakura Tomomi were able to adopt a more moderate Korean policy.[41] While managing to avoid an immediate war, the Ōkubo government nevertheless decided to put maximum diplomatic pressure upon China and at the same time resort to gunboat diplomacy in dealing with Korea, imitating what Commodore Matthew C. Perry had done to Japan in 1853 and 1854.

Thus, on the one hand, Japan in early 1876 sent the Mori Arinori Mission to China to persuade the government to advise Korea to negotiate with Japan and to clarify China's relations with Korea. Despite disagreement on the status of Korea, Mori was successful to the extent that China did in fact advise Korea to come to terms with Japan.[42] In addition, Japan also signed the Treaty of St. Petersburg of 1875 with Russia, securing tacit understanding that Russia would not interfere in case of a Japanese war with Korea. On the other hand, the Japanese—who had earlier successfully used gunboat diplomacy in the Taiwan venture—once again adopted in late 1875 the same kind of "armed diplomacy," sending a vessel, the *Unyō*, to survey the forbidden inland waters around Kanghwa Island where the Koreans had expelled the French and the Americans.[43]

Again the Koreans fired on the intruders. This action provided the Japanese government with a golden excuse to dispatch a naval force, consisting of six ships and four thousand men, led by General Kuroda Kiyotaka as ambassador plenipotentiary and Inoue Kaoru as vice-envoy. Within a month of their arrival at Kanghwa, the Korean-Japanese (Kanghwa) Treaty of 1876 was negotiated and signed. Despite strong opposition by the semiretired Taewŏn'gun and other powerful conservative forces in Korea, the conclusion of the treaty proved possible largely because of the Chinese advice of 1874 and partly because of Kojong's strong support for it.[44]

In order to place Korean–Japanese–Chinese relations in historical perspective, it is important to note that the Korean-Japanese Treaty of 1876—*unlike* the Sino-Japanese Treaty of 1871 (which had been concluded on the assumption of a genuine equality between two countries) and *like* the unequal Treaty of Shimonoseki of 1895 (in which a victorious Japan compelled the defeated China to concede inclusion of a most-favored-nation treatment clause)—was definitely unequal, to the disadvantage of Korea.[45] For example, Article 10 of the treaty provided for extension of extraterritorial jurisdiction to Japanese subjects in Korea. During the negotiations the Japanese also demanded a most-favored-nation treatment clause. The Koreans replied that the insertion of such a clause would not be necessary, since Korea had no intention of concluding any treaties with Western nations.[46] Yet Article 12 did provide that the Japanese would receive a most-favored-nation treatment in case Korea should sign a treaty with a Western power, which the Japanese expected to occur sooner or later but which many Korean leaders still believed avoidable. Worse still for Korea, the treaty had no provisions whatsoever for tariffs on import and export goods. This defect contrasted sharply with the provisions of the treaties Japan had concluded with Western powers, which, though depriving Japan of its tariff autonomy, had still stipulated that Japan had the right to collect import and export duties within the limits approved by the treaty powers (5 percent).

Although the Korean leaders failed to grasp its significance, the issue of foreign import and export duties, being directly related to their meager government revenue, was very important. In the case of the United States, about 50 percent of its government revenue was derived from tariffs in the early 1880s. As early as 1871, unhappy with the 5 percent tariff stipulated by the treaties Japan had concluded with Western powers, the Japanese government, through the Iwakura Mission, attempted to persuade the United States and other Western treaty powers to permit it to raise the tariff rate, but without success. In view of the fact that Japan had had tariff relations with Western treaty powers since the 1850s and was quite familiar with the issue, the Japanese negotiators could have initiated, and inserted, a tariff stipulation into the Korean-Japanese Treaty of 1876, but they completely ignored the subject. In a significant way Japan initiated modern diplomatic relations with Korea on a basis even more unequal than that underlying Western power relations with Japan. Commenting upon the treaty, British minister Harry Parkes stated in Tokyo that the Japanese government, which had lately complained of the extraterritoriality provisions of foreign treaties with Japan, had been careful to insist upon the right of jurisdiction over its own subjects in Korea.[47]

On the other hand, the treaty turned out to be a first step toward making Korea independent of China. For example, Article 1 of the treaty provided as follows:

Chosen [Korea] being an independent (autonomous) state enjoys the same rights as does Japan.
In order to prove the sincerity of the friendship existing between the two nations, their intercourse shall henceforward be carried on in terms of equality and courtesy, each avoiding the giving of offense by arrogance of manifestations of suspicion.

Thus, Japan recognized the independence and sovereignty of Korea and meant to use the treaty as a rejection of China's claim to suzer-

ainty over Korea.[48] As for China, it failed to realize the full implication of such a provision.[49] By its silence in the face of the Japanese
recognition of Korean independence, it in fact defaulted on its exclu-
sive claim over Korea. A most significant and pertinent question,
then, from the standpoint of East Asian interstate relations was this:
How did the provision affect the international status of Korea? The
conventional thesis on the subject is that the traditional status of
Korea was not affected by the treaty and that Korea remained a
dependency of China, regardless of what its provisions stated.

That interpretation of the status of Korea after 1876 has been
increasingly challenged, however, by a new one. It seems that, in
view of the fact that the treaty brought Korea, at least partly, into the
framework of the Western international system, Korea must have
become, at least partly, an independent and sovereign nation.[50] To
be sure, upon the conclusion of the treaty the Korean leaders
believed that the controversial provision was merely a reaffirmation
and reclarification of the traditional status of Korea vis-à-vis Japan
and so were slow to recognize its importance. Within a few years,
however, Kojong and some of his advisers, such as Ŏ Yun-jung,
came to understand the significance of the provision and the new
status it created for Korea. Thus, in November of 1881 Kojong proposed to Viceroy Li that negotiations be conducted for—among
other things—the termination of Korean tributary missions to
China and the stationing of a Korean commission (a diplomat) in
Peking.[51] Unfortunately for the cause of Korean independence and
progress, the Chinese leaders rejected Kojong's proposal. Kojong's
proposal indicates that even before the conclusion of the Korean-
American Treaty of 1882, the Korean monarch, influenced by the
Japanese diplomats in Seoul, made a feeble but significant attempt
to modernize Korea's tributary relations with China and even considered making his kingdom independent of China. As will be
shown, after 1882 he took several steps that were quite a bit more
daring to distance his country even further from China.

## The United States as Source of Korea's New World Order

The increase in Japanese diplomatic and economic activities in
Korea was a source of anxiety for Chinese leaders. Adding to their

uneasiness, Japan in 1879 formally incorporated the Ryūkyū Islands into its empire as Okinawa prefecture.[52] Many Chinese leaders began to worry that Korea might be next. Right or wrong, Li Hung-chang believed that Korea was strategically more important for the defense of Peking in north China than such southern Chinese coastal provinces as Kiangsu and Chekiang.[53] He correctly believed that the greatest danger to Korea and eventually to China as well would be from Japan. Another power that troubled Viceroy Li was Russia, which had pressured China to give up a Siberian territory larger than the state of Texas by concluding two treaties—the Treaty of Aigun of 1858 and the Treaty of Peking of 1860—and with whom it was having additional troubles over Ili in Sinkiang in the 1870s and early 1880s. Despite the Treaty of St. Petersburg of 1881 (which replaced the Treaty of Livadia of 1879), under whose provisions Russia returned most of Ili area to China, the Chinese leaders were worried about a Russian march into Korea, Manchuria, and Sinkiang.

As will be discussed later, so far as the reality of the Russian policy toward Korea in the early 1880s was concerned, the St. Petersburg government was interested mainly in concluding an agreement with Korea for limited trade and in resolving issues involving Korean immigrants in Siberia and the boundary between two countries rather than in territorial aggrandizement at the expense of Korea. However, the Chinese perception of Russian ambitions and of their threat to Korea was genuine.

In order to solve China's Korean problem, Li proposed to apply the principle of the balance of power to Korea—*i-i chih-i* (using barbarians to control barbarians).[54] He sincerely believed that balance-of-power politics had kept China from being exploited any more than it was and that in Europe and the Middle East the British had been skillfully applying balance-of-power diplomacy since the Crimean War of 1853 and 1856. His strategy was to persuade Korea to enter into treaty relations with the United States and other Western powers in order to check the ambitions of the Japanese and Russians there. In retrospect, it seems that Li was unwise in attempting to use the United States to enhance what he perceived to be China's interests in Korea.

To begin with, while Korea might be vitally important to China, strategically or otherwise, this was not necessarily so with the United

States, located thousands of miles away. Li should have realized—in view of the fact that President Franklin Pierce had rejected Commodore Perry's proposal for occupying the Ryūkyūs, the Bonin Islands, and Taiwan in the mid-1850s—that American interests in China, Korea, Japan, and the rest of East Asia must be rather limited. Bitterly disappointed with President Ulysses S. Grant's obvious failure in mediating the issue of the Ryūkyūs and dismayed by American discrimination against Chinese immigrants in the United States,[55] he should have known that even if the Americans had wanted to play a dominant and constructive role in Asia, events might not work out the way he wished. American treatment of immigrants from China should have warned him that the United States might not be respectful toward Chinese desires. Moreover, he should also have been able to see that his strategy of balance of power with regard to Korea would never work because not only was Russia stronger than China but even Japan was strong enough to challenge China.

Despite Viceroy Li's lack of knowledge and far-sightedness in international politics, the Ch'ing court generally agreed with his assessment of the Korean problem and situation. Thus, in 1881 the Chinese emperor placed Li in charge of Korean affairs, relieving the conservative Board of Rites of its responsibility in dealing with Korea.[56] Thereafter, Li directed Chinese policy toward Korea until the Sino-Japanese War of 1894 and 1895, after which Russia and Japan became dominant in the peninsula.

Even before Li was formally appointed to handle Korean affairs, he and other Chinese leaders were advising the Korean government to enter into treaty relations with Western powers. By 1879 and 1880, King Kojong and some of his important advisers were already in favor of opening Korea to the United States, although the majority of the literati and public were opposed to concluding modern treaties with Western "barabarians." In 1879 Li had advised Yi Yu-wŏn, a Korean leader visiting China, that Korea should try to cope with the ambitious nations of Japan and Russia by opening itself to friendly Western powers, particularly to the United States. Li argued that in Europe such small nations as Belgium and Denmark coexisted with the great powers because they were members of the international community and benefited from the protection of international law and the international balance of power. If Korea would enter into international treaties with the United States, France, Germany, and Great Britian, Li urged, then it would enjoy the same protection.[57] Li's attempt to compare the international status of Belgium with that of Korea under forthcoming treaties with the Western powers was grossly wrong, because when the "perpetual neutrality" and independence of Belgium had been guaranteed by the European powers at the London Conference of 1838 and 1839, none of the involved powers had meant to treat the country as if it were a vassal or colony. In the case of Korea, Li meant to expand and intensify China's already dominant influence rather than to jointly support and guarantee the independence and neutrality of the country. As for comparing the status of Korea with that of Denmark, the two situations can hardly be analogous, in spite of Denmark's thorny relations with Sweden. As misleading as his comparisons were, Li's advice still had an important impact upon Kojong and his supporters.

The most important source of Kojong's becoming pro-American, however, was probably the booklet *Chao-hsien ts'e-lüeh* (A policy for Korea), written by Huang Tsun-hsien, the Chinese counselor to the Chinese legation in Tokyo. In 1880, Huang and Ho Ju-chang, Chinese minister in Tokyo, urged Ambassador Kim Hong-jip of the Korea mission to Japan to deliver the essay to King Kojong. In it, Huang warned that the most urgent task for Korea was "to defend itself against Russia," whose troops had been stationed at the mouth of the Tumen River since 1860, and urged Korea "to become intimate with China, develop a friendly association with Japan, and conclude an alliance with the United States." So unlike Li, who considered Japan as potentially the most dangerous enemy to China and Korea, Huang regarded Russia as the most troublesome power. Huang also suggested that the Korean king "memorialize the Chinese Emperor to grant permission for a Korean envoy to reside in Peking permanently and also to allow Chinese merchants to trade in the open ports of Pusan, Wŏnsan, and Inch'ŏn, so as to prevent a monopoly by the Japanese merchants." So far as the United States was concerned, Huang had portrayed it as a powerful industrial state and yet as an anti-imperialistic, Christian, and moralistic country that usually supported weaker states against aggressive countries. Huang's perception of the United States was naive and only half-truthful at best. Unfortunately for Korea, however, and for his political career, Kojong was convinced of the veracity of Huang's artless misperception of the United States.[58] It should be clearly noted, on the other hand, that for the Koreans as well as the Chinese, it was nothing new to view the world order and political system in terms of morality or ethical rules. After all, both regarded the East Asian world order in terms of the Confucian teachings of *li*.

Kojong, therefore, on balance quite favorably disposed toward the United States, played a constructive role in opening his country to the American in 1882. In fact, Kojong played a much more positive role in 1881 and 1882 than either Emperor Tao Kuang had done in China in the early 1840s or Emperor Kōmei had done in Japan in 1853 and 1854 in opening their respective countries to the West.

The actual negotiation (January–April 1882) was conducted in Tientsin, China, between the self-appointed "plenipotentiary" Li and Commodore Robert W. Shufeldt. Although Kojong was strongly in favor of signing a treaty with the United States, there was much opposition to it by conservative literati and the followers of his own father, the Taewŏn'gun.[59] To overcome such opposition and resolve other pertinent problems, Kojong wanted the Chinese government to issue an edict ordering Korea to conclude a treaty with the United States. Li rejected the idea but still made himself a "plenipotentiary."[60] This was a radical departure from China's policy in the 1830s through the 1860s and even the early 1870s, when it repeatedly and loudly disclaimed any responsibility for Korea's actions. As for the American government, impressed with the Japanese success of 1876, it had decided to make yet another attempt to negotiate with Korea. American attempts to sign a modern treaty in the 1860s and 1870s had all been in vain. Commodore Shufeldt, who had been sent to Korean waters in 1867 to investigate the fate of the *General Sherman* and its crew, had maintained a strong hope and desire to bring Korea into the realm of "modern civilization" by concluding a treaty with it.[61] Having failed to negotiate with the Korean government through Japanese good offices, he had accepted Li's invitation to meet in Tientsin in 1880. After returning to the United States for new and furthur instructions, he and Li met again at Tientsin and concluded the treaty in the spring of 1882.[62] Shufeldt then proceeded to Inch'ŏn (Chemulp'o), where the treaty was signed on May 22 by himself for the United States and by Sin Hŏn and Kim Hong-jip for Korea.[63]

From the standpoint of the United States the most important provision of the treaty was the protection of American seamen and the
opening of trade, which it had sought since the 1860s.[64] So far as the
Korean government was concerned, however, the most important
part was the "good offices" clause of Article I, providing that the
other party would exercise good offices if either party should be
treated "oppressively or unjustly" by a third nation.[65] To the United
States, the term "good offices" implied no special obligation; it was
merely a sign of friendship couched in diplomatic language. But to
the Koreans the "good offices" clause meant that, henceforth, the
United States had not only a legal but a moral obligation to help
them diplomatically or otherwise in the event of an international crisis in Korea.[66] With a tragic history of being invaded and sacked by
the Mongols, the Japanese, the Manchus, and even by the French
and Americans in more recent years, being surrounded by neighbors larger and stronger than itself, and convinced that China could
no longer aid it when it needed help, Korea looked to the United
States as a kind of new "elder brother" that would willingly offer
"good offices" and other assistance in times of distress.

It is important to note that, unlike the Korean-Japanese Treaty of
1876, which had no provisions on tariff issues, the Korean-American Treaty of 1882 (in Article 5) set the import tariff on articles of
daily use at 10 percent *ad valorem,* on luxury goods at 30 percent, and
the export tariff on native products at 5 percent *ad valorem.*

Another important effect of the treaty was that it undoubtedly
strengthened the independence and sovereignty of Korea (along
with other treaties that Korea concluded subsequently). Korea's
treaty with Japan in 1876 had made it partly independent; its treaty
with the United States made it more independent, although one
could not argue that in 1882 it became completely independent
because, whether compelled or not, it kept sending tributary missions to China until 1894.

From the standpoint of China, the most important part of the
treaty was not any provision within the treaty itself but a separate
letter that the king of Korea sent to the president of the United
States. At the time of the Li-Shufeldt negotiations in Tientsin, Li
had insisted on inserting a statement into the text of the treaty stating that Korea was a dependency of China, although it was autonomous in both internal and foreign affairs.[67] Li contended that a writ-

ten statement of Korea's dependent status was necessary, so that other powers would not cause difficulties later on.[68]

What the distinguished Viceroy Li Hung-chang wanted was quite clear to Shufeldt. On the one hand, Korea was to deal with the United States as a sovereign and independent nation; on the other, Korea was to remain a faithful dependency of China; and in so far as the United States was concerned, it should support this dual status by agreeing to the insertion of this peculiar statement into the treaty provisions. Shufeldt vehemently rejected Li's ploy on the grounds that his government would conclude a treaty only with a fully sovereign and independent nation and that, moreover, the United States Senate would never ratify such a treaty as that proposed by Li. The result was a compromise whereby the king of Korea would write a separate letter to the American president, acknowledging Korea's dependent status in respect to China, which Kojong did.

Li believed that he had won at least a partial diplomatic victory and was quite certain that from then on he could use the United States to check Japanese and Russian expansionism into the peninsula and at the same time keep Korea as China's dependency.[69] Unfortunately for the Chinese government, however, the United States virtually ignored the existence and significance of Kojong's letter in diplomatic dealings with Korea and China. Even the Korean government itself, while conducting normal diplomatic relations with the United States, did not treat the letter as of much importance, although it did respond when reminded of the letter's existence and significance by the Chinese. It should be noted that whenever the Chinese wanted to justify their interference in Korean affairs vis-à-vis the United States, they referred to this controversial letter.[70]

The Japanese reaction to the Korean-American treaty was mixed. The Japanese disliked the fact that Shufeldt had concluded the treaty with Chinese rather than with Japanese help and that Shufeldt had accepted the Chinese insistence on the letter acknowledging Korea's dependent status, which they considered quite contrary to the spirit and letter of the Korean-Japanese Treaty of 1876.[71] On the other hand, Japanese leaders were pleased that—legally as well as diplomatically—the independence of Korea was strengthened by the new treaty and that Korea would soon and easily conclude modern treaties with other Western powers, thereby discrediting China's claim to suzerainty over Korea.[72]

From the viewpoint of the system of traditional East Asian world order, the Korean-American Treaty of 1882 proved to be one of the severest blows that China had suffered. In spite of the fact that the Korean-Japanese Treaty of 1876 had made Korea partly independent in terms of modern international relations, Korean leaders failed to grasp its importance until 1881 and as a result did not take full advantage of the treaty in the interests of their country. After 1882, Kojong and his adherents came to understand the implications of the treaty with the United States and realized that its provisions could be employed to gain more independence from China and to work toward the modernization of Korea.

Soon after Korea had signed the treaty with Shufeldt, it concluded a similar treaty with Vice-Admiral George Willes (the Willes or Anglo-Korean Treaty), Commander of Britain's China Station, representing the British government.[73] The next month the Korean-German Treaty was signed, with Max von Brandt, German minister to China, representing the German government.[74] In each case, Ma Chien-chung, one of Li's Western-educated aides, served as mediator. Ma tried to persuade Willes and von Brandt to agree to a treaty formally affirming Korea's tributary ties to China, but he was unsuccessful. After the conclusion of the treaties, however, the Korean king through the British and German envoys sent to their rulers letters identical to the communication of May 15 delivered to the president of the United States.[75]

Kojong was delighted to learn that the U.S. government had decided to send as its first minister to his country Lucius H. Foote. In fact, Kojong is said to have "danced with joy" when Minister Foote arrived in Seoul in May 1883, because the monarch hoped that the Americans would support the independence and progressive reforms of his kingdom. Before a day had passed after the exchange of the treaty ratification, Kojong granted Foote an audience.[76] It is interesting to contrast this promptness with the fact that the Chinese emperor refused to receive foreign envoys for nearly thirty years after the ratification of treaties with Western powers and that the Japanese emperor did the same for nearly fifteen years.[77]

Among other things, Foote told Kojong in that first audience that, in concluding the treaty, the United States had been motivated mainly by concern for the welfare and happiness of the Korean people and that in this world there is such a thing as moral power more potent than armies.[78] This is the kind of sentiment that Kojong was

hoping and expecting to hear from an envoy of the newly rising
"moral" power. In view of the intrinsic nature of international
power politics, however, and of American foreign policy based upon
national self-interest and realism, it would have been much better if
Foote had given Kojong the kind of advice that German Chancellor
Otto von Bismarck had given to the Iwakura Mission from Japan in
1871—if Japan wanted to become a respectable and influential
nation, it must first develop its own national strength and then rely
upon it rather than upon international law or morality. In fact, not
only Foote but all of his successors—including George C. Foulk,
Hugh Dinsmore, and others—made various contributions to the
development and strengthening of this unrealistically pro-American
policy and attitude on the part of the Korean leaders and government. Kojong's pro-American posture and sentiment was correct in
view of his strong desire to modernize his country in imitation of the
Unites States but (as it turned out) was questionable and unrealistic
in the light of the lukewarm and indifferent attitude toward Korea
exhibited by the United States as time went on.

An important question intrudes here: Why did Kojong hold such
a misperceived and naive faith in the United States? As stated earlier, Kojong's previous knowledge about the West was based mainly
on information he received from and through China and Japan.
Kojong took at face value the (distorted) image of the United States
as a benevolent and moralistic power of the kind presented to him by
such Chinese leaders as Counselor Huang and Viceroy Li. Second,
he was impressed with the constructive and positive roles Americans
had been playing in modernizing Japan, believing that probably
they could do the same in his country. Third, familiar with the Confucian concept of *li* governing inter- and intra-state relations in the
East Asian world order, he tended to perceive modern (Western)
international rules of behavior in moralistic terms. Reinforced in his
faith in the United States by Minister Foote and by other American
diplomats who were later appointed to the American legation in
Korea, Kojong was strongly inclined to regard and accept the
United States as Korea's new elder brother. Most important of all,
however, geopolitical factors forced Kojong to seek "protection"
from the United States—the emerging and supposedly powerful
Christian nation situated thousands of miles away across the Pacific.
Surrounded by stronger and larger neighbors, intimidated by the

newly aggressive Chinese, still doubtful of rising Japan's "reliability and ability," and knowing very little about an expanding Russia in the north, Kojong felt compelled to seek a senior ally elsewhere that would have no colonial or territorial ambitions in East Asia. In the early 1880s and thereafter that power in Kojong's perception was the United States.

It should be emphasized, therefore, that if Korea had been surrounded by countries weaker and smaller than itself at the time, it would not necessarily have sought a new protective elder brother after having become supposedly independent. Rather, it would have tried to use the United States essentially the same way the Japanese used American and other aid to modernize the country, not to assert and strengthen the country's national independence. In other words, Korea's search for a new elder brother after 1882 was dictated, at least in part, by its geopolitical settings and new political factors both within and without Korea. Consequently, Kojong's strong inclination in seeking a new senior ally should be explained (1) in terms of traditional suzerain-dependency relations and (2) in terms of new international and geopolitical circumstances. As time went on and as the powers became more imperialistic in and toward Korea, international and geopolitical factors became more important to the behavior and policy of Kojong and of his advisers.

In the meantime, both before and after the conclusion of the Korean-American Treaty, but especially during initiation of its implementation, the behavior and policy of Kojong toward China began to change significantly. While he still sometimes acted as if he were a dependent king, he frequently behaved like a sovereign and independent ruler, acknowledging that the once-almighty China was crumbling and that a new age had come to the East Asian world. He was no longer willing to put all of his hopes in the decayed vortex of China; instead, he wanted to place them under the shield of the United States, distancing himself from the weakened sinitic power. Kojong and his followers regarded the United States as the symbol of a beneficent and benevolent power that would protect or guarantee the integrity and independence of Korea and viewed the Korean-American Treaty as an instrument to free Korea from Chinese domination.[79]

There is no doubt that Kojong wanted the United States to intercede for Korea in the way that China had done in the past, acting even against China if it should interfere in Korea. This was a quite new and radical reorientation of policy on the part of Kojong and his adherents. However, a certain caution is required in assessing this reorientation. Whereas Kojong definitely prized the United States in its role as a new elder brother in place of China, he never wanted to terminate Korea's traditional ties with China completely. After all, as a good Confucian monarch he was not about to repudiate bonds based on *li*. He wished to maintain a historical relationship with China but on the basis of Korea's new status under modern international rules. Thus, when he failed to win China's consent to his idea of terminating Korea's tributary missions to China and of establishing a permanent mission in Peking, Kojong continued to send tributary missions to China until the latter was compelled by Japan to renounce its claim to suzerainty over Korea in 1895.[80] All in all, Kojong wanted to loosen Korea's traditional ties with China while continuing nonetheless to profit from what little aid China was still willing and able to provide to Korea, making sure at the same time that the United States would become a kind of new elder brother in place of China and would, as such, help with his modernization programs and with his efforts to make his kingdom more independent of China. Kojong's new policy, however, had one serious problem: the more he tried to get away from China, the more tightly China tried to dominate Korea—doing so, to be sure, in the name of suzerain-dependency relations but actually in an imperialistic way.[81] As for Kojong, the more China tried to control him and his country, the more he tried to distance himself from China. By 1882 China's posture and policy toward Korea had become quite interventionist and even imperialistic.

## China's New Imperialism in Korea

Although the Ch'ing government never admitted that its direct and outright interventionism in Korea after 1882 was a kind of new imperialism, and even though many East Asian historians in the school of sinocentrism[82] failed to recognize the new character of China's expansionistic policy toward Korea after 1882, it is clear that there was an important shift in policy. Beginning in the mid-1870s, China offered strong and clear-cut advice on how Korea should conduct its relations vis-à-vis Japan and the Western nations; in and following 1882, China moved from a noninterfering and merely advice-giving policy to one of direct interference and aggression. It did so largely because of its fear of Japanese annexation of or Russian encroachment upon the small country situated so close to its own capital.

To be sure, the Chinese government attempted to justify its policy of intervention in Korea in the name of suzerain-dependency ties in order to lend it an air of historical legitimacy. In whatever name and whatever manner the Chinese leaders tried to rationalize their expansionistic policy, however, it was definitely imperialism. Explaining the nature of Sino-Korean relations after 1882, Key-Hiuk Kim correctly states that "the traditional suzerain-vassal relationship between China and Korea (after 1882) gave way to a new type of relationship between an imperialist power and a colonial dependent."[83] As time went on, Viceroy Li and his government intensified their imperialistic policy toward Korea, especially after the failure of the *Kapsin* Coup of 1884, always in the name of suzerain-dependency relations, which caused American minister Hugh Dinsmore in Seoul to comment that China's pretended seriousness about the dependent status of Korea was mainly "to assist in bringing about a relation which has never before existed," and it could not be justified by the historical relations of two countries.[84] Even American minister Charles Denby in Peking, who usually sympathized with the Chinese position, wrote to Secretary of State Thomas F. Bayard that China's claim to suzerainty over Korea after 1882 was not based on its former status but on newly established relations between two nations.[85]

No doubt, Viceroy Li Hung-chang was intelligent enough to understand the changes brought into the relations between China and Korea. However, because of what he perceived to be strategic and political reasons and because of his strong desire to give an air of historical legitimacy to China's new imperialism in Korea and to create foreign diplomatic support for it, he pretended to be most serious in his insistence that Korea was still a vassal of China. He and his associates continuously maintained this dubious (or clever) posture toward Korea until they were driven out of the peninsula following the Sino-Japanese War of 1894 and 1895.

It is not only interesting but also important to compare Li's policy with that of the *ch'ing-liu tang* (the Party of the Purists) in their attempts to cope with the Western and Japanese encroachments upon China's tributaries and territories. Beginning in the 1870s this *ch'ing-liu tang*—a group of patriotic, stubborn, and conservative Confucian scholars—stood opposed to Western learning and advocated a reinvigoration of traditional Chinese ideas and virtues. Led by Chang P'ei-lun, Chang Shih-tung, and Huang T'i-fang, they strongly advocated a hard-line policy toward the Western powers and Japan. Lacking a sufficient understanding of international affairs and any specific knowledge of China's military strength vis-à-vis the Western nations and despite their brilliant Confucian scholarship, they insisted upon an active and rigid foreign policy aimed at retaining Chinese territories and tributaries.[86]

At the time of the Ili Crisis in the 1870s and early 1880s, for example, they advocated defending the Sinkiang area against Russia at all costs, thereby indirectly and in a small way influencing the Peking government to renegotiate the one-sided Treaty of Livadia of 1879 and to conclude the Treaty of St. Petersburg of 1881 in place of that humiliating agreement.[87] At the time of the Ryūkyū-Taiwan Crisis in the 1870s, the leaders of the *ch'ing-liu tang* advocated a more consistent and aggressive policy vis-à-vis Japan. And after the Japanese annexation of the Ryūkyū kingdom in 1879, they charged that China's vacillating, weak, and inconsistent policy had led to the loss of one of its three most important tributaries (along with Korea and Vietnam).[88] Some harder-line purists, such as Chang Chien, urged that Korea be placed under the control of a Chinese royal supervisor *(Chien-kuo)* somewhat as the Mongols had done at the time of the Koryŏ Kingdom in the thirteenth and fourteenth centuries.[89] But Viceroy Li was opposed to the taking of such drastic measures toward Korea—at least for the time being. It was not until 1885, when Li sent Yüan Shih-k'ai to Korea, that the Chinese policy of control over Korea became so radical.

China's first opportunity to intervene in Korea came in 1882 when the *Imo* Revolt (the Soldiers' Revolt of the *Imo* Year) broke out in Seoul. It was anti-reform, anti-Japanese, and anti-foreign, opposed to the corruption of the existing government—the kind of revolt that the reactionary and semiretired Taewŏn'gun was glad to see and exploit. The trouble started in July, when the unhappy regular army revolted against the progressive policies of the dominant

Min clan, who favored Kojong's reforms, and also against the Japanese in Seoul, who were identified with the reforms. The regular army—poorly fed, paid, and clothed—believed that such reforms helped the Special Skills Force (Pyŏlgigun) of about 3,000 men under the training program of a Japanese military instructor, Second Lieutenant Horimoto Reizō, who had been the Military Attaché of Japanese minister Hanabusa Yoshimoto in Seoul. Kojong favored the Special Skills Force and hoped that it would develop into the nucleus of a large modern army. Among several causes of the riot, one contributing factor was clearly the display of anti-Japanese feeling by the Korean people, who objected to Japan's refusal to pay any duties on imports and exports, to the Japanese importation of rice and other grains from Korea, and to the exportation by Japan of cheap goods to Korea.[90] Within a few days of the outbreak, the Min clan was overthrown; Kojong, though physically safe, became a virtual prisoner in his own palace; and Queen Min had to flee the capital and go into hiding for safety.[91] The Taewŏn'gun was able to return to power and proceeded to repeal many of Kojong's reform programs.[92]

Thus the Taewŏn'gun was on the scene again, taking advantage of the unfortunate rebellion[93] in somewhat the same manner that the Empress Dowager Tz'u-hsi would in cooperation with the Boxer Rebels in 1900 in China. Although the Taewŏn'gun told Minister Hanabusa that he would not return to his earlier anti-Japanese and anti-Western policy, he had already caused serious damage to his son's policy of modernization. Soon the revolt became a mutiny and the mutineers killed Lieutenant Reizō, three of his aides and four Japanese civilians, and attacked the Japanese Legation.[94] Unable to secure protection from the Korean authorities, Minister Hanabusa returned to Japan via Inch'ŏn. The Japanese government, at the recommendation of Gustave E. Boissonade, a legal adviser, decided to send Minister Hanabusa back to Korea with warships and with full discretionary power to investigate the situation and negotiate with the Korean government.[95] Minister Hanabusa then demanded harsh terms from the Korean authorities, which the Taewŏn'gun rejected.[96]

Meanwhile, the report of the imminent dispatch of Japanese troops, one battalion strong, alarmed the Chinese government. Without consulting the Korean government or obtaining an invita-

tion from it, China sent 2,000 troops to Korea under Admiral Ting
Ju-ch'ang and General Ma Chien-chung, ostensibly to mediate
between Korea and Japan, but actually to keep an eye on the Japanese soldiers in Korea.[97] The Ch'ing court arrived at this decision
from the vantage point of a recommendation made by Governor-
General Chang Shu-sheng, a stand-in for Li, who was on leave to
mourn the death of his mother.[98] General Ma, Admiral Ting, and
Admiral Wu Ch'ang-ch'ing carried out a prearranged plot to kidnap
the Taewŏn'gun. A young Chinese officer by the name of Yüan
Shih-k'ai, an aide to Admiral Wu, helped his superiors in carrying
out the plot.[99] Ma charged the Taewŏn'gun with treason against the
king, whom the Chinese emperor had "invested." "Do you know,"
asked Ma, "that the Korean King was invested by the Emperor?"
He replied: "I know." Then Ma continued: "To deceive the King is
actually to slight the Emperor. This crime should not be forgiven;
but since you are the father of the King we are being lenient." Then
Ma arrested the troublesome Taewŏn'gun, ending his one-month-
old regime, and sent him to Tientsin in order to avoid conflict with
Japan, which this reactionary ruler might easily have caused.[100]

On the day of the Taewŏn'gun's abduction, General Ma, Admiral
Ting, and Admiral Wu Ch'ang-ch'ing jointly issued a proclamation
declaiming that

> Korea is China's dependent state. . . . [Chinese] troops have arrived
> by land and sea with a total of twenty battalions, and more are to
> come [sic]. If you consider that you can compete with our forces, we
> are ready to fight at any time. Otherwise, you should repent your
> guilt and punish the leaders [of the rebellion]. . . .[101]

Now Kojong was worried lest the Chinese perpetrate the same out-
rage on him that they had done to his father. Kojong tried to save his
father, but in vain, because the situation was beyond his control.[102]

The actual negotiations between Hanabusa and plenipotentiary
Yi Yu-wŏn, assisted by Kim Hong-jip, took only three days. The
final agreement, the Treaty of Chemulp'o of 1882, met most of the
demands made by the Japanese, inasmuch as Yi and Kim failed to
persuade Hanabusa to moderate the Japanese claims.[103] During the
negotiations, the frustrated Kim wrote to General Ma that "Hanabusa persisted and would not make any concessions . . . , urging

[threatening] us to sign at noon tomorrow."[104] The treaty provided, among other things, that Korea was to pay an indemnity of 500,000 yen, that Korea was to punish the ringleaders of the revolt, that Korea was to build and maintain quarters for the Japanese soldiers, and that Korea was to send a special envoy to Japan to apologize for the unfortunate incident. An additional convention provided for complete freedom of movement of Japanese officials and their families in the interior of Korea.[105]

In view of Kojong's noninvolvement with the rebels and of Korea's sorry economic conditions at the time, the terms of the treaty—and especially the huge indemnity—were too harsh.[106] They should have provided the Korean leaders a great lesson: that if they were to fail in protecting the safety of foreign diplomats and their properties in Korea, the consequences could be detrimental, if not fatal, to the interests and honor of their country. It was the kind of lesson that the Japanese had learned quickly enough during and after the Western allies' punitive action following the murder of a British diplomat, C. L. Richardson, by Japanese in 1862 and following the Japanese attack on the American, French, and Dutch ships at Shimonoseki Strait in 1863. It was a lesson that the Chinese leaders repeatedly failed to learn as late as the Boxer Rebellion in 1900. In comparison with the anti-Western and confusing role that Emperor Kōmei had played in 1862 and 1863 in Japan and with the destructive and self-defeating actions of the Empress Dowager Tz'u-hsi during the Boxer Rebellion of 1900, however, Kojong prior to and during the *Imo* Revolt was much more positive and constructive in serving the interests of his kingdom as well as those of foreign diplomats in Korea.

As for the Taewŏn'gun, Li removed him from Tientsin to the prefect of Paoting, where he was held under survelliance until October 1885. After the pacification of the *Imo* Revolt, King Kojong requested that the Ch'ing court repatriate his father to Korea, but Li rejected the request "to avoid further political complication."[107] The Taewŏn'gun's own petition for freedom was also denied.[108]

This was not the first time that the Taewŏn'gun had been involved in a plot against King Kojong, nor would it be the last. That the old ex-regent participated in a campaign against Kojong's attempt to come to terms with Japan in 1876 and the United States in 1881–1882 has already been noted. After being permitted to return to

Korea from China in 1885, the old man became a willing tool of Chinese Resident Yüan Shih-k'ai in their combined effort—never successful—to carry out a plot whose object was to overthrow Kojong, as we shall see in chapter 7. In 1894 after agreeing to "collaborate" with the Japanese, whom he much despised, to bring about reforms for Korea, which he had always found objectionable, the father of Kojong then began to work closely with the anti-Japanese *Tonghak* rebels. A year later he cooperated with the Japanese to assassinate Queen Min, his daughter-in-law and archenemy, despite the fact that he had himself arranged her marriage to his son. His whole career and behavior, public or private, indicate that this one-time de facto regent was not only an intellectual anachronism but an individual of weak ethical standards without much integrity and kingly dignity.

To be objective, it must be admitted that he possessed a strong-willed and compelling personality, which his son did not. But he was not open-minded, pragmatic, flexible and far-sighted, as Kojong was. Unlike his son, who after 1874 became willing and interested in learning about what was going on in China, Japan, and the rest of the world and was realistic enough to make necessary adjustments to the new situation, the Taewŏn'gun showed no interest or curiosity about the rapidly changing world. Thus, he was incapable of realizing what kinds of policies and programs might be good for his country and for his people on a short-term as well as a long-term basis. Worst of all, however, his moral sense was deficient: whenever he felt that it served his own personal interests, he was willing to collaborate with the Chinese, or the Japanese, or any other group, notwithstanding his strong personal convictions to the contrary.

After the settlement of the *Imo* Revolt, the Chinese troops hunted down and executed its leaders and then remained in Korea. But so did the Japanese soldiers. Thus, for the first time since the 1630s, and only shortly after Korea had supposedly become independent and sovereign, foreign troops moved freely into Korea—the Japanese in order to guard their legation and the Chinese in order to check Japanese influence in Korea.

The Special Skills Force was disbanded. At Kojong's request, China was to start a new military training program. Yüan Shih-k'ai was placed in charge of training the Korean army by Admiral Wu Ch'ang-ch'ing. And, at least initially, King Kojong was pleased with what little "progress" Yüan was making in modernizing this army. But all turned out to be in vain in the end. What China could not do for itself, it certainly could not do for Korea.

While Li wanted to avoid a confrontational diplomacy with Japan in Korea, he wanted also to increase China's commercial, political, and diplomatic influence in Korea after the revolt, and, in fact, he succeeded in doing so. Originally it was Kojong in 1881 who sought Li's advice as to how Korea could revise its tributary trade relations with China, reduce or limit the ever-increasing Japanese commercial activities in Korea, and modernize Korea's traditional relations with China. But Li had taken no action on the Korean proposals before the conclusion of the Korean-American Treaty of 1882. After the *Imo* Revolt, Li, contrary to what Kojong had proposed, instructed Ma Chien-chung and Chou Fu to draft an agreement as between suzerain and dependency, not as between two sovereign and equal nations, so that other treaty powers might not demand the same rights in Korea as those enjoyed by China on the basis of most-favored-nation treatment.[109] When Ŏ Yun-jung, a Korean leader then in China as a member of a special mission, read the proposed draft, he argued that the regulations should be negotiated on an entirely commerical, rather than political, basis and, moreover, should be signed on an equal basis between China and Korea. But Ma and Chou rejected Ŏ's argument on the grounds that Korea was a dependency.[110] Frustrated and helpless, the Korean envoys—Ŏ, Kim Hong-jip, and Cho Yŏng-ha—were compelled to sign the so-called "Regulations for Maritime and Overland Trade Between China and Korea Subjects."[111] Among other things, the regulations placed the superintendent of the Northern Ports, Li Hung-chang, on an equal footing with the king of Korea; allowed the Chinese to travel in the interior, under passport; permitted the Chinese and Koreans to trade at some cities at both the Yalu and the Tumen rivers with duties to be 5 percent *ad valorem* on all goods except red ginseng; and stipulated that, in the case of Korea, the king was to appoint the trade commissioners whereas, in the case of China, the superintendent of the Northern Ports was to appoint the trade commissioners to reside at the open ports.[112] In brief, the regulations gave a definite superiority to the Chinese in Korea, something that other treaty powers did not possess in the peninsula. It is ironic to note that, whereas the Chinese, following the conclusion of the

Treaty of Chemulp'o, had complained about how badly and unfairly the Japanese had treated the Koreans by imposing such harsh terms, they themselves had now imposed even more unfair regulations on Korea. This imposition the Chinese characterized as "the elder brother caring for [loving] the younger brother."

In connection with the Trade Regulations, three important observations should be made. First, with their implementation, the Chinese government meant to control the political and economic affairs of Korea very closely. Second, however Li and his associates attempted to justify or rationalize their interventionist policy in Korea, it was, in reality, a clear-cut case of a new imperialism. Lastly and most important, just as Japan in 1876 had started modern diplomatic relations with Korea on a basis that was even more unequal than that of the Western powers with Japan, now, in 1882, China initiated new relations with Korea that were even more unequal than those of the Western powers with China.

## Kojong's Unsuccessful Attempt to Hire American Advisers

Japanese and Chinese troops were able to move freely into Korea and to remain there mainly because the Korean government had no forces with the capabilities of resisting the foreign soldiers. Thus, Kojong realized that one of the most urgent tasks facing his government was to hire foreign military instructors to train and modernize his army. Since his experiences with Japanese- and Chinese-directed military training programs had been unfortunate, and since he held such an optimistic and strong faith in the United States, he naturally conceived the idea of inviting American military instructors.

The issue of foreign military instructors for the training of Korean troops was important to those powers who had an interest in Korea. Because it was assumed that any power that supplied military instructors to Korea would have a greater influence over the Korean forces and affairs, the question of who would supply them became a matter of great concern to those who had treaty relations with Korea. All eventually agreed on or recognized the urgent need for the modernization of Korea's military forces, but they could not agree on who should provide military instructors. So far as King Kojong was concerned, however, his first choice was to solicit military advisers from America. The first opportunity to ask the American government formally to send military and political advisers to Korea came when he dispatched the 1883 Korean Mission to the United States.

The first Korean mission to America was sent at the advice of Minister Foote, who suggested it as a means of showing the world that, after all, Korea had become sovereign and independent and also to bring the benefits of American civilization to Korea.[113] Kojong was more than happy to follow Foote's suggestion. While in the United States, the Korean envoys, among other things, asked the American government to send military and political advisers, teachers, technicians, and agricultural scientists, and they received a favorable reply.[114] At the same time the Korean envoys were in Washington asking for American advisers of all kinds, Minister Foote had an audience with King Kojong, during which Kojong himself asked Foote to persuade his government to send military and political advisers to Korea as quickly as possible.[115]

Thus, beginning in October 1883, Minister Foote repeatedly asked the U.S. Department of State to send American military and diplomatic advisers.[116] Secretary of State Frederick T. Frelinghuysen, having eagerly supported the idea of opening Korea to the United States and having promised to send American advisers to Korea, was in fact strongly in favor of complying with the king's wish. However, it was not until November 1884, that he took appropriate action. The main reasons for the delay were largely constitutional and bureaucratic. To begin with, Foote's initial dispatch had been mislaid, which needlessly caused about one year's delay.[117] Then, there were necessary legal and technical procedures to be followed—such as winning the approval of the secretary of war, of the president, and above all of the Congress, as Article I, Section 9, of the United States Constitution states: "no person holding an Office of Profit or Trust under them shall, without the Consent of Congress, accept any present, Emolument, Office, or Title of any kind whatever, from any King, Prince, of foreign state." Frelinghuysen wrote to Foote in November 1884 that "I have today fully and urgently presented the matter to the Secretary of War, in a letter summarizing your several dispatches, and have asked that he give the subject his immediate attention and favor me with his response."[118] On January 30, 1885, President Chester A. Arthur

finally recommended to Congress the adoption of a joint resolution
authorizing him to send American military officers to Korea for
service with the Korean government. But the issue was buried in the
Congress, inasmuch as it failed to act on the president's recommendation.[119]

Meanwhile, since Admiral Shufeldt had previously conferred with
the Korean mission while it was in the United States and expressed a
willingness to go to Korea, Foote, at the request of the king, asked
Shufeldt "to come at once." But the admiral did not do so.[120] In
November 1884, Foote complained to Frelinghuysen that "the truth
is that the King's patience is exhausted with the long delay . . . ;
had he asked Great Britian or Germany to perform a like service, it
would have been done at once."[121] Thus, in the words of George M.
McCune and John A. Harrison, "the net result of American delay
was to shake the confidence of Korea in the United States and to
make the United States impotent in East Asian affairs for another
decade."[122] Although McCune and Harrison might have overstated
the case, there is no doubt but that Kojong and his pro-American
advisers were deeply disappointed with the American delay, especially since they were not fully aware of the constitutional issues
involved in such a case. The American government's delay in sending a sufficient number of military and technical advisers to Korea
was perceived by King Kojong as unwarranted and incomprehensible. This seeming procrastination impelled the monarch to try to
hire nationals other than the Americans. In the circumstances that
actually prevailed, however, even before Kojong attempted to
employ American advisers, he had already been able to obtain the
services of one German national diplomat, Paul Georg von Möllendorff, who started to work for the king and his government beginning in December 1882.

## CHAPTER 2

# Paul Georg von Möllendorff in Korea

## Von Möllendorff and Kojong

At the time when the kingdom of Korea came to conclude treaties with Japan in 1876 and with the United States in 1882 on the basis of modern (Western) concepts of international rules, it lacked the benefit of any services that might have been rendered by Western foreign policy advisers, who could have promoted the interests of Korea vis-à-vis its counterparts.

After concluding the treaty with the United States in 1882, Korea proceeded to negotiate further treaties with various powers. To do this, Korea badly needed a competent foreigner who could advise king and government on issues of foreign policy and the customs service. Viceroy Li seized this opportunity to engage in certain manipulations that led the Korean government to ask him to recommend a capable adviser.[1] In the early 1880s there were already several hundred Western advisers and employees in China, most of them serving in the Maritime Custom Services or operating in other areas which the Chinese had been traditionally unfamiliar. At the formal request of the Korean government and after about six months of tedious negotiations between Chinese and Korean governmental officials and Paul Georg von Möllendorff, Viceroy Li recommended and sent to Korea the German diplomat, whom he described as "a good natured and sincere man."[2]

Paul Georg von Möllendorff was born on February 17, 1847, into a well-known aristocratic family in Zedenik, a small town in the district of Ückermark, in the Prussian province of Brandenburg (north of Berlin), now in East Germany. Among his famous ancestors was Field Marshall Wichard Joachim Heinrick von Möllendorff, who won awards for his distinguished service to the state from Frederick William (1713–1740) and his successor, Frederick the Great (1740–1786). Paul's own father was a well-educated government official (Ökonomiekommissionsrat) in Zedenik, who was later transferred to Görlitz, in the district of Lausitz, southwest of Berlin. It was in Görlitz that Paul attended a gymnasium, where he displayed a remarkable and precocious aptitude for classical and foreign languages.[3]

When Paul von Möllendorff reached adulthood, he was a tall, lean, and stern- and athletic-looking young man, although in middle-age he tended to be overweight and unhealthy-looking. He passed away in 1901 at the age of fifty-four—rather an early age even according to the standards of the time. In 1865 he entered the University of Halle located by the Saale River in Sachsen, now in East Germany. At Halle he studied, among other subjects, jurisprudence and Oriental as well as Occidental languages.[4] Thus by academic training he was not only a jurist but also a philologist and linguist; he eventually became capable of doing research not only in such Aryan (Indo-European) languages as, of course, his own native tongue, German, and English, French, Italian, Spanish, Russian, Polish, Dutch, Danish, and Serbian but also in languages as diverse as Hebrew, Chinese, and the Ural-Altaic languages such as Manchurian, Korean, and Japanese (with some difficulties, to be sure, in the case of the latter two). In due time, he became one of the most formidable and astute European philologists as well as sinologists of his time, publishing a number of books, monographs, and articles in studies of Chinese, Manchurian, and other languages and laws.[5]

In 1869, at the age of twenty-two, he went to China as an assistant secretary in the Chinese Imperial Maritime Customs, with an understanding from the German government that after five years or so he would be given an appointment in the German diplomatic service in China. After working in the customs service between 1869 and 1874, he entered the German foreign service and eventually became German vice-consul at Tientsin. While serving at Tientsin, he developed close relationships with Ma Chien-chung and Chou Fu, both close to Li Hung-chang, and with Viceroy Li himself. In

1879 von Möllendorff helped Li to purchase some weapons and war-ships, from two German firms, Krupp and Vulkan.[6] It was during this period at Tientsin that von Möllendorff cultivated a cordial rela-tionship with Takezoe Shinichirō, the Japanese consul and future Japanese minister in Korea (1882–1885), and also an especially effective and intimate friendship with Karl Waeber, the Russian con-sul and future Russian chargé d'affaires and minister in Korea (1885–1897).

After leaving the German diplomatic service in 1881 on account of personal problems with German minister Max von Brandt in Pe-king, who unfortunately became his lifelong enemy, he joined Li's staff.[7] Li argued that if, at the time of the negotiation of the Korean-Japanese Treaty of 1876, Korea had enlisted someone like von Möl-lendorff to manage the negotiations, the Japanese would never have been so high-handed.[8] In July 1882, when von Möllendorff learned from Chou Fu that he was being considered for the position of adviser to the Korean government and king, he had started learning the Korean language. By this time he had an excellent command of the Chinese language, which he had been busily studying and pol-ishing since his arrival in China in 1869, and it was not too difficult for him to learn the written and spoken Korean language, although his command of Korean never became as good as that of Chinese or Manchurian.

King Kojong learned of Li's recommendation of von Möllendorff from Kim Hong-jip, Cho Yŏng-ha, and Yi Cho-yŏn who, having just returned from China, had also reported on the new trade regu-lations with China.[9] When the appointment of von Möllendorff became known, there was some opposition to it. The first opponent was Minister von Brandt. Von Brandt told the Tsungli Yamen that von Möllendorff should not be recommended to Korea for the rea-son that two more years remained in his ten-year contract with the German government. This problem was solved, however, by von Möllendorff himself by obtaining official confirmation from his gov-ernment that his contract had expired on October 1, 1882. Opposi-tion also came from Robert Hart, a Germanophobic British servant and the inspector general of the Chinese Imperial Maritime Cus-toms. Hart disliked the idea of sending the German diplomat to Korea to organize and head the Korean Customs Service and advise Korea on foreign policy because he feared that the appointment might lead to the extension of German influence into Korea at the expense of his and British interests. Besides, he wanted to pick his own man for the position.[10] But Ma Chien-chung strongly supported von Möllendorff with Viceroy Li, referring to him as the "most confident man for the job." American minister Russell Young in Peking, who wanted to send an American to the post, also opposed the appointment.[11] Viceroy Li overruled all of these opponents and decided to abide by his original decision.

Hart believed that Li's selection of von Möllendorff, who had not held any distinguished diplomatic post in China or elsewhere, was "to have low-class men who will obey orders rather than better-class men who will give advice."[12] No doubt, by the term "low-class men" Hart was referring to those who worked at the low or middle echelons of diplomatic or governmental services (such as von Möllendorff who had served as German vice-consul in Tientsin and in the Chinese Customs Service under Hart), rather than to someone who came from a nonaristocratic family background or lacked a good education. Von Möllendorff's background and education certainly did not make him a "low-class" man in the general sense of the term.

Cho Yŏng-ha, one of King Kojong's confidants, left Seoul at the end of October in order to escort von Möllendorff from Tientsin on November 11, 1882, and became the first Korean to meet him the following day. He told von Möllendorff that Li had already officially notified the Korean king of his appointment.[13] As soon as von Möllendorff's appointment was approved by King Kojong, a draft contract was drawn up. It was reviewed by Cho and Ma Chien-ch'ang and then approved by Viceroy Li on November 18. The definitive draft of the contract, written in both Chinese and English, was finally signed by Cho for the Korean government and by Ma Chien-ch'ang for the Chinese government. It contained six articles: (1) von Möllendorff was to assist with the foreign affairs of the Korean government; (2) he was to establish and administer the Korean Customs Service, and in case foreigners were to be employed, the exact years of their services should be stipulated; (3) the administration of the Korean Customs Service was to be under the control of the Korean government; von Möllendorff's jurisdiction was to include planning, evaluation, and reporting of customs affairs; (4) his monthly salary was to be three hundred silver taels, and other expenses such as rent and travel allowances were to be covered separately; (5) the Korean government reserved the right of dismissal in case von Möllendorff did not observe the contract, and each could terminate the contract giving notice three months in advance; and (6) the contract was to be signed by von Möllendorff and Cho Yŏng-ha, and ratification by the king of Korea was required, to be reported to Viceroy Li by Cho.[14]

Examination of the contract reveals that the Korean government had effective control over von Möllendorff and could dismiss him at any time should he violate its terms. Yet von Möllendorff was completely happy with his new appointment, as he wrote in his diary: "If the contract is signed, I will assume the most powerful position in East Asia. . . . It's like a dream."[15] The principal reason von Möllendorff was so gratified with the contract was this: Under its authorization he could exercise almost unlimited power in matters of foreign policy and of the customs service during his tenure in Korea. His handsome monthly salary of three hundred taels, or approximately $400, which exceeded what he made in China as German vice-consul in Tientsin or as an official with the Chinese government through its customs service, together with a liberal allowance, was understandably appealing to von Möllendorff. Before leaving Tientsin for Korea, von Möllendorff was visited by many seeking his favor in employment and for business ventures in Korea. Among them was the Russian delegation asking his aid in negotiating the Russo-Korean treaty.

Arriving at Seoul via Inch'ŏn on December 13, 1882, von Möllendorff first had an audience with King Kojong, on December 26. After prostrating three times to the king (according to custom) he told the king in Korean: "I thank you for letting me come to your country. I will do my best. I ask Your Majesty please to trust me." With these greetings, von Möllendorff became the first Westerner whom the king had ever had occasion to meet. The king seemed extremely pleased with von Möllendorff's demeanor and asked him to put his eyeglasses back on (which, again according to custom, he had taken off in front of the monarch). The king also inquired about his family (his wife and child), who were supposed to join him after he had made housing and other necessary arrangements in Seoul (Rosalie, his wife, who was pregnant, stayed in Tientsin). Von Möllendorff was equally delighted with the monarch's appearance and affectionate kindness toward him.[16] The German diplomat was immediately made a noble and appointed councillor to the Office of Foreign Affairs.[17]

As the king had hoped, von Möllendorff identified himself with the Koreans. He elected to live in an entirely Korean style, wearing the official Korean dress of a nobleman and conforming in many respects to Korean habits in the same idealistic spirit as present-day Peace Corps volunteers. Soon he developed a fairly good command of the Korean language. In due time King Kojong came not only to admire von Möllendorff for his linguistic and intellectual ability but also to extend to him the same kind of trust that he had asked from the German toward himself, entreating his loyalty toward the monarch. It should be emphasized that von Möllendorff understood the difficulties involved for a Westerner to become easternized or Koreanized.[18] Nevertheless, he adjusted himself to the Eastern living better than any Westerner in Korea or China at this time.

As happy as he was about his appointment in Korea, he did not plan to stay there permanently. Rather he thought about staying for about five or six years (though his plan was flexible, as was his contract on the issue) to initiate and then complete whatever reform and modernization projects he envisioned for Korea. Moreover, there is no doubt but that, while serving in Korea, he meant to devote his total energy and resources to its development and welfare and that he immensely impressed King Kojong with his political ability and knowledge in the Chinese and Korean languages. In Korea he even adopted the Korean name Mok In-dŏk and was known as *Mok ch'amp'an* (Möllendorff, vice minister).

On December 26, 1882, when the Office of Foreign Affairs (*T'ongni Amun*) was established, von Möllendorff was appointed as a councillor (*ch'amui samu*). Rapidly advancing, he was promoted, in mid-January 1883, to vice minister of the Office of Revenue and Port Administration (*Chonggaksa*). Within four more months, he became vice minister of the Foreign Office and Inspector General of the Korean Customs Service.[19] Kojong came to have a strong faith in him.[20] As vice minister of the Foreign Office, von Möllendorff became a key figure in all Korean negotiations with Westerners.

Although some historians charge that Li and Kojong were indiscreet and naive in appointing a Westerner to such an important position in the Korean government,[21] the fact is that Korea then needed

many more Western advisers like von Möllendorff in high government positions who could start various necessary reform projects.
Some insist that Li's primary motive for sending von Möllendorff
was to control Korean foreign affairs and customs through him.[22]
Others assert that Li's main objective was not necessarily to
strengthen Chinese interests and suzerainty in Korea but to check
Japanese penetration into the peninsula and to help the Korean government in foreign affairs and in organizing the customs service.[23]
Still another view is that Li recommended the German diplomat
because he happened to be "available" at the time and that Korea's
employment of von Möllendorff reflects its wish and quest for an
independent foreign policy.[24] According to Kim Yun-sik, who was
involved in hiring von Möllendorff, Li had been convinced that the
Japanese were afraid of the Germans—especially of von Möllendorff
—and that making this German an important adviser to the Korean
government would halt the Japanese advance into Korea.[25]

Nonetheless, the evidence indicates that Li sent von Möllendorff
to Korea not only to guard against Japanese ambitions but also to
further Chinese control over Korea in a manner that he deemed
might be acceptable to the other powers that would sooner or later
conclude modern treaties with Korea. Certainly, Li did not send von
Möllendorff to Korea in the expectation that he could help Korea to
escape from Chinese domination.

And yet, that is exactly what von Möllendorff did. He soon came
to identify himself more with Korea than with China. Among other
things, he sponsored a great many reform programs in industry,
communications, and other areas. And, worst of all from the standpoint of China, he busied himself with furthering the interests of
Korea rather than those of China.

## The Establishment of the Customs Service

As the inspector general of the customs service, von Möllendorff had
first the urgent task of establishing the Korean Maritime Customs
Service. The ratification of the Korean-American Treaty, which provided for customs duties, was to be consummated on May 19, 1883.
It was also anticipated that the Korean government would conclude
certain trade regulations and a tariff agreement with the Japanese

government in the near future. Therefore, it was imperative that von Möllendorff set up the customs service as soon as feasible. To do so, however, and to open Korea to the West, the Korean government needed huge sums of money—which it did not have. In fact, as von Möllendorff fully realized, he needed not only funds but also personnel to establish and run the Korean Customs Service.

Thus, in order to arrange for financing and to recruit personnel, King Kojong sent a mission to China, on January 22, 1883, consisting of von Möllendorff as chief envoy and Min Yŏng-ik as vice envoy. Kojong asked von Möllendorff to use Korean mining, customs, and railroad assets as mortgages. Prior to von Möllerdorff's appointment, Kojong had sent Cho Yŏng-ha to China to consult Li on the issue of Korean modernization. With Li's active aid and through the good offices of T'ang T'ing-shu, the director of the Chinese Steam Navigation Company, some Chinese businessmen at Tientsin had agreed to grant a private loan of 500,000 taels at 8 percent interest to the Korean government. The preliminary agreement stipulated that the loan be used for establishing a Korean Customs Service, not for the payment of indemnity to Japan.[26] This prearrangement made von Möllendorff's mission to China and the loan transaction process much easier. In Shanghai, the Korean mission was able to conclude an agreement for a loan in the amount of 200,000 taels, and von Möllendorff was able to recruit twenty-eight men, most of them personally known to him from the Chinese Imperial Maritime Customs. Of the twenty-eight recruits, twenty-three were Europeans, four were Chinese, and one was Japanese.[27] It is probably a tragically fateful fact for Korea that it had to borrow money from the Chinese, who had to borrow the same from the Russians, who in turn borrowed money from the French—all for diplomatic, political, and economic reasons.

While in China von Möllendorff exploited the possibility of enlisting Chinese government aid for a variety of projects, and he sought foreign investors for the development of Korean mining, railroads, telegraph, and other industrial interests. Von Möllendorff strongly believed that in order for Korea to become truly independent, it must develop, among other things, a productive industrial base. For that purpose he wanted to develop its natural resources, especially a mining industry, since Korea had great potentials in coal, steel, lead, gold, and silver. He also contacted the Chinese Imperial Telegraph concerning the installation of marine and land cables between Shanghai and Seoul, and from Seoul to Vladivostok. He made several trips to textile factories in Shanghai to ascertain whether he could introduce the textile industry to Korea. He sought and obtained a medical doctor to set up a government-sponsored medical college in Korea and made a preliminary agreement with Jardine, Matheson and Co. to initiate regular steamship service on a tri-weekly basis between Shanghai and Nagasaki via Pusan and Inch'ŏn. In order to establish postal service and communication systems in Korea, he hired as his secretary an Englishman, W. D. F. Hutchinson, who had once been deputy director of the Post Office of Hong Kong. For the purpose of improving Korean forestry, he decided to import 100,000 mulberry trees to plant in Korea. While in Shanghai, he discussed the issue of the ratification of the Korean-American Treaty with American minister Russell Young and explored the prospects for the conclusion of treaties with the Russian and Austrian consuls.[28] Von Möllendorff was most happy to see his family and one of his sisters, who was visiting China from Germany at the time. Now that he was able to take a Western medical doctor with him, he planned to move his family to Korea sometime after the birth of his second child in the spring. After spending almost three busy months in Tientsin and Shanghai, he returned with a part of the Chinese loan,[29] which he used for the establishment of the customs service.[30]

Two days after returning from China, he moved into a large, newly remodelled house, attractive according to Oriental style and standards, located in Pakdong, not too far from the royal palace. The house was rumored to be haunted by "a ghost-appearance," inasmuch as it used to belong to Min Kyŏm-ho, who had been tragically killed in the *Imo* Revolt of 1882; it had remained vacant since then. Actually, the king had arranged for this house for von Möllendorff even before his arrival in December 1882, but he was worried about this ominous gossip. Von Möllendorff, however, laughed at the rumor and was more than glad to make the house his residence. He and his family, who joined him in summer 1883, were content with the house except for one inconvenience: the low ceilings of its rooms bothered his tall Western guests.[31] Of course, nothing adverse happened to the von Möllendorffs during the three years of their residency in the house.

In connection with the establishment of the customs service, one of the first problems that von Möllendorff had to confront was what to do with the port superintendent (the *kamni*). Prior to 1883 the port superintendent had been attached to the provincial governors's office to administer coastal-region and maritime affairs. The Korean-Japanese Treaty and Trade Regulation Annex had entrusted the port superintendent with the implementation of the treaty's stipulation concerning the administration of treaty ports and the collection of harbor dues, but not with the collection of import duties. Reflecting the traditional policy of isolationism pursued by the late Yi dynasty, the port superintendent generally tended to reduce the volume of Korea's foreign trade rather than trying to expand it. Von Möllendorff's initial wish had been to discontinue the office of port superintendent, but he decided not to urge such action overtly, lest he should offend the royal court and the port superintendent himself. Instead, he separated the office of port superintendent from the customs service and placed it technically under the jurisdiction of the newly created Ministry of Foreign Affairs (1883). Nonetheless, von Möllendorff was able to supervise the port superintendents closely, inasmuch as their salaries were paid by the customs service.[32] He also had the European commissioners at the treaty ports work closely with the port superintendent officials.

Upon returning from China von Möllendorff visited three open ports—Inch'ŏn, Pusan, and Wŏnsan—to decide upon the exact locations of the customs service. His objective was to open up the customs service in all three ports by late June of 1883. Despite his efforts, however, only the Inch'ŏn Customs Service was opened in accord with his original schedule. He placed A. B. Stripling, a British national and one of his appointees, in charge of Inch'ŏn customs as its commissioner.[33] Meanwhile, the Korean government appointed Cho Pyŏng-jik as the port superintendent at Inch'ŏn in September 1883.[34] Wŏnsan customs was not opened until October 1883. Another of his appointees, T. W. Wright, also a British national, was put in charge of the port. Chŏng Hyŏn-sok had been appointed as the port superintendent at Wŏnsan one month earlier.[35]

Because of the increase in trade transactions by the Japanese merchants at Pusan and because of the conclusion of the Korean-Japanese Trade Regulations and the Tariff Agreement (to go into effect beginning November 3, 1883), von Möllendorff wanted to open the

Pusan customs in early November at the latest—which he was in fact able to do. A German national, W. N. Lovatt, was his choice as the commissioner.[36] Since September, Yi Hŏn-yŏng had been serving as the port superintendent at Pusan. Thus, by the end of 1883 the customs service was functioning at all three treaty ports. In January of the following year Kim Ki-su, who had led the 1876 mission to Japan was assigned to Ŭiju, where Korean trade with the Chinese was expanding.[37]

In spite of the fact that both Viceroy Li and Robert Hart believed that the Korean customs should be an appendage or a part of the overall Chinese Maritime Customs, von Möllendorff thought it should be as independent as possible from Chinese control, just as he believed that Korea should become as independent of China as possible diplomatically and politically. Thus, he made every effort to manage the Korean Customs Service independently of the Chinese Maritime Customs and its influence—which annoyed Viceroy Li thoroughly. Chinese merchants would receive no preferential treatment, despite the Trade Regulations of 1882 between China and Korea, which required such preference. However, von Möllendorff ran into difficulty supervising his personnel because the majority of his staff were still on the payroll of the Chinese Maritime Customs under Hart. Moreover, due to his excessive overload, von Möllendorff had to delegate the administration of each customs house into the hands of each commissioner. Furthermore, each levy of customs revenue was at first so small that many staff members were inadequately paid. Despite all of these initial difficulties, however, he was able to establish and administer the Korean Customs Service without any financial aid from the Korean government and quite independently of Chinese control. Because of his independent actions, however, Chinese commissioner Ch'en Shu-t'ang became hostile to him and Viceroy Li summoned von Möllendorff to Tientsin in the summer of 1884 for a good explanation. Although the two disagreed, they parted with good feelings toward each other.[38] Commenting on the Li–von Möllendorff controversy, Hart said, "I hear Li is *inwardly* wild over this, but *outwardly* says its what he intended! —I must confess v M. has gone ahead very cleverly: perhaps he'll end by being King of Corea (with German support)!"[39]

There was at least one respect, however, in which von Möllendorff was pleasing Li: He was anti-Japanese. Moreover, von Möllendorff

was also anti-American and anti-missionary while in Korea. Thus
he soon became a chief rival to American minister Lucius H. Foote
and to American naval attaché George C. Foulk.[40] Although von
Möllendorff was in favor of reforming and modernizing Korea, he
sided with the usually conservative Min faction as opposed to the
Korean Progressives, who were liberal-minded reformers, because
the latter were strongly pro-Japanese. Von Möllendorff was especially close to such government officials Min Yŏng-ik and Min Yŏng-
mok. Viceroy Li could have pressured the Korean government to
dismiss him, but Li allowed the German diplomat to stay in Korea
because of his anti-Japanese posture.[41]

Despite this posture, von Möllendorff believed that if necessary,
he should be resigned to doing business with the Japanese. Thus, in
1883 he negotiated a $24,000 loan from the First National Bank of
Japan located in Seoul at the rate of 10 percent interest per year. He
used the collection of duty monies as surety for the loan. The money
was intended to meet the expenses of the customs houses, to purchase office equipment and uniforms, to make partial payments
toward the salaries of his employees, and for other necessary items
for the maintenance of the customs. In addition, von Möllendorff
arranged with the First National Bank of Japan to act as the customs
service bank by setting up one account for customs revenues primarily from import and export duties and a separate account for the ton-
nage and harbor dues. Since there were no banking institutions at all
in Korea, except for this Japanese bank, and since at this time more
than half of the total volume of foreign trade was conducted with
Japanese nationals, these kinds of business transactions with the
Japanese were inevitable.

However, von Möllendorff's willingness to do business with the
Japanese was limited. This is made clear, for example, by his reaction to the suggestion of the Korean government. Concerned that
von Möllendorff had overstaffed the customs service with Europeans
(who required rather high salaries by Oriental standards) out of the
still-meager customs revenue, it suggested that he hire less expensive
Japanese personnel. Von Möllendorff, however, would have nothing
to do with the idea, which, good or bad, indicated that he was loyal
to those whom he hired.[42]

Another of von Möllendorff's achievements in the area of customs
affairs was the drafting of the General Trade Regulation of 1883,

which became applicable to all commercial treaties with Korea. Compiled by von Möllendorff, this regulation consolidated all of the general trade regulations provided in each of the separate treaties with Korea. Containing thirty-nine articles and an annexed table of tariff rates, it was intended to be a codification of the procedures for all customs matters and was designed to simplify them.[43] However, since the General Trade Regulation had to be approved by the treaty powers and since its terms could in no way deviate from any of the provisions in the existing (or even forthcoming) treaties of trade,[44] the regulation inevitably tended to favor the treaty powers. In fact, it specifically stipulated that none of the treaty provisions might be altered or amended without the consent of the treaty powers. Von Möllendorff's concessions, seemingly favorable to the treaty powers as written in the regulation, were made not from any desire to sell Korean interests down the river for the sake of the treaty powers but rather because he had no choice but to bow to the structures of existing treaty provisions.

## The Conclusion of the Korean-Japanese Trade Regulations and Tariff Agreement of 1883

One of the earlier accomplishments of von Möllendorff in Korea was the negotiation and conclusion of the Korean-Japanese Trade Regulations and Tariff Agreement of July 1883. It should be recalled that, unlike the Korean-American Treaty of 1882, the Korean-Japanese Treaty of 1876 had no provisions for tariffs, either on import or export items. During the negotiations for the treaty, the Korean delegates did not ever raise the subject of duties, let alone push for their inclusion in the treaty. The Korean government belatedly realized that, in light of the ever-increasing trade with the Japanese since its ports were opened and in view of the mutual recognition of the issue of tariffs in Sino-Japanese relations and of the concessions they had made on this point, their oversight had been a mistake. Thus the government repeatedly asked Japanese minister Hanabusa Yoshimoto to negotiate for a tariff agreement. At first, Hanabusa refused to engage in such negotiations on the grounds that the Korean-Japanese Treaty of 1876 had provided for no such arrangements.[45] Then in the summer of 1879, Hanabusa informed the Korean government that his own government might be willing to accept a "reasonable" tariff. Soon after the opening of Wŏnsan in May 1880, the Korean government dispatched the Kim Hong-jip Mission to Tokyo to find out, among other things, the attitude and opinion of the Japanese government on the tariff issue and then to advocate mutual negotiations on the matter.[46] The Japanese government, though unhappy about its own unequal treaties with the West and with its loss of tariff autonomy vis-à-vis the Western treaty powers, was lukewarm toward the idea of concluding a fair and equitable tariff agreement with the Korean government. Moreover, Kim, despite his high intelligence and open-mindedness toward Japan and the West, was neither well informed on tariff matters nor well prepared for negotiating with the Japanese officials on a tariff agreement. In talking and negotiating with the Japanese Foreign Office officials, therefore, Kim relied upon Chinese minister Ho Ju-chang in Tokyo. The Japanese government proposed a 5 percent *ad valorem* duty on all imports and exports. Influenced by Minister Ho, Kim rejected the Japanese proposal and instead proposed that Japan and Korea sign a tariff agreement identical either to the one then existing between Japan and China or to the new one that Japan was about to sign with the Western treaty powers. Since the Japanese refused Kim's offer, however, and made no appealing counterproposal, no agreement was reached in 1880.[47]

Even so, Kim was able to obtain a statement from Foreign Minister Inoue Kaoru to the effect that his government would study the tariff issues in relation to Japanese-Korean trade for a few years and then appoint a Japanese plenipotentiary to negotiate a tariff agreement with Korea.[48] It was at this time that Kim was provided with Counselor Huang Tsun-hsien's *Chao-hsien ts'e-lüeh* to be delivered to King Kojong upon his return to Korea, as discussed in chapter 1. Rather than waiting for a few years, however, the Korean government, in late 1881, sent another mission to Tokyo headed by Cho Pyŏng-ho. As a result of Cho's importunate requests, Inoue finally entered into negotiation with him. In accordance with his government's instructions, Cho insisted upon 10 percent duties on all imported articles and upon prohibiting the export of rice and red ginseng into Japan. Inoue countered, however, with a 5 percent tariff and insistence on the free and unlimited purchase and import of Korean rice and red ginseng into Japan.[49] Inasmuch as the negotiators were unable to come to mutually agreeable terms, Cho's mission also failed, as had Kim's earlier mission.

At the time of the Li-Shufeldt negotiations in Tientsin where, among other things, the subject of tariffs between Korea and the United States was also discussed, the Japanese government decided that it would do well to conclude a tariff agreement with Korea lest it be placed in a disadvantageous position later on. As instructed by his government, Minister Hanabusa entered into negotiation with a team of Korean delegates headed by Kim Po-hyǒn and Kim Hong-jip.[50] By June, when Hanabusa and the two Kims began serious negotiations on tariffs, the Korean-American Treaty had already been signed embodying the principle of a 10 percent tariff and a ban on rice exports from Korea. Thus, the two Kims strongly insisted upon a minimum 10 percent tariff rate on imports and a prohibition of rice exports, utilizing the example provided in the Korean-American Treaty. However, Hanabusa persistently demanded a 5 percent rate.[51] While the negotiations were still in progress, however, the *Imo* Revolt of 1882 broke out, and they were postponed indefinitely.

On December 14, 1882, just one day after von Möllendorff's arrival in Seoul, Takezoe Shinichirō was appointed as the new Japanese minister in Korea. There is some evidence showing that Takezoe's assignment to Seoul was made, in part, because of his old acquaintance with von Möllendorff at Tientsin, where he had served as Japanese consul, and that the appointment reflected the Japanese government's desire to have a minister who could influence von Möllendorff toward a pro-Japanese policy in general and toward a tariff agreement advantageous to Japan in particular.[52] Inoue and his advisers, thoroughly familiar with the tremendous impact of Western advisers (such as Charles W. LeGendre, Gustave E. Boissonade, and others) upon Japanese foreign and domestic policies and anticipating such an influence by von Möllendorff on Korean affairs, intended that Takezoe should influence von Möllendorff, and through him the Korean government, to formulate and implement pro-Japanese policies. Like Viceroy Li earlier, the Japanese leadership misjudged von Möllendorff's political orientation and commitment. Once he became an adviser to the king and government of Korea, von Möllendorff was almost totally devoted to the interests and welfare of his adopted country, not to those of China or Japan.

It should be emphasized, herewith, that this was not the only time that the Japanese government tried to influence Korean policies through indirect means—by influencing Korea's Western advisers or by placing in the Korean government those Westerners (their own spies) who would promote Japanese interests rather than those of Korea. In April 1895 at the end of the Sino-Japanese War, the same Inoue, now an old Korea hand, advised then Foreign Minister Mutsu Munemitsu to install "our [Western] advisers" into the Korean government so as to enhance Japanese interests in the peninsula without arousing suspicion or opposition on the part of foreign countries.[53] And in the mid-1900s the Japanese government successfully placed Durham White Stevens, an American citizen and its former employee, in the Korean government as an adviser, and Stevens secretly worked for the Japanese annexation of Korea.[54]

Be that as it may, Foreign Minister Inoue, in his new instructions to Takezoe, made it clear that the minister should seek a 5 percent tariff rate and a most-favored-nation treatment clause for Japan.[55] When Minister Takezoe visited von Möllendorff and unofficially sought his favor in the forthcoming negotiations with the Korean government, von Möllendorff made it abundantly clear that the Japanese minister should not count on such favors. In preliminary talks between the two, Takezoe argued that a high tariff rate (10 percent) would hurt Japanese traders in Korea, who lacked strong capitalization, and would therefore be detrimental to Japanese-Korean trade. Thus he proposed a lower tariff rate. Von Möllendorff replied that since the treasury of the Korean government was so poor, it considered the revenues from tariffs to be its most plausible source of income.[56] Therefore, von Möllendorff suggested a high tariff rate.

Although Min Yŏng-mok was appointed as Korea's chief plenipotentiary for the actual negotiations, beginning on July 18, 1883, the real work was conducted by von Möllendorff and Takezoe. In view of the persistence of the Korean government's request for a 10 percent rate, Inoue now sent new modified instructions to Takezoe—a 7.5 percent rate on duties. In the end both sides agreed on an 8 percent rate on general commodities and 10 percent on certain other items. As for the export of rice, it was agreed that Korea could place a ban on it in times of famine and other emergencies, provided that it would give a month's advance notice to the Japanese government. As for the red ginseng, the Japanese would receive the same treatment as that proffered to Chinese traders. Article 42 of the agreement included a clause stipulating most-favored-nation treatment for Japanese subjects in Korea.[57] In view of the fact that the Korean-American Treaty of 1882 included such a most-favored-nation provision, von Möllendorff had no choice but to accede to Takazoe's demand. Besides, at the time of the Korean-Japanese Treaty of 1876, it was clearly understood that if ever Korea should grant most-favored-nation treatment to a Western power, it would grant the same right to the Japanese government. The Korean-Japanese Trade Regulations and Tariff Agreement, containing forty-two articles, was signed on July 25, 1883, and its ratification was exchanged on August 17. It went into effect beginning on November 3, 1883.

## Von Möllendorff's Other Activities in Korea

Von Möllendorff strongly believed that in the modern world Korea must develop and maintain industrialization and modern educational systems not only in order to gain and keep its true independency but also to win respect from neighboring countries and the world community—a vision that truly materialized some hundred years later, at least, in the case of South Korea. Among other things, he insisted that a Korea of ten million people should have 8,000 elementary schools, 84 secondary schools, a college of natural sciences, one of engineering, and one of foreign languages.[58] In order to initiate and develop modern industry and education, von Möllendorff was deeply involved in various reform and modernization projects. In March 1884, he was placed in charge of directing the Minting Bureau and centralizing the several existing government minting operations. He ordered minting machinery from Germany to improve the quality of the coinage and invited a German geologist to explore Korea's mineral resources.[59]

He became involved in installing and maintaining a Machine Hall, a workshop for manufacturing and repairing military equipment as well as a training center for Korean machinists.[60] He also contributed to the building of the first steam-operated electric generator in Korea.[61] He helped the Korean government to establish a foreign-language school and hired a British language instructor.[62] As a vice minister of the Foreign Office, von Möllendorff participated

in the initiation and compilation of the country's daily events, doing
so in the name of *T'onggi* or *T'ongsŏ Ilgi* (Diary of Office of International Trade and Diplomatic Affairs).[63] He was mainly responsible
for the invitation to a German sericulturist to come to Korea and for
introducing certain modern agricultural techniques to Korea.[64] In
early 1883, von Möllendorff negotiated with Commissioner Ch'en
Shu-t'ang a navigation agreement on the basis of Article VII of the
Sino-Korean Trade Regulations of 1882. By this agreement the
China Merchant's Steam Navigation Company obtained an exclu-
sive right to service the route from Shanghai through Inch'ŏn and
Pusan to Nagasaki, Japan thus dominating Korean foreign trade
and reaping profits from exporting Korean goods and re-exporting
Western goods from China.[65] Though the agreement proved benefi-
cial mainly to the Chinese, Korea nonetheless needed this kind of
agreement in order to transport its import and export goods.

During his tenure in Korea, therefore, not only did he organize
and run the customs service independently of China but he also initiated much-needed reforms in the educational, industrial, commercial, and financial fields.[66] In addition, there were many ideas, projects, and programs that von Möllendorff suggested or considered
proposing for the modernization of Korea. He believed that the
expenses of the royal court were too high and that the government
should increase its revenues by exporting and auctioning off ginseng
abroad (in Hong Kong and Macao), by taxing the licenses for mining and the forestry industry, by improving and exporting the fish-
ery industry, and by reforming Korea's tax systems. He further
believed that the archaic, inhumane, and cruel Korean judicial system, based on that of Ming China (1368–1644), should be reformed
and modernized and that the powers of the parasitic nobles (such as
*Namin, Soron,* and *Pugin*) in mercilessly exploiting the masses should
be drastically curtailed. His reform projects for Korea's future also
included the importation and utilization of milch cows (not necessarily milch lambs, which would devastate what little pastureland
Korea had), the conservation of forests and overused soil, the building of railroads, replacement of the handcraft industry with a modern machine industry and exportation of the products abroad, and
the national and official use of the Korean vernacular language
*(Han'gŭl)* in place of archaic Chinese characters. As an exceptionally
brilliant philologist and linguist, he strongly believed that *Han'gŭl*

was a language rich in vocabulary and yet very simple and logical in structure. He was convinced that the Korean people were superior to the Japanese and might surpass the islanders in the learning of Western sciences—an unusual observation in those days, because Westerners generally insisted that it was the other way around. Although he had strong reservations about the Korean type of absolutism existing during the 1880s, mainly because he felt that King Kojong was not strong and decisive enough to make the system work effectively, he never believed in nor advocated the political democratization of Korea.[67]

He proved to be an innovative and imaginative modernizer. But the problem was that Korea then needed many more men, all of whom had to be as vigorous and far-sighted as von Möllendorff, to help in these multifarious works, but it had only one. Under these circumstances, therefore, von Möllendorff had to try to be at the same time a linguist, diplomat, financier, organizer, and executive in all these works. Despite demands on his time and energy, he was still able to initiate numerous reform projects.[68] Unfortunately for the Koreans, however, many of his modernization projects were discontinued after his dismissal, largely because of a lack of the necessary zeal, funds, and support for such projects on the part of the government leaders and bureaucrats.

## Treaties with Other Powers

Von Möllendorff believed that Korea, to enhance its independence, should conclude treaties with as many powers as possible. He reasoned that the establishment and maintenance of foreign legations in Seoul would in itself be a great boost to the idea that Korea was a sovereign and independent nation.[69] Thus, he eagerly represented the Korean government in negotiating and concluding treaties with England and Germany. In 1883, the Korean government had to renegotiate treaties with the British and Germans because the treaties it had signed with them in 1882 had been rejected by them for their too "liberal" tariff rate (10–13 percent) and for some other stipulated provisions. The British had been opposed to implementation of the Korean-American Treaty of 1882 for the same reason, but had had no success with their opposition. They were, however, able to induce the German government to renegotiate new treaties with Korea.

Harry Parkes, the new British minister in Peking, was instructed to proceed to Seoul to represent the British government, while Edward Zappe, German consul general in Tokyo, represented the German government. Prior to his departure for Korea, Parkes visited Viceroy Li in Tientsin and informed him of his mission to Korea.[70] During the negotiations, von Möllendorff, as vice minister of the Korean Foreign Office, strongly argued against the attempt of Parkes to impose his will on the weak Korean government. On one occasion von Möllendorff became so infuriated with Parkes' arrogance that he walked out of the conference room.[71] In the end, however, Parkes prevailed, representing as he did the mightiest empire in the world. The revised treaties were signed by Min Yŏng-mok, minister of the Korean Foreign Office, for his government, and on the same day (November 26, 1883) by Parkes and Zappe, respectively, for their governments. These treaties provided that duties on imports were to be paid on an *ad valorem* basis, the rates varying from 5 to 20 percent. Thereafter, goods, when transported inland, were to be exempt from further taxation.[72] After the exchange of ratifications in April 1884, the London government made its diplomatic establishment in Seoul an appendage to the British legation in Peking and appointed the minister at Peking as concurrent minister to Korea, installing a consul general in Seoul and a vice-consul at Inch'ŏn. Unlike the governments of Japan and the United States, both of which began to treat Korea as an independent and sovereign nation after the conclusion of their treaties with it, the British government showed no interest whatsoever in promoting the idea that Korea had become an independent kingdom. Its concerns were for the acquisition and expansion of its trading rights and interests there and the use of some of the Korean islands for strategic and military purposes vis-à-vis Imperial Russia. This almost totally one-sided policy toward Korea on the part of the British would eventually generate friction with von Möllendorff and the Korean government, as will be discussed in the following chapters.

The low rate of tariff conceded in the Anglo-Korean Treaty that went into effect on April 28, 1884, created problems for the Korean government with regard to the Chinese and Japanese traders in Korea. The Chinese commissioner, Ch'en Shu-t'ang, and the Japanese minister, Takezoe, both demanded that their nationals be accorded the same treatment as that stipulated in the newly concluded Anglo-Korean Treaty.[73] At first the Korean government evaded these demands and was relectant to comply with them. As Takezoe persisted, however, the three port superintendents at Inch'ŏn, Pusan, and Wŏnsan were all instructed, on August 16, to allow the Japanese and Chinese merchants to pay the lower tariff, as provided by the Anglo-Korean Treaty.[74] For certain confusing reasons, however, the Korean government reversed its position the next day and recalled its instructions.[75] Minister Takezoe was then asked to consider the possibility of applying the low rate of tariff provided for in the Anglo-Korean Treaty only to certain commodities imported from Japan.[76] Inasmuch as Takezoe absolutely refused such a consideration, the Korean government in the end had to notify not only the Japanese legation but also all other legations as well as the Chinese commissioner that it would henceforth collect duties on imports and exports from and to the treaty powers at the lowest rate stipulated in the Anglo-Korean Treaty (November 10, 1884).[77] Then on November 21, the government sent the new instructions to the port superintendents and commissioners at the three open ports and charged them to follow the orders.[78] Thus, it was not until November 1884 that Korea came to have a uniform code for all import and export goods.

Thanks to British imperialism and the practice of most-favored-nation treatment, which every treaty power and even China now enjoyed in Korea, the tariff rates gradually decreased. Between May 1883 (when the Korean-American Treaty went into effect) and November 1883, America's "liberal" tariff rate (10 percent on general commodities and 30 percent on luxury items) was applied in the Korean trade; between November 1883 and April 1884 the more parsimonious Japanese tariff rate (8–10 percent) was applied; and after April 1884, when the Anglo-Korean Treaty went into effect, the lowest tariff (5–7.5 percent) was forced upon all imports into Korea. A rate of only 10–20 percent rather than 25–30 percent was to be charged on all luxury items.

According to the standard of nineteenth-century big-power imperialism vis-à-vis the weak nations of the world, the British treatment of Korea was not exceptionally unfair or severe. Besides, the provisions of the treaties that Korea had concluded with the United

States, Great Britain, and Japan were only marginally different, although the policies of these countries toward Korea were significantly different. Moreover, in view of the fact that even China and Japan had been subjected to unequal treaties by the Western powers, King Kojong had been taking such one-sided treaties realistically and as a matter of course. Thus, the monarch concentrated on utilizing the newly established relations with the United States, Japan, and others as a means of making his kingdom more independent of China and also to modernize it—as, for instance, the Japanese leadership had been doing with the Western powers ever since the 1860s. However, insofar as von Möllendorff was concerned, the tendency of the British and the Japanese to take advantage of weak and seemingly helpless Korea, with little or no regard for the welfare of the Koreans, soured him and hardened his anti-British and anti-Japanese posture during his tenure in Korea.

In 1884, Korea concluded two more treaties, one with Italy and another with Russia. Von Möllendorff was particularly pleased to meet and negotiate with Karl Waeber, the Russian consul at Tientsin and an old acquaintance of his, for a treaty with Russia. Although Kim Pyŏng-si was the chief Korean plenipotentiary, von Möllendorff played the more dominant role. The negotiations went smoothly, and the Russo-Korean Treaty was concluded on July 7, 1884, while ratifications were exchanged in October of 1885. The provisions of the Russo-Korean Treaty of 1884 were identical to those of the treaties that Korea had concluded with other Western nations, except in a few areas. As he had done at the conclusion of treaties with the United States and other Western powers, King Kojong sent a letter to Czar Alexander III stating that Korea, though a dependency to China, was still autonomous in all domestic and foreign affairs. In spite of the fact that Waeber's instructions suggested that he need not negotiate any overland trade provisions, he nonetheless agreed with von Möllendorff and Kim Pyŏng-si upon the inclusion into the final treaty of a provision stipulating future negotiations for an overland trade agreement between two nations. By 1884 Kojong and his advisers had, in fact, become anxious to conclude an overland trade agreement with Russia. It is particularly significant that, in Article VIII, the treaty provided that warships of either country had the right to visit any port of the other contracting party, for Korea had not granted such a right to any of the other signatory powers.[79] Clearly, by granting the right exclusively to Russia, the Korean government meant to encourage the Russian government to establish close relations with it, an idea that was largely von Möllendorff's. As we shall see, von Möllendorff's pro-Russian posture and policy were strengthened even more strongly during the *Kapsin* Coup of 1884.

## CHAPTER 3

# Korea's Search for a New World Order

## The *Kapsin* Coup of 1884

When the United States proved to be slow in providing aid and support for Korea, Kojong became interested in the ideas of the Korean Progressives, a group of liberal reformers who were convinced that the salvation of Korea lay in breaking the old submissive ties with the weak and decadent China and in adopting and imitating what Japan had been doing since the Meiji Restoration.

Although Kojong had never been a great admirer of Japan and, historically speaking, very few of his countrymen had been either, it should be recalled that the conclusion of the Korean-Japanese Treaty of 1876 was possible partly because of the king's strong support for it, despite opposition from the still-influential Taewŏn'gun and the conservative militant literati. By 1883 and 1884, Kojong had learned—largely from the members of the Korean missions that had been to Japan—enough about the tremendous progress that the Japanese had been making since the Meiji Restoration to lead him to conclude that Korea had a great deal to learn from Japan, regardless of Korea's traditionally unhappy relations with the island nation.

The leadership of the Progressives arose from those who had visited Japan on diplomatic or cultural missions in 1876, 1881, and 1882 and also from those who had been members of the first Korean mission to the United States in 1883. The Progressive reformers in Korea were also known as the Party of the Enlightenment *(Kaehwa Tang)*, the Party of Independence *(Tongnip Tang)*, the Progressive

Party *(Chinbo Tang),* or the Pro-Japan Party *(Ch'inil Tang).*[1] Although
they were a tiny minority, they became vocal and effective between
1882 and 1884. The most important of them were Kim Ok-kyun, a
councillor of the Foreign Office and the boldest; Pak Yŏng-hyo, a
brother-in-law to Kojong and the commissioner of the City of Seoul;
and Hong Yŏng-sik, the founder of the Party of Independence. All of
them belonged to the Korean nobility and held government positions of secondary importance.

These reformers were neither profound philosophers nor great
theoreticians; rather, they were idealistic, reform-minded, pro-Japanese and pro-Western, and yet strongly nationalistic politicians. The
main source of their inspiration was Japanese liberalism. They were
immensely impressed with the progress that the Japanese had been
making in imitation of the West. They were ideologically and intellectually inspired and influenced, in particular, by the ideas of Fukuzawa Yukichi, the greatest liberal westernizer of Japan during the
nineteenth century.[2] In fact, some of them maintained close personal
contacts with Fukuzawa. Among other things, they wanted modernization of the army; development of modern education and industry; the founding of newspapers; many other social, legal, and political reforms; and above all, elimination of Chinese influence from
Korea, which they considered detrimental.[3] All of these goals and
more the Progressive wanted to accomplish with Japanese aid and
under its protection. They were also pro-Russian. While visiting
Japan in the early 1880s, Kim Ok-kyun and Pak Yŏng-hyo called
upon the Russian minister in Tokyo and, seeking Russian aid in
winning more independence from China, expressed their desire to
conclude a modern treaty with Russia on the basis of sovereign
equality, and to do so as soon as was feasible.[4]

The position the Kojong took toward the Progressives is intriguing. He liked the ideas, goals, and aspirations of these reformers,
and he began to entertain some sort of admiration toward Japan for
its rapid and efficient modernization. He was quite willing to let the
Progressives try to implement whatever goals and ideas they might
have. However, he did not officially identify himself with them by
giving them active political and public support for three reasons.
First of all, Kojong's faith in the new Japan was somewhat limited
and shallow, reflecting Korea's traditionally anti-Japanese attitude
and also the relative youthfulness of the new Japanese civilization.

Kojong was only partly sure that Japan could serve as a source of Korea's new order—to be not only a model for Korean modernization and independence but also an ally, protector, or a new elder brother in the modern international community into which Korea had drifted.

Second, Kojong was still reluctant to offend China by giving open and active support to the essentially anti-Chinese Progressives, because China, though weakened, was still powerful enough to punish Korea, if it so chose. Lastly, Kojong felt that he was not in a position to repudiate and rebuke the powerful Min faction (supported by his own strong-willed wife) by openly siding with the Progressives. Although Kojong was an absolute autocrat, in fact his real power and authority were seriously limited by such powerful clans as the Mins and also by powerful bureaucrats. For all these reasons, the only thing that Kojong felt he could do for the Progressives was to become a silent, secretive, and unofficial partner to them.

Inasmuch as the Progressives and Kojong meant to modernize Korea and make it truly independent of China under Japanese tutelage, it seems that they conceived of making Japan the senior and protective ally—a new elder brother—rather than making their country truly equal to Japan. Thus, it was obvious that the traditional suzerain-dependency concept still pervaded the nature and conduct of a supposedly new foreign policy of Kojong and his enlightened advisers.

However, that was probably only one side of the story. The other side was that if the realities of East Asian international politics and geopolitical and internal factors in Korea in the 1880s had been different from what they actually were, then king and Progressives, being enabled to strengthen Korean independence and modernize the country more or less on their own, would have planned to achieve their goals without undue aid and protection from Japan. After all, the Koreans had always considered themselves superior to or at least equal to the Japanese. Moreover, even the admiration that Kojong and the Progressives had developed toward the Japanese was reserved and limited—unlike the traditional Korean attitude toward China, especially Ming China. The whole argument put in historical perspective, it should be emphasized that had Korea been more powerful and larger than its neighboring countries, then by the mid-1880s Kojong and his advisers would surely have been debating how, irrespective of historical relations, they could promote and advance the interests of their country at the expense of their neighbors rather than arguing how they could interest Japan, one of the their bigger neighbors, to help them to avert exploitation by another aggressive neighbor in the form of China.

The immediate political enemies of the Progressives were the ruling Conservative elites,[5] consisting of the Min faction and their associates—such as Min T'ae-ho, minister of the Home Office and father of Min Yŏng-ik, who in turn was vice minister of the Foreign Office; and Min Yŏng-mok, Yi Cho-yŏn, Yun Tae-jun, Han Kyu-jik, and Cho Yŏng-ha.

In comparison with the Taewŏn'gun, the Mins were reform-minded in the same sense as were the leaders of China's self-strengthening movement, which has attempted to reinvigorate the Ch'ing dynasty by means of Western technologies—in particular, those of military science—while coping with Western penetration. In general, however, the Mins were not interested in modernizing and westernizing Korea along the same line as the leaders of Meiji Japan had been following. In that sense, the Mins were conservative. Moreover, the Mins were probably more interested in promoting their own interests than in serving the welfare and well-being of their countrymen. Initially, the Progressives had tried to work within the framework of the Min-dominated self-strengthening movement. But eventually they were disillusioned and disappointed with the Mins' half-hearted approach to modernization and their subservient attitude toward China. By October 1884 the gap between them became irreconcilable and the Progressive concluded that they must physically eliminate the ruling Min faction before they could launch genuine reforms with the Japanese aid.

In some ways, it was unfortunate that von Möllendorff and the Progressives were not in the same camp, inasmuch as they had at least three things in common: (1) they both wanted to make Korea truly independent of China; (2) both were devoted to the modernization of Korea; and (3) both were pro-Russia in that they all believed that Russia might be in a position to help Korea to become truly independent of China. However, both sides were diametrically opposed to each other on another important issue: whereas the Progressives were strongly in favor of collaborating with the Japanese to achieve their goals in Korea, von Möllendorff was equally strong in opposition to Japanese influence and domination. In addition, they disagreed on some important fiscal and economic matters. For example, Kim Ok-kyun wanted to finance a modern military unit that Pak Yŏng-hyo had been planning to establish with the aid of two graduates of the Japanese military school.[6] But von Möllendorff was opposed to such a project, and Viceroy Li Hung-chang readily agreed with him.[7] Von Möllendorff, like Viceroy Li, was against any kind of policies or projects that might increase Japanese influence in Korea. Even though von Möllendorff was opposed to the Progressives and their pro-Japanese policies, he had no choice but to maintain a less-than-benevolent neutrality before and during the coup attempt, because he was well aware that King Kojong was deeply, though unofficially, involved in the plot.

In view of the deepening hostility and deteriorating relations developing between the Progressives and the Conservatives, some moderate Korean leaders, such as Ŏ Yun-jung and Kim Hong-jip, tried to bring about a reconciliation or compromise between these two antagonistic groups. They made this attempt by emphasizing the importance of winning reforms by gradual means and the necessity of building a strong national defense. In addition, they made a proposal for the neutralization of Korea and for mutual cooperation among Korea, China, and Japan as a means of checking Western encroachment upon East Asia.[8] In retrospect, it seems that the suggestions made by Ŏ and Kim—reconciliation between the Progressives and the Conservative Min faction; gradual reforms for the modernization of Korea; and the neutralization of the peninsula—were the most sensible and appealing solutions to the problems of Korea in the 1880s. It would have been good for Korea if Kojong, von Möllendorff, the Progressives, and the Conservatives had somehow been able to see the merits of these proposals and work together to achieve them peacefully. Unfortunately for the future of Korea, however, none of these endeavors succeeded, because none of the parties in power paid any attention to the proposals.

The Japanese liberal leaders insisted that their government should help the Korean Progressives to rid their country of China's domination and to modernize. To the Japanese government in the 1880s, however, the most important and urgent diplomatic issue was the revision of its unequal treaties with the Western powers.[9] Furthermore, avoiding a war with China at that time was more important than helping the Korean rebels at the risk of war. Moreover, from the standpoint of the Tokyo government, it was legally difficult, if not impossible, to give active diplomatic and economic support to the Korean Progressives, since they had never been officially in charge of the government (except some secondary- or third-level positions). Thus, all in all, the Japanese government leaders sympathized with the aspirations of the Korean Progressives but refrained from doing anything that might lead to a conflict between Japan and China. Contrary to the official policy of his own government, however, Minister Takezoe lent active support and encouragement to the Korean Progressives.[10]

In the meantime, China's vacillating attitude toward its tributaries was once again being expressed in its handling of Annam, vis-à-vis the French, actions which strengthened Kojong's conviction that China would no longer be of much use to Korea and that, therefore, he must seek a new ally or protector elsewhere. Through inept diplomacy and without clearly defined political objectives, without the popular support of its people, and without sound military and naval strategy and tactics, China drifted into an undeclared war against the French over the kingdom of Annam between May 1883 and April 1885. In the end, China's policy—or nonpolicy—of procrastination, compromise, indecision, and drift in dealing with the French over Annam eventually brought a humiliating defeat to the Chinese and a political and military victory to the French.

It should be noted that at the beginning of the Vietnam Crisis of 1884 and 1885, Li advocated a policy, unlike that of his aggressive stance toward Korea, of negotiation and accommodation with the French—for he believed that Vietnam (Tongking and Annam) did not constitute a force of vital importance to the security of Peking. Thereupon, the *ch'ing-liu* leaders accused Viceroy Li of being cowardly and guilty of defeatism and appeasement. Even though the Ch'ing court and Li did not want war with the French over Vietnam, they were eventually dragged into it, partly if not mainly because of the outcries of the *ch'ing-liu tang*. Following the Chinese defeat and loss of Annam to the French, the *ch'ing-liu tang* was held to be partly responsible for the disaster and began to be discredited.[11]

In retrospect, one suspects that what China should have done was to avoid another inglorious military defeat by granting the French what they had already won in 1874 in a less humiliating diplomatic manner, since the Peking government had neither the will nor the military capability to force the French out of Annam. By taking vacillating and shifting courses of action, China in the end lost both Annam and what little honor and prestige it had retained up to that time. The loss had a significant impact on Burma, Japan, and Korea. Encouraged by the French victory, the British made Burma its protectorate in 1885. And further north, the Korean Progressives in Korea and the Japanese Liberals in Japan decided that this might be a golden opportunity for them to oust the Chinese from Korea.[12]

From von Möllendorff who just returned from Tientsin Kojong learned that the Chinese army had been humiliated in Annam and that seven Chinese warships had been sunk by the French within thirty minutes on August 22, 1884.[13] Kojong and his advisers wondered whether the Sino-French War might force China to withdraw all its troops from Korea and asked Minister Foote about it.[14]

The Japanese supporters of the Korean Progressives advocated using the French against the Chinese in support of the Korean Progressives. For example, Gotō Shōjirō and Itakagi Taisuke advocated an alliance whereby Japanese volunteers would help the French against the Chinese in Annam in return for French support of Korean independence and a loan of one million yen to the Korean Progressives.[15] Although the idea was not adopted in the end, the Korean court, the Progressives, and the Japanese Liberals all believed that, if and when the coup being planned by the Progressives were to be implemented, the Chinese government might choose not to intervene because of their deep involvement with the French in Annam.[16]

Both Minister Lucius H. Foote and American naval attaché George C. Foulk, an intimate friend of the Progressives, were aware of the projected coup attempt. When the Progressives told Foulk of the plot, he tried to discourage their use of assassination as a method for achieving political change.[17] On November 2, 1884, Minister Takezoe, who had returned to Seoul in October after a ten-month leave of absence, had an audience with Kojong and informed him that the Japanese government had decided to cancel Korea's 400,000 yen balance of the 1882 indemnity.[18] But he also demanded and received for Japanese merchants in Korea the same most-favored-nation treatment provided for Chinese merchants in the Sino-Korean Trade Regulations of 1882.[19]

The scene of the *Kapsin* Coup was the inauguration party for the new Post Office in Seoul on the evening of December 4, 1884. Among the guests attending the party were the leaders of the Progressives—Kim Ok-kyun, Pak Yŏng-hyo, Sŏ Kwang-bom—and the leaders of the Min clan and their associates, including Min Yŏng-ik, Yi Cho-yŏn, and Han Kyu-jik; and certain foreign guests, including von Möllendorff, Minister Foote, British consul general William G. Aston, Chinese commissioner Ch'en Shu-t'ang, and Shimamura Hisashi, the chief aide of Minister Takezoe, who excused himself from the party. The most joyful and talkative among them were von Möllendorff and Min Yŏng-ik. In the confusion created by a cry of "Fire!" about 10:00 P.M. in the midst of the festivities,[20] Min Yŏng-ik was severely wounded; his father, Min T'ae-ho, and some other leaders of the conservative faction, including six ministers, were later assassinated.[21] The staggering and bloody Min Yŏng-ik fell into the arms of von Möllendorff, who, covered as he was with Min's blood, was also thought to be wounded. Von Möllendorff did whatever he could to stop Min's bleeding and, taking him to his own residence, called for Dr. Horace N. Allen, an American missionary doctor and the resident physician at the royal household, who was able to take care of Min's wounds. Dr. Allen did not personally care for the German diplomat and considered von Möllendorff anti-American and antimissionary, but his own sense of duty as a physician compelled him to come to von Möllendorff's residence in order to save the life of the pro-Chinese conservative leader Min.[22]

Von Möllendorff was genuinely afraid that he himself might become a target of the assassins, because of his intimate ties with the Mins. He spent that night dreadfully, in fear of his own life. Cho Yŏng-ha, who had escorted von Möllendorff from China to Seoul late in 1882 and had been the first Korean official to meet him, came to see him in the middle of the night. Soon after he left von Möllendorff's residence to see the king, Cho was cut down, along with some other ministers of the conservative faction. Von Möllendorff was genuinely sorry for Cho's death, because he had respected his opinions and valued his friendship. He later suspected that the reason he had not been killed in the 1884 coup was that many believed both Min and he had died earlier. In reality, however, there had been no real danger whatever for his life, because the Progressive leaders had never contemplated assassinating von Möllendorff. One wonders whether von Möllendorff, during a night like that, might have thought about "the Min ghost" that the Koreans were so worried about before he moved into his "haunted" house in early 1883.

These murders were all committed without the involvement of Kojong, but still in his name. At the coup leaders' request, moreover, the king readily sent a written appeal (though without the royal seal) to Takezoe asking for his protection. Thereupon Takezoe led two hundred legation guards in to protect the royal family.[23] On December 5, the Progressives proclaimed a new government, headed by Yi Chae-wŏn as Left State Councillor and Hong Yŏng-sik as Right State Councillor. The government drafted a Fourteen Point Proclamation for radical reform in Korea. It called for a radical revision of Sino-Korean relations, immediate return of the Taewŏn'gun, equal rights for all people, and a reform in land taxes.[24] That same day the newly instituted cabinet leaders invited certain Western representatives—American minister Foote, British consul Aston, and German consul general Zembsch—to the palace to see them and the king. They apparently wanted to win their approval or recognition for what they had just done. On the way to the palace the representatives dropped in at von Möllendorff's residence to discuss their plans for dealing with the new government. Zembsch was especially anxious to hear his opinion, because when he had arrived in Seoul in October 1884, he had been instructed by the Berlin government to work closely with von Möllendorff. Moreover, since von Möllendorff's contract with the old government had not been terminated and because he was therefore still the only foreign policy adviser (in reality) to the king, the Western representatives believed that, whatever they should do with or against the new government, they should seek his advice. Von Möllendorff argued, however, that without the presence of the Chinese representative they should not make the final decision on whether or not to support the new government. While Zembsch agreed with von Möllendorff's view, others felt otherwise. Without the support of von Möllendorff, they proceeded to the palace.[25] Disappointed, von Möllendorff considered leaving Korea for China, but decided not to do so. When Foote, Aston, and Zembsch met Kojong on December 5, the monarch had little to say, clearly indicating the timid manner in which he approved of the radical turn of events in Korea.[26]

Learning of the outbreak of the coup on December 4 and uncertain of China's rights and obligations, Commissioner Ch'en Shu-t'ang and General Wu Chao-yu were hesitant to take any action against the rebels. But the younger and more daring Yüan Shih-k'ai decided otherwise, insisting that there was no time to lose.[27] On December 6, Yüan led 1,500 Chinese soldiers to Ch'angdŏk palace, where the frightened royal family was quartered under Japanese protection. Outnumbered and overwhelmed by the Chinese, the Japanese retreated to their own legation.[28] The reformist-rebels then asked Takezoe to remove Kojong to Inch'ŏn, but the Japanese minister refused. Hong Yŏng-sik and Pak Yŏng-gyo stayed with the king and were killed by Yüan's troops.[29] Other Progressives—such as Kim Ok-kyun, Pak Yŏng-hyo, Sŏ Kwang-bom, and Sŏ Chae-p'il—followed the Japanese minister. In the midst of this crisis Yüan, angered by Kojong's involvement in the coup, proposed to dethrone the king, but his superior, General Wu Chao-yu overruled him and, instead, placed the king under Chinese "protection." In the Chinese camp, Kojong was pressured to void all decrees and appointments made by the rebel government and to declare all members of the coup to be "traitors."[30] Easily forcing the weak-willed Kojong to go along with his scheme, Yüan was able to turn the revolutionary tide in his favor and take command of the situation. Although von Möllendorff was "sickened" by all the fighting and killing, he was pleased that the pro-Japanese government was overthrown and that the Conservatives, his political friends, were about to regain the power.

The excited mobs turned anti-Japanese, killed many Japanese, and looted Japanese houses.[31] As the Japanese legation buildings were burning, Takezoe, the Korean rebels, and some Japanese nationals fled to Inch'ŏn, as his predecessor, Minister Hanabusa, had done in 1882. Takezoe stayed in Inch'ŏn to greet Japanese foreign minister Inoue Kaoru. Kojong, still in Yüan's "protection," ordered the arrest of the surviving leaders of the coup. Von Möllendorff, an avowed enemy of the Progressives, and Cho Pyŏng-ho then rushed to Inch'ŏn to prevent the rebels from fleeing to Japan but they were unsuccessful.[32]

On December 7, after three days of turmoil and fighting, the reform government was overthrown. The Conservatives were restored to power and von Möllendorff was reinstated. Sim Sun-t'aek was appointed chief state councillor, Cho Pyŏng-ho was appointed

minister of the Foreign Office, and Kim Yun-sik was made another
vice minister to the same office.[33] On December 10, Kojong was
finally able to return to his palace from the Chinese custody and
restored normal government function.[34] Meanwhile, the news of the
coup reached the Chinese and Japanese governments on December
10 and 11, respectively, after its complete failure. Altogether, more
than three hundred persons lost their lives in the three days of riot-
ing, Koreans constituting the majority of the victims although they
had done the least fighting. The Chinese troops were victorious in
the end, as they outnumbered the Japanese seven to one. The Western representatives in Seoul asked von Möllendorff to do everything
he could to restore and maintain order and peace. Viceroy Li himself sent a telegram to von Möllendorff, asking him to do his utmost
to mediate the deteriorating relations among Korea, Japan, and
China. Von Möllendorff made many trips between Seoul and
Inch'ŏn to persuade Minister Takezoe (who was waiting there for
the arrival of more Japanese troops and a plenipotentiary) that
Japan should not start a war against China by bringing in more soldiers.[35]

In Japan the public was outraged by the Chinese actions in
Korea.[36] But the Japanese government decided to avoid any conflict
with China.[37] Even Foreign Minister Inoue, who had wanted to
exploit the Sino-French war, changed his attitude in favor of a peaceful settlement with China. He volunteered to go to Korea for negotiations aimed at carrying out the Japanese policy of "peace with
honor" and preserving Korean independence through a peaceful
settlement.[38] With regard to Minister Takezoe's role in the coup, the
Japanese government, though unhappy with his "clumsy" and
unauthorized conduct, decided to cover up his misconduct by sending Japanese investigators to Korea.[39] On December 20, Foreign
Minister Inoue was appointed as a special ambassador to Korea to
negotiate with the Korean government and also with the Chinese
officials, if feasible.[40]

Meanwhile, the Peking government sent Commissioner Wu Ta-
ch'eng and Admiral Ting Ju-ch'ang, with a force of five hundred
soldiers, to Korea ostensibly to investigate the incident and also to
"help" the Korean government in restoring peace and order.[41]
Commissioner Wu advised the king, Kim Hong-jip, and the new
foreign minister Cho Pyŏng-ho to put the entire blame on Minister
Takezoe.[42] Even Yüan Shih-k'ai became the target of Wu's investi-

gation, and on January 31, 1885, Yüan was sent back to China.[43] Once again Kojong's conciliatory and moderate approach prevailed over the relatively hard-line approach advocated by the Chinese and by pro-Chinese Korean officials. In order to smooth Korean relations with Japan, Kojong's recommendation was to put the blame upon the Korean rebels.[44] In a conciliatory move, he appointed Sŏ Sang-u and von Möllendorff as special envoys to Japan to pacify and negotiate with the Japanese government.[45] He also asked Minister Foote, Consul Zembsch, and Consul General Aston to mediate between Japan and Korea; he even requested that the president of the United States send Foote to Japan to exercise his good offices.[46] The king further asked if Foote would accompany a Korean envoy to be sent to Japan "invoking the good offices of the United States to bring about an amicable settlement," as provided by the Korean-American Treaty. Leaving Naval Attaché Foulk in charge of the legation, Foote, on December 22, went to Inch'ŏn with the intention of going on to Japan. But he changed his plans because Foreign Minister Inoue had himself come to Korea.[47] Sensing the seriousness of the situation in Korea, Foote requested Rear Admiral Lee Davis, commander of the American Naval Forces in the Far East, to send the American warship *Trenton* and some marines to the American legation in Seoul for "such duty" as he might assign them.[48]

Before any actual negotiations took place between plenipotentiary Kim Hong-jip and Foreign Minister Inoue, Foote had talks with both of them. Foote advised Kim to show "prudence and conciliation" in the negotiations with Inoue.[49] And he advised Inoue that acquisition of any portion of Korean territory would "be most unwise" and that "Japan could afford to treat Korea liberally and at the same time maintain her own honor." Inoue agreed with Foote.[50] In an interview with Foote, Commissioner Wu Ta-ch'eng assured him that "he was instructed to use his utmost endeavors to bring about an amicable settlement" but that he had no power to settle any questions that may have arisen between China and Japan.[51]

## Von Möllendorff's Despair with the Japanese

Meanwhile, Foreign Minister Inoue, who arrived at Inch'ŏn on January 1, 1885, accompanied by three warships and two thousand soldiers, had an audience with the king. He threatened to return to

Japan immediately if the Korean government were to put the blame on Takezoe and to reject Japanese demands.[52] Receiving a conciliatory response from the king, he decided to stay.

On January 7, Inoue and Kim Hong-jip, assisted by von Möllendorff, started negotiations. Although Inoue had already heard a great deal about von Möllendorff this was the first direct encounter between the two men. It should be recalled that, soon after von Möllendorff had arrived at Seoul in December of 1882, Inoue appointed Takezoe as the Japanese minister to Seoul partly because he believed that the German diplomat, an old acquaintance of Takezoe, might help in promoting Japanese interests in Korea. As it turned out, however, von Möllendorff was completely devoted to promoting the welfare and interests of Korea, making concessions to the Japanese and doing business with them only when it was absolutely necessary. In fact, given that von Möllendorff's stance in Korea became distinctly anti-Japanese, no doubt Inoue resented von Möllendorff. Thus, while von Möllendorff's presence on the Korean delegation might not have hurt the Korean government, it certainly did nothing to help the Korean cause. Besides, in view of Japan's superior military strength and Inoue's strong determination to impose Japanese terms on Korea, von Möllendorff had no actual leverage for negotiation. Thus, on the very next day the Treaty of Seoul was imposed on them. Among its provisions were that the Korean government must send a letter of apology to the Japanese government; pay an indemnity of 110,000 yen to the relatives of those Japanese who had suffered; punish those who had killed or injured Japanese subjects; and provide the site and costs for constructing a new Japanese legation building.[53] Thus, the consequence of Kojong's tacit support for the Progressives' plot for making Japan a senior partner of Korea was its imposition of a humiliating treaty on his kingdom.

More than anyone else von Möllendorff was sickened by the Japanese and their selfish and unreliable policy toward Korea. On February 5, the king sent Sŏ Sang-u and von Möllendorff to Japan on a mission of apology. Entirely disgusted with both the Japanese and the Chinese behavior in the policies toward Korea, von Möllendorff became strongly convinced that the salvation of his adopted country lay in forming an alliance, not with decayed China, not with selfish Japan, and not with a far-away and indifferent United States, but with nearby Russia. Thus, it was during this trip to Japan that von

Möllendorff conferred with Russian diplomats in Tokyo about a possible alliance between Korea and Russia, as explained in detail in the following chapters. Unlike von Möllendorff, Foote, having been concerned with the real possibility of harsher Japanese terms—such as the annexation of a portion of Korean territory—felt that the provisions of the treaty turned out to be most creditable to Japan and most liberal to Korea.[54]

In the meantime, in Korea there was a panic, due to the rumor that the Japanese might start a war against China.[55] The Korean leaders feared that either China or Japan might take King Kojong into protective custody in case of such a war. Accordingly, they asked Sir Harry Parkes, the British minister to China, to send some British soldiers to protect the safety of the king, but the British refused.[56] Unfortunately, neither Japan nor China consulted with the Korean government or informed it of a forthcoming conference in Tientsin, where the central issue was the future of Korea. Viceroy Li and Prince Itō opened the negotiation, whose purpose was to settle the wider and broader implications of the Sino-Japanese conflict in Korea. Unwilling to offend the Chinese or Japanese, the Seoul government had neither requested that the governments of Peking and Tokyo inform or consult it about the conference nor protested when they did not. Thus, eight years after Korea's independence had been officially recognized by Japan in a written treaty and two years after the same was upheld by the United States, the fate of Korea was about to be negotiated by two of Korea's neighbors without Korean participation or knowledge.

The result of the Li-Itō negotiation was the Tientsin (Li-Itō) Convention of April 1885. The agreement provided that each side was to withdraw its troops from Korea within four months after the signature of the treaty; that each side would encourage the king of Korea to hire foreign military instructors for training a peace-keeping force in Korea; and that in case of future disturbances in Korea, one signatory was to give advance notice in writing to the other if it wanted to send troops to Korea.[57] In July 1885 both Chinese and Japanese troops were withdrawn.

From the standpoint of von Möllendorff, Kojong and his reform-minded advisers, the failure of the *Kapsin* Coup, the Treaty of Seoul, and the Tientsin Convention all meant that, henceforth, the Japanese, be it the government or its Liberal leaders, could not be relied to provide the political, military, and other support necessary for the modernization of Korea. Von Möllendorff already held a dim view of the Japanese policy vis-à-vis Korea and had no faith in Japan's willingness to help Korea in its modernization efforts; now he was disturbed by the harsh terms imposed on Korea by Foreign Minister Inoue. The king too was obviously disappointed with the whole fiasco of the coup attempt. And it was indeed unfortunate for Kojong and his kingdom that the *Kapsin* Coup had failed, because its failure had a harmful effect on the reform and modernization movement, which was strategic to the king's policies.

The coup failed largely because of Chinese intervention. If the Chinese had not intervened and the coup leaders had been able to accomplish their objective, then Kojong might have been able not only to make his country completely independent of China but also to modernize and develop Korea's industry and economy with technical aid and a financial loan from Japan. If all of these eventualities had happened in the 1880s and early 1890s, there might then have been no Sino-Japanese War of 1894 and 1895, nor any Russo-Japanese War of 1904 and 1905. To be sure, the Japanese policy of domination in East and Southeast Asia a half-century later—in the 1930s and early 1940s—would have come under any circumstances. But if the *Kapsin* Coup had been successful, then the timing and the method of the Japanese takeover of Korea might have been quite different from what they in fact were.

In the meantime, Foote left Korea in January 1885, and Naval Attaché Foulk became chargé d'affaires ad interim, in charge of the American legation in Seoul;[58] and in Washington, D.C., Thomas F. Bayard replaced Frelinghuysen as secretary of state in March 1885. Foulk was even more interested in helping the Korean government with American aid than Foote had been. Foulk was, in fact, very well aware that the king was unhappy with the results of the *Kapsin* Coup and that he was anxious to declare and maintain Korean neutrality in case of war between China and Japan. That Kojong could not undertake such action was apparent, because he feared China, which was demanding that Korea apply for further assistance from the Chinese government. In this situation, Foulk strongly believed that the Korean government should organize and train its military forces in a more effective way and that his own government could help the Korean to do so.[59] Foulk also felt that the *Kapsin* Coup had arisen, in a measure, from the American government's delay in heeding the king's request for American military instructors.[60] He thus repeatedly urged his superiors in Washington to comply with the king's desire. He wrote that Korea's most pressing need in its present deplorable straits was to hire a number of competent Western military instructors, preferably American.[61] It seems, however, that Bayard was even less interested in sending American advisers to Korea than Frelinghuysen had been. To Foulk he wrote that the Korean desire for Americans to be sent out with the sanction of the United States government was most friendly and flattering, but that it could not be acceded to without Congressional consent; that, therefore, the urgency of the Korean appeals for the immediate dispatch of such advisers was almost "embarrassing"; and that, moreover, there is the most abundant evidence that the suggestion of so employing American army officers is not of the nature of a selfish proposal.[62] In short, owing to the inaction of Congress, the United States government had to delay any action on the matter.[63] Naturally, the king felt deeply disappointed at the delay and presumably considered hiring nationals from some other country.

Concerning the king's alleged vacillation in seeking foreign aid from different countries, M. Frederick Nelson strongly charges that, "with a habit of subservience to a stronger power extending over centuries, she [Korea] vacillated between the alternate overlordship of her two strongest neighbors, Russia and Japan."[64] Although Nelson's harsh indictment is not incorrect, it should nonetheless be noted that a small dependent nation like Korea, which had lived under the cultural and political influence of suzerain China for so long, could not be expected to behave all of a sudden like a completely independent and sovereign country, particularly in view of the fact that China—despite the treaties that Korea had concluded with other powers—tried to control Korea too tightly. Furthermore, Kojong felt that if he could win aid from the United States, or Japan, or Russia, he might be able to limit or even eliminate the Chinese influence from his kingdom. Without any such aid from a powerful third power, he realized he had absolutely no chance of removing the Chinese. Accustomed to the traditional suzerain-dependency system, therefore, Kojong was searching for a new protective elder brother in the old fashion in which China had been such to his country in the past. On the other hand, as the subject was already dealt with and will be discussed further, it should be stressed at this point that if Korea had been stronger and bigger than its neighbors, then by the mid-1880s Kojong would not have still been seeking a new elder brother who would supersede its historical suzerain-dependency ties with China.

In light of the Chinese perception of Korea as being strategically more important to Peking than such southern provinces as Chekiang and Kiangsu, and in view of the vital Chinese commitment to the policy of keeping Korea under their influence, it was unrealistic and naive for the Progressive leaders and Kojong to think that they might be able to establish a pro-Japanese government by eliminating pro-Chinese officials and by expelling the Chinese from Korea and that the Chinese, after being ejected, would quit the country permanently. They should have realized that China would never stay out of Korea in the 1880s, regardless of their conflict with the French over Annam. The Chinese commitment to their policy of dominating the peninsula was so strong that, in the 1880s, they would have gone to war against Japan to prevent Korea from falling under Japanese domination. That is exactly what happened in the mid-1890s.

The question as to whether or not China's policy of dominating Korea at the risk of war with Japan in the 1880s and early 1890s was a wise and farsighted one is an entirely different matter. In view of the fact that China's imperialistic policy toward Korea during a decade and a half period led it into a humiliating and fatal defeat at the hands of the Japanese following the Sino-Japanese War of 1894 and 1895, it would have been better and wiser if China had adopted a noninterventionist policy in Korea and had concentrated on strengthening its own government, industry, technology, army, and navy, in the 1880s. In retrospect, therefore, one could well argue that what the Ch'ing court should have done was to let the Korean Progressives take over the government, thereby providing them and their king with some chance of modernizing their own country in their own terms. But the Manchu and Chinese leadership in the 1880s was not that farsighted nor was it enlightened enough to perceive Sino-Korean relations in such a long-term perspective or in view of such remote goals. Furthermore, before the Ch'ing court had ample opportunity to study the riotous situation in Korea, the highly energetic and aggressive Yüan, unlike the more cautious and careful Ch'en and Wu, had already gotten himself and his Chinese troops deeply involved in fighting against the Japanese soldiers under Takezoe. Thus Yüan, without consulting Viceroy Li or the Ch'ing court, had initiated what their course of action would have been: a military intervention in the *Kapsin* Coup in Korea.

In view of the fact that Japan finally attacked and occupied Manchuria in 1931, and even some parts of mainland China soon thereafter, the Japanese seizure of Korea would have taken place in any case, as a preliminary step toward conquering China. After all, the peninsula was directly on the route of Japanese Asian expansion. Japan's eventual control or domination of Korea was inevitable, even if Korea had escaped Japanese domination of 1905. Yet if the *Kapsin* Coup had been successful in 1884 and 1885, Korean leaders could have had some golden opportunities to modernize and strengthen their country, with Japanese aid, before and after the mid-1880s, thereby making their peninsula a reasonably strong and prosperous nation. Inasmuch as a stable, prosperous, and genuinely independent Korea would have undoubtedly served as a buffer state for China vis-à-vis Japan and the success of the coup would have been the beginning of the process of developing Korea into a strong nation, its failure may be seen to have been unfortunate not only for Korea but, ironically, for China as well.

Although von Möllendorff was essentially opposed to the coup attempt, he tried to maintain a neutrality. But he was dragged into the incident, mainly because of his importance as the only adviser (and influential) to the Korean king and government. When the Western representatives seemed inclined to deal officially with the newly established pro-Japanese government, von Möllendorff let them know that they ought not to do so unless the Chinese representative was heard and was found to agree. So when the Chinese army under Yüan toppled the new government, he was more than happy about it. And he did play a role in convincing Takezoe and other Japanese leaders that, as bad as the whole situation was in Korea, it did not warrant Japan's launching of a full-scale war against China. Yet he was plunged into utter despair at the harsh terms that Japan imposed upon Korea following the failure of the coup. He became even more mistrustful about the Japanese vis-à-vis Korea. In his perception, the Japanese Liberal leaders and even some officials (such as Minister Takezoe) not only encouraged but instigated the coup. When things became difficult due to the Chinese military intervention, they backed down. Then, after the failure of the coup, their government imposed harsh terms on the feeble government of Korea. Even from the beginning, von Möllendorff was dubious of the Japanese ambitions and the intentions in Korea. Following the failure of the coup, he became convinced that the Japanese influence in Korea would be nothing but detrimental to Korea.

An interesting and important question arises here: What would have happened to von Möllendorff's career in Korea if the coup had been successful? In view of the Chinese government's strong commitment to maintenance of its supremacy in Korea and the Japanese government's limited political interest in Korea in the mid-1880s, the *Kapsin* Coup was destined to fail, and so the question is purely hypothetical but pertinent and significant. If the coup had been successful and, therefore, the pro-Japanese government formed at the initial stage of revolt had lasted, Kojong, fond as he was of von Möllendorff, would probably have kept the German diplomat in charge of important governmental projects or duties. Still in Korean governmental service, von Möllendorff would likely have been placed in some kind of domestic reform and modernization projects (in addition to running the Customs Service) rather than in formulating a new Korean foreign policy. Von Möllendorff, therefore, would not have been given a chance to try to make Russia the new protector of Korea, which is the topic of the next chapter.

*King Kojong of the Late Yi Dynasty of Korea*

*Paul Georg von Möllendorff in the Costume
of Korean Nobility, 1882–1885*

*Von Möllendorff's Residence at Pakdong in Seoul*

*Paul Georg von Möllendorff at the Age of Twelve*

*Von Möllendorff as German Vice-Consul at*
*Tientsin in 1879*

*Von Möllendorff in China, sometime after returning
from Korea in 1885*

*Von Möllendorff's Grave at a Cemetery in Shanghai*

CHAPTER 4

# Von Möllendorff's Search for a New Order

## Von Möllendorff and the Americans

Of all the accomplishments, programs, and policies for which von Möllendorff was, either directly or indirectly, responsible in Korea between 1882 and 1885—establishment of the Maritime Customs Service; conclusion of the Trade Regulations and Tariff Agreement with Japan; negotiation and ratification of treaties between Korean and other powers; establishment of Western-style schools; erection of an arsenal; initiation of match- and glass-making; initiation of minting; exploration of Korean mineral resources; installation of a steam-operated electric-generator; initiation of modern agricultural science and sericulture; and many other reform activities—his attempt to make Russia a senior ally of Korea turned out to be the most thorny and controversial. Von Möllendorff reasoned that, in light of the unfortunate geopolitical factors to which Korea was subject and of its tragic historical experiences with its neighbors, Korea must possess a strong army as well as a reliable and strong protective ally. After starting to work for the Korean king and government, he became convinced that both China and Japan were already too influential in Korea and therefore detrimental to its progress and independence.

In order to free Korea from the harmful influences of China and Japan, he wanted at first to obtain American and British support and approached American minister Foote and British minister Harry Parkes in Peking to this end. But he concluded that neither of them was interested in helping him. In fact, he was convinced that they supported either Japan or China in furthering alien control of Korea. Foote, in turn was highly critical of von Möllendorff, feeling that the German adviser was trying to restrict legitimate intercourse between his legation and the Korean Foreign Office.

Actually, the initial relations between von Möllendorff and Foote had been very cordial. When Foote arrived at Seoul in May 1883, he stayed at von Möllendorff's residence at the invitation of the latter. And in the ceremony involving the exchange of ratification of the Korean-American Treaty of 1882 that same month, Vice Foreign Minister von Möllendorff assumed an important role, serving as a sort of interpreter for Foote and others. Even after Mrs. Foote joined her husband some time later, the Footes continued to stay at von Möllendorff's residence, since their own house had not yet been made ready for occupancy.[1]

Troublesome relations between these two Western diplomats started when Foote, without consulting with von Möllendorff in advance, influenced the king to send a diplomatic mission headed by Min Yŏng-ik to the United States in the summer of 1883.[2] During this time von Möllendorff remained at home owing to illness and could not participate in deciding if the mission should be sent to the United States.

A basic divergence of opinion between these two men centered on von Möllendorff's contention that the mission itself was unnecessary, since he believed that the United States would hardly be willing to play any significant role in Korean affairs. Even more pointedly, von Möllendorff felt that Foote should have first consulted with him on the issue of a mission. There subsequently ensued ill-feeling and a struggle for power and influence between von Möllendorff, a proud and strong-willed "official" adviser to the king, and an equally strong-willed and sensitive Foote, whose advisership to the monarch was of an "unofficial" nature.

An American naval surgeon George W. Woods of the USS *Juniata*, who visited Korea in the spring of 1884 and received von Möllendorff's invitation to his house, described the von Möllendorff–Foote controversy as follows:

> Mr. von Mohlendorff also came down, and will visit the ship in a few days. Though on bad terms with our Minister, he was very courteous

to the officers he met on shore, and invited any of us to make his house our home during our visit to Seoul; but of course we could not accept without offending Mr. Foote. He has become thoroughly denationalised, and wears the Corean costume of a high official. His jealousy of the Americans is extreme, and we understand he has forbidden the Customs-House officials to give us any information.[3]

There were some technical economic issues on which von Möllendorff and Minister Foote disagreed. Von Möllendorff was opposed to Foote's proposal that American traders make good payment of duties on imports, and exports, doing so in "the American Trade Dollar." Von Möllendorff insisted that the General Trade Regulations he had complied and codified should replace the provisions of the Korean-American Treaty of 1882; however, Minister Foote contended that the regulations should be subject to any provisions of the Korean-American Treaty. On both accounts Foote strongly protested to the Korean government and won, superseding von Möllendorff's objection—a circumstance that made the German very hostile toward the American minister.[4]

But there was a much more important and broader point of contention between these two Western diplomats. As the representative of the first Western nation that had concluded a modern treaty with Korea; as the first Western minister to be dispatched to Seoul; and as an envoy in whom the Korean king held an abiding faith in his capacity as a kind of unofficial adviser, Minister Foote demanded that he have as much access to the Korean king and government as he wanted. At the same time von Möllendorff, as the only Western and legal adviser to the Korean government and as a confidant of the king, maintained that he should be the most important foreign adviser, official or unofficial, to the monarch and his government and that he should have the power to regulate or influence the relations between the Korean Foreign Office and Western representatives in Seoul. In addition, von Möllendorff mistrusted Foote, because he believed that the American minister was excessively pro-Japan. Inasmuch as the minister was also strongly pro-Korean, Foote's seemingly pro-Japanese posture should not have bothered von Möllendorff, but apparently it did.

There remained some additional sources of disagreement between von Möllendorff and Foote. While von Möllendorff, though an advocate of the modernization and independence of Korea, was on good terms with the Mins, the leaders of the conservative pro-China faction, Foote was more in sympathy with the increasingly visible and vocal leaders of the anti-Chinese and pro-Japanese Progressives. Moreover, Foote came to conclude that von Möllendorff was too anti-American in diplomatic and other terms. Foote's conclusion was shared by other American leaders in Korea, including Dr. Horace N. Allen and George C. Foulk, the American naval attaché and later chargé d'affaires.

In particular, Dr. Allen, "the dean of the Seoul mission colony and ruler by the right of seniority," an American legation physician, a royal doctor, a future American legation secretary, a future American minister in Korea, and, above all, a confidential and unofficial adviser to King Kojong, complained that von Möllendorff was even "more anti-missionary than the Koreans themselves" and was disproportionately hostile toward American interests in Korea.[5]

The actual situation was that von Möllendorff liked and supported the idea that Korea establish or strengthen its diplomatic relations with as many nations as possible, including the United States, so that it could join the international community and assert its own independence. In the instance of the United States, however, not yet a great world power and located thousands of miles from Asia, the German scholar-diplomat strongly believed that since it would not be significant in Korean development, its representatives, whether diplomatic or business, should have a low profile in the kingdom's affairs. Obviously, the Americans involved should definitely not go over his head and establish a direct link with the king, at least during the time that he was serving as the only official Western adviser to the monarch. Foulk eventually became a mortal enemy of von Möllendorff, in spite of the fact that they both believed in the same things for the future of the kingdom. They both advocated the modernization and independence of Korea; they both strongly believed that while Westerners should assist Korean modernization in the industrial, educational, and diplomatic fields, they should not introduce Western religions and try to impose them on the Koreans,[6] because the Koreans, like the Chinese and the Japanese, had their thousands-years-old and well-systemized religions and Western religions might not do anything productive for the modernization of Korea. In other words, both von Möllendorff and

Foulk were in favor of only "secular missionary work"—the kind of work modern-day Peace Corps volunteers undertake in many parts of the world. In spite of their agreements and beliefs in common, von Möllendorff did not like Foulk, partly because he represented American interests in Korea and partly because he, too, became an influential unofficial adviser to King Kojong, a situation that caused dismay for the German diplomat.

## Pro-Russian Posture and Policy

Disappointed with Minister Foote and the American "laxity" in sending military and political advisers, von Möllendorff thought about inducing or inviting German advisers to Korea.[7] But soon he decided against hiring German military advisers. It is not only interesting but also important to note that von Möllendorff invited and hired many German nationals for service in the Korean customs and for other reform projects that he had initiated in Korea, as explained in chapter 2. The use of German nationals as military instructors for the Korean government would have been an ideal and splendid choice, something to which King Kojong would have given his whole-hearted support, if only von Möllendorff had recommended it. After all, the prestige and quality of the Prussian army had become famous following the Franco-Prussian War of 1870 and 1871. Moreover, unlike the Japanese, Chinese, and Russian governments, which supposedly had partisan and one-sided interests in Korean affairs, Germany was neutral toward Korea—whether officially or otherwise. Under the circumstances, German military instructorships in Korea would have been acceptable to all of the powers involved in the affairs of the peninsula. In fact, on the eve of the Li-Itō negotiations at Tientsin in 1885, Hsü Ch'eng-tsu, the Chinese minister to Tokyo, advised Viceroy Li to recommend and send German military advisers to Korea precisely for those reasons.[8]

But von Möllendorff never seriously contemplated recommending that Kojong hire German military instructors. Von Möllendorff thought that whatever country provided military instructors to Korea should also be the one that would play a dominant role in the diplomatic and political matters of Korea. In his opinion, that country should be nearby Russia, not far-away Germany. Moreover, von

Möllendorff correctly believed that, since his own newly rising country had no possessions in East Asia, it would take no interest in the fate of such a tiny kingdom as Korea.

Another reason he thought that Russia and not Germany ought to be involved in the training of the Korean army is that such a plan would probably fit perfectly into the German foreign policy of "Wilhelmstrasse to lure the Russian bear to the Far Eastern pasture" during this period.[9] Since he was in the service of the Korean government, not of the German government, luring Russia into playing an important role in Korea rather than in Europe was not the most significant reason for his pro-Russian policy in Korea; but he did feel comfortable with it, because it was in accordance with Germany's overall Far Eastern strategy. Even before he had left China for Korea in late 1882, he had tended to be pro-Russia, influenced by E. K. Birtsov, the Russian minister in Peking, and also by Karl Waeber, the Russian consul in Tientsin and a good friend of his. Prior to his departure for Korea, he had been paid a courtesy call by a Russian delegation and had been asked to help Russia in concluding a treaty with Korea.[10] When Waeber, in fact, came to Korea in 1884 hoping for a treaty, von Möllendorff gladly represented the Korean government in negotiating and concluding the Russo-Korean Treaty of 1884.[11]

Thus, even before the *Kapsin* Coup, but especially at the time of and after the coup, von Möllendorff was convinced that Korea should seek military and political assistance from Russia—not from Japan, China, France, Germany, and not even from the United States. He reasoned that Japan was too ambitious toward Korea and could not be trusted; that China, though aggressive toward Korea, was too weak and backward to help it (which was very true); and that France was actively confronting China in Vietnam. Germany, he argued, was not an important power in international politics; England was confronted with Russia in the Near and Middle East and was seeking an alliance with Japan; and the United States was too far away and lacked the will to assist Korea. In his view, Russia was the most qualified country, most able to provide the aid that Korea so badly needed.[12] Von Möllendorff further believed that the fact that, in the early 1880s, China was struggling with France over Vietnam and with Japan over Korea might be a boon to Korean independence and development. The exertion of Japanese pressure upon China, he argued, would force China to leave Korea alone. And once China ceased its interference in Korea, Japan would become more conciliatory and friendly. Moreover, von Möllendorff believed that some powerful third power should help both China and Japan in maintaining the balance of power in the Korean peninsula, and that this third power should be Russia.

Actually, von Möllendorff at first analyzed the Korean problem in terms of three alternative solutions: (1) that Russia, China, and Japan should jointly guarantee the neutrality and integrity of Korea, in which case Korea was to become like Belgium in Europe; or (2) that Russia should provide military aid to Korea and form an alliance with it; or (3) that Russia should become the protector of the integrity of Korea.[13]

In the summer of 1884 while visiting China, von Möllendorff had an opportunity to talk to the Russian military attaché, Colonel Shneur, at the Russian legation in Peking and also to a high-ranking Russian naval officer, Rear Admiral Kroun, at Chefu, China. He proposed to these Russian officials that the Russian government should initiate a plan for a joint international guarantee of Korean independence modeled after Belgium but was told by them that he ought to establish a direct contact with their government. Both Colonel Shneur and Admiral Kroun, however, dutifully reported von Möllendorff's proposal to their government in St. Petersburg.[14] With William G. Aston, the British consul general at Seoul, von Möllendorff talked about the possibility of a neutralization of Korea not only by agreement with Russia, China, and Japan but also with the European powers.[15] But like Ministers Foote and Parkes before him, Aston gave no positive and satisfactory response to von Möllendorff. Thus von Möllendorff, too easily disappointed perhaps with the multilateral or multinational approach to the internationalization of Korea, soon dropped the idea of pursuing neutralization of the peninsula. And, unfortunately, as it turned out for the future of the Korean people, he then began to feel that a bilateral alliance between Korea and its "powerful" neighbor, Russia, would be much more feasible and realistic.

As a strong Russophile in Korea, therefore, von Möllendorff thought that, since both the Chinese and the Japanese troops that had been dispatched to Korea during the *Kapsin* Coup were soon to be withdrawn, the Korean government should, in the meantime, strengthen its army by hiring about a thousand Russian military instructors in order to avoid becoming a target in any future Sino-Japanese struggles.[16] He further reasoned that it might be in the interest of Russia for Korea to become strong and stable and that the issue as to whether Russia would take an active interest in Korean affairs or not would depend upon what benefits Korea could offer to Russia.[17] Because Korea had shared a common border with Russia since 1860 and possessed some excellent ice-free ports that Russia would presumably covet, von Möllendorff reasoned that Russia could be persuaded to be actively involved in Korean affairs. Korea should seek Russian aid to strengthen its independence from China and to modernize its army, offering Russia some ice-free ports in return.

Although von Möllendorff did not spell out the exact nature of the relationships to be developed between Korea and Russia, it is clear that he was thinking of making Korea either a protectorate or a junior military ally of Russia rather than a completely equal military partner. He was not so naive as to believe that in the age of nineteenth-century imperialism, Russia, an expansionistic country that was geographically the largest in the world, would be interested in becoming an equal political and military partner to a small kingdom like Korea. Besides, he also knew that Kojong was not seeking a completely equal political partner—a radically new concept to a strongly Confucianistic monarch and his people—but a senior or protective ally after the fashion of the old Confucian concept of the elder brother. He was convinced that, in view of America's lukewarm attitude and of the Japanese failure to become Korea's new elder brother, the idea of making Russia a protective ally would appeal to Kojong and his adherents. There is no doubt that when he finally approached Kojong with his proposal, the monarch gave his whole-hearted support to it, believing that it would be not only desirable but possible to enlist his new giant neighbor as the chief resource for the rise of Korea's new order.[18]

It is interesting and important to note that even after Kojong realized that his Hermit Kingdom had become independent in terms of modern-day international rules and practices, he was seeking a new world order that was still traditional in the sense that the security and interest of his kingdom would be protected by an elder brother. He had looked to the United States to fill this role following the conclusion of the Korean-American Treaty of 1882. He had done the same, with reservations to be sure, with regard to Japan on the eve of the *Kapsin* Coup of 1884. Now in 1885, after what he saw as the disastrous failure of the Japanese, he was doing it again—this time with Russia. In an interesting way, this is a classic case of how important the traditional and historical experiences of a country can be to its latter-day actions and policies. For example, even after such a radical event as the Marxist-Leninist revolution in Russia and the equally radical Marxist–Leninist–Maoist revolution in China, the weight of their respective historical and traditional experiences have had a tremendous impact upon the two countries' Communist policies and systems. It was certainly to be expected that Korea's historical and traditional factors would similarly influence, if not dominate, its diplomacy and policies even after it entered into the international community. And no doubt von Möllendorff, a highly competent philologist and sinologist, understood the role that traditional factors would play in shaping and formulating a new course for Korea's foreign policy. In light of Korea's history and tradition, and in view of what Kojong desired, von Möllendorff's idea indeed makes a great deal of sense.

Since the importance of one side of the coin in an analysis of the story of historical and traditional continuity in the political behavior and policy of Korea has been gone over, there is reason now to present the other side. As stated in chapter 1, as early as 1881 Kojong had attempted to modernize Korea's tributary relations with China and to make his kingdom more independent of China. After the arrival of the American diplomats Foote and Foulk, Kojong was repeatedly complimented on the fact that Korea had become sovereign and independent on the basis of modern international rules and was reminded of the fact that his kingdom did not have to be subordinate to China, which the monarch in any case considered a decaying state. Kojong dispatched modern diplomatic missions to Japan and to the United States—in the case of the latter a revolutionary act —and was extremely happy with the immediate and potential consequences of those missions. In addition, he now enjoyed advisers, both official and unofficial—other than overbearing Chinese—whom he happened to be immensely fond of (von Möllendorff, Foote, and Foulk). All of this was possible because his kingdom was supposedly independent and sovereign. Thus, it is reasonable to insist that Kojong would have tried to make his kingdom genuinely independent and sovereign if Korea's geopolitical and international circumstances had permitted him to do so. The important point is this: regardless of its traditional suzerain-dependency ties with China, the monarch would have attempted to make his kingdom truly independent if Korea had been strong enough to resist foreign aggression or, better still, if by comparison with its neighbors Korea had been stronger and larger enough to deter any further challenge from them. Commenting on Korea's troubled history from the standpoint of geographical factors, James William Morely aptly contends that one of the reasons for "the dynamic of intervention" in the peninsula is that "Korea was too small and too weak to maintain its independence against such determined intervention" on the part of its stronger neighbors.[19] Consequently, Kojong's search for a new elder brother even after 1882 should be explained not only in terms of Korea's political heritage but also with respect to the hard realities of the geopolitical situation.

The same argument goes for von Möllendorff. If in the mid-1880s Korea had been more powerful militarily or otherwise than its immediate neighbors, which was almost an impossibility in view of the small size and "backwardness" of Korea at the time, von Möllendorff would have spent his time in promoting the interests and welfare of Korea rather than in striving to secure a protective senior ally as a counterweight against its other aggressive neighbors. Thus, the search for an ally—this time Russia—on the part of von Möllendorff and Kojong, while dictated in part by Korea's traditional concepts and practices, was mainly dictated and necessitated by geopolitical factors. Unless this search is understood in terms of such dualism, the pro-Russian posture of Kojong and von Möllendorff becomes needlessly complex and incomprehensible. Although their new policy sounds, moreover, as if it was based on two contradictory factors (make Korea independent of one country—China—but a protectorate of or subordinate to another—Russia), in actuality it was quite understandable for just this reason. So far as the perceptions of these two men were concerned, their posture seemed ideal because it was not only historically and politically right but was also the best solution for their new military problems, both international and internal.

So here were two young men who were very important in the history of modern Korea: the 38-year-old von Möllendorff, a product of Western civilization and its political system, and the 33-year-old King Kojong, a product of East Asian civilization and the Confucian world order. How was it possible that these two men, from entirely different cultural and political backgrounds, so easily agreed on the delicate future course of action for the salvation of Korea? The answer seems to be that, regardless of their diverse cultural and political training, both came to realize that Korea, owing to internal weakness and geopolitical factors, should depend on the aid and protection of a big neighbor that would be powerful and interested enough to do such a job, and that power ought to be Russia, a new and giant neighbor of Korea.

So it was that Kojong and von Möllendorff were merely following a universal and fundamental political principle: seek an alliance when one's country is weak and threatened by outsiders. As simplistic as it might sound, that explanation must be valid to explain the seemingly surprising mutual consent of these diverse individuals for the future course of Korea. Any attempt to mystify the behavior and policies of Kojong and von Möllendorff in terms of the peculiarities or uniqueness of traditional East Asian and Confucianist pattern— or the too-often quoted phrase "East is East, West is West, and never the twain shall meet" (Eastern civilization is so different from that of the West that Easterners should be understood only in terms of Eastern standards and culture, not those of the West, and Eastern countries will never become like Western nations), as traditionalists (for example, M. Frederick Nelson) have done—would not only be like chasing a wild goose but would confuse this complex and much-debated subject. To be sure, Confucian political tradition played a significant role in Kojong's and von Möllendorff's search for a new protector, but geopolitical factors, good or bad, played an even more important and dominant role in their casting Russia for the part, although both of them conceptualized the new world order according to the traditional system of elder brother–younger brother (suzerain-dependency) relations.

Kojong's ready willingness to think of Korea's new senior partner (be it the United States, Japan, or Russia) in terms of the traditional concept of elder brother–younger brother relations is similar to Viceroy Li's justifying the shift in China's policy toward Korea in terms of traditional suzerain-dependency relations. After 1882 Li came to realize that China's interventionist policy in Korea was essentially a new imperialism, but he attempted to justify and explain it in old suzerain-dependency terms in order to create a sense of historical legitimacy and make it acceptable to the new international community. Kojong, on the other hand, came to understand, though slowly, that the new international treaties had made his kingdom sovereign and independent. Frequently threatened by Chinese interventionists and strongly believing that the kingdom could not stand alone, he realized that he needed a new senior ally that could not only keep China away from Korea, but also help him in strengthening and modernizing his kingdom. Following the disastrous *Kapsin* Coup, Kojong wholeheartedly agreed with von Möllendorff that Korea's new elder brother should be Russia.

However, the other powers that had vital or secondary interests in the peninsula would have absolutely nothing to do with von Möllendorff's pro-Russian concept. According to his strategy, moreover, Korea was to play a secretive game of intrigue rather than a more open and dignified diplomatic role. Realizing the weak position that the kingdom was in, von Möllendorff reasoned that Korea should not give the impression of actively seeking an alliance with Russia; instead, it would do better to maintain the image of strict neutrality in dealing with the various powers.[20]

Von Möllendorff's strategy for King Kojong (and his pro-Russian advisers) to play only a covert role in arranging a Russo-Korean alliance suited the monarch well for several reasons. First of all, as an absolute monarch (at least in theory), Kojong wanted to maintain the appearance of staying above the usual political struggles and intrigues. Even in the *Kapsin* Coup of 1884, he tried to look as though he remained aloof from all the political and diplomatic maneuvering, although he was, in reality, deeply involved. Second, Kojong did not want to go against the powerful pro-China faction (supported by his foreign minister Kim Yun-sik) by publicly embracing von Möllendorff's scheme, which would establish a pro-Russian government and eliminate the sinophile bureaucrats. Third and most important, Kojong was afraid of offending China by openly supporting von Möllendorff because China was still carrying a big stick, at least in Korea, and was still acting like a suzerain to

Korea according to Confucian teachings, which this Confucian monarch still revered.

In view of the deteriorating political, economic, and agricultural conditions prevailing in Russia in 1882, before and after the assassination of Czar Alexander III, von Möllendorff's reasoning that Russia was the ideal ally is hard to accept. Strongly committed to the reactionary policies of autocracy, orthodoxy, and nationalism, and beset and tormented by the activities of internal radical revolutionists (such as the members of the Will of the People), the Imperial Russian government under Alexander III (1881–1894) was hardly in a position to become involved in the affairs of the Korean peninsula. Moreover, even if the Czar and his foreign policy advisers had been interested—which they in fact were not—they would not have been able to render constructive aid militarily, materially, or otherwise. Somewhat like the Chinese government at about the same time, the St. Petersburg government was unwilling and unable to promote the welfare of its own people, let alone extending to such a far-away kingdom as Korea the kind of benefits that would have helped the government and people of Korea. Nevertheless, von Möllendorff believed that Russia in the 1880s could accomplish much good for Korea, and he flatly proposed that the Korean government "reject China and ally itself with Russia." It seems that not only the king but also some of his independent-minded advisers such as Han Kyu-sŏl, Yi Cho-yŏn, and Cho Chŏng-hi accepted von Möllendorff's proposal. And by the mid-1880s even the Mins had joined Kojong and von Möllendorff in seeking Russian support as a means of counteracting any Japanese, Chinese, or British aggression in Korea.[21]

## Russia as a Source of Korea's New Order

Von Möllendorff's first opportunity to try to induce Russia to play a role in Korean affairs came during and after the *Kapsin* Coup of 1884. Russian foreign minister N. K. Giers, worried about the possibility that a Sino-Japanese War would erupt in Korea on account of the coup, instructed A. P. Davydov, Russian minister in Tokyo, to advise the Japanese government not to occupy any Korean port.

And owing to the fact that Giers considered the maintenance of the status quo in Korea to be of "paramount importance" to Russia, he also had Alexis de Speyer, first secretary at the legation there, dispatched to Korea to do his best to prevent the war.[22] Giers's instructions were given in response to Davydov's earlier report to him, in which the minister had notified the foreign minister that von Möllendorff, a German adviser to the Korean government, had shown an interest in the establishment of a Russian "protectorship" over Korea. In the middle of December 1884, at the height of the crisis that followed the failure of the *Kapsin* Coup and before the final settlements were made between Korea and Japan and also between China and Korea, von Möllendorff, genuinely worried about the safety of the king and the future of Korea, made a proposal to Minister Davydov, through the Russian consul at Nagasaki, Japan. He suggested that the Russian government consider the possibility of establishing protectorship over Korea and that it send warships along with two hundred soldiers to Inch'ŏn to protect the king. In Korea, Davydov instructed de Speyer to find out more pointedly what von Möllendorff had in mind.[23] Thus, de Speyer arrived at Inch'ŏn for this purpose on December 28, 1884.

In a conversation with de Speyer, von Möllendorff explained that to implement the Russian protectorship of Korea, Russia could lease any port on the eastern Korean seaboard. To avoid any alarm on the part of those powers interested in the peninsula, this could be done under the pretext of leasing it to a Russian firm. Should the Russian government find this arrangement disagreeable, then it might propose to other European nations that they grant an international guarantee to protect the independence of Korea in the same way that they had done for Belgium. It should be recalled that the independence of Belgium (from the Dutch) was guaranteed by the major European powers at the London Conference between 1830 and 1831.

After conferring with von Möllendorff and Foreign Minister Cho Pyŏng-ho, de Speyer, a future Russian minister to Korea (1896–1898), won an audience with the king. At this audience, de Speyer, a strong advocate of Russian expansionism into Korea, explained that the Russian government would deplore a war in Korea, which had a common border with Russia, but would be willing to protect the king and his country if war did break out between China and

Japan.[24] At this opportunity, von Möllendorff advocated Russo-Korean cooperation and alliance. The king became keenly interested in von Möllendorff's proposal. De Speyer then left for Japan on January 7, 1885, having scored a diplomatic success, and duly reported his conversation with King Kojong and von Möllendorff to his superior, Minister Davydov. Davydov informed Foreign Minister Giers of de Speyer's mission in Korea and requested due instruction. Giers advised Czar Alexander III that the establishment of Russian protection over Korea at this time might bring more liability than advantage to Russia, inasmuch as it would lead to conflicts with China and Japan, for which the Russian government was not prepared either militarily or otherwise. But he also convinced the Czar that Russia should keep the Korean hope of a Russian protectorship alive for future eventualities. Alexander III felt very much complimented and flattered by the Korean king's voluntary invitation for Russia to become the protector of his kingdom, but he essentially agreed with Giers's cautious approach to the situation and had Giers direct Davydov to advise the Korean government not to seek protection from any other power, assuring it that a Russian representative soon to be dispatched to Korea would examine how to ensure the integrity of the peninsula.[25]

As for other subjects proposed by von Möllendorff, Alexander and Giers wanted to devote more time to further study and to consult first with Baron A. N. Korf, governor general of the Amur region. The Czar instructed Korf to formulate and recommend to him a Russian policy toward Korea. In response, Korf proposed that Russia should strengthen the independence of Korea and urge the withdrawal of both Chinese and Japanese troops from Korea. Consequently, the Russian government decided to promote the simultaneous evacuation of all Chinese and Japanese soldiers from Korea and then gradually to formulate a policy toward Korea as events developed in the peninsula.[26]

Meanwhile, in February 1885, after Japan's imposition of harsh terms upon Korea (the Treaty of Seoul of January 1885) and before the conclusion of the Tientsin Convention of April 1885 between China and Japan, Kojong sent a confidential mission to Vladivostok, consisting of four emissaries and headed by Kwŏn Tong-su and Kim Yong-wŏn, on the pretext of buying arms but actually for the purpose of conferring with Korf. As a means of facilitating and complementing their scheme, von Möllendorff agreed with Kojong in sending this secret mission to Vladivostok.[27] Kwǒn and Kim informed Korf that it was the wish of their king that Russia become the new protector of Korean independence and its ports (vis-à-vis Japan and China), accelerate the ratification process of the Russian-Korean Treaty of 1884, and also conclude an overland trade agreement with Korea as soon as possible.[28] Upon receiving due instructions from the St. Petersburg government, Korf assured the Korean envoys that his government would hasten to send a diplomat to Korea for the exchange of ratification of the Russo-Korean Treaty and for the conclusion of an overland trade agreement and also for discussions with the Korean government about guaranteeing the integrity of the country from external aggression. In addition, Korf assured Kwǒn and Kim that the Russian navy would be interested in looking after Korean coasts.[29]

Analyzing this meeting between Korf and the Korean envoys, some Soviet historians, such as M. N. Pak, insist that what Korf did was to stress "the importance of strengthening the independence of Korea and the withdrawal of Chinese and Japanese troops from Korea."[30] That statement is only halfway truthful. Actually, Korf not only asserted "the importance" but also led the Korean emissaries to believe that the Russian government would in fact be sincerely interested in "doing something about" maintaining the independence of Korea and the integrity of its ports against foreign encroachment. To be sure, Korf made no commitment to the issue of Russian protection of Korean independence and of its coasts. Still, he conveyed enough of an impression to Kwǒn and Kim that the Russian government cared sufficiently about them; and that is what the envoys reported to Kojong when they returned to Seoul. In fact, studies made by other Soviet historians, such as B. D. Pak and A. L. Narochnitsky, make it reasonably clear that Korf's assurances to Kwǒn and Kim included the Russian government's interest in "doing something about" maintaining the integrity of Korean ports and independence.[31] On the issue of a Russian lease or use of Korean ports, Korf was chiefly interested in preventing others from taking them over rather than in Russia's physical occupation of them. In other words, Russia was interested in defensive measures rather than in offensive ones, so far as Korean ports were concerned. All of these considerations make it quite clear that, on the issue of

Russian protection of Korean independence and ports, there still was no concrete or definite agreement between Korf and the Korean envoys; there was merely a favorable reaction from Korf.

Whatever understanding or agreement the Korean envoys accomplished with Korf, it was not exposed until June 1885—one month after the return of the mission to Seoul. And when this secret mission became no longer a secret, the Chinese and Japanese diplomats in Seoul were strongly, but incorrectly, convinced that the deals that Kwŏn and Kim had made with Korf included the Russian lease of Port Lazareff in return for the dispatch of military instructors to Korea and warships to protect Korean interests against any power.[32] As explained, however, Korf had never made such a promise or guarantee to the Korean envoys, even though his government was favorably disposed to those ideas.

Regardless of the success of the Kwŏn and Kim Mission, however, Russian interests in Port Lazareff and Port Hamilton (Kŏmundo) were well known.[33] As early as 1854, a Russian ship, the *Pollada,* under Vice-Admiral Evfimii V. Putiatin—a rival of the famed Commodore Matthew C. Perry, who succeeded in opening Japan in 1854 —surveyed Broughton Bay (Yŏnghŭngman) and then discovered and named Port Lazareff (Songchŏnman), farther inside the bay. Vice-Admiral Putiatin on his own authority had tried to establish trade relations with the Korean government, but was unsuccessful.[34] In 1857, Putiatin attempted to establish a coaling depot at Port Hamilton off the southern coast of Korea, but had to abandon the idea owing to a lack of support from the Russian Admiralty.[35] In 1859, during the Taiping Rebellion in China, Count Nikolai N. Muraviev, the governor general of East Siberia, feared that, in case the British and French were to capture Peking, China might be compelled to give up some of the ports of Manchuria or Korea to the Europeans, which, in his opinion, would create a threat to Russia.[36]

Concerned that a hostile power (such as the British or French) might occupy Korea, or Manchuria, or Mongolia in case of the breakdown or demise of the Ch'ing dynasty, the Russian government instructed Governor General Muraviev to do his best to maintain the status quo in those areas.[37] From the standpoint of Russia, it was partly because of this kind of potential threat from the British and the French that, in 1860, when the British and French did capture Peking, the Russian government compelled the Chinese government to give it the Maritime Province, the coastal region of Siberia southeast of the Amur and Sungri rivers. Thus, the Russian annexation of the Maritime Province was not only an offensive but also a defensive measure, so far as the Russian government was concerned. Following 1860, when Russia came to share a common border with Korea, the Russians not only increased their unofficial and semiofficial contacts with the Koreans but also became even more keenly interested in what the powers might do in the peninsula.

The Russo-Korean border was now demarcated by the Tumen River with twenty *li* (five miles, or eight kilometers) along the left bank from the mouth of the river belonging to Russia and all of the right bank to Korea. The Russians, however, were worried that, in case of the demise of Korea, an adversary might take advantage of the strategic position in the peninsula and close the Korean strait to Russian ships; thus, Russian policy (or rather desire) was to assure maintenance of the status quo in the peninsula kingdom.

Therefore, in 1866, when a French expeditionary force was sent to Korea to punish those Koreans responsible for persecuting French missionaries, the Russian minister to China, A. E. Vlangali, was instructed to reject American minister Anson Burlingame's invitation to participate in sending an international expeditionary force to open Korea.[38] While the Russian government was not interested in joining an international expeditionary force to punish Korea for the "crimes" supposedly committed against the French nationals, neither did it wish to see any French occupation of Korean territory or ports. Therefore, in 1869, it sent a gunboat to Kanghwa Island, where the battle had taken place between the French and the Koreans in 1866, in order to investigate the rumor that the French were still in occupation of the island.[39] After some unfortunate incidents between the Russian sailors and the local Korean authorities, however, the Russian ship withdrew from the area.

Meanwhile, throughout the 1860s and the 1870s certain ambitious and adventurous Russian naval officers had come on occasion to Port Lazareff and had made several unofficial or semiofficial attempts to secure a treaty with Korea.[40] The Japanese government for its part was so concerned with the Russian interest in Port Lazareff that, at the time when the Korean-Japanese Treaty was negotiated and thereafter, it tried to persuade the Korean government to make it an open city. But the Korean government rejected the suggestion because there were royal tombs of progenitors around the city.[41]

Russia's sharing of a common border with Korea created an entirely new problem for both countries. Attracted by an area that was agriculturally more fertile and by the exaction of less (or even no) taxation in the area of South Ussuri, Korean peasants and laborers, beginning in 1863, started to emigrate into the region. At first, the Russian authority under the govenor general of East Siberia, M. S. Korsakov, welcomed these Korean immigrants as a source of cheap labor for farm work. But as the number of Korean immigrants grew excessive—thereby creating housing, sanitary, and other problems—the Russian authorities asked the local Korean authorities of Hamkyŏng Province to stop them from entering Siberia.[42]

Actually the Seoul government was even more opposed to Korean emigration into Siberia than the Russians were, for two reasons: emigration onto foreign soil ran contrary to Korea's traditional law and isolationistic policy; and emigration to a foreign country meant the loss of tax revenues into the Korean treasury.[43] Thus, the Korean government tried to stop emigration of its subjects into Siberia by strengthening the northern border's military and security system, hoping that such measures would provide a better check on the emigration movement and better supervision and surveillance for the security of the region.[44]

As news of the advantages of a "better life" in Siberia spread, however, and as conditions in Korea continued to deteriorate, more Koreans moved to the north, especailly in and after the famine of 1869, there by bringing the number of Koreans living in the region to something more than seven thousand by 1869.[45] The Korean government, without fully understanding the Russian government's position on the issue of Korean emigration into Siberia and in accord with traditional Korean policy—to deal with foreign governments through China—repeatedly asked the Board of Rites of China to persuade the Russian government to discourage the immigration. Although the board then asked the Tsungli Yamen to negotiate with Russia on behalf of Korea, the Tsungli Yamen rejected the request on the grounds that such negotiations should be undertaken by the Korean government itself.[46] In 1871 the Russian minister in Peking approached the Tsungli Yamen about the possibility of stopping

Korean emigration into Russian territory but was told that the Russian government should deal directly with the Korean government
about it.[47]

Meanwhile, the Russian authorities in Siberia had become interested in trade with the Koreans. The Russian military authorities in
East Siberia were especially interested, because it was cheaper to
import Korean cattle and food supplies than to bring them in from
European Russia. As mentioned already, as early as in 1854 Admiral Putiatin had attempted to establish trade relations with Korea,
but in vain. In 1865, Minister Vlangali was instructed to determine
whether it would be feasible to negotiate with Korea through Chinese mediation. Vlangali replied that, whatever China's position
may have been on the subject of the conclusion of a Russian treaty
with Korea, in reality Russia's entrance into direct diplomatic and
trade relations with Korea might arouse suspicion or jealousy on the
part of the Chinese government and also certain European powers.
He recommended that Russia should initiate only a modest frontier
trade with the Koreans.[48]

On the basis of Vlangali's recommendation the St. Petersburg
government in September of 1865 instructed Governor General
Korsakov to start talks with the Korean authorities for the development of frontier trade. Accordingly, in the late 1860s and 1870s
attempts were made by the local Russian officials to conclude a trade
agreement with Korea; but all such efforts were rejected by the
Koreans.[49] Thus, Russia's official policy toward Korea in the 1860s
and 1870s was to adopt a wait-and-see posture rather than physically
forcing the country to open itself to Russia. In fact, the Russian government would rather have seen Korea kept in isolation than opened
by European powers, which might then use the peninsula in a manner inimical to Russian interests. Even after the conclusion of the
Korean-Japanese Treaty of 1876, Russia maintained this wait-and-
see approach, especially since none of the Western powers had been
successful in establishing treaty relations with Korea.[50] In the
absence of a trade agreement between the two nations, therefore,
Russian-Korean trade was carried on unofficially. By 1881, the
trade amounted to 500,000 rubles ($250,000). It should be noted,
though, that before and at the time of the Li-Shufeldt negotiations
(1880–1882), the Russian government tried to discourage the Chinese government from helping with the conclusion of a Korean-

American treaty. Russia considered an American or European presence in Korea undesirable, because these nations might use the peninsula as an instrument against Russia.[51] Besides, the Russian government disliked the fact that China and others were using the idea of Russia as a "threat" to Korea as a reason for prompt conclusion of a Korean-American treaty. Moreover, the Russian leaders felt that, since Russia's military strength and economic resources in East Siberia were weak at the time, they were in no position to compete with the Americans or British in Korea. Thus, they preferred that Korea remain in isolation and considered that the Chinese suzerainty over Korea was a useful obstacle to its domination by the Japanese or Americans. Once Korea was brought into the international community, however, Russia changed its policy and became willing to conclude a treaty with Korea, so that it would not be barred from the peninsula.[52]

Following the conclusion of the Korean-American Treaty of 1882, therefore, the Russian minister in Peking, Eugene de Butzow, approached the Chinese government about a trade agreement with Korea. Ma Chien-chung conveyed the Russian desires to the Korean government, but Yi Ch'oe-ŭng, the chief state councillor of the Korean government, frustrated Russian wishes, urging them "to wait for another day."[53] Thus, even before—but especially after—the Korean conclusion of treaties with Japan and the United States, many Russians were keenly interested in negotiating a treaty with Korea—mainly for trade and for the settling of some ill-defined immigration issues between two countries and not necessarily for territorial aggrandizement at the expense of Korea. It should be emphasized, however, that this Russian interest in Korea (and possibly also in Port Lazareff) was a constant cause of great anxiety among the Chinese and the Japanese and even among the British.[54]

It is interesting and pertinent to ask whether this anxiety was justified. It might appear that since many Russians—adventurers, diplomats, admirals, and soldiers—did indeed display an aggressive interest in Korea and in particular Port Lazareff, their apprehension about the Russian presence should have been understandable. But what the Russian government wanted in concessionary terms after 1882 was only the conclusion of a treaty with Korea, along the lines of those of Japan and America. Thus, seen in retrospect, this anxiety was clearly unjustifiable. Nevertheless, in the early 1880s, the Japanese perception, and to some extent the British, of Russia's ambitions in Korea, like that of the Chinese, was probably real—whatever the grounds for the perception may have been.[55] It is important to emphasize herewith that, although Chinese and Japanese fears of a Russian threat in the Korean peninsula were genuine, and even the British concern over the possibility of Russia's expansion into the peninsula was not totally unjustified, the British government was still foxy enough in addressing the Chinese and Japanese to exaggerate in the grossest manner the alleged "danger" posed by Russia's aggressive policy, so that the East Asian nations would join Britain in checking whatever southward movement Russia might make. And in the mid-1880s the British were very successful in their enterprises around and in the Korean peninsula.

Returning now to the Kwŏn and Kim Mission and the ensuing contacts with the Russians, it will be recalled that when, in May 1885, these emissaries returned to Seoul, they had in hand some kind of understanding with Korf—a development that deeply worried Chinese commissioner Ch'en and Japanese chargé Kondō Masuki.[56] King Kojong's next move, a subtle follow-up of the Kwŏn and Kim Mission, was to send von Möllendorff to accompany Sŏ Sang-u on a mission to Japan on February 15, 1885. Sŏ was heading the so-called "apology mission" for the *Kapsin* Coup dispatched to the Japanese government in fulfillment of the provisions of the Treaty of Seoul. Von Möllendorff's real mission, however, was to confer secretly with Russian minister Davydov concerning Russian aid to Korea.[57] Arriving in Tokyo, which von Möllendorff considered a very pleasant city, he and Sŏ had an audience with Emperor Meiji. He found Minister Davydov, who had studied at a German university and was fluent in German, to be friendly and cooperative. Von Möllendorff was also happy to see First Secretary de Speyer, who had earlier been in Seoul and had conversed with him on the possibility of a Russian protectorship of Korea. The Korean emissaries, including von Möllendorff, stayed in a Japanese house and ate Japanese foods while they were there.[58] With Kojong's blessing but still without official or bona fide credentials, von Möllendorff conferred with Minister Davydov on the feasibility of engaging Russian military officers to train the Korean army and discussed the possibility of obtaining Russian protection for Korea in return for the cession of Port Lazareff to Russia.

Von Möllendorff wrote down his proposals in German and signed them and then handed the papers to Davydov.[59] According to Davydov, von Möllendorff suggested that Russia could even occupy Port Hamilton.[60] Favorably disposed once again toward von Möllendorff's ideas, Davydov sent them to his government in St. Petersburg. Upon receiving the proposals, the provisions of which were essentially similar to those of Davydov's earlier report and from Governor Korf, Czar Alexander III became vitally interested in the idea of sending Russian military instructors to Korea. He ordered Foreign Minister Giers to study the general international conditions with regard to Korea and the credibility of von Möllendorff's proposals, and to instruct Karl Waeber—soon to be assigned to Korea as chargé d'affaires of the Russian legation in Seoul—to cultivate friendly relations with the Korean government. As for the possibility of Russian protection of Korea and use of its port, the Czar stated that this would depend upon the future development of political conditions in Korea.[61] Flattered as he was by the Korean invitation, Alexander III was concerned that such a move would lead to friction with Japan or China; he preferred to continue a policy of noncommitment—neither rejecting the Korean proposal outright nor embracing it wholeheartedly right away—essentially the same position that he had taken earlier on this issue. Moreover, he and Foreign Minister Giers agreed that it would be important to keep Korean hopes alive and future options open.[62]

Commenting on Alexander III's position on the issue of a Russian protectorship over Korea, M. N. Pak flatly stated that "the Russian government did not dare make any official statement in this regard."[63] But this is a highly misleading assertion, because in dealing with von Möllendorff the Russian diplomats who were in communication with Foreign Minister Giers never rejected the idea of a Russian protectorship over Korea and instead kept encouraging von Möllendorff by using highly obscure and diplomatic language, just as Governor Korf had done to the Kwŏn and Kim Mission earlier in Vladivostok. And yet, as of 1885, Foreign Minister Giers had authorized Minister Davydov to make official deals with the Korean government only in the matter of the Russian dispatch of military advisers.

Despite the limited official interest in Korea displayed by Giers and Alexander III, however, certain Russian officials—such as de

Speyer—were interested in more than just sending Russian military instructors to Korea. Von Möllendorff himself was eager for a far more comprehensive alliance with Russia. Returning to Seoul on March 5, 1885, he secretly reported to the king his negotiations with Davydov and received the monarch's approval. Von Möllendorff's activities in Japan were kept so secret that even the first state councillor, Sim Sun-t'aek, the second state councillor, Kim Hong-jip, and the new foreign minister, Kim Yun-sik, were for a while unaware of them.

CHAPTER 5

# The Reaction to British
# Imperialism in Korea

## Britain's Seizure of Port Hamilton (Kŏmundo)

The von Möllendorff–de Speyer intrigues in the meantime became intertwined with an Anglo-Russian crisis in Central Asia. Throughout the nineteenth century, Great Britain had been opposed to Russian expansion into the Near East, Central Asia, and the Far East, and yet Russia was able to penetrate into Central Asia and Siberia, even annexing the Maritime Province in 1860. In the process of its expansion in Central Asia, Russia came into conflict with Afghanistan and thus soon with England, which had a great interest in this region.[1] In November 1884, British and Russian commissioners met to adjust the disputed boundary between Russia and Afghanistan, but they could reach no agreement. In March 1885, General Kanasov's forces expelled the Afghans from the disputed areas, thereby creating the Pendjeh crisis. In England, Parliament voted 11,000,000 pounds, the largest vote of credit since the Crimean War, for war preparations; and the Gladstone government (1881–1885) mobilized the reserves. An Anglo-Russian war became imminent.

The British apparently thought that if an Anglo-Russian war should erupt they would need a naval base near Korea from which to attack Russia at a weak point in its far-flung possessions, just as they had assaulted the Kamchatka area during the Crimean War. So, with Vladivostok as the objective, and without formally asking or notifying Korea, the British government decided, on April 11, 1885, to occupy Port Hamilton, and the Admiralty ordered Vice-Admiral

William Dowell of the China Station to occupy the port on April 14. Thus, the cabinet of Gladstone, supposedly a sympathizer with the underdogs in international politics, was quite willing to protect what it perceived to be British interests in Central Asia by illegal means in the Far East. On April 15, three British warships occupied the port. Dowell was instructed not to hoist the British flag until Russian ships actually entered the harbor.[2] But on May 10, when a Russian ship came into sight, the British flag was prematurely raised.

Port Hamilton, called the "Gibraltar" of the Orient, consists of a group of three islands just 18 miles off the southern coast of Korea; it is located 35 miles from Chejudo, 850 miles from Vladivostok, and 1,200 miles from Hong Kong. From the British point of view, the port occupied a strategic position in the Yellow Sea and the Sea of Japan.[3] Thus, possession of the port would give the British fleet a good northern naval base similar to Hong Kong in the south, from which they could not only protect their commerce in North China but attack Russian bases in Vladivostok, if such action should become necessary.

Actually, this British interest in Port Hamilton was not new. As early as 1845, a British surveyor named the islands after the British admiral, Lord George Hamilton. In 1875 and 1876, the British were interested in occupying the islands as a means of checking a possible Russian occupation of Korea.[4] Then in 1882 (at the time the Anglo-Korean Treaty was negotiated), they again thought of leasing the islands for strategic and naval purposes.[5] In particular, Northbrook, the First Lord of the Admiralty, believed that the British navy might need the port as a base against Vladivostok in case of war with Russia.[6] When Harry Parkes finally concluded the Anglo-Korean Treaty of 1883, he observed that Korea occupied a valuable strategic position.[7] The British had noted that, despite the huge investment that the Russians had committed to the fortification of Vladivostok in 1877–1879, the harbor was not an ice-free port; they generally believed, therefore, that Russia was searching for an ice-free naval base such as Port Lazareff on the Korean coast.

There seems to be a great deal of dispute as to whether the British government decided to occupy Port Hamilton before or after learning something about the alleged secret Russo-Korean agreement. Many distinguished diplomatic historians claim, or leave a strong impression, that the British occupied the port because of the rumor of this secret agreement.[8] However, that does not seem to be the case. It was the British minister at Tokyo, Francis Plunket, who first detected the Russo-Korean intrigue; but he did so early in June 1885, almost two months after the British seizure of the islands. In fact, he reported what he had learned to the British Foreign Office and to British chargé N. R. O'Conor at Peking on June 4, 1885.[9]

What actually happened is that, before learning anything about the Russo-Korean intrigue, the British government decided to occupy Port Hamilton in order to use it as a springboard for attacks on Vladivostok and other Russian possessions in the Pacific in case of an Anglo-Russian war; the British later tried to justify their action as a response to the conclusion of the Russo-Korean agreement.[10] To borrow the words of Lord Dufferin, the viceroy of India, the British goal in occupying Port Hamilton was to "make the dog drop his bone by squeezing his throat [that is, blockading his ports, etc.], instead of taking it out of his mouth."[11] By occupying Port Hamilton and thereby showing their willingness and readiness to fight against Russia, the British wanted to bring Russian actions in Central Asia to a halt. Nevertheless, it is wrong to assume that both Gladstone and his foreign secretary, Lord Granville, handled the crisis with a clear and well-thought-out plan. In fact, they handled the crisis in a quite clumsy manner, as they did other colonial matters, partly because Gladstone was in poor health and Granville was too old and partly because both of them lacked a creative and innovative foreign policy.[12]

The British seizure of Port Hamilton without any sort of agreement with the Korean government was "an open violation of international law" and of their treaty obligations;[13] but that did not bother the British. The British had no significant interest in Korea and regarded the peninsula kingdom only in relation to the balance of power in the Far East. Unlike the United States, which was committed to the independence of Korea, the British were not particularly concerned with its integrity and independence. In view of and because of Russia's perceived aggressive expansion into Siberia and the Maritime Province during the middle of the nineteenth century, the British regarded the Korean peninsula as Russia's stepping-stone to China and possibly to Japan, and so decided to support the Chinese claim to suzerainty over Korea in order to thwart Russian expansion in the Far East. The British preferred Chinese domination over Korea to Russian control or colonization; and in fact, they not only considered China as their unofficial ally but used every opportunity to increase China's suspicion of Russian expansionist aims.

## The Japanese Response and Diverse Proposals for the Internationalization of Korea

When the Japanese government learned of the British seizure of Port Hamilton, it not only asked the British government to explain the arrangement it had made with Korea but warned that, if the British were to remain in the port, the Russians might occupy Wŏn-san or Pusan or Chejudo. It even sent warships to the treaty ports in Korea as well as to Tsushima and started to build fortifications on the island.[14] Although the Japanese government had decided to adopt a passive policy toward Korea after the failure of the *Kapsin* Coup, it was still keenly interested in what the Chinese, the Russians, and the British might do there. It should be recalled that even at the negotiation of the Tientsin Convention of April 1885, which mitigated the problems created by the *Kapsin* Coup, Japanese pleni-potentiary Itō Hirobumi had made no concessions to Chinese pleni-potentiary Li on the issue of military intervention in Korea. The convention had provided for the withdrawal of their troops from Korea; but it had also stated that, in case of future disturbances, nei-ther signatory would send troops without notifying the other. It was generally agreed that Japan had now gained a position of equality with China in the matter of military intervention, something Japan had not possessed before.

At about this time, there were also some diplomatic pressures and proposals for the internationalization of Korea, following perhaps examples such as that of Belgium. German vice-consul Herman Budler submitted a proposal to the Korean government for the joint protection of Korea by the great powers, and the suggestion was for-warded to Viceroy Li; but both Li and the Korean foreign minister, Kim Yun-sik, rejected the proposal without careful examination.[15] In May 1885, the Japanese minister to China, Enomoto Takeaki, made a proposal to his government for joint Sino-Japanese protec-tion of Korea, but it too was turned down, on the grounds that it would be contrary to the spirit of the Tientsin Convention.[16] It should be noted that, in 1882, Enomoto proposed to American minister Russell Young at Peking that an international meeting, with representatives from the United States, Great Britain, Russia, Germany, France, and Japan, be held in Tokyo to deal with the possibility of the neutralization of Korea. Enomoto wanted to do something about the Chinese claim to suzerainty over Korea by means of an international guarantee of its neutrality; but Young rejected it. He did not want to venture "into the atmosphere of romance and hyperbole which surrounds these Oriental claims" to suzerainty.[17]

As a stimulus for Sino-Japanese-Korean cooperation vis-à-vis Western expansionism in East Asia and as a means of improving Korea's deteriorating domestic and international positions, some Korean moderates—such as Ŏ Yun-jung and Kim Hong-jip—suggested, as stated earlier, a neutralization proposal for Korea.[18] In July of 1885, American chargé Foulk also suggested to Secretary Thomas F. Bayard that there should be an international guarantee of the neutrality of Korea in case it were to accept Russian military instructors.[19] The Chinese minister to Russia, Liu Jui-fen, also recommended to Viceroy Li that China should either incorporate Korea into China or "put Korea under joint protection of Great Britain, the United States and Russia."[20] K'ang Yu-wei, a prominent Chinese intellectual leader, made a similar proposal for joint protection of Korea.[21] Even some Korean intellectual leaders like Yu Kil-chun proposed in 1885 the neutralization of Korea after a model combining features of the neutralization of Belgium with that of Bulgaria. In Yu's plan Korea's neutralization would be initiated by China and guaranteed by China, England, France, Japan, and Russia.[22] Japanese foreign minister Inoue Kaoru, who had earlier rejected Minister Enomoto's idea, did finally propose to Viceroy Li a joint Sino-Japanese condominium, with Li assuming the executive responsibility.[23] In April 1886, British Foreign Secretary Rosebery made a proposal to the Chinese government for an international guarantee of the integrity of Korea.[24]

Unfortunately for the future of the Korean peninsula and people, Li Hung-chang rejected all of these ideas and proposals,[25] doing so for three reasons: (1) the neutralization of Korea would be contrary to his conception of the country as a tributary of China;[26] (2) apprehension on his part that neutralization, if guaranteed by the concerned powers, might have the effect of bringing England and Russia together against China;[27] and (3) in light of China's increasing influence before and after the *Kapsin* Coup, he believed that little good would result from such a compromise of China's predominant and favorable position in the peninsula kingdom.[28]

In view of the fact that Viceroy Li, whose objective was to maintain a balance of power in the kingdom, had encouraged Korea to enter into treaty relations with the Western powers and aided in bringing it about, the neutralization or joint protection of the independence of Korea would have been consistent with his own purposes. It follows, therefore, that Viceroy Li should have pursued the neutralization of Korea as an ideal policy for China; but he did not undertake it because of his strong desire to gain and maintain a paramount and preponderant domination of the kingdom in contravention of the Tientsin Convention. All in all, it can be safely said that in the mid-1880s China missed a golden opportunity to provide and maintain a stable and independent Korea by means of international neutralization or joint protection without Chinese loss of vital interests in the peninsula.

Given that Viceroy Li's policy of trying to dominate Korea eventually led his country into a disastrous war with Japan in 1894, one could argue in hindsight that a more far-sighted and wiser policy toward Korea on the part of China in the 1880s would have been the neutralization or joint protection of Korea by the powers that had vital and secondary interests in the peninsula. Moreover, it would have been much better for both China and Korea if the Chinese had concentrated all of their resources and efforts on modernizing and strengthening their own country, leaving Korea alone, so that Korea too could modernize on its own terms. Regretfully, however, such an enlightened policy was not the one China pursued or even conceived of in the 1880s and early 1890s.

As for the king of Korea and his advisers, except for a few of the latter, they failed to strive for the neutralization of their weakly situated country partly because the idea was so novel and alien to them that they were unable to see its advantages and also because the Chinese leaders were firmly opposed to it.[29] In view of the fact that, after all, the policy of searching for a new elder brother failed in the end and that neutralization was not seriously attempted in the 1880s, one may wonder in retrospect whether Kojong and von Möllendorff might not have met with less opposition if they had pursued neutralization. It is unfortunate that Kojong was not enlightened and forceful enough to see the merits of neutralization and pursue it persistently and consistently, however contrary to or different from Korean tradition the effort might have been.

As for Foreign Minister Kim Yun-sik, by and large he did what the Chinese suggested or told him to do—which raises an interesting and pertinent question: Was he a hopeless Chinese puppet, selling the interests of his own country, or was he a great and faithful Confucian statesman acting as a loyal official of a supposedly tributary state for the interests of suzerain China? It should be recalled that, in 1887, he faithfully carried out the wish of Resident Yüan Shih-k'ai by declaring George C. Foulk as *persona non grata* and thereby causing him to leave Korea, quite contrary to the wishes of Kojong and to the interests of his own country.[30] Since Korea was supposed to have become an independent and sovereign nation, its foreign minister should have been more concerned with promoting the interests and welfare of his country than with trying to remain faithful to China in Confucian terms. In fact, Kojong, repeatedly disappointed with Kim's excessively pro-Chinese behavior, felt compelled to dismiss him in 1887.

As for von Möllendorff, it was unfortunate that he missed or ignored these opportunities to pursue the neutralization of Korea, something he had told William Aston, the British consul general at Seoul, that he wanted; the international climate for the internationalization of Korea was so favorable at that time that it might have been worthwhile for him and the Korean government to consider it seriously.[31]

## The Chinese Response to the British Act

While the Japanese reaction to the British seizure of Port Hamilton was distinctly unfriendly, if not hostile, China's initial reaction was rather favorable. Ever since Russia took the Maritime Province by the Treaty of Peking in 1860, China had been worried about what the Russians might do next in Manchuria and Korea. But China's concern over Russian expansionism was not confined to the Far East; it was equally worried about Russian moves in the Sinkiang area to the Northwest. Moreover, Viceroy Li believed that, in case of war between Russia and England, it would be to China's advantage to be on the British side. Therefore, Li was worried over the Russian move in Korea, but was not anxious about the British move. He told British chargé O'Conor that he would not oppose the British occupation of Port Hamilton, although he could not consent to it publicly.[32] He reasoned that the British occupation of Port Hamilton would deter Russia from expanding southward.[33] As a means of checking Russian expansionism in Korea and Central Asia, Li even proposed an Anglo-Chinese alliance to Byron Brenan, the British consul in Tientsin. O'Conor, in Peking, liked the idea and worked diligently for it.[34] Although the alliance was never consummated, it was against such a background that the temporary occupation of Port Hamilton by the British won Li's "disguised blessing" during its initial stages. Thus he instructed Commissioner Ch'en Shu-t'ang in Seoul:

> British occupation of Port Hamilton does not seem likely to be ended. They hope Korea will grant a temporary lease with an annual rent of 20,000 taels. The subjects and administration are still to be under the Korean government. In a secret pact, Britain will guarantee never to injure Korea. Please convey this secretly to the Korean government. If it is acceptable, negotiations can be carried on with the British Consul-General. If not, it should not be made public.[35]

In Korea, Viceroy Li was quite willing to recognize the legality of the British occupation, if the British government would guarantee China's special rights in Korea and protect Korea against any Russian or Japanese aggression.[36] Even though Korea had become de jure independent by 1882, Viceroy Li still treated the kingdom as if it were a dependency and was ready to let the British have Port Hamilton if they would protect the Chinese suzerainty over Korea. Chinese minister Tseng suggested in London that the British government sign an agreement providing that the British government, in return, confirm Korea's vassalage to China to frustrate any Japanese attempt to destroy the suzerain-dependency relations between China and Korea.[37]

The British government welcomed China's pro-British and anti-Russian policy with regard to Korea. In spite of the fact that Britain had established diplomatic relations with Korea as a sovereign power and that Port Hamilton belonged to Korea, not to China, it entered into negotiations with China as if Korea were a part of China. Foreign Secretary Granville notified Minister Tseng in London that the sudden decision on the part of the British was made to prevent the "probable occupation of these islands by another power." In addition, Foreign Secretary Granville proposed an agreement binding China to acknowledge the British occupation of the port as lawful and obliging the British government to pay Korea for any revenues accruing from these islands, one stipulation being that there would be a deduction in payment to Korea for money that would have gone normally as a tribute to China.[38] But the Chinese government decided not to go so far as to authorize Tseng to sign the British proposal, largely because of fear of Russia's negative reaction to it.

## The Russian Response to the British Act

The Russian government took the British occupation of Port Hamilton very seriously and warned the London government that it could not remain indifferent to the British seizure of the port.[39] The Russian minister to China, Sergei I. Popov, also warned the Chinese government that if China condoned the British occupation, then Russia might be forced to take similar action against some other target of opportunity.[40] Some Russian newspapers were already advocating retaliatory action against England by occupying Port Lazareff and a strip of land running from the port to the Tumen River.[41] Thus, the situation in Korea was steadily deteriorating. Although the idea of occupying Port Lazareff was not an official policy of the Russian government,[42] there is no doubt that Russia used the proposal as a threat to put pressure on China and gain its support in forcing the withdrawal of the British from Port Hamilton.[43]

Fearing the possibility of Russian occupation of some Korean territory, something which he should have expected even before Russia's "warning," Viceroy Li decided to push for the evacuation of the British fleet from Port Hamilton. Li sent Admiral Ting Ju-ch'ang to Korea with a letter for the king advising him not to lease or loan the islands to the British under any circumstances, since Russia and even Japan might not stand idly by if the British took them. Li further warned the king that the British usually took territories by first leasing them, as they had done with Hong Kong.[44]

Meanwhile, Chargé O'Conor in Peking, under instructions from Granville, sent a formal notification to the Korean government, dated April 14, 1885, ten days after the actual occupation had occurred, but received on May 19.[45] O'Conor wrote that the port was a "trivial island"; that the British had taken it as a coaling station only temporarily and to prevent others from doing so; and that the Koreans and Chinese should appreciate the service that the forces of circumstance had thus rendered there.[46] Thoroughly annoyed, von Möllendorff had the Korean government reject the British argument that a temporary seizure of the territory should be excusable in order to "forestall its occupation by the enemy."[47] In view of the fact that the Russian government had no concrete design to occupy Korean territory at that time, the British argument that their seizure of Port Hamilton was done to prevent its occupation by Russia was nothing but a cover for their true intentions.[48] The British behavior "evoked natural and justified protest" by the Korean government.

Furthermore, in spite of the fact that, by May 2, the Anglo-Russian crisis over Afghanistan had largely dissipated,[49] the British fleet remained in continuous occupation of the islands, neither annexing them formally nor abandoning them. Under the circumstances, von Möllendorff advised the Korean government to dispatch commissioners to Port Hamilton to inspect British activities there. Among the commissioners were Ŏm Se-yŏng, von Möllendorff himself, and Admiral Ting.[50] They found that six British warships and two merchant steamers were at anchor in the ports; that its harbors were being improved; that the British flag was raised over the islands; that mines were laid in the surrounding waters; and that some telegraphic wires had been installed.[51] The commissioners protested to the British commanding officer, Captain J. P. Maclear, against such actions and then proceeded to Nagasaki, Japan, where they protested on May 19 to Vice-Admiral Dowell, the British naval commander in the Far East. Dowell explained that he was acting under orders from his government and that the occupation was only temporary.[52]

## Von Möllendorff and the Korean Response to the British Act

In Seoul, angered by the high-handed proceedings of the British and feeling that Korea's dignity and sovereignty were at stake, von Möllendorff urged the Korean government to act. On May 20, one day after receiving the formal notification of the seizure, von Möllendorff advised Foreign Minister Kim Yun-sik to send a strong note of protest to acting British consul general W. R. Carles.[53] As agitated as von Möllendorff was, he realized that the only thing the Korean government could do was to protest diplomatically to the British government for its "naked" violation of international law and of the spirit and letter of the Anglo-Korean Treaty of 1883. He knew very well that Korea's weak armed forces were in no position to drive the British war vessels out of Port Hamilton. Rather the British behavior affirmed his conviction that Korea needed a strong protective ally such as Russia, that with Russian help it must protect its independence, and that it must develop a strong army as soon as it was feasible to do so.

Although the Korean government had learned of the British move as soon as the port was occupied, it had decided to withhold protest until receiving a formal note from the British, partly because of George C. Foulk. Chargé Foulk advised Foreign Minister Kim that Korean resentment against the British seizure of the islands was "premature and out of place" in view of their lack of information on British intentions and on the details of the incident.[54] While the United States government maintained a policy of neutrality and indifference in regard to the Port Hamilton affair, Foulk showed a definite pro-British sentiment. Because Kojong had faith in Foulk and regarded him as one of his "unofficial advisers," even von Möllendorff often had to pay attention to what this American naval-diplomat said and did in Korea. It is no wonder that von Möllendorff considered Foulk to be his chief rival (among Westerners in Korea at the time) and not surprising that the relations between these two Westerners were so bad, in spite of the fact that both of them were champions of the independence and modernization of Korea.

In a note to Carles, Foreign Minister Kim protested that the British had no right to "protect" the port without Korea's consent and should evacuate the islands immediately. Von Möllendorff went so far as to warn Carles that if the British disregarded the Korean request for a British withdrawal it would be impossible to grant a proposed mine concession to the British company Jardine, Matheson and Co.[55] At von Möllendorff's recommendation, Kim sent diplomatic notes to all of the foreign representatives in order to solicit their support.[56] Von Möllendorff correctly reasoned that, whereas Korea could not coerce the British into withdrawing their ships from Port Hamilton, they would certainly be concerned with the opinions of the international community in this matter. Japanese chargé Kondō Masuki and German consul general Zembsch advised the Korean government to make it clear that the British occupation of Port Hamilton without Korean permission was contrary to British treaty obligations. The Chinese commissioner, Ch'en Shu-t'ang, sent an evasive reply, saying that the decision would have to be made by Viceroy Li. American chargé Foulk, however, was more concerned with what Russia might do to Korea. He advised the Korean government that the British action was only temporary and friendly and that the Koreans should assure the Russians that Korea would never permit any country to use its territory for military purposes.[57]

Needless to say, von Möllendorff strongly disagreed with Foulk's argument. Foulk was a staunch Anglophile and distinctively anti-Russian; and for his pro-British attitude Carles thanked him.[58] His bias might have been a reflection of the general American public attitude toward the two countries at this time. In Korea, however, Foulk might have reasoned that, for the progress of the country, British influence could be positive whereas Russian influence would be negative.

Having received the Korean protests, Foreign Secretary Granville instructed Chargé O'Conor at Peking to negotiate for an annual rental of $5,000 through the Chinese government with the main purpose of stopping the Korean protest.[59] In the actual negotiations with the Chinese officials, however, O'Conor was told that the Empress Dowager Tz'u-hsi had forbidden interference in such Korean matters.[60]

Thus the British government faced not only a moral but a legal dilemma: How to explain and justify its illegal occupation of Port Hamilton to the governments of Russia, Japan, and above all, of Korea. Of the countries maintaining direct interest in the British seizure of the islands, only China had been willing to cooperate or con-nive with the British in this action, provided that the latter would support China's claim to suzerainty over Korea. After being intimi-dated by the Russian government, however, even China worked for the British evacuation from Port Hamilton. At this critical juncture the British diplomats in Korea, Japan, and China were able to expose the von Möllendorff–de Speyer plot and began to use it as an excuse to justify and prolong their seizure of the islands.

## CHAPTER 6

# Von Möllendorff's Downfall

## The Reaction to the von Möllendorff–de Speyer Intrigue

It was in early June 1885 that the Japanese, Chinese, and British governments learned of the secret Kwŏn and Kim Mission to Vladivostok and of their return to Seoul in May. In spite of the fact that Kwŏn and Kim and Governor General Korf had not officially signed any written agreement for the Russian lease of Port Lazareff in return for Russia's dispatch of military advisers to Korea, the governments of Japan, China, and Great Britain mistakingly believed that the alleged secret Russo-Korean understanding involved Russian protection and military aid for Korea in return for Russian acquisition of Port Lazareff. The pro-Chinese Korean foreign minister, Kim Yun-sik, had been deeply worried about the pro-Russian policy advocated by von Möllendorff and approved tacitly by King Kojong. Kim had even warned Kojong that Korea would receive no benefits from Russia and should remain under Chinese influence. Kim did not explain how Korea could benefit from China. As foreign minister, Kim was eventually able to uncover some (not all) of the facts about the secret Kwŏn and Kim understanding with Korf and also about the agreement that von Möllendorff had supposedly reached with the Russian legation officials in Tokyo. Confused and frightened, Foreign Minister Kim revealed them to Chinese commissioner Ch'en Shu-t'ang and Japanese chargé Kondō Masuki; they in turn sent secret (and distorted versions of) reports about it to their respective governments.[1]

Upon receiving Chargé Kondō's report, Foreign Minister Inoue showed it to British minister Plunket and Chinese minister Hsü Cheng-tsu at Tokyo. Plunket immediately reported it to the British Foreign Office and Chargé O'Conor at Peking, and O'Conor directed Consul General Aston at Seoul to investigate any such agreement.[2] Minister Hsü also reported it to his government, as Commissioner Ch'en in Seoul did as well.[3] The Chinese felt that Russian policy was to draw Korea further away from China whereas British policy was to bring it closer to China. Viceroy Li reasoned that the British imperialism in Korea would be compatible with Chinese imperialism there. The British policy in Korea, he argued, would complement and strengthen the Chinese policy, whereas the policy of the Russians, who had no intention of cooperating with the Chinese in Korea, would be harmful to the interests of China in the peninsula. Therefore, Viceroy Li decided to reverse once again China's stand toward the British occupation. Li instructed Commissioner Ch'en to investigate the alleged agreement between Korea and Russia. Ch'en then vigorously protested to the Korean government about the agreement.[4] The Chinese government refused to support the Korean demand for the evacuation of the British from Port Hamilton. Instead, Viceroy Li decided once more to propose an Anglo-Chinese alliance against Russia by supporting the British occupation of the islets.[5] However, the Chinese added one condition: they asked the British government to guarantee the integrity of Korea before committing their government openly to the British occupation of Port Hamilton. But the British government was not willing to give China such a broad guarantee. In pointed to Russo-Korean intrigue as sufficient justification for British retention of Port Hamilton.[6]

Meanwhile, the Gladstone ministry of the Liberal Party was replaced by that of the Conservative Salisbury who, on June 24, became foreign secretary as well as prime minister. Salisbury's policy toward Korea, however, remained for some time the same as that of the previous ministry. As for the Korean government, since it had not received a formal British reply to its note of protest of May 20, it decided to bring the treaty powers into the dispute and asked the foreign representatives for mediation. For whatever reason, the British government and representatives proved to be extremely sensitive to the idea that the treaty powers should get involved. Throughout the whole period of the Port Hamilton affair, the British would become very receptive—and even willing (or at least pretending to be willing) to negotiate the matter amicably—every time the Korean government threatened to ask the treaty powers for mediation. The only weapon the Korean government had in the crisis was to appeal to the principles of international law and to the treaty powers. Finally, in July, Foreign Minister Kim formally requested mediation by the foreign representatives at Seoul, but he withdrew the request within two days inasmuch as Aston promised an amicable settlement.[7]

The Japanese government was more alarmed at the alleged Russo-Korean intrigue than by the British seizure of Port Hamilton. It is true that Foreign Minister Inoue instructed Minister Enomoto in Peking to urge the Chinese government to negotiate with the British to terminate the occupation; but he also suggested to Viceroy Li that he take appropriate action for the removal of pro-Russian ministers from the Korean court.[8] Inoue also conferred with Chinese minister Hsü in Tokyo and urged him to persuade Li to advise the king of Korea to dismiss von Möllendorff and employ a new, American, adviser.[9] The Japanese government apparently preferred Chinese control over Korea to Russian control and tried to achieve a detente with China to check the Russians in the peninsula. Thus, through their common fear of Russian designs in Korea, Sino-Japanese relations became somewhat closer.

The British now waged a full-scale campaign against von Möllendorff. The British press charged that von Möllendorff was incompetent in running the Korean Customs Office and that he hired mainly German nationals for the top positions in Korea and sold Chejudo to Russia by signing a secret agreement with it—which was, in fact, totally incorrect.[10] Consul General Aston presented a strong protest against von Möllendorff on the grounds that "he had acted treacherously against Korea and for Russia."[11] Chargé O'Conor accused von Möllendorff of not being a "safe adviser" to the Korean government and urged Viceroy Li to dismiss him from the Korean service. He wrote to his superior in London that von Möllendorff was "an unscrupulous agent in any matter in which he can serve his own private aims."[12] All of these charges and accusations were grossly exaggerated and one-sided. Whatever von Möllendorff did, he did with the tacit consent of the king, although he seemed on occasion to have gone too far.

## Von Möllendorff between de Speyer and Foreign Minister Kim Yun-sik

It was at this juncture that Alexis de Speyer was again sent to Korea. What happened is this: In May, when von Möllendorff visited Nagasaki to negotiate with Vice-Admiral Dowell over the Port Hamilton issue, he told Russian consul Vasili Kostylev in the same city to inform Minister Davydov that the agreements they had reached in February in Tokyo had been approved by King Kojong. It turn, von Möllendorff was told that the Russian government was prepared to send military instructors to Korea. But Davydov wanted some financial compensation in the form of Russian management of Korean mining, telegraph, and mail services.[13] Immediately after the exchange of communications with von Möllendorff, Minister Davydov instructed de Speyer to proceed to Korea as *agent provisoir* for the consummation of the secret Russo-Korean agreement and also to discover what were the British intentions in seizing Port Hamilton.[14] De Speyer was specifically instructed to make promises to the Korean government about the dispatch of Russian military instructors only after the Korean king had officially stated his desire to commission the Russian advisers to train the Korean army.[15] Upon his arrival in Seoul, de Speyer made it clear to the Korean government that if it were to lease or sell Port Hamilton to the British, then his own government would make similar demands.[16] In an interview with American chargé Foulk, however, de Speyer, reflecting his role as an adversary, stated that the Russian government regarded the British occupation of Port Hamilton as an act of hostility against it. Then he declared that he had "instructions to take steps for the annexation of ten times as much Korean territory as had been occupied by Great Britain unless the latter withdraws from Port Hamilton."[17] It is not clear as to who had given him such an instruction. Probably it came from his immediate superiors at the Russian embassy in Tokyo, if indeed he had gotten any such instruction at all, or most likely he said it on his own initiative, because Foreign Minister Giers had sent no such instruction to Tokyo.

It is true, however, that Kojong had requested of Alexander III, through the Russian embassy in Tokyo and Governor General Korf, that Russia should become a protector of Korea in return for Port Lazareff. Although the Czar at first thought it was "a good opportunity," he refused to comply with the request, but still kept Korean hope alive for future options.[18] The Russian government, to be sure, had neither the intention nor the desire to lag behind the Western powers in the struggle for influence in Korea, sharing a common border with it, and in 1884 Russia did in fact conclude a treaty with Korea. However, even after 1884, the Russian government—because of its backward economy, poor financial resources, and lack of adequate communication and transportation systems between St. Petersburg and Siberia—did not aspire to any political and territorial changes in the Far Eastern countries, for fear that its rivals rather than Russia itself might profit the most from such changes. Thus, in spite of the expansionist character of Czarist policy, the Russian government refused to be "an initiator" of imperialistic ventures in the Korean peninsula.

In fact, and right or wrong, the Russian government believed that "the real threat that menaced Korea at that time came from Great Britain, the United States, and Japan."[19] Russia was keeping only 18,000 armed men east of Lake Baikal in 1885. And in 1886, the Russians had only 15,000 men in the Far East, with 11,000 of them stationed around Vladivostok; Siberia had no troops to spare; and the nearest base for reinforcements was 4,000 miles away in European Russia. It would have taken eighteen months for the Russian government to send troops from European Russia to the Maritime Province region.[20] Moreover, Russian naval forces in Far Eastern waters were smaller than the Chinese forces. Even during the *Kapsin* Coup of 1884, Russia did not send any warships to the Korean waters, while the other treaty powers did. Also, construction of the Trans-Siberian Railroad did not start until 1891. Under the circumstances it is doubtful that the Russian Foreign Office would have given de Speyer such a reckless instruction. So far as Alexander III and Giers were concerned, therefore, all that they officially wanted as of 1885 was to send Russian military instructors to Korea and persuade the Korean government not to cede Port Hamilton to the British.[21]

Even so, de Speyer's bold and seemingly unauthorized statement was not completely out of line with the spirit of the foreign policy of Czar Alexander III and Foreign Minister Giers. While the Russians met only a part of King Kojong's requests by deciding to dispatch Russian military instructors to Korea as of 1885, they still did not officially reject the possibility of becoming a "protective ally" or senior partner of Korea in the future. Their policy was to wait and see how political conditions might develop in Korea before making the final decision. Being well aware of the flexibility and of the option retained by his superiors in St. Petersburg, de Speyer was talking not about what his government would necessarily do, but what it might or could do in case the British fleet remained in occupation of Port Hamilton. Thus, de Speyer's apparently unauthorized and offensive statement was not completely contrary to the thinking and posture of his government in St. Petersburg.

Moreover, probably because de Speyer was ambitious and wanted to accomplish so much on his own, he made further claims that, on the basis of the most-favored-nation treatment clause, Russia should be entitled to send troops into Korea under certain circumstances in accordance with the privilege of Article III of the Tientsin Convention of April 1885. He and von Möllendorff then drafted a paper to document the secret agreement on the basis of the arrangements that Davydov and von Möllendorff had made earlier in Japan; and the king gave tacit approval to the document.[22] Von Möllendorff's approach was to present a fait accompli to Foreign Minister Kim and to force him to sign the document, using the king's approval as pressure. But before von Möllendorff could take any action, Kim managed to secure a copy of the draft. Frightened and puzzled, Kim consulted Chargé Kondō and Commissioner Ch'en in Seoul. Kim then successfully persuaded Sim Sun-t'aek, Kim Hong-jip, and Kim Pyŏng-si to join him in requesting the king to change his mind on this matter.[23] Kim's role during this crisis seemed so crucial that Frederick Foo Chien goes so far as to say that "without the vigilence of Kim Yun-shik [Kim Yun-sik], the secret agreement and the advance of Russia in [into] Korea could very possibly have succeeded."[24] But Chien's statement reflects a gross misunderstanding of Russia at that time because, as explained above, in the mid-1880s Russia was neither ready nor willing to play an active role in the Korean peninsula, regardless of what de Speyer and von Möllendorff had been doing.

As for de Speyer, without being fully aware of what had been going on in Seoul, he began to negotiate with Foreign Minister Kim; but he discovered that everything had changed. Because of Chinese pressure and intervention, the Korean government repudiated the secret Russo-Korean agreement unilaterally. He was told that the king and his government wanted American military instructors, not Russians, and that they had already requested American instructors. De Speyer was astonished and demanded that the Russians be formally invited.[25] Von Möllendorff sided with de Speyer and urged Kim to finalize the agreement, but Kim refused to do so.[26] Instead, Kim complained to von Möllendorff about the secret diplomacy used in negotiating the agreement. He further declared that, henceforth, important diplomatic negotiations should be conducted with his knowledge and approval.[27] Moreover, Kim persuaded Sim Sun-t'aek and Kim Hong-jip to denounce the unauthorized activities of von Möllendorff and the secret agreement. He also won support from Commissioner Ch'en and Takahira Kogorō, the new Japanese chargé ad interim.[28] However, some Korean officials close to the king secretly approached de Speyer and told him that although the monarch still desired to hire Russian military instructors, he was very much afraid of the Chinese pressure.[29] In order to get Dr. Horace N. Allen, an influential American confidant of King Kojong, to support his seemingly lost cause, von Möllendorff offered him a position in the customs service at twice the doctor's salary. But Allen, who resented von Möllendorff's high-handed manner of doing business and his generally anti-American stance, declined the offer.[30] Being astute, Allen accurately sensed, moreover, that von Möllendorff was about to be forced out of Korea.

At this juncture, on July 2, 1885, Foreign Minister Inoue sent Li his "Eight Points of Opinion" on Korean foreign and political affairs. In it, Inoue advised Li that von Möllendorff should be replaced by an American adviser, that Commissioner Ch'en should also be replaced by a more capable Chinese official, and that the diplomatic conduct of the Korean government should be carried out under instructions from Viceroy Li—but that Li should confer in advance with Inoue before dispatching any instructions to the Korean government.[31] Li received Inoue's advice with mixed feelings. He liked Inoue's idea of making the Korean government more subordinate to his own instructions, but he had no intention of implementing his policy in concert with the Japanese Foreign Office, virtually giving what amounted to a veto power to the Japanese foreign minister. So Li politely refused Inoue's suggestion. On August 15, therefore, despite the Tientsin Convention, Inoue decided to adopt a policy of noninterference toward Korea without receiving the same guarantee from China, so long as Li were to remove von Möllendorff from Korea.[32] As a result, the king and von Möllendorff faced opposition from the king's own ministers as well as from the Chinese and Japanese governments. It is important to note that the Japanese government, which had been committed to the proposition that Korea had been independent since 1876, in 1885 encouraged Chinese control of Korea to the detriment of the very independence earlier espoused. It preferred China's domination of Korea to that of Russia, mainly because the Japanese leaders believed that China was an essentially impotent nation not to be feared, while Russia was a formidable and expanding military power that Japan might find it hard to eliminate from the peninsula, if it were ever to establish a stronghold there. In any case, "the truth is that Korea became the unfortunate victim of the imperialist powers, China, Japan, and England."[33]

Not only the Japanese but also the British government wanted to see von Möllendorff removed from the Korean scene. O'Conor strongly "urged" both Viceroy Li and the Tsungli Yamen to withdraw the controversial German.[34] In the face of such strong opposition on the parts of both the British and Japanese governments against von Möllendorff, Li felt that even if he had wanted to keep him in Korea, he had no choice but to bring him back to China. Following the exposure of the von Möllendorff–de Speyer intrigue, however, Li himself did not wish to let the German diplomat stay in Korea, where he could plot against Chinese interests there. So he decided to "advise" the Korean king to dismiss him from all the positions he held and send him back to China. Even so, it seems that the overwhelming reason for Li's advice on von Möllendorff's dismissal was that he felt the force of British and Japanese pressures. The very fact that Li later sent the supposedly "reformed" German back to Korea in 1888, as discussed in detail in chapter 8, indicates that Li's disappointment with von Möllendorff's "intrigue" in connection with the Russian officials in 1885 was most likely not as intense as that of British and Japanese officials. Nevertheless, as of the summer of 1885 Li decided to remove him from the Korean political scene.

In late July 1885, Li sent a letter to the Korean king with instructions that the Korean government should hire American military instructors as soon as possible and officially proclaim the nullification of the secret Russo-Korean agreement. As for von Möllendorff, Li charged that "he has concentrated too much power in his hands and is hated by officials of other countries and so he should be dismissed for his action and be replaced by an American adviser." Li added that Japanese foreign minister Inoue had agreed on the dismissal of von Möllendorff and that Kim Hong-jip, Kim Yun-sik, and Ŏ Yun-jung, being highly regarded by other countries, should be appointed to important government positions. Li further stated that the Chinese army would be withdrawn from Korea, but that Chinese warships would be dispatched to remain at Inch'ŏn to "contend with any crisis" in Korea. He also revealed his plan of releasing the Taewŏn'gun, presumably as a deterrent to the Mins, who had sided with von Möllendorff and the Russians.[35]

Meanwhile, de Speyer insisted that the Korean officials, while visiting the Russian legation in Tokyo, had said that Russian military instructors should train the Korean army, after the withdrawal of the Japanese and Chinese troops. Kim explained, on the contrary, that the official position of the Korean government was to nullify any negotiations conducted by von Möllendorff without official authorization. As to the legality of the secret agreement between the Russian minister in Tokyo and von Möllendorff, de Speyer argued in return that it was valid because the negotiation had been conducted by von Möllendorff in his official capacity as vice minister of the Office of Foreign Affairs of the Korean government.[36] Furthermore, de Speyer insisted that the Korean request to the Russian government for Russian military instructors had been made in writing. Kim thereupon asked von Möllendorff whether he had sent a written request for Russian military instructors to the Korean government. Turning to de Speyer, von Möllendorff stated—in French—that a Russian official wrote down in German what he had said in his conversation with Minister Davydov. Von Möllendorff used French so that the Korean official keeping the minutes of the three-sided conversation could not understand what he said. Annoyed by von Möllendorff's ambiguity, de Speyer still insisted that Kim and the Korean government must honor the earlier agreement, because the Russian Czar had already acted on the matter of sending Russian military instructors to Korea, and that whether von Möllendorff's request had been written or not was irrelevant. Von Möllendorff then pushed for de Speyer's position by arguing that, in international negotiations, so long as the negotiators know each other, documents are not crucially important. Without being fully aware of the British and Japanese campaigns against him and behind his back, and without realizing that his contract with the Korean government was about to be terminated, von Möllendorff still took sides with de Speyer in favor of a Russo-Korean alliance.

Then de Speyer threatened Kim by declaring that he would return and report to the Russian government and the Czar. Russians, he urged, must be the military instructors, even if the Korean government did not wish it. Otherwise, there would be great difficulties for Korea.[37]

In order to find out who or what was responsible for changing Kojong's mind on the issue of hiring Russian military instructors, de Speyer had talked with the French bishop in Seoul, Msgr. Blanc. Blanc explained that, so far as he knew, Kojong would hold fast to his original idea of inviting Russian military instructors, if he were left alone; however, he would change his mind if the Chinese were to interfere in the matter.[38] De Speyer's next move was to discover what the Chinese position on the issue was. He asked Commissioner Ch'en's view on the matter. Ch'en slyly replied that Korea would be free to invite advisers from any country, after the withdrawal of the Chinese and Japanese troops.[39] With this assurance, he saw Kim again and declared, "If you do not accept the American army instructors, there would be no loss, but if you do not take the Russian officers, you must lose a great deal. . . . If you break with America in this, there is no loss, but if you do with Russia, trouble lies [in wait]. . . . America is far away from Korea, and cannot be of any benefit to your country."[40]

Somewhat intimidated and cowed, Kim proposed a compromise whereby the Korean government would invite an equal number of military instructors from both the United States and Russia, but de Speyer rejected the ploy. Kim then made another proposal: mining technicians would be invited from Russia and military officers from the United States, but de Speyer turned it down also. He would settle for nothing short of the employment of Russian military instructors. Finally, Kim told de Speyer that the Korean government could broach the matter with the Russian minister when he came to Korea. De Speyer intimated that there would be no Russian minister coming and that the Korean government should be prepared for serious consequences.[41]

Apparently disappointed with his pro-Chinese superior, von Möllendorff told Kim that "ten Chinas cannot be compared with Russia. Why should you depend on the undependable, and not rely on the reliables?" Kim replied that even if Russia were powerful and China weak, Heaven would be offended if China were not consulted on such an important matter as this. After all, Korean ties with China had been bound by *li*. Von Möllendorff then questioned why in the world the Korean government was so submissive to other powers and yet so hostile toward Russia.[42]

Although de Speyer won another audience from the king and received the monarch's seemingly favorable but nonetheless noncommittal response on the issue of Russian dispatch of military advisers to Korea, he was still unable to find a way to implement the von Möllendorff–Davydov agreement because of Kim's strong opposition.[43] Before he left for Tokyo, de Speyer heard the rumor that the American government had finally decided to send four military instructors to Korea but demanded a prior payment of $2,400 in travel expenses for them. Now de Speyer told Kim that the Russian government would make no such request for prior payment and that the Korean govenment could rightly refuse American military instructors on the grounds of such a request; but Kim refused to consider de Speyer's new proposal.[44] Before leaving for Tokyo, de Speyer had another conversation with Foulk, who thought that de Speyer was a "blustering" diplomat. He explained to Foulk that he was now aware that the matter of the Russian military instructors had originated with and was negotiated by von Möllendorff, who had not been authorized to act (which is inaccurate). However, since Czar Alexander III had already acted upon the treaty, he insinuated that Russia might force Korea to accept Russian military instructors.[45] In his last dispatch to Minister Davydov before leaving Korea, however, de Speyer rationalized his "incorrect" and "unauthorized action" in dealing with the Korean government on the grounds that he himself had been misled by King Kojong and deceived by von Möllendorff. He claimed, therefore, that he was the "victim" not the "offender" in the whole situation.[46]

So far as the issue of Korean employment of Russian military advisers was concerned, de Speyer's charge that he became the "victim" was essentially correct. However, he apparently failed to perceive that, with respect to the idea of a Russian protectorship of Korea, von Möllendorff and King Kojong might have become victims, because the Russian Czar and foreign minister never flatly and unequivocally rejected the Korean offer and, instead, deliberately encouraged the idea among Korea's pro-Russian leadership. Moreover, de Speyer's conversation with Foulk and dispatch to Davydov seem to indicate that he was not only uncertain about the complex role that von Möllendorff had played in this Russo-Korean intrigue but was not positively sure about the exact role that Kojong had played in the matter. Having accomplished nothing, he left Seoul on July 7 after a month of activities there. Soon after de Speyer's return to Tokyo, a small Russian military mission under Colonel Shneur did arrive at Seoul; however, it decided to return to Russia immediately in view of what had taken place in Korea.[47] Despite de Speyer's uncertainty or confusion and despite assertions by some distinguished historians that von Möllendorff had acted on his own,[48] there is overwhelming evidence to the contrary. Von Möllendorff acted on the matter, as he himself acknowledged,[49] under a tacit understanding with the king and with some of his important officials.

Foulk was concerned that the Russian negotiators might try to establish "Korea as the protectorate of Russia" and that Korea might have to accept only Russian officers should the United States not speedily expedite the request made by the king. In case Russian officers were hired in Korea, he thought they should be accepted and serve only under a Korean neutrality well guaranteed by the powers. Thus, he again urged the U.S. Department of State to take action on the king's request.[50]

While de Speyer was pressing his demands, the Korean government formally invoked the good offices clause of the American-Korean Treaty of 1882 in a letter to Foulk asking for assistance in the Port Hamilton affair. British consul general Aston in Seoul told Foulk that England would relinquish Port Hamilton only if and when the secret Russo-Korean agreement was formally denounced and declared to have been unauthorized.[51] Foulk forwarded to his government the request of the Korean government. However, the position of Secretary of State Bayard on this subject was that the Korean-American Treaty did not empower the United States to interfere on behalf of either party.[52] Besides, on July 5, the Korean government withdrew the request for American good offices, inasmuch as the British representatives in Seoul promised negotiation on the issue.[53]

Because of Foulk's strong sympathy with the king and deep involvement with the dubious activities of de Speyer and von Möllendorff in Seoul, Bayard reminded him of the neutral and impartial policy of the United States. He warned Foulk that "it is clearly the interest of the United States to hold aloof" from all the intrigues in Seoul involving China, Russia, England, and Japan.[54] After all, de Speyer was right when he told the Korean officials that "America is far away from Korea and cannot be of any benefit to your country."

In light of the fact that Chargé Foulk campaigned for the removal of von Möllendorff from Korea, it would be interesting to compare the ideas and personal qualities of these two Western diplomats. Although von Möllendorff and Foulk disliked each other, in many ways they were very much alike: both were highly idealistic, lofty, towering, romantic, brilliant, and colorful diplomats. Both believed in progressivism and modernization for the welfare of Korea, and that China's retarding influence must be eliminated. Both held strong reservations about missionary work in Korea. Both were liked and trusted by King Kojong and many of his independent- and progressive-minded advisers, which helped make the two men jealous of each other. Von Möllendorff was, officially, a diplomatic, political, and financial adviser to King Kojong and his government, while Foulk was regarded and treated by the monarch as an unofficial but confidential adviser. Both also possessed a high degree of integrity—Foulk even more than von Möllendorff. Both were ideologically consistent and somewhat inflexible—again Foulk moreso than von Möllendorff. Ironically, both ended their professional careers in Korea in a most unfortunate way and held no significant posts after they left the peninsula.[55]

Of course, Foulk was also quite different from von Möllendorff. Besides the age difference (von Möllendorff was nine years older than Foulk), Foulk was much more charming and conciliatory. Foulk, the naval officer and diplomat, was an Anglophile, whereas von Möllendorff, the scholar (philologist) and diplomat was a Russophile. Moreover, Foulk was sinophobic, as his predecessor Foote had been, but von Möllendorff, a sinologist, was a sinophile except in Sino-Korean relations, in which case he was mildly but distinctively sinophobic. But his anti-Chinese sentiment was confined mainly to China's seemingly unfair treatment of and unwarranted interference in Korea. Furthermore, von Möllendorff was much more secretive and intrigue-minded (as King Kojong himself was) than Foulk. Von Möllendorff passed away at the age of fifty-five while Foulk died at thirty-seven. In terms of scholarly contributions, von Möllendorff's accomplishments were outstanding, but Foulk left no achievements in the area. Because of his high intelligence and linguistic and other scholarly abilities, Foulk too would have undoubtedly turned out to be a first-rate and superior scholar if he had lived longer and had chosen to be a specialist in Oriental studies. It should be noted that most of the more important scholarly researches of von Möllendorff were conducted and published after he left Korea and returned to China in late 1885.

## The Fall of von Möllendorff

As an easy way out of the difficult situation, the Korean king and government decided to put the entire blame on von Möllendorff, using him as a scapegoat. Although the turn of events showed in retrospect how "pliable and ill-planned" Kojong's pro-Russian policy had been,[56] it was actually von Möllendorff who had originally proposed that Korea should not give the impression of actively inviting the Russians into Korea and that, instead, Korea should maintain relations with the treaty powers on the basis of strict neutrality and impartiality.[57] Moreover, von Möllendorff himself never complained about the king's official disavowal, although he felt that Kojong was not a man of strong will and decisiveness.[58] Pliable or not, Kojong's approach was to sell von Möllendorff down the river rather than face up to the Chinese.

The question arises here: Was Kojong being wise or clever or cowardly? The nature of Kojong's statemanship and character is one of the most controversial and interesting subjects of the period of the late Yi dynasty. Some historians charge that Kojong was a weak, incompetent, confused, and intrigue-minded monarch.[59] Others portray him as a pragmatic, bold, innovative, and reasonably intelligent reformer—at least in the 1870s and 1880s.[60] To be sure, Kojong was neither an inspiring and charismatic nor a dynamic and forceful ruler. Intellectually and politically, however, he was a progressive-minded ruler who displayed a keen instinct for what the future of his kingdom should be, and he tried to modernize his country and make it more independent of China—which happened to be the right course of action for Korea in the 1880s and the 1890s. Yet, as a good Confucian younger brother, he was still not only deeply respectful but even fearful toward his elder brother, China, though it gradually dawned upon him that his brother had steadily declined to the point where he would no longer be useful to Korea. In terms of his personality, Kojong was rather timid, secretive, and intrigue-minded. In addition, Kojong, in trying to modernize his country, allowed himself to be constantly obstructed by overpowering and self-interested bureaucrats.[61] Worst of all, Kojong suffered constant interference and hampering from the decadent but yet still "mighty" Chinese (mighty, at least, in the minds of most Korean bureaucrats and people)—something that his counterpart in Japan, Emperor Meiji, did not have to contend with at all. As it turned out, in due time Japan became a strong and modernized empire, whereas the kingdom of Korea was eventually absorbed by Japan. So Emperor Meiji emerged a winner, while King Kojong became a loser; and it is very easy to praise a winner and criticize a loser.

Be that as it may, in 1885, Kojong showed neither the initiative nor the courage to save his gifted and favorable German adviser. Instead, he sought the least controversial way out by dismissing him and returning him to China, though admittedly very reluctantly. Accordingly, the king sent a mission to Tientsin, headed by Nam Chŏng-ch'ŏl and Pak Che-sun, to "explain" the whole episode to Viceroy Li. The king's letter stated that the secret Russo-Korean agreement had been initiated and negotiated by von Möllendorff without authorization from the Korean government and that the Korean government intended to dismiss von Möllendorff and would like to ask the Chinese government to recommend a suitable person to replace him as head of the Korean Customs Service. As for the secret Kwŏn and Kim Mission to Vladivostok, the note stated that, to avoid an international crisis, the Korean government refrained from any punitive action against them.[62] Significantly, the note did not state that the mission had never reached an understanding with a Russian official at Vladivostok. Rather what the note implied was that even though Kwŏn and Kim had committed or might have committed an action worthy of punishment, the Korean government should not in fact take any punitive action against them lest the Russian government should be offended.

In Seoul, a rumor was spreading to the effect that von Möllendorff might be treated as a Korean subject and as such be tried for "high treason."[63] Foulk was opposed to such a drastic action, as it might precipitate trouble with Chancellor Otto von Bismarck of Germany. But he strongly urged the Korean government to dismiss von Möllendorff for using "puerile invective to vent his personal feeling by using the name of the [Korean] Government."[64] Despite Kojong's strong confidence in him, von Möllendorff was finally removed, officially "for the moment," from the position of vice minister of the Office of Foreign Affairs on July 27 and of inspector general of the Korean Customs Service on September 5. There is no doubt that Kojong's reluctant dismissal of von Möllendorff was largely because of pressure from Li.[65] By the same token there is no doubt that in the final analysis Li's recommendation to Kojong for the dismissal of von Möllendorff was made largely because of pressures placed upon him by the British and Japanese governments. Whatever role may have been played by Foulk and others was only marginal. The fact that Kojong repeatedly asked von Möllendorff to remain in Korea after his "dismissal" of the German (until the latter's departure in December 1885) and that the monarch repeatedly urged him to return to Korea even after his exit to China strongly indicates that Kojong retained his confidence in the German scholar-diplomat.

It was clear that once von Möllendorff was removed from Korea under Chinese pressure, it would be most unlikely, probably impossible, that he would be rehired by the Korean government. Some historians argue that Li's real reason for recommending von Möllendorff's dismissal was that he had acted independently in administering the Korean Customs Office; and that Li hoped, with his dismissal, to make the Korean Customs Office subordinate to the Chinese Maritime Customs as a part of China's political and trade expansion into Korea.[66] However, such an argument is only partly correct, because von Möllendorff's involvement in the Russo-Korean intrigue played a dominant role in his downfall, as explained above.

Even after losing the position of inspector general, von Möllendorff did not have to return to China right away. Apparently the king wanted to keep him in Korea to use him again for secret negotiations with Russia; so he was permitted to wait for the coming of Karl Waeber, the first Russian chargé, to Korea on October 3, 1885. After the exchange of treaty ratifications on October 16, Waeber presented von Möllendorff, on behalf of his government, with the decoration of Saint Anna in appreciation of his aid in the negotiation of the Russo-Korean Treaty.[67]

Unlike the dictatorial and undiplomatic de Speyer, Waeber proved to be a conciliatory and agreeable man. Moreover, he was specifically instructed by Foreign Minister Giers to avoid any controversy with China over Korea.[68] In an interview with Foulk, he said that de Speyer, "being a young man, had assumed unwarranted authority" in his method of conducting Russo-Korean negotiations and that the Russian government had no intention of pursuing an aggressive policy in the Korea peninsula.[69] De Speyer was destined eventually (in 1896) to replace Waeber as the Russian minister to Korea and to push hard for Russian penetration—economic, political, and military—into Korea. His American counterpart in Seoul, Minister Horace N. Allen, characterized de Speyer as "an impudent pup, a most arrogant and boisterous man," and "a bitter enemy of the United States."[70] British consul John Jordan described the Russian as an extremely unreasonable and tactless diplomat.[71] Later de Speyer was placed in charge of the Russian legation in Tokyo. While serving as the Russian minister in Japan, he advocated equally aggressive policies for the furtherance of Russian interests in Japan as in Korea. Baron Roman Romanovich Rosen, who succeeded de Speyer as the Russian minister to Japan, commented that the latter was "one of those young diplomatic hopefuls who are always ready to recommend to their governments [a] 'forward policy' in the hope of thereby acquiring credit for activity and patriotism."[72] Philip Jaisohn (Sŏ Chae-p'il), an American-educated Korean patriot and a Progressive reformer, although praising Waeber as "one of the ablest and most faithful" Russian diplomats in East Asia, disliked de Speyer for being too "coarse and ignorant."[73] There is no doubt that, in general, Waeber—unlike de Speyer—was liked and trusted by the king, the queen and many of their advisers.

Stripped of his official positions and learning that Viceroy Li had already sent a Chinese ship to transport him to China, von Möllendorff and his family had no choice but to prepare for departure. During all of this time, however, King Kojong and Queen Min repeatedly urged von Möllendorff to remain in Korea. In fact, the king did so not only in many letters but also privately and directly in many audiences he gave the German. But the situation seemed beyond the control of the monarch and also of von Möllendorff himself. Even the Tsungli Yamen informed Viceroy Li that, under the stormy conditions existing in Korea—for which von Möllendorff was held responsible—it would be prudent to remove the controversial diplomat from Korea. Feeling that King Kojong would be impotent in face of the massive international campaigns against him, von Möllendorff explained to the monarch that under the circumstances it might be wiser and better for everybody concerned if he went back to China, strongly implying that he would wish to return to Korea after the situation calmed down. Kojong reluctantly agreed, naively feeling assured that he could be easily rehired.

On December 5, 1885, when the von Möllendorffs left Inch'ŏn, thousands of Korean well-wishers came to see them off.[74] After arriving at Tientsin via Chefoo, von Möllendorff provided Li with a detailed report about the unfair way he had been treated and denounced by the foreign diplomats—especially the British. Viceroy Li, who liked von Möllendorff's anti-Japanese posture but was annoyed at his pro-Russian scheme, decided to keep him on hand, with an idea that perhaps in the near future this "barbarian" could be "reformed," enlisted in support of the Chinese policy toward Korea, and used against some of the other "barbarians." Also, Viceroy Li, essentially a parochial and narrow-minded politician, believed that the linguistic talents and administrative ability of the German scholar-diplomat could be utilized in his own service. So Li hired von Möllendorff as his "personal secretary" and translator, providing him with piles of insignificant paperwork rather than endowing him with some research fellowship or with a professorship at an academic institution for the development and furtherance of Chinese studies.

Despite the dismissal of von Möllendorff and the Korean renunciation of the secret Russo-Korean agreement, Li decided to strengthen Chinese control of the kingdom. He now visualized a Korea dominated completely by China. In order to implement his aggressive imperialistic policy toward Korea, Li decided to return the kidnapped royal father, the Taewŏn'gun, to Korea and to replace Ch'en Shu-t'ang with the more energetic Yüan Shih-k'ai.[75] Li hoped that the Taewŏn'gun would check the pro-Russian sentiment of the Korean government and become Yüan's collaborator vis-à-vis the king and the Min faction. These officials, accompanied by Henry F. Merrill, an American who had served in the Chinese Customs Service under Robert Hart, reached Korea in October 1885. Merrill was nominated by Hart to succeed von Möllendorff as the head of the Korean Customs Service.[76] As for the position of adviser to the king and the Korean Foreign Office, in April 1886 Li recommended and sent Judge Owen Nickerson Denny, an American diplomat who had served as American consul at Tientsin and later as consul general at Shanghai.[77] Because of Li's unfortunate experiences with von Möllendorff and his mistrust of Hart, who had exercised great influence on Chinese foreign affairs, he decided to divide these two functions.[78] Denny arrived at Seoul on May 28, 1886.

CHAPTER 7

# More Storms in Korea after von Möllendorff's Exit

### The Establishment of Yüan Shih-k'ai as the Chinese Resident in Korea

Viceroy Li was determined to control Korea even more tightly than he had done before following the fiasco of the von Möllendorff–de Speyer intrigue. The Japanese government, clearly preferring Chinese control of Korea over that of Russia despite the Tientsin Convention of 1885, urged Viceroy Li to replace the mild-mannered commissioner in Seoul, Ch'en Shu-t'ang, with a more energetic agent. Even if the Japanese government had been reticent on the desirability of a more vigorous Chinese agent in Korea to check the pro-Russian Korean movement, Viceroy Li would have undoubtedly replaced Commissioner Ch'en with a more aggressive agent anyway, not only because the performance of the commissioner had been generally "unsatisfactory" (from the standpoint of China) but also because of the vital importance that the viceroy attached to keeping Korea under China's influence even after the removal of von Möllendorff from Korea. However, confirmed now by the Japanese government's recommendation and support for such a move, Li felt quite safe and comfortable in dispatching the aggressive Yüan Shih-k'ai to Korea.

In October of 1885, in his petition to the Chinese emperor on behalf of Yüan, Li explained that "the Korean King has been affecting gratitude toward Your Imperial Majesty *outwardly*, while *inwardly* he harbors the interest of promoting (his own) self-interest with the help of foreign powers." Describing King Kojong as a "recalcitrant monarch," Li recommended that Yüan be sent to Korea for the purpose of "maintaining the local Korean situation to our advantage."[1] With the emperor's approval in hand, Li was then more than happy to send Yüan to Korea.

Viceroy Li had some difficulty in formulating an exact title for Yüan. After much consideration, he decided on *Tsung-li Ch'ao-hsien t'ung-shang chiao-shih shi-i* (literally, "Stationing in Korea to administer negotiations and trade affairs"—i.e., to manage diplomatic and commercial affairs in Korea) thus the title "Manager of Diplomatic and Consular Affairs in Korea," which appeared quite harmless to Korea.[2] Although Li skillfully or cunningly hid his true intention in sending Yüan to Seoul, Yüan's mission was not only to take care of normal diplomatic and consular business but also to control and supervise the "recalcitrant monarch" of Korea to the advantage of China. In the same petition to the emperor, Li also stated that "one inch we gain in strengthening our capacity to preserve this country is an inch added to our national interest."[3] In other words, the main job of the new agent was to milk the Koreans as much as possible and, in any and every way that he could, to do so for the interest of China, regardless of the wishes and welfare of the Koreans and their leaders. So here was in fact China's, or rather Li's, version of an "elder brother" taking care of the "younger brother."

In informing King Kojong of Yüan's new appointment, Li stated that "Yüan is loyal and intelligent. . . . Whenever you have important matters of internal and foreign affairs, implement them by consultation with him."[4] In Korea, Yüan introduced himself to foreign representatives with a name card bearing an English translation of his position as H.I.C.M. Resident, Seoul ("The Resident in Seoul Sent by His Imperial Chinese Majesty"); he was commonly referred to as "resident."[5]

It is an interesting and important fact that by 1885 Yüan was not only recognized as an "expert" on Korea by Viceroy Li and other Chinese leaders but was also welcomed by King Kojong as China's new agent in his kingdom. Ever since the *Imo* Revolt of 1882, Yüan had served in Korea in several different capacities and had even on occasion pleased King Kojong, which led the monarch to ask Viceroy Li for Yüan's service in Korea. In 1882, Yüan had helped Admiral Wu Ch'ang-ch'ing in suppressing the *Imo* rebels and in abducting the Taewŏn'gun and sending him to China.[6] Following the fiasco of the *Imo* Revolt, Admiral Wu had placed Yüan in charge of organizing and modernizing the Korean army. Recognizing Yüan's contribution to the training of the Korean army, Kojong had expressed his appreciation to him in an audience in September 1882.[7]

In April 1884, following the partial withdrawal of the Chinese troops from Korea, Li appointed Yüan as director-general of the Military Secretariat and the concurrent associate director of Korean Military Affairs to be attached to Admiral Wu Chao-yu.[8] And in September of the same year Kojong even asked Li to appoint Yüan as a military adviser for the military affairs of his country—not necessarily, however, as resident.[9] The king also appreciated Yüan's role in "rescuing" him and the queen from the hands of the rebels, who had become "blood-thirsty" during the *Kapsin* Coup of 1884[10] (despite Yüan's suggestion for dethroning the king, of which, at first, Kojong was unaware).[11]

King Kojong's recommendation that Yüan be appointed as a military adviser for his royal army shows how ill-informed and ill-advised the monarch was of Yüan's professional qualifications. Although Yüan was a daring and aggressive individual—probably a good quality for a competent soldier—he possessed no expert knowledge and professionally earned experience, to speak of, on modern military strategy, tactics, discipline, and organization and, therefore, was utterly incapable of training and modernizing the Korean army, though admittedly he was no worse than most of Kojong's own Korean military officers. Unlike Chiang Kai-shek, who systematically studied military science in China, Japan, and even in Russia for a brief period, Yüan had no formal education and training in military science in China or elsewhere. Having failed the civil service examination twice in his youth (in 1876 and 1880) and made the decision not to pursue the career of scholar-bureaucrat, he could have devoted his time and energy to studying modern military science, thereby eventually earning the title of "the Father of Modern Military Science" in China, but did not. Instead, he eventually became a "curse" to the political and military modernization of China by allowing himself in the 1910s to become "the Father of Warlords" in China. Besides, Yüan did not want to see Korea develop and maintain a strong and modernized army. That became obvious while he served as the Chinese resident in Korea between 1885 and 1894.

Be that as it may, as of 1885 Kojong's appreciation of Yüan's services in Korea—though based on Kojong's misperception of Yüan's qualifications and intentions—clearly indicate that Yüan had an excellent chance to develop and maintain cordial and effective working relations with the Korean monarch, despite Kojong's earlier involvement in von Möllendorff's pro-Russian scheme. Moreover, the monarch was so frightened and intimidated by the Chinese after the von Möllendorff–de Speyer fiasco that he would have refrained from making another request for Russian protectorship so quickly if Yüan and the Chinese government had treated him with some respect and with due concern for the sovereign rights and autonomy of his kingdom in and after 1885. Especially since he was unaware of the true function and mission of Yüan in Korea, Kojong was ready and willing to work in a cordial manner with the new Chinese agent. All Yüan had to do was to promote the interests of China in Korea without sacrificing too much of the welfare of the Koreans and without undermining too seriously the dignity and autonomy of the Korean monarch and his people; but he did quite the opposite, thereby virtually forcing King Kojong to seek another protectorship elsewhere.

To begin with, Resident Yüan held a low opinion of King Kojong and described him as a "dim-witted monarch" easily dominated by his "obstinate and stubborn" queen.[12] Yüan believed that King Kojong should have been deposed at the time of the *Kapsin* Coup, as he had proposed to his then-superior General Wu Chao-yu. He hated the monarch for his involvement in the von Möllendorff–de Speyer intrigue of 1885 and resented the fact that this "unreliable" king was still in power in Korea. Determined to dethrone the monarch or make him look like his own puppet, Yüan did everything he could "to weaken the Korean royal authority in the eyes of officials and subjects alike."[13]

Yüan refused to attend conferences of the foreign representatives in Seoul on the excuse that he was not a member of the regular diplomatic corps. He insisted on exercising his privilege of being carried through the palace gates to the audience hall and of remaining seated in the presence of the king to prove that his position was equal to or superior to that of Kojong, while other foreign representatives had to dismount at the palace gates, proceed on foot, and stand in the presence of the monarch. Naturally, King Kojong resented

Yüan's abusive behavior and gross violation of the long-established sacred customs of the Korean royal court. As resentful as he was, however, the king at first tried to be conciliatory and cordial to Yüan but eventually decided that it would be better to minimize his contacts with the overbearing Chinese. Often Yüan would demand an audience with the king and then would lecture the monarch on the "virtues" of loyalty and obedience toward China. Clearly, the 27-year-old Chinese resident was trying to dictate to the 34-year-old monarch in every way that he could. On January 23, 1886, Yüan complained to Viceroy Li that the king and his anti-Chinese advisers seemed "to follow my advice to my face, but defy it behind my back"; that the possibility of the Taewŏn'gun's emergence as a political power seemed remote; and that further Chinese interference in Korean affairs could be "extremely unwelcomed" and resented by the Korean government.[14]

The reception of the Taewŏn'gun in Korea had been rather cool, in spite of the fact that in 1882, when he had been kidnapped by the Chinese, the king and the people had resented it and petitioned Viceroy Li for his release. Now, in 1885 and 1886, out of fear of the possibility that the Taewŏn'gun might be able to incite his followers against the Min-dominated regime under Kojong, a number of those who had followed or collaborated with him in the *Imo* Revolt of 1882 and had been imprisoned for it were executed. In addition, a special decree was issued forbidding free contact between the Taewŏn'gun and any outsiders.[15] Yüan disliked all of these restrictions placed upon the Taewŏn'gun, whom he described as "the ablest man in Korea."[16] Yüan admired the Taewŏn'gun not because he felt that the ex-regent would become a far-sighted statesman capable of bestowing great benefits upon his people and country but because he believed that the old man would most likely maintain close relations with China, thus serving the interests of China in Korea as he had promised to do before his release. Yüan even scolded the king and Queen Min for their cold reception of Kojong's father.[17]

Whatever he had promised Viceroy Li before being released in China, it is doubtful that the Taewŏn'gun, once in power, would have served as nothing but a puppet of Yüan; for it was clear that the majority of high-ranking Korean government officials disliked Yüan and also that anti-Chinese feelings had been growing among the

Koreans ever since 1882. It should also be remembered that, contrary to the advice given by the Chinese emperor to the Korean government, the Taewŏn'gun had campaigned against the negotiations for a treaty with Japan in 1875 and 1876 and also against the conclusion of a treaty with the United States in 1881 and 1882; he had even instigated a riot (the *Imo* Revolt) directly against King Kojong and indirectly against the Chinese policy toward Korea in 1882. Furthermore, the old father of the young Korean king was too obstinate, too nationalistic, and too strong-willed to become and remain a willing tool of this young Chinese (young enough to be his own son) and of Yüan's policy of control and eventual annexation of Korea. Thus in the long run, the Taewŏn'gun would eventually have had a final showdown with Yüan, had he been placed in power in 1885 or thereafter, although in the end the Chinese resident would have been able to crush the Taewŏn'gun as he did Kojong in 1886.

Despite all of these possibilities, and perhaps without being aware of them, Yüan, in 1885 and 1886, definitely preferred the Taewŏn'gun to King Kojong, but he feared that the situation in Korea was not moving his way. And Yüan was able to sense that, so long as Kojong and the Min faction were in control of the government, the Taewŏn'gun would hardly be in a position to play any significant role, let alone to take over the government. Thus, he came to the conclusion that his best strategy would be to dethrone King Kojong and install one of the members of the royal family as the new monarch under the regency of the Taewŏn'gun, so that he could win firm and undisputed control over Korea with the possibility of eventual annexation into the Chinese empire.[18] All that he needed was some kind of excuse, so that he could propose such a plan to Viceroy Li.

## The Western Diplomats in Korea
### (Waeber, Denny, Baber, Merrill, and Foulk)

Unlike the aggressive and coarse Alexis de Speyer, Karl Waeber, the first Russian chargé in Korea, proved to be a cautious and prudent diplomat. King Kojong, Queen Min, and many of their advisers found Waeber a very agreeable and likable man. Ironically, even some British diplomats, for example, Chargé O'Conor, who had had contacts with Waeber in China, characterized the Russian as "mild and conciliatory."[19]

Waeber had been instructed to do his best to avoid unnecessary complications with China or Japan over Korea, but he had also been told to assure the Korean king and government leaders that Russia would support Korea in case its integrity and independence were threatened. He was to explain, however, that an international guarantee of Korean independence would be unworkable inasmuch as none of the powers far away from Korea would be in a position to compete against any Chinese pressure; and that if the Korean king should again express his desire for Russian protection of his kingdom and Russian military instructors to train his royal army, Waeber was not to discuss these issues directly with the Korean officials and should, instead, forward them to St. Petersburg.[20] It is extremely important to note that Waeber had not been instructed specifically to reject or even discourage any Korean proposal for a Russian protectorship over Korea, but merely to refer it to St. Petersburg.

Waeber's relations with the Korean government were not all rosy, as there were some controversial issues such as Korean emigration or the flight of "fugitives" into Siberia. Soon after his arrival, Waeber entered into a series of negotiations on the Korean emigration issue, trade regulations between the two countries, and the opening of Puryŏng as a treaty port.[21] Despite the involvement of Owen N. Denny, however, in the talks beginning in October of 1886, negotiations did not go well over the issue of Korean emigration. The Korean side insisted that Russia should return the Korean "fugitives," while Waeber persisted in supporting the Russian government's position that they were voluntary "immigrants" driven by starvation and tyranny and thus not to be forcefully repatriated. It was not until August 20, 1888, that the Russo-Korean Trade Agreement was amicably concluded, largely through the skillful efforts of Denny.[22] Despite the prolonged delay in the negotiation of this Trade Agreement, however, Waeber, along with Foulk and Denny, was one of those Westerners liked and trusted by the king; thus he was able to win the king's confidence in him and his country. Moreover, Waeber's personal closeness to Denny helped him to remain on good terms with the Korean officials, especially with the more independent-minded and anti-Chinese officials.

As for Denny, in recommending him as an adviser to the Korean government and king, Viceroy Li hoped to win loyal support for his policy toward Korea. Rather than striving to maintain Korea's dependency on China, however, the independent-minded Denny became an outspoken champion of the independence and progress of Korea. Thus, an inevitable friction developed between Denny and Yüan, particularly since the latter considered himself the only foreign adviser to the Korean king and his government; something he openly and flatly claimed in conversations with Foulk and others and which was in fact quite contrary to Li's original intention but was tolerated by the viceroy in view of Denny's anti-Chinese standing.[23]

Yüan sought to place Denny in a position subordinate and inferior to himself, but the strong-willed American lawyer-diplomat was vehemently opposed to Yüan's efforts and acted as a bona fide and independent adviser to the Korean king and his government, which he regarded and treated as that of a full-fledged sovereign and independent nation. In the summer of 1886, during the negotiation of a Franco-Korean treaty, Viceroy Li instructed Denny to leave the negotiations to Yüan. When the king asked Denny to assist in the negotiations as a vice plenipotentiary for the Korean government, however, Denny complied with the king's wish, ignored Li's instruction, and thus helped Plenipotentiary Kim Man-sik in negotiating and concluding the Franco-Korean Treaty of June 4, 1886.[24] As time passed, the hostility between Denny and Yüan worsened.

Unlike Foulk, an Anglophile, Denny was a Russophile and thus developed warm relations with Waeber both in Tientsin and in Seoul. Moreover, from the beginning of his service in Korea, Denny encouraged Russian interest in Korea as an aid to its independence, which Waeber appreciated and supported.[25] Unlike von Möllendorff, however, Denny neither advocated nor initiated the idea of a "protective alliance" between Russia and Korea.

It should be noted that Chargé O'Conor under instruction from London had attempted to negotiate with the Chinese government for the lease of Port Hamilton, but had been told that the Empress Dowager Tz'u-hsi had been opposed to China's interference in such Korean matters. Thereupon, O'Conor instructed Consul General Aston in Seoul to negotiate directly with Foreign Minister Kim Yun-sik, presenting the offer as coming through Viceroy Li and taking Korea's financial stress into consideration, something which the British public servants had never considered nor cared about when they had pressured the Korean government to agree to the lowest possible tariff rate in concluding the Anglo-Korean Treaty of 1883. In July 1885, when Aston made an offer to pay annual rent to the Korean government for Port Hamilton, Foreign Minister Kim refused and Aston complained that "the support we receive from China . . . is not very effective."[26] Furthermore, the Salisbury ministry soon decided not to spend the money for the port, although O'Conor and Aston felt that the prospect for a settlement seemed to have improved since von Möllendorff's removal.[27] Actually, neither the Gladstone nor the Salisbury cabinet was genuinely interested in leasing or purchasing Port Hamilton; they wanted to remain in the port as long as they felt necessary without incurring any expenses, using the idea of rent as a diplomatic trick.[28] All of these developments made the mission of Acting Consul General E. Colborne Baber, who succeeded Aston in October 1885, very difficult. He apparently felt that he should, if possible, find some excuse to justify and prolong the British occupation of Port Hamilton.

Unlike von Möllendorff, his predecessor, Henry F. Merrill, an American but a protege of Robert Hart and the new chief commissioner of the Korean Customs Service, generally supported China's policy of tight control of Korea.[29] Like Baber and W. W. Rockhill, soon-to-be American chargé, he also maintained good relations with Yüan in Korea.[30] Initially, the king and his independent-minded advisers resented the arbitrary manner that Li and Hart employed in selecting and sending Merrill to Korea.[31] Once again, however, the monarch did not register his protest with Viceroy Li, mainly because Merrill was an American and therefore might become a good friend of the Korean cause.

Hart too was concerned that Merrill might indeed become a second von Möllendorff—a champion of the progress and independence of Korea. He warned Merrill not to make the kind of "mistakes" that the German had made, advising that he "not be tempted to hook on, or drop your moorings, elsewhere" and that he try to incorporate the Korean Customs Service into the Chinese Imperial Maritime Customs in order to demonstrate that "Korea is China's tributary."[32] Hart advised Merrill that since von Möllendorff's only responsibility was to hand over to him—Merrill—everything, including archives, statistics, accounts, balance, and so on, he should "be friendly but firm" with the former adviser and "not explain any programme to him or express any instructions—keep your own counsel." Merrill was further urged to do his best at integrating the Korean customs into that of China in order to make Korea more dependent upon China and also to make Hart's position as inspector general of China's Maritime Customs Service much more powerful. Interestingly enough, Merrill was instructed to implement Hart's design without letting the Korean king and government know of it beforehand and also without giving any impression of direct intervention in Korean internal affairs.[33]

With regard to the Korean desire for independence, Hart acknowledged that Merrill might find himself sympathizing with the "Korean aspiration and angry over China's interference and system of vetoing." But he advised the young American to serve the interests of China rather than those of Korea, since China would rather fight anybody or any nation than allow independence to Korea.[34] While serving in Korea (1885–1889), Merrill faithfully carried out his mentor's instructions, although even he eventually became disgusted with Yüan's ruthless and dictatorial behavior and finally joined Denny and others in asking the Chinese government to recall Yüan from Korea.[35] As the chief commissioner of the Korean Customs Service, Merrill was especially disturbed with Yüan's involvement in ginseng smuggling into China.[36] The highly agitated Merrill sent a report of the incident to Viceroy Li. Thereupon, Li reprimanded Yüan and ordered a fair investigation and trial of those Chinese "hoodlums" and smugglers with whom Yüan had either direct or indirect ties.[37]

It should be recalled that in July 1884, the American legation in Seoul had been reduced from the grade of envoy extraordinary and minister plenipotentiary to that of minister resident and consul general, owing to the new Diplomatic and Consular Appropriation Act of Congress. After Minister Foote left Korea early in 1885, the American legation was headed by Foulk as chargé d'affaires *ad interim*. Following the failure of the *Kapsin* Coup of 1884, Viceroy Li saw that this fiasco might offer a golden opportunity to end the U.S. recognition of Korean independence by having the American government subordinate its legation in Seoul to that in Peking. Thus, through and with the full support of Charles Denby, who had succeeded John Russell Young as American minister at Peking, Li asked Secretary of State Bayard to make the American legation in Seoul an appendage of the American legation in Peking.[38] After all, that was what the British government had been doing ever since 1883. But Bayard rejected Li's request.[39] American policy toward Korea around that time was that inasmuch as the United States had concluded the Korean-American Treaty of 1882 and had been dealing with Korea on the basis of sovereign equality between two nations, it would, and indeed must, treat Korea as a full-fledged and bona fide independent country. On the other hand, the U.S. government and diplomats in Korea should not be involved in the internal affairs of the kingdom. As for Korea's repeated requests for American military advisers, Bayard informed Foulk that he could do nothing until and unless the Congress took action on it.[40]

In February 1886, after a one-and-half-year delay, William H. Parker was appointed as American minister resident and consul general in Seoul. He arrived at Seoul on June 8, 1886. In spite of his seemingly impressive past as the superintendent of the Confederate Naval Academy and the president of Maryland Agricultural College (but with no experience in diplomatic service), he turned out to be a hopeless dipsomaniac and failed to perform his duties at all.

Despite Parker's obvious misfit, King Kojong nonetheless treated him well because of his nationality and even requested that he "ask President Cleveland for permission for Mr. Foulk" to serve in the Korean government as a military adviser.[41] Parker stayed in Seoul for only about seven months, during which time the Korean officials and foreign diplomats were unable to conduct normal business with him; then he was recalled.[42] Consequently, Foulk, who had been on vacation in Japan on account of ill health, was asked to take charge again of the American legation temporarily.

With Parker gone, Foulk was again in charge of the American legation and could not be hired by the Korean government. With the support of Denny and Dr. Allen,[43] Admiral Robert W. Shufeldt, visiting Korea in October 1886, was asked by the king to become a military adviser to Korea; but the old admiral rejected the offer mainly for personal reasons.[44] The king, hoping that somehow the American government could still be persuaded to let Foulk become an adviser to his government, continuously entertained the idea of hiring Foulk, which greatly disturbed Yüan.

Then in December 1886, W. W. Rockhill was placed in charge of the American legation as chargé d'affaires.[45] Unlike Foulk, who fought Yüan for the progress and independence of Korea, Rockhill maintained good relations with the Chinese resident, for which (among other reasons) he was offered the position of adviser to Yüan in 1914, when he made himself president of the Republic of China after "betraying" Dr. Sun Yat-sen.[46]

The new American minister resident, Hugh Dinsmore, was not appointed until January 1887, after the storm over the Yüan dethronement plot (discussed below) had subsided and after the Chinese resident had become even more oppressive toward the Korean king and government. Reporting to Bayard concerning China's debilitating influence on Korea, Dinsmore stated that were it not "for China's interference, all would go smoothly and well here, and the country would advance rapidly in prosperity and enterprise."[47] Lamenting Yüan's arbitrary behavior, he informed Bayard that the Chinese resident "memorializes, provides, dictates, and directs all under a system of intimidation mixed with an affection as disinterested kindness" thus effecting the stagnation and degeneration, not the development and progress, of Korea.[48]

## Kojong's Pro-Russian Scheme and the Yüan Dethronement Plot of 1886

Observing Yüan's dictatorial and arbitrary behavior and policy, Kojong came to realize that the Chinese government was trying to tighten its control over his kingdom and that the true mission of Resident Yüan might well be to make Korea a virtual province of China. Kojong and his independent-minded advisers had no intention of allowing their country to become a *de facto* province by default. So they decided to seek Russian protection once again. It should be emphasized again that, as instructed by Foreign Minister Giers, Waeber had never completely disavowed the idea of a Russian protectorship for Korea.

Korea's independent-minded and pro-Russian officials were Cho Chon-du, Kim Ka-jin, Kim Hak-u, Kim Ryang-muk, and Ch'ae Kyŏn-sik. These men were personally close to King Kojong and Queen Min and strongly urged them to seek an alliance with the United States or with Russia as a means of making Korea truly independent of China.[49] Since the Unites States seemed indifferent to the fate of Korea, they advised the king to form an alliance with Russia even after the fiasco with von Möllendorff a year earlier. The king wholeheartedly agreed with them. As a result, there began a series of negotiations between the king's emissaries and Waeber.

In order to pave the way for a Russo-Korean alliance, Kojong dismissed his pro-Chinese and anti-Russian foreign minister Kim Yunsik on May 19, 1886, and put pro-Russian Sŏ Sang-u in charge of the Foreign Office as acting foreign minister. Yüan was furious at Kim's dismissal but thought that the incident might provide him with a new opportunity for his political plot.[50]

It is not clear exactly when King Kojong became determined to approach Waeber with a proposal for a Russian protectorship of Korea. As early as July 1886, he sent his emissary to Waeber to negotiate an alliance.[51] Yüan learned of this secret negotiation between Waeber and the Korean emissary from none other than Min Yŏng-ik—a "double dealer."[52] In 1883 and 1884, Min was on the side of the Progressives but later deserted his colleagues and joined his own, conservative Min faction against the Progressives. Now in 1886 he deserted the pro-Russian Min faction and secretly and willingly served as a spy for Yüan against the king and the Mins. At the same time, he was able to keep the king's confidence and served as a confidential messenger between the king and Waeber. Then in the midst of the Yüan dethronement plot, he turned against Yüan, who favored the establishment of a new government under the regency of the Taewŏn'gun, a mortal enemy of Min himself, and so now spied on Yüan for the king and Denny.

On July 17, 1886, Min notified Yüan of the king's readiness and preparations to approach the Russians. On August 4, he reported to Yüan that the king had asked for Russian protectorship through Waeber and that the Russian chargé had asked for and received a written document of request. Min further told Yüan that the king had asked his (Min's) opinion on the matter and that he (Min) had agreed to the king's idea in his presence but decided secretly to inform Yüan about the proposal.[53] This was the kind of opening that Yüan had been waiting for even before, and especially after, the dismissal of Foreign Minister Kim. Yüan concluded that this was an excellent chance to depose King Kojong and make Korea a province of China. Thus Yüan initiated what appeared to be "the boldest imperialistic plan" ever contemplated by the Ch'ing dynasty toward Korea in more than two hundred years of relations.[54]

On the next day, August 5, Yüan secretly proposed to Viceroy Li a plan for dethroning King Kojong and replacing him with some other member of the royal family (e.g., with Yi Chun-yong, the son of the elder brother of Kojong and one of the grandsons of the Taewŏn'gun) under the regency of the Taewŏn'gun with the idea of eventually annexing Korea. He suggested that, with thousands of Chinese reinforcement troops, the scheme could be accomplished within three or four days and thus before Russia could take any action.[55] Viceroy Li agreed with Yüan's plot in principle but feared "the likelihood of protests from foreign powers."[56] Taking advantage of British support for China's policy of control of Korea and their concern over Russian domination of the peninsula kingdom, Yüan explained to Acting Consul Baber of Kojong's pro-Russian ploy and asked Baber to request some British warships to patrol Korean waters in order to check the movement of Russian ships.[57] Baber expressed his full support for whatever plan Yüan had in mind.

At this juncture one of the most controversial documents in the annals of Korean history appeared. It is an allegedly "forged" document, dated August 9, 1886, bearing a royal seal as well as the official seal of Sim Sun-t'aek, chief minister of the Office of Internal Affairs and the first councillor of the State Council. This document shows Korea's official request for a Russian protectorship and for the dispatch of warships to Korea against China. Usually diplomatic documents or correspondence of the Korean government were issued to foreign representatives through the Office of Foreign Affairs, bearing the official seal of the minister of Foreign Affairs, not that of the Office of the State Council. Whoever it was who authored or doctored or forged the document, it is obvious that it was made under strict secrecy and by-passed the Office of Foreign Affairs.

There has been considerable debate as to who was responsible for this controversial document. According not only to Denny and Foulk, who were either directly or indirectly involved in the incident, but also to some prominent historians, it was Yüan himself who "forged" the document—an act that he often committed while serving in Korea—and sent it to Viceroy Li in order to plunge him into genuine worries about the possibility of a Russian move and thus get him to approve of his dethronement plot.[58] Other distinguished historians insist that it was Baber who "forged" the docu-

ment in order to use it to justify Britian's continuing occupation of
Port Hamilton.[59] In either case, the implication is that the document
had been sent to Tientsin but not to St. Petersburg; or if it had been
sent to the Russian Foreign Office, then it must have by-passed
Chargé Waeber, who would surely have examined the authenticity
of the document after what had happened to de Speyer in 1885.

An examination of studies based on the Russian archives, however, makes it quite clear that it was Waeber who, at the king's
request, did indeed send such a proposal to his superiors in St.
Petersburg. Apparently, the king had his proposal, dated August 9,
1886, delivered to Waeber, stating in it that he resented China's
"detrimental" influence on his kingdom; that he wished his country
"might become equal with other nations of the world"; and that he
desired that Russia would protect Korea "in a spirit of mutual cooperation" and send Russian ships if other countries should interfere
in Korea.[60] At about the same time Russian minister Popov at Peking informed Foreign Minister Giers that the Chinese government
had concentrated a large number of troops at the Sino-Korean border and that the British were spreading a rumor about the establishment of a Russian protectorship over Korea in order to win
increased Chinese support for their illegal occupation of Port
Hamilton.[61]

Upon receiving these reports from Seoul and Peking, Giers
explained to Waeber that a Russian dispatch of warships to Korea
would lead to Chinese military intervention and seizure of Korea,
which would most likely cause "disadvantageous" conditions for
Russia. Accordingly, Giers instructed Waeber to advise the Korean
king not to take any action that might provoke China. But the Russian chargé was also instructed to assure the king of "Russia's good
will and support." As instructed, Waeber notified the king through
Min Yŏng-ik of his government's negative decision on the request
and advised Min to suggest to the king that he try to improve his
relations with China.[62]

On August 9, 1886, the same day that he obtained a copy of the
now-controversial document dated August 9, 1886, supposedly
through Min Yŏng-ik, Yüan cabled Viceroy Li stating:

The king, as you may recall, caused trouble in 1884 by pursuing a
policy of befriending Japan in repudiation of China. Now he repeats

this policy by seeking Russian help against China. . . . I submit that China dispatch marines to Korea and carry out the deposition of this dim-witted monarch in favor of a more sagacious scion from the Yi royal line. . . . If Russia realizes that our troops have landed first and completed the installation of a new king, it will abandon its schemes. . . . If we delay our action until Russian troops arrive, I am afraid things will develop beyond our control.[63]

Upon receiving Yüan's cable, Li immediately instructed Liu Jui-fen, the Chinese minister in St. Petersburg, to persuade the Russian government not to accept the Korean request for a Russian protectorship and not to send Russian warships to Korea.[64]

After consulting Prince Ch'un and the Chinese emperor, Viceroy Li ordered Admiral Wu K'ang-an of the Southern Fleet to proceed to Inch'ŏn with four warships and secretly instructed Yüan to delay his dethronement plan pending further investigation and to cooperate with the Taewŏn'gun in curbing those members of the Min clan who had actively participated in the pro-Russian scheme. He also dispatched Ch'en Yün-i to Korea to investigate the whole incident independently of Yüan.[65]

Upon receiving Li's instruction, Yüan decided to forge a document in order to force the king to back down on whatever pro-Russian ploy he might have had in process. Yüan's forged document claimed that seventy-two battalions of Chinese army troops had boarded ships and were on the way to Seoul.[66] Yüan showed it to Acting Foreign Minister Sŏ and the commanding generals of the Korean royal army and demanded that the king arrest and execute all officials connected with the pro-Russian plot and officially withdraw the secret proposal from the Russian government.[67] Yüan was very successful in intimidating the king with this forged document, for the weak-willed monarch became frightened and decided to comply with Yüan's demands. Only through the intervention of Denny, Allen, Merrill, and German consul general Kempermann, were the lives of Cho Chon-du, Kim Hak-u, Kim Ka-jin, and Kim Ryang-muk saved; they were merely exiled.[68]

When the Korean government asked Waeber to return Kojong's written request, the Russian diplomat denied any knowledge of the entire episode and of the alleged document and, instead, protested that the Korean government had banished innocent officials under

pressure from the Chinese—assertions that had the effect of minimizing the embarrassment all around: that of King Kojong, the pro-
Russian Korean officials, himself, and his own government.[69] Still
unsatisfied and angry, Yüan reported to Li that "if I had 500 soldiers, I could dethrone the King and abduct all the criminals to
Tientsin for investigation."[70]

On August 20, however, Li received an important message from
Ch'en Yün-i stating that the Taewŏn'gun and his associates would
be a poor choice for taking over the monarchy. At about the same
time, he also received another important report, this time from Minister Liu Jui-fen in St. Petersburg, that the Russian government had
denied receiving the controversial document from the Korean government and promised not to accept from it any document dealing
with a Russian protectorship and dispatch of warships to Korea.
Russia's vice foreign minister, A. E. Vlangili, who had been the
Russian minister at Peking between 1864 and 1873, asked the Chinese government (through Minister Liu) to restrain Yüan from taking any action against the Korean king and government that might
entail complications in Korea.[71] Chinese minister Hsü in Tokyo also
reported to Li that the Japanese government had advised him that
any overreaction by China over the episode would be highly undesirable.[72] While the Japanese government preferred China's domination of Korea over that of Russia, it was definitely opposed to China's dethronement of King Kojong or annexation of Korea to its
empire. Consequently, Li decided not to capitalize on the king's pro-
Russian scheme, as Yüan had proposed, and advised him that, since
the Taewŏn'gun's political power was not yet strong enough for a
takeover, he (Yüan) should "quiet down and not incite things."[73] As
reluctant as he was, Yüan had no choice but to comply with his superior's instruction. During the crisis the new Russian minister to
Japan, Dmitri E. Shelvich (1886–1892), who replaced Davydov,
reported to Foreign Minister Giers that, so far as he could tell, both
Foreign Minister Inoue and Viceroy Li wished to avoid any complications over Korea, but warned that this might not necessarily be
the case in the future.[74]

Meanwhile, Min Yŏng-ik was placed in an awkward situation. He
had favored China's domination of his country over that of Russia
and therefore had at first betrayed his own king and Min clan by
informing Yüan of the king's pro-Russian plot. Learning then that

Yüan's scheme included placing the Taewŏn'gun, his and his clan's bitter enemy, into the new government he then betrayed Yüan and informed the king and Denny of Yüan's dethronement plan. Commenting on Min's role, Denny wrote that, without the "integrity of Prince Min Yong Ik [Min Yŏng-ik] one of the ablest of Korean subjects, who . . . faithfully reported its different phases [from] time to time to His Majesty as well as myself," the plot to overthrow King Kojong would have been accomplished.[75] Commenting on the same subject, Viceroy Li stated to Denny that "while Yüan was in it, yet it was all the fault of Min Yong Ik [Min Yŏng-ik] who laid the plot and induced Yüan to go into it and that for his stupidity in letting himself be drawn into such a thing, he had been severely reprimanded."[76] Denny was wrong on one important point: Min was far from being a man of "integrity," while Viceroy Li was equally wrong on another important point: Min did not lay the plot to dethrone Kojong.

While Yüan was compelled to drop his dethronement plot, he was still able to do several things to assure the supremacy of China in Korea and to discourage further efforts by the king and his anti-Chinese officials to initiate more anti-Chinese activities. First, as mentioned, he had pro-Russian officials exiled and forced the king to renounce any document he might have sent to Russia.[77] Second, he pressured the king to reappoint Kim Yun-sik to the position of foreign minister.[78] Third, he forced the Korean government to send a circula signed by Kim Yun-sik to all foreign representatives explaining that any document henceforth communicated to them would be valid only if countersigned by the minister of Foreign Affairs.[79] Fourth, he compelled the Korean government to send a special mission led by Sŏ Sang-u to China to apologize and explain the entire episode to Viceroy Li, the Board of Rites, and the Tsungli Yamen.[80] Fifth, Yüan wrote several essays of less-than-marginal value and sent them to the king as a sort of guideline for the future course of Korea. One of them was entitled *Yü-yen ssu-t'iao* (Four Points of Verbal Order). In it, Yüan stated that "Korea is like a sinking ship . . . and the King and his subjects are passengers on the ship"; and he (Yüan) is like a good captain, and so his Korean "passengers" should obey him. Also he stated that since the "Korean sickness is almost hopeless" and he is like a "good doctor," the Koreans must follow his advice.[81]

Thus, even before the Japanese used the rationalization that the

misgoverned Korea would be better off under their wise rule to justify their colonization of Korea in the 1900s, Yüan had used the similar argument that "sick" Korea would be better off under China. It
is interesting to note that the American expansionists under President William McKinley used the same assertion in annexing the
Philippines following the Spanish-American War of 1898 and 1899.
In the case of the Japanese and American claims, however, there was
at least some justification for this stance in that these two countries
were then rapidly growing industrial and political powers capable, if
they so desired, of doing a great deal of good for their colonized peoples in terms of modernization and development.[82] But the problem
with Yüan's claim was that even if China had wanted to modernize
and develop Korea, which it clearly did not wish, it was incapable of
doing so, since it was in fact unable even to modernize itself, let
alone Korea. What Yüan really wanted was the establishment and
intensification of China's new imperialism in Korea, even though
he, Viceroy Li, and other Chinese leaders slyly applied the argument of suzerain-dependency relations in order to lend an air of historical legitimacy to their new imperialistic policy toward Korea.

In another essay entitled *Shih-pi shih-k'uan* (Contemporary Evil-
Practices and Ten Suitable Treatments), Yüan advised that "these
so-called modernization programs are not urgent things for Korea"
and everything would become fine if "the king should try his utmost
to be pro-Chinese."[83] This statement shows that Yüan failed to grasp
the spirit of the age in which he was living and was essentially an
anachronistic politician, radically different from one of his most
important contemporary Chinese peers, Dr. Sun Yat-sen, whom he
later double-crossed. In still another essay entitled *Chao-hsien ta-chü-
lun* (Views on the Korean Public Interest), he stated that even
though Korea was "the world's poorest country, incapable of autonomy without the protection of a big power," it should not "depend
on a protector such as Great Britain, France, Russia, Germany, the
United States, or Japan, because they were either territorially ambitious or indifferent toward Korea." He concluded that, so long as
Korea had China's aid, no foreign power could ever encroach upon
it; and so Korea should depend upon China "absolutely."[84] As it
turned out, ironically, within fewer than ten years after Yüan had
made this statement, Japan was able not only to encroach upon
Korea, but to expel China from the peninsula. Unfortunately for the

Koreans, this was the man who in many ways was more in charge of the destiny of their country than was their own king between 1886 and 1894.

Returning to the subject of Yüan's initiation of the dethronement plot, strictly speaking, from the standpoint of modern international law, Yüan should have been charged with the crime of attempting to overthrow the head of the state to which he was accredited. To be objective about the whole incident, however, it should be admitted that, because of the peculiar relations that existed between China and Korea before and even after 1882, the case is not so clear. Those who insist that even after 1882 Korea remained a vassal to China speak with some validity in urging that modern international rules should not be applied to the relations between China and Korea nor to Yüan's behavior in Korea. On the other hand, judged even by traditional Sino-Korean rules and laws, Yüan's plot against King Kojong was out of line, because the king, like his predecessors, had been "invested" by the Chinese emperor, whom Yüan was pledged to serve. It should be recalled that after the *Imo* Revolt of 1882, the Taewŏn'gun was arrested and shipped by the Chinese generals (aided by Yüan himself) to China on the grounds that he had attempted to overthrow the king, who had been invested by the Chinese emperor.[85] Thus, for his "crime" Yüan should have been at least recalled, if not tried. Of course, the defenders of Yüan could insist that the Chinese Resident had proposed or attempted to dethrone King Kojong because of his anti-Chinese ploy—which was very true. But it was equally true that Kojong tried to rid Korea of China's influence because he believed that after 1882 his country had become independent and he wanted to develop his kingdom and deal with other treaty powers in whatever way he wished without any "retarding" interference from China. Moreover, according to traditional Sino-Korean suzerain-dependency rules, it should have been the Chinese emperor, or at least Viceroy Li himself, not Yüan, who reprimanded the king of Korea or proposed his dethronement, if there was ample justification to do so. Instead, Yüan plotted the scheme, though in vain, thereby violating not only modern international law but also traditional Chinese and Korean laws.

Legalities aside, moreover, it would have been politically and diplomatically wise if Viceroy Li had replaced Yüan with another Chinese representative more acceptable to the king and to the diplomatic corps in Korea—a move that in the long-run might have delayed the Sino-Japanese War of 1894 and 1895, or might even have made the war unnecessary. In fact, numerous requests, some through official channels and some through unofficial ones, were made for the recall of Yüan from Korea. While in China, Sŏ Sang-u complained about Yüan's dictatorial behavior, and the Tsungli Yamen instructed Li to replace Yüan with a more desirable official. But Li was able to keep Yüan in Seoul, although he found it necessary to advise him to behave better.[86] Even Merrill, one of very few Westerners in support of China's policy of domination of Korea, became disgusted with Yüan's behavior and believed that he should be recalled from Korea. Merrill reported to Hart that, if the Korean request for a Russian protectorship had indeed been made, then it would have been the result of Yüan's "ruthless and disrespectable behavior." Thus, he and Gustav Detring, Viceroy Li's personal German adviser, soon joined in with Denny's effort to persuade Li to recall Yüan from Seoul.[87] While visiting Li in Tientsin in September 1886, Denny had complained about Yüan's behavior and asked Li to recall Yüan. Li strongly defended his protege in Seoul by claiming that Yüan's dethronement scheme had actually been initiated by the British representatives in China, who had recommended that the Chinese goverment should "incorporate Korea" into the Chinese empire.[88]

On October 31, 1886, the Korean king himself sent an official memorandum to the Tsungli Yamen requesting the replacement of Yüan. Again, because of Li's strong support of Yüan, the Chinese government decided to retain him in Korea.[89] Early next year Kim Ka-jin and Min Yŏng-ik persuaded the king to make another attempt to get rid of Yüan. Accordingly, the king dispatched Kim Myŏng-gyu to Tientsin with a request to replace Yüan with someone else; but again Li refused.[90] In August 1888, the king instructed Sŏng Ki-un, the Korean commercial commissioner in Tientsin, to approach Viceroy Li for Yüan's recall. Sŏng asked Li to replace Yüan with either Ma Chien-ch'ang or Yal Wen-tsao; but again Li stuck with Yüan.[91] The result of these failures on the part of the Korean king and government to have Yüan recalled from their country meant that they had to wait until the Japanese compelled him to leave Korea on the eve of the Sino-Japanese War of 1894 and 1895.

## Yüan vs. Foulk and Minister Dinsmore, 1887

As if he had not caused enough storms by trying to dethrone King Kojong, Yüan soon precipitated another crisis, this time against Foulk. In this attempt against an American sympathizer with the Korean cause, Yüan was successful in killing two birds with one stone, or at least in killing one bird (Foulk) and severely wounding another (King Kojong).

Ever since Yüan had come to know Foulk in 1883 in Seoul, he disliked the bright American naval attaché who was three years his senior for the reasons that he was a champion of Korean independence and modernization and that he served as a sort of unofficial adviser to the king. In view of American indifference toward his repeated requests for American advisers and of his fondness for and trust of Foulk, Kojong tried to hire Foulk as his military adviser,[92] and that effort really disturbed Resident Yüan. Because of the constitutional issues involved and of his own reservations about such a position in Korea, Foulk was unable and unwilling to accept the king's offer.[93] From Yüan's standpoint, however, it was desirable to change the situation, as long as there was any possibility that Foulk might indeed become an adviser to the Korean government. For Yüan, it was bad enough to have Denny present in Korea; it would be worse if Foulk were to remain at the American legation; and it would be worst of all if the American were to be appointed as another adviser. Consequently, Yüan decided to get rid of Foulk from Korea once and for all.

Yüan apparently realized that, as powerful as he was in Korea, he was still not empowered or authorized to ask an American secretary of state to recall his representative from Korea and that only the Korean foreign minister could legally ask Secretary of State Bayard to recall Foulk by declaring him *persona non grata*. Thus, he decided to use Foreign Minister Kim Yun-sik, his own puppet, in getting rid of Foulk.

It was in November 1886, while Rockhill was still in charge of the American legation in Seoul, that Foreign Minister Kim filed his protest about the report Foulk sent to the State Department prior to the *Kapsin* Coup of 1884. In this report, Foulk candidly wrote about the Korean politicians, both the Progressives and Conservatives, and of the physical infirmities of the Crown Prince and predicted a coup d'état by the Progressives, which in fact became a reality only a few months later. Unfortunately for Foulk's career, the State Department published his report in full in 1885, thereby making it available to the public.[94] *The North China Daily News* of Shanghai thereupon printed distorted and mistranslated versions of the report.[95] Those newspaper articles became the weapons of Foreign Minister Kim and therefore, in turn, of Yüan.

Beginning in December 1886, Kim protested to Chargé Rockhill, charging that Foulk "tried to establish that the traitors to our country [the Progressives] are loyal subjects . . . maligning our high nobility."[96] Rockhill, after carefully studying Foulk's report and the newspaper articles, was able to calm Foreign Minister Kim with an explanation that the articles "are partly made up of extracts" from a report that Foulk had sent to the State Department and that he was not responsible for its publication in such a distorted manner.[97] Bayard essentially approved of Rockhill's handling of the matter,[98] and Kim dropped the charge, or so Foulk and others believed. Apparently, what happened is that Yüan, a good friend of Rockhill, decided not to go through with an anti-Foulk plot while Rockhill was in charge of the American legation in Seoul.

Then in April 1887, soon after the new American minister resident, Hugh Dinsmore, arrived and relieved Rockhill, Foreign Minister Kim renewed the old charge against Foulk, officially declaring him a *persona non grata,* and thereby making Foulk's recall legally mandatory.[99] But Dinsmore, partly because of his reliance on Foulk for his linguistic and many other talents and partly because of his awareness that this was a struggle not only between Yüan and the king over the destiny of Korea but also involved China's policy of treating Korea as its vassal and America's policy of treating it as an independent nation, strongly defended Foulk and urged Bayard to let Foulk stay in Korea. Dinsmore explained to Bayard that the king and many of his officials (but not Foreign Minister Kim) had urged him to let Foulk remain in Korea.[100] During the crisis, Russian chargé Waeber supported Dinsmore while the Japanese representative kept his neutrality and the British and German representatives took sides with Foreign Minister Kim.[101] Learning that Foulk might be in physical danger, Dinsmore asked, through American minister Hubbard at Tokyo, for an American vessel of war. Thus, the USS *Marion,* under Commander Merrill Miller, arrived at Inch'ŏn on May 16, 1887.[102]

Knowing that Yüan was behind the entire plot, Dinsmore confronted the resident directly asking for a good explanation of his anti-Foulk campaign. But the cunning warlord told Dinsmore that he personally had no grievance or charge against Foulk and that the whole issue was between the Korean Foreign Office and Foulk.[103] Despite this statement, however, Yüan asked Viceroy Li to instruct the Chinese minister in Washington to put pressure on the secretary of state to have Foulk recalled from Korea.[104] The minister then told Bayard that "the continuous residence of Mr. Foulk in Korea is a source of peril to relations between Korea and China," because he, "in concert with some evil disposed person of Korea, is planning a rebellion against China."[105]

Although Bayard did not believe the charge against Foulk and sympathized with Foulk and Dinsmore's efforts to save him, he felt that he was bound by international law to recall Foulk from the American legation in Seoul, because the diplomat had been officially declared *persona non grata* by the Korean foreign minister. Thus, he relieved Foulk as naval attaché and ordered him to report on board the USS *Marion*.[106] On June 21, 1887, Foulk left Korea for Japan, where he died in 1893 at the age of thirty-seven while teaching at Doshisha College, a missionary-connected institution in Kyoto.

It should be noted that, unlike Foulk, whose career ended tragically and who died at so young an age, Yüan became the most successful and important foreigner in Korea between 1887 and 1894. He emerged as a strong foe of all who advocated the modernization and independence of Korea, making himself a curse to the interests of Korea and its people. In trying to keep Korea under Chinese control, he often overstepped the instructions of Viceroy Li and the Ch'ing court.[107] As noted earlier, Denny went so far as to characterize Yüan as a "smuggler, conspirator, and diplomatic outlaw." Though it is usually advisable for a diplomat or a historian not to use excessive language, in the case of Yüan, Denny might just as well have added some other descriptive words, such as "double-crosser," or "traitor," because of what he did against Sun Yat-sen and his own country.[108] After reaching an agreement with Dr. Sun in 1911 whereby Dr. Sun was to step down in favor of Yüan, who then became the provisional president of the Republic of China with an understanding that he would make China a republic, Yüan, "The Father of Warlords," treacherously double-crossed Dr. Sun, "The Father of the Chinese Revolution," by proclaiming himself emperor of China in 1915, thereby plunging China into a disastrous and tragic period of warlordism (*Tuchunism*, 1916–1927).[109] The important point is that Yüan proved to be as much of a "curse" to the salvation of his own country in the 1910s as he was to Korea in the 1880s and early 1890s, in view of his major contribution to the outbreak of the Sino-Japanese War of 1894 and 1895.

In light of the fact that in and after 1885 Viceroy Li's policy toward Korea was tighter control than before 1885 and in view of the fact that even after 1885 King Kojong's ultimate desire and intention was to make his kingdom independent of Chinese domination, a sort of showdown between Kojong and Yüan was inevitable. Nonetheless, the showdown would not have had to come in the way that it did nor so soon after the von Möllendorff–de Speyer intrigue if Yüan had been far-sighted enough to be able to perceive Sino-Korean relations in a long-term perspective as well as on a short-term basis; to grasp the spirit of the age in which he was living; and to deal with King Kojong and his independent-minded officials on the basis of mutual respect and with due respect to the long-established traditions and customs of Sino-Korean relationships.

To begin with, Yüan's mission in Korea was to exploit the country for the interests of China and to place and keep the country under the close surveillance of China, but not just for a few years and not necessarily at the risk of war with Japan or any other power for that matter. Moreover, despite some specific instructions given to Yüan before his departure for Korea in 1885, Yüan's function in Korea was flexible and broad enough for him to develop and pursue a policy that would have served the interests of both China and Korea and that also would not have antagonized King Kojong and his advisers as much nor so quickly. The fact that it was Yüan himself, not Viceroy Li nor the Ch'ing court, who initiated such drastic actions as Foulk's ouster from Korea, the dethronement plot, and many other schemes strongly indicates the scope of his power and authority in Korea. Consequently, Yüan could have become an instrument for initiating a policy positive, constructive, and beneficial to both China and Korea, thereby creating reasonable, amicable, and cordial relations between himself and King Kojong.

Furthermore, since originally it was King Kojong himself who had suggested that Viceroy Li send Yüan to Korea, though admittedly not as the resident, he most likely would have tried to remain on good terms with Yüan if the resident had behaved reasonably and had worked to promote the interests of China in Korea with due respect also to the welfare of Korea itself. But Yüan did quite the opposite, treating King Kojong as if he were his subordinate and trying to expand the interests of China in complete disregard to the feelings and interests of the Korean government and leaders.

Because Yüan had been so abusive and oppressive of King Kojong and his government and had violated traditional Korean and Chinese laws as well as modern international law by trying to overthrow him, many attempts were made to have Viceroy Li recall Yüan from Korea. But largely because of Li's faith in and support of him, Yüan stayed in Korea until he was practically driven out of the country by the Japanese in 1894 on the very eve of the Sino-Japanese War.

As tricky as von Möllendorff's pro-Russian ploy might have been, it was not as bizarre or grotesque as Yüan Shih-k'ai's plot to dethrone King Kojong in order to install a pro-Chinese ruler in Korea, whom he could easily manipulate. Technically speaking, von Möllendorff had never violated any point of international or Korean law in negotiating his secret treaty with the Russian diplomats, inasmuch as whatever he did with the Russians bore the full though tacit authorization of King Kojong. In the case of Yüan's anti-Kojong plot, on the other hand, he violated both international law and certain Sino-Korean rules by trying to overthrow the king in favor of his own hand-picked ruler.

World history is replete with secret negotiations and agreements among the sovereign nations. And, of course, the same world history records many incidents in which a foreign agent has tried to overthrow the head of a government to which he is accredited. Yet there is a fundamental difference between the two: for a sovereign nation to try to conclude a secret agreement with another independent nation is in no sense a crime, while it is certainly a crime for a foreign agent to plot the overthrow of a legitimate government to which he is accredited. Admittedly, in the case of Yüan's plot in Korea, the problem was somewhat complicated because, as perceived by the Chinese, neither was Korea a fully sovereign and independent nation nor Yüan, strictly speaking, an accredited diplomatic agent in Korea. Even so, he violated traditional Chinese and Korean laws by trying to dethrone King Kojong, who had been "invested" by his own emperor, for whom he had been sworn to serve. The only crime worse than what Yüan had tried to commit would have been an effort to assassinate King Kojong, which apparently he did not attempt.

To be sure, from the vantage point of the short-term interests of China in the Korean peninsula, Yüan's accomplishments between 1885 and 1894 were indeed outstanding. Jerome Ch'en insists that "as a struggling young man in Korea, Yüan had served the throne well."[110] One of Yüan's impressive accomplishments in Korea was China's monopoly of loans to Korea. He insisted that loans "would be very practical instruments to control the Korean government and strengthen China's suzerain rights over Korea."[111] Whenever the Korean government and king sought loans from other countries than from China, Yüan successfully blocked the effort, which eventually irritated not only the king but also the Japanese government.[112] Another of Yüan's accomplishments in Korea was China's control of the telegraph service, which also eventually made the Japanese government angry.[113] Yüan also successfully increased China's trade with Korea. During his tenure in Korea, he was able to increase China's trade in Korea sixfold. As for control of Korean Customs Service, he did not have to worry about it, because Merrill, under the instruction of Hart, did such "a good job."

Above all, he had been so successful in having the independent-minded pro-Russian officials exiled or checked in and after 1886, that the king would not resort to another pro-Russian scheme until 1896, this time because of the Japanese threat. It should be added, however, that Yüan was not successful in destroying Kojong's independent-minded spirit. Angered by Yüan's success in ousting Foulk from Korea, the king, supported by Denny and Dr. Allen, and after plenty of troubles with Yüan, was able to establish the permanent legation in the United States in 1887, thereby proving that after all his kingdom was indeed sovereign and independent.

From the long-term standpoint, however, and with respect to the long-range interests of China itself, Yüan's accomplishments, inciting as they did the irritation of the Koreans and the anger of the Japanese, do not look that great. Under the illusion that what would be good for Korea would be bad for China and what would be bad for Korea would be good for China, Yüan hampered and even thwarted most of Korea's modernization efforts in diplomatic, economic, and military spheres, and "broke the backbone of the reform-minded

Korean leadership, replacing it with a corrupt and incompetent one,"[114] thereby eventually providing with the Japanese an excellent justification for their intervention in Korea. The Japanese intervention led to the Sino-Japanese War of 1894 and 1895, after which the defeated China, among other things, was forced to relinquish its claim to suzerainty over Korea, to pay an indemnity of 200 million taels, to cede Taiwan, and to grant most-favored-nation treatment to Japan. It should also be stressed that, if it had not been for a certain "blessing in disguise"—the shooting and wounding of Chinese plenipotentiary Li by a Japanese fanatic—the Japanese terms would have been much harsher, and that China's defeat in the war soon led to the "battle of concessions" among the treaty powers in China—"the cutting up of the Chinese melon." For all of these tragic consequences, direct or indirect, of their policy in Korea, both Li and Yüan should have shared between them a large amount of the responsibility. In fact, because Viceroy Li was held responsible for China's defeat in the war and for the disastrous policy toward Korea, he was not permitted to play any significant role in Chinese politics and diplomacy after the war, although Yüan was able to escape severe criticism and would eventually play a role even more destructive and tragic between 1911 and 1916.

In retrospect, therefore, one may argue that Viceroy Li's decision to retain Yüan in Korea, despite the Tsungli Yamen's recommendation for his recall and despite King Kojong's repeated request for his replacement, was not a good one for China's future. The main problem with Yüan was that, unlike many contemporary Japanese leaders, he was ignorant of contemporary world affairs and was unable to perceive the spirit and trend of his time in universal terms. Moreover, even in the context of China's traditional standards, Yüan was not a brilliant scholar-militarist nor scholar-politican. He had failed the provincial civil service examination twice before turning to a military career, without any formal or professional military training.[115] He was made the resident largely because of the dominant role that he played in Korea before and during the *Kapsin* Coup of 1884 and partly because Viceroy Li regarded him as a sort of "expert" on Korean affairs.

It might have been much better for Yüan, for Li himself, and above all for China, if Li had recalled Yüan from Korea in 1866 and had sent him to the Chinese legation in the United States or in some

European country. Who knows but what, in Western countries, Yüan might have been able to open his eyes and become a far-sighted and visionary statesman capable of seeing China's interests and security issues in a context of both short-term and long-term goals? With that kind of cosmopolitan and worldly diplomatic experience, Yüan, given the same opportunity at the time of the Republican Revolution of 1911 and 1912, might have accepted and promoted the idea of republicanism in China rather than betraying and double-crossing Sun Yat-sen's republicanism and might thereby have avoided the evils of civil war and warlordism in the 1910s and 1920s.

It should be emphasized that in the case of Japan, before many of its leaders had become foreign ministers or prime ministers, they had typically served abroad—not only in Korea and China but also in Russia, the United States, and European countries, or traveled a great deal (as had Itō, Komura, and others). Consequently, as a whole their outlook toward the world and for the future of Japan became much more enlightened, broad, and far-sighted than that of Yüan who, partly because of ignorance of the rapidly changing world and of his parochialism, precipitated for Korea the tragedies of the late 1880s and early 1890s, and ultimately for China itself those of the early 1900s.

CHAPTER 8

# The Convenient Settlement

## The Anglo–Chinese–Russian Agreements of 1886 and 1887

In the end, ironically, it was not only the Korean government but both the British and Viceroy Li who pushed for a final settlement. Seeing that the possibility of an Anglo-Russian war had evaporated and that Russia was not about to occupy Port Lazareff, Li repeatedly and strongly urged Chargé O'Conor to persuade the British government to make some arrangement with the Korean government. The Korean government, however, insisted on outright and immediate withdrawal. O'Conor told Li that the time was not opportune for a decision on evacuation, due to impending elections in England; but he still urged his government to approve Li's proposal. The negotiations dragged on into January 1886, involving many proposals and counter proposals. The main ideas of Li's proposals were that the British should (1) guarantee Korea's integrity in case of China's recognition of the British occupation of Port Hamilton; or (2) withdraw from Port Hamilton, maintaining a warship at Inch'ŏn ready to reoccupy the port in case of need; or (3) lend money to Korea as a mortgage, taking the port as security, with the provision that Korea was to return the money whenever the British should withdraw from the port.[1] The British government rejected any idea of payment in cash or a loan. Instead, it again asked the Chinese government either to occupy the port itself or to extend a guarantee that no other European power would seize it when the British withdrew. China replied that it could neither occupy it nor give such a guarantee, since the port belonged to Korea.[2]

In the meantime, several British naval experts reported that Port Hamilton, once thought to be the Gibraltar of the Orient, was actually a poor location and could not be maintained except at large expense. Admiral George Willes, Vice-Admiral Dowell, and Sir George Bowen, the governor of Hong Kong, all agreed with that view. When the Gladstone government ordered Vice-Admiral Dowell to occupy the port, it did so without studying all of the pertinent factors concerning the island. In September 1885, when Vice-Admiral Richard Hamilton succeeded Dowell, the Admiralty ordered him to study the matter and report fully upon it. Hamilton's report was in agreement with his predecessor's evaluation of the port: in time of peace, it would be useless or unnecessary; in time of war, it might be a source of weakness to the British navy. At best, the port might be useful for offensive operations, but not good enough for defensive purposes. Endorsing Hamilton's report, the Admiralty urged the government to take steps to evacuate the port.[3]

Before the Conservative government took over the cabinet as the result of the elections, Prime Minister William Gladstone, during the interlude, employed Archibald P. Rosebery, a Liberal, as Foreign Secretary (between February and July 1886). The Admiralty turned over the same report to Rosebery that it had given to the Salisbury ministry earlier. As for a final solution, the government of Korea persistently pressed for an immediate British action. Gladstone and Rosebery had no objection to withdrawal; the question was how to obtain Russian assurance not to seize either Port Hamilton or Port Lazareff after the British evacuation from the former. They devised a ploy to have the Chinese government prevent Russia from occupying Port Hamilton. In April 1886, Rosebery drew up a memorandum proposing that China either must assume responsibility for the security of Port Hamilton or must persuade the Russians and other powers to conclude an international agreement for the integrity of Korea, to which Great Britain too would be a party.[4] China refused to give such a guarantee alone, or to enter into an international agreement, for obvious reasons: Li thought that China was simply not strong enough to back up such a guarantee. As for the idea of an international guarantee of the integrity of Korea, Li again rejected it out of hand, before studying the feasibility and wisdom of the suggestion, because China's policy toward Korea during the 1880s called for Chinese domination or preponderant control, despite the Tientsin Convention of 1885.

Thereupon, the British made another proposal. British minister John Walsham, newly appointed to serve concurrently in China and Korea, received several notes of Korean protest concerning the continued British occupation of Port Hamilton. He proposed to the Korean government that he would do his best to improve relations between his country and Korea and that he would visit the king of Korea to present his credentials in person.[5] Then he recommended that both Port Hamilton and Port Lazareff be constituted treaty ports open to all treaty powers, so that no one hostile power could seize them. In London, the new prime minister, Robert A. Salisbury and the new foreign secretary, Lord Iddesleigh, approved of Walsham's idea.[6] However, the Korean government and Viceroy Li rejected it on the grounds that Port Lazareff was too close to Wŏnsan, already a treaty port, and that Port Hamilton was a desolate island unsuited to be a treaty port. Owen N. Denny, the new American adviser to the Korean government, was also opposed to Walsham's proposal. He strongly argued that the best solution to the problem was a British withdrawal. While serving in China, Denny had become a close friend of Karl Waeber, the first Russian chargé d'affaires in Seoul. After communicating and negotiating with Waeber, Denny, on June 13, 1886, sent Li a so-called "private and confidential" letter that he had received from a Russian official (Waeber). In the letter the Russian official stated that "if England continues much longer to hold temporary occupation of Port Hamilton, in my opinion the Russian Government in self-defense will be compelled to follow her example and take 'temporary possession' of Port Lazareff."[7] After further meetings with Waeber on June 29, Denny sent Li another letter, in which he stated that "there is no danger at all of any other nation [Russia] occupying Port Hamilton in the event of the withdrawal of the English. Such an idea is advanced only as a pretext to continue in possession. Russia does not want Port Hamilton, but does want Lazareff, and if the British continue to hold the former, Russia will make the precedent as an excuse for taking similar possession of the latter."[8] No doubt Denny's message, coming initially from Waeber, had some positive influence on Li. But Li's problem was the British demand that the Russian government must certify its intention of refraining from occupying Port Lazareff.

Meanwhile, in August of 1886, Viceroy Li received through

N. F. Ladyzhensky, the Russian chargé d'affaires at Peking, the Russian government's assurance that it would not occupy Port Hamilton after the evacuation of the British fleet from the island.[9] Deciding to take advantage of this timely message from St. Petersburg, Viceroy Li invited Ladyzhensky to Tientsin. In several conferences, Ladyzhensky told Li that he had been instructed by his government to inform the Chinese government that Russia had no intention of seizing Port Hamilton or any other port of Korea. Li, in turn, explained to Ladyzhensky that the British demanded a Chinese guarantee that no third nation would seize the port and that he would therefore appreciate a Russian pledge of nonoccupation. Ladyzhensky replied that his government might be ready to extend such a guarantee to the Chinese government, but not to the British government. Li insisted that Ladyzhensky write down a Russian pledge of nonoccupation of Port Hamilton following the British evacuation of it. But Ladyzhensky refused, asserting that doing so would imply that Russia had such an intention from the beginning.[10] Thus, Li had to be satisfied with Ladyzhensky's verbal pledge. In some ways, the verbal pledge of nonaggression pleased Li, because it would enable China, jointly with Russia, to keep Japan in check. Also, Li reasoned that an agreement in written form might restrain China's future actions in Korea.[11]

During the Li-Ladyzhensky negotiations, Minister Walsham wanted to visit Korea to negotiate directly with the government about Port Hamilton, but Li objected to it, as he considered himself the de facto foreign minister of Korea in charge of the whole matter. Here again is a case where "the elder brother," who is utterly incapable of coping with the various challenges presented by the Western treaty powers, not only puts all kinds of pressures on his "younger brother" that prevent the latter from learning how to be self-reliant and independent but also tells the other treaty powers not to treat the younger as an independent and sovereign entity. This is what the Chinese called the "elder brother" caring for or loving the "younger brother."

In November 1886, Viceroy Li notified Minister Walsham of the verbal pledge he had received from Ladyzhensky. As a precaution, Foreign Secretary Iddesleigh instructed Walsham to obtain a written note from the Tsungli Yamen, guaranteeing that no power would occupy Korean territory. After receiving such a written note from the Chinese government, Walsham notified the Korean government that, despite his wishes, circumstances had prevented him from visiting Korea and that, therefore, he was sending a letter through a British agent in Seoul.[12] On January 21, 1887, the British acting consul in Seoul, T. Watters, handed Walsham's dispatch to Foreign Minister Kim. Then, after more than another month of delay, the British finally withdrew their fleet from Port Hamilton on February 27, 1887. After all of this mistreatment, deceit, procrastination, and duplicity on the part of the British, the Korean government, in recognition of Britain's "good faith," expressed its desire for friendly relations between the two countries.[13] The Seoul government felt that it had no choice but try to get along with the British government and its diplomats, despite the "wrongs" they committed.

Consequently, the Li-Ladyzhensky Agreement of 1886 produced an amicable resolution of Anglo-Russian tension over Port Hamilton. It also provided a degree of satisfaction to the governments of China, Japan, Russia, Great Britain, and Korea. Moreover, on December 12, 1886, after the conclusion of Li-Ladyzhensky agreement and before the British evacuation of its fleet from Port Hamilton, the Russian government officially rejected the necessity of acquiring Port Lazareff or any other ports outside its own territory on the grounds that Vladivostok was already the most favorable naval base in Russia's Far Eastern waters.[14]

As for von Möllendorff, who had worked so hard for the British evacuation of Port Hamilton, he was indeed pleased with the news. After returning to China, where he became known as the "ex-king of Korea"[15]—a romantic title that von Möllendorff never took up but which the British officials used sarcastically—he was not offered any distinguished public or academic positions. Although he worked as personal secretary and translator for Viceroy Li from early 1886 and on, what he wanted more than anything else was to be invited and reappointed as an adviser to the Korean king and government.

## Von Möllendorff's Brief Return to Korea, 1888

In May 1888 Viceroy Li sent von Möllendorff back to Korea in order to see if the supposedly "reformed" German could replace Judge Owen N. Denny, who had succeeded him in 1886 as an adviser to the Korean government. During his two years of tenure in Korea, Denny had vigorously campaigned for the cause of Korean independence and progress vis-à-vis both the Chinese interventionistic policy in general and Yüan's arbitrary and even illegal activities in Korea—thereby annoying Li, Yüan's superior. In early 1888, because of his bitter feud with Yüan and his own ill health, Denny thought about not renewing his contract with the Korean government, provided that the American minister resident in Seoul, Hugh A. Dinsmore, be permitted to resign from the American diplomatic service and accept Kojong's offer to be his adviser as Denny's successor. According to Denny's own account, his poor health was partly due to "the excitement and worry" he had been experiencing in his struggle against "China's unjust and high-handed treatment" of Korea. Corresponding with his friend, Senator John Mitchell of Oregon, Denny bitterly complained that China's "apparent determination . . . to furnish another example of the 'lion and lamb lying down together' with the lamb inside, has been too much for me and I find my health giving way in consequence." He further stated that he was so aggravated with Viceroy Li and Yüan that he might not return to Korea even if his health were to improve.[16]

Kojong was perfectly willing to renew the contract with Denny, or to appoint Dinsmore in place of Denny if the latter were to leave Korea. Dinsmore himself was interested in this new and challenging position, and Chargé Waeber gave strong support to the plan as conceived by Denny, Kojong, and Dinsmore. However, Secretary of State Bayard disapproved of Dinsmore's request to serve as adviser to the Korean government on the grounds that his new position "might make it exceedingly difficult for your [Dinsmore's] successor to conduct the business of the [American] legation," and also might complicate American relations with China. Fully aware of Dinsmore's intention to fight the Chinese claim to suzerainty over Korea if he were to succeed as adviser, Bayard further reminded him that "it certainly would be considered a disregard by the United States of the Chinese claim, if we consented to our representative leaving our service in order to assume the position of adviser to the Corean Government."[17] Consequently, Minister Resident Dinsmore could not and did not become an adviser to the Korean government.

Since Dinsmore was thus unable to succeed him, Denny decided to renew his contract with the Korean government for another two-year term, and on May 14, 1888, he did in fact sign the new contract. By this time Denny felt better, as his health had apparently improved.[18] Another important factor influencing Denny's decision to stay in Korea might have had something to do with Korea's obligation to pay the remainder of his salary. Resident Yüan, Denny's avowed enemy, and Cho Pyŏng-sik, the pro-Chinese Korean foreign minister, tried to do financial harm to the American adviser by preventing a final settlement of the wages that were still outstanding to Denny from his original contract. King Kojong, who assertively desired the continuous services of the American judge, used this situation to his advantage by informing Denny that he would pay the back wages if the American adviser were to renew the contract. Thereupon, Denny readily accepted the monarch's offer. It should be noted that Denny (whose monthly salary, according to his original contract, was 1,000 taels or about $1,200) was willing to accept a somewhat reduced monthly payment of $1,000, which still was much more than von Möllendorff's wage of 300 taels per month during his tenure in Korea between 1882 and 1885.[19]

It was during this transitory period before Denny renewed his contract that Viceroy Li sent von Möllendorff back to Korea with the hope he would succeed the "undesirable" American, Denny. To be sure, when Denny, who as early as October 1887 had thought he would not renew his contract (which was to expire in April 1888), consulted King Kojong in February 1888 and decided to renew it later that spring (early April),[20] he did so without knowing that von Möllendorff was about to be sent to Seoul to succeed him. Immediately after his arrival at Inch'ŏn on May 14, 1888, von Möllendorff reported the news of his arrival to the Seoul authority and learned to his discomfiture that Denny, who had been promised the remainder of his salary from the first contract, had decided to remain in Korea and had begun the process of negotiating his second contract with the Korean government. When von Möllendorff actually reached Seoul the next day, Denny and the Korean government had concluded their negotiations and settled the contract. No doubt, Denny and the Seoul authority did make haste, since they learned on May 14 that von Möllendorff had arrived at Inch'ŏn on that day and anticipated his arrival in Seoul forthwith.

The exact timing of Denny's signature on the new contract is not only interesting but also controversial. According to Minister Dinsmore, who was deeply involved in the whole matter, it was on May 14 that Denny officially signed the new contract.[21] However, according to von Möllendorff, it was between 5:00 P.M. and 6:00 P.M. on May 15, when he was already in Seoul but before he was able to make contact with the proper Korean authority, that Denny in fact renewed his contract with the king.[22] Because von Möllendorff's account of these proceedings was based mainly on hearsay and that of Minister Dinsmore on his official relations with the Korean government and with Denny himself, the American minister's version should be considered more accurate. Besides, from the time von Möllendorff arrived in Inch'ŏn, the Korean authority tried to avoid any official contact with the German owing to the reason for his return to Korea: he was in the country at the command of Viceroy Li and not necessarily in compliance with the king's repeated invitations. In any case, however, what was more important than the timing of the contract renewal was the fact that Denny had more or less decided to sign a new contract for another two more years even before von Möllendorff had left Chefoo, China, on May 12, 1888. Apparently, neither Viceroy Li nor von Möllendorff was aware of this fast-changing circumstance in Seoul.

There were important reasons why Li decided to send von Möllendorff back to Korea in May 1888. Li believed that Denny would soon definitely leave Korea, since his two-year contract with the government was to expire in 1888, and that the Korean king and authority would surely require the services of another Western adviser like von Möllendorff. By the spring of 1888 Li believed that he had ample evidence that von Möllendorff had been reformed and reconstructed so as to be trusted again and that therefore he would be an ideal successor to Denny. Moreover, Li was well aware of the fact that the Korean king had repeatedly urged von Möllendorff to come back to Korea as his adviser and was therefore reasonably sure that the Korean government would rehire the German diplomat.

As for von Möllendorff himself, he too was quite certain that he would be rehired. After all, von Möllendorff knew that, even after the exposure of the von Möllendorff–de Speyer intrigue in the summer of 1885, Kojong would have retained him had it not been for the pressure placed upon the Chinese government by the Japanese and British governments. He was further aware that when Viceroy

Li recommended Denny and sent him to Korea as his successor, Kojong and his more independent-minded Korean advisers had strong reservations about Denny, because of Li's arbitrary manner of selecting and dispatching the American diplomat to Korea— although the king soon developed a firm faith in the American owing to his nationality and his unquestionable devotion to the cause of Korean independence and progress.[23] Furthermore, even after von Möllendorff's return to China in December 1885 he had been repeatedly asked by the king and his messengers to come back to Korea, presumably to resume his old position. In fact, von Möllendorff was so sure of his reappointment that he even took his wife and three children with him on his return to the country for which he held a feeling of "sorrowful affection."[24]

In an interesting way Viceroy Li believed that he was playing a shrewd game: using a "reformed barbarian" (von Möllendorff) against an "undesirable barbarian" (Denny) in Korea. There were many reasons why Li believed that he could have von Möllendorff "checkmate" or "replace" Denny by exploiting the hostilities existing between these two barbarians. One of the main reasons for the ill-feeling between these two was von Möllendorff's jealousy of Denny. Von Möllendorff resented Denny's takeover of his position, a post he felt he should resume after the storm that he had helped to cause subsided.[25] For his part, Denny believed that von Möllendorff's secretive approach in trying to induce Russia to become Korea's protector through the back door was not only wrong but also unworkable, and he referred to the whole scheme as "Möllendorff's blunders."[26] Another reason was Denny's American nationality. Von Möllendorff, having experienced hostile relations with American diplomats in Korea, such as Minister Foote and Chargé Foulk, and strongly believing that the U.S. government was in no position to do much good for Korea, could not see how Denny's appointment would be beneficial to the Koreans.

But there was still another much more tangible reason for the bad relationship between these two diplomats. Denny, frustrated by China's unprecedented interference in Korea in general and angered by Resident Yüan Shih-k'ai's bullying mistreatment of the Korean king and officials, wrote and published in the summer of 1888 a pamphlet entitled *China and Korea*.[27] In it he categorically condemned every phase of China's new imperialism in Korea, mainly on the basis of the modern Western concept of international law and relations. Denny argued that not only had Korea become more sovereign and independent through its treaties with Japan in 1876 and with the United States in 1882, but it had been independent even *before* the conclusion of the treaties. Denny admitted that Korea had been historically a tributary to China, but not a vassal. He contended that a tributary could be a sovereign and independent nation, as Korea had been. Borrowing the theories of such distinguished Western jurists as Henry Wheaton, Emeric de Vattel, Hugo Grotius, and John Austin, Denny based the independent status of Korea on both historical and newly created factors (the conclusion and implementation of the treaties between Korea and treaty powers). Korea had the right to diplomatic negotiation, the right to appoint and dispatch ministers to the treaty powers, the right to declare war or peace; it did not sign an international agreement with China recognizing its vassalage to the latter; and it concluded the Trade Regulations of 1882, providing extraterritorial rights to the Chinese in Korea. Discussing Yüan's plots of July–August 1886 to overthrow King Kojong and replace him with a pro-China ruler and his involvement in smuggling and other illegal activities in Korea, Denny condemned him as a "smuggler, conspirator, and diplomatic outlaw."[28]

Moreover, in 1887, a year before publishing the controversial *China and Korea,* Denny, together with Dr. Horace Allen and Min Yŏng-ik (former vice minister of the Korean Foreign Office and a new enemy of Resident Yüan), had persuaded King Kojong to establish permanent legations in the United States and Europe in order to show the world that Korea was, after all a sovereign and independent kingdom.[29] As if he were a full-fledged and absolute monarch, King Kojong attempted to dispatch his ministers without prior permission from the Chinese emperor.[30] Although threatened by Yüan and intimidated by the Chinese government,[31] Kojong was eventually able to send his missions after petitioning for and obtaining permission from the emperor—thereby proving that though he might be only "half-sovereign," his kingdom had become independent and sovereign according to modern diplomatic and international rules.[32]

In an essay entitled "A Reply to Mr. O. N. Denny's Pamphlet Entitled: 'China and Korea,' "[33] von Möllendorff repudiated Denny's contention that Korea had always been a sovereign and independent nation. Utilizing studies by John Ross, E. H. Parker, and others, he insisted that Korea had been historically a dependency of, or subordinate to, China. Quoting the theories advocated by such legal scholars as Calvo, Hallek, and Heffter, von Möllendorff rejected the validity of every point Denny had tried to prove. He further disagreed with Denny's view that China was guilty of "oppression and unjust treatment" of Korea.[34] He even rejected the thesis that Korea had become independent and sovereign in and after 1882. As if he had forgotten that in 1884 and 1885 he himself asserted that China was no longer in a position to remain the "protector" or "elder brother" of Korea and so had attempted to replace "China's protection" with that of Russia, now, in 1888 von Möllendorff flatly stated that "Korea is rather in want of China's protection, as she cannot alone resist 'those powers' whose assistance Mr. D. [Denny] implores."[35] In view of the fact that von Möllendorff had never felt that Korea was strong enough to become genuinely independent and sovereign on its own, his argument that Korea needed a "protector" is nothing new. What is new and surprising is his assertion that Korea now needed "China's protection."

Defending Yüan's activities in Korea, von Möllendorff described him as "a pure handed official and quite above suspicion."[36] With regard to Yüan's plots to overthrow King Kojong, von Möllendorff charged that "the whole story seems to rest on Mr. D.'s too vivid imagination and his too great animosity towards Yuen [Yüan]."[37] Since both Korean and Chinese sources confirm Yüan's initiation of and involvement in anti-Kojong plots in 1886 (and on another occasion),[38] we have to surmise that von Möllendorff tried to discredit Denny by praising Yüan, without investigating or knowing all the facts.

With regard to Denny's involvement in Kojong's decision to establish permanent legations in the United States and elsewhere, von Möllendorff charged: "By sending off missions to Europe and the U.S. he [Denny] thought to steal a march on China. Denny's advice was hardly as well considered as he calls it on p. 15 [of *China and Korea*]. The King has obeyed the orders from China in this question, because they are in conformity with his vassal relations; Denny, however, without sufficient knowledge of the true relationship gives advice to the contrary."[39]

He concluded his essay in a bitter and most undiplomatic manner, with the accusation that "this is the perspective of the kind of service which Mr. D. in his ignorance of all circumstances wants to render to Korea."[40] Thus, more than anything else, von Möllendorff strongly questioned Denny's qualifications in serving the Korean government. In other words, he himself, not Denny, was best qualified to serve the interests of the Korean government.

The most striking thing about von Möllendorff's essay is that it is not a well-researched scholarly paper; rather it was poorly documented and hastily written. It is full of subjective criticism and personal vindictiveness against Denny and his activities in Korea. Compared with the fine quality of his many scholarly works, this article is cheap political propaganda. In fact, during his tenure in Korea, von Möllendorff had not believed in, and therefore rejected, much of what he professed in the essay to be factually and historically accurate.

Two inevitable questions therefore arise: Whose contentions were accurate vis-à-vis the international status of Korea? Why did von Möllendorff change his mildly anti-Chinese animus (with regard to Korea) to a strongly pro-Chinese position? It must be admitted that Korea had been historically a subordinate or dependency to China and the sovereignty of the king of Korea had been limited, at least in theory, and even in practice occasionally. Although von Möllendorff had utilized sources of marginal value to support his argument, he was accurate on the status of Korea before 1876. In an effort to prove that Korea, in the 1880s and thereafter, should be treated as a full-fledged sovereign and independent nation, Denny appeared to have oversimplified the complex Confucian suzerain-dependency relations between China and Korea in terms of contemporary Western international law and rules.[41]

Concerning the new international status created by the modern treaties Korea had concluded with Japan and Western powers, there are still debates between traditional-minded historians, who insist that Korea remained a dependency to China even after it had entered into modern treaty relations with other nations, and revisionists, who proclaim that the peninsula kingdom became at least partly independent and sovereign following the conclusion of the treaties.[42] This study advocates the new and revisionist thesis that Korea, which had become partly independent in 1876, became even more sovereign and independent in and after 1882. Thus, on the issue of whether after 1882 China should have left Korea alone, treating it as a fully sovereign nation, it must be contended that Denny's argument had much more validity and credibility than von Möllendorff's. It should be emphasized that even von Möllendorff, during his tenure in Korea, had taken and maintained a position similar to Denny's: China should leave Korea alone, regardless of their historical ties.

All of this leads to the next, extremely interesting, question: Why did von Möllendorff reverse his earlier convictions and take an unduly and overly sinophile posture by vigorously and unfairly attacking Denny's position?[43] The main reason von Möllendorff adopted this pro-Chinese outlook was that he desired to regain Li's confidence so that he might again be recommended and sent to his old post in Korea. After all, at the time when von Möllendorff wrote his essay in 1888 he was at the mercy of Viceroy Li (as far as his livelihood was concerned) owing to his status as Li's "personal secretary" and translator, yet he desired more than anything else to return to Korea. Thus he wanted his boss to believe that he had been "reformed" in favor of China's policy of control of Korea and against the policy of Denny and others, who had been campaigning for the cause of Korea. Von Möllendorff's willingness to compromise his beliefs in order to achieve his goal may reflect a certain realism or even opportunism in this otherwise essentially idealistic and romantic diplomat. In any case, inasmuch as Denny was publicly championing the independence of Korea while von Möllendorff was challenging Denny's apparently anti-Chinese policy, Viceroy Li considered exploiting the Denny–von Möllendorff controversy to China's advantage and interest and so dispatched the German to Korea. Before von Möllendorff left China for Korea, Viceroy Li gave him the advice to be "prudent" in Korea this time.[44]

Only three days after leaving Chefoo, on May 12, 1888, von Möllendorff arrived in Seoul via Inch'ŏn. Learning of Denny's new contract, he was utterly disappointed but decided to remain in Seoul in the hope that he might be hired in another capacity by the Korean king. He did not hesitate to make his view known that his original contract with the Korean government should have priority over any contracts Denny had signed, because his had been signed much earlier, in 1882.[45]

Although Viceroy Li and von Möllendorff planned the latter's trip to Korea in secret in order to be discreet and present a fait accompli to others (the Japanese and British), many people soon came to know of von Möllendorff's re-entry into Korea and wondered about his mission. For example, *The Chinese Times* of Tientsin reported (more than one month, however, after his arrival in Korea) that von Möllendorff reappeared in Korea either "to aid Yuen in his struggle with the King, or to bring the King to the side of Yuen; also to seize charge again of the Customs, whose control is now vested in the Inspectorate General [Hart] at Peking." The paper warned that von Möllendorff's mission would "make the Japanese restive and suspicious" toward the Chinese government.[46]

Learning of von Möllendorff's trip to Korea, Hart believed at first that "he will probably give me some troubles, but I fancy that he will burn his own fingers in the end."[47] Since von Möllendorff was extending his stay in Korea, Hart began, however, to worry and wrote to James D. Campbell, his confidant and agent in London, that "I am on the tie-toe of expectation regarding Corea where von Möllendorff is again located." In yet another letter he complained that "von Möllendorff is still in Corea and an explosion of some sort may be looked for this autumn."[48] In view of the hostility Hart exhibited toward the German diplomat, a brief comparison of what von Möllendorff accomplished and later desired to achieve in Korea with what the British servant achieved in China would be revealing. To be certain, Hart, who became the inspector general of the Chinese Maritime Customs Service in 1863, came to have "more influence on the ruling Chinese than any other foreigner" during his service in China of more than fifty years. Demonstrably, as an employee of the Chinese government, Hart served the interests of not only his mother country, Great Britain, but also those of China. He pushed for the modernization of China in the industrial and economic as well as in the political and diplomatic areas. In undertaking this task, Hart hired more British subjects than those of any other nationality: for example, in 1875 the Chinese Maritime Customs Service under Hart's supervision had 252 British employees and only 156 from other Western backgrounds. What Hart did for so long in China, supposedly for the sake of the Chinese, von Möllendorff more or less wanted to do for the Koreans, and in a much more genuine manner. Unfortunately, nothing that von Möllendorff did and wanted to do was likely to satisfy Hart, who had a prejudicial and condescending attitude toward von Möllendorff because of his being German and because of his having hired mostly German employees in Korea as a matter of policy. It seems that Hart's perspective amounted to the following: if he, Hart, robbed a bank, whether robbing is good or bad, that was acceptable; if someone else robbed a bank, that was not acceptable—a mentality that was typical of nineteenth-century British imperialism.

Even von Brandt, the German minister in Peking and a bitter enemy of von Möllendorff, campaigned against his reappointment in Korea. He urged German acting consul Krien in Seoul not to aid von Möllendorff in Korea and requested the Tsungli Yamen to withdraw him from Korea. In fact, von Brandt attempted to drive von Möllendorff out of not only Korea but China. But Viceroy Li complained to the German minister that his interference in the matter was unjustifiable and unacceptable.[49]

Altogether von Möllendorff stayed in Korea for about two months, during which time he repeatedly asked for an audience with the king but was always rejected. Much to his dismay and consternation, even Karl Waeber, the Russian chargé, who had been one of his friends while he was serving as Russian consul in Tientsin where von Möllendorff had been German vice-consul, who had negotiated with him and concluded the Russo-Korean Agreement of 1884 in Seoul, and who had even presented the decoration of Saint Anna to him on behalf of Czar Alexander III in appreciation of the agreement, had now become an intimate colleague of Denny and himself an unofficial confidant of King Kojong. Worst of all from the standpoint of von Möllendorff, Waeber now deliberately avoided him, taking sides with Denny against China's policy of controlling Korea.

Kojong, who had repeatedly urged von Möllendorff to return to his country, was "offended" because he believed that the German had reappeared in Korea not at his own request but at the command of Viceroy Li. When von Möllendorff was finally given an audience, the monarch was very "cold" toward him, which undoubtedly made him feel like "a jilted lover." Kojong also disliked von Möllendorff's "reformed" position in favor of China and his disputes with Denny, whom the monarch trusted.

It is interesting to ask why Viceroy Li did not push for von Möllendorff's reappointment in Korea by vigorously advising King Kojong to rehire him. After all, by this time Li preferred von Möl-

lendorff to Denny as an adviser to the government, or at least felt
that the German was a lesser evil than the American. It appears that
the main reasons for Li's nonintervention related to Denny's nationality, legal status, and personality. Li believed that von Möllendorff
should succeed Denny only if the latter did not renew his contract
with the Korean government or leave Korea voluntarily; that if the
American retained his post in Korea, there was no realistic way for
him to compel Denny to leave the country. Li realized that if he were
to attempt to replace Denny with von Möllendorff after the American had decided to stay in Korea, he could expect difficulties with
the Washington government, and that that would be too much for
him to handle, especially in view of the assertive opposition shown
by the British and Japanese toward von Möllendorff's previous as
well as the rumored new appointment. Besides, Li was persuaded
that Denny, a seasoned, strong-willed, proud, and independent-
minded diplomat and lawyer, was not the kind of person who could
be readily pushed around and kicked out of Korea, as, for example,
George C. Foulk had been. Li was aware of another significant difference between Foulk and Denny: Foulk, as an accredited diplomat
officially declared to be *persona non grata* by the Korean foreign minister, had been obligated by international law to depart from Korea;
whereas Denny, who was wanted by the Korean king and his officials and had just signed another contract with the government,
could not, as a private citizen, be asked to leave Korea even by the
American government itself, unless he had committed a crime in
Korea, which, of course, he had not. Li recognized that the American government had all the obligations and rights to protect the
interests of Denny in Korea, so long as he and the Korean government agreed that he should remain in that country for one reason or
another.

There was still another important reason Li decided not to push
his luck. Knowing that Denny had on his side many influential leaders of the Republican Party in the United States, such as Senator
John H. Mitchell of Oregon, former President Ulysses S. Grant,
and others; that he knew how to use them against the Chinese government, if necessary; and that he would fight back fiercely if the
Chinese were to strive to remove him from Korea, Li wisely decided
to let the king have his way this time.[50] Two additional factors are
germane to this situation: (1) von Möllendorff arrived at Seoul after

Denny's contract with the Korean government had been legally renewed; and (2) even if Denny had left Korea in the spring or summer of 1888, a circumstance that would have made von Möllendorff's reappointment in Seoul feasible, there would have been so much opposition to him by the British and the Japanese that his reinstatement in Korea would have been very brief or even impossible.

Kojong still had a great deal of confidence in von Möllendorff, however, and sent Min Ŭng-sik to him with the message that if he were to be rehired now, it would cause a "loss of face" to the king, because he had been sent to Korea by Viceroy Li, and that the king would invite him back after a return trip to China. Min told von Möllendorff that he could even leave his family in Korea.[51] Halfway believing in Min's assurances, von Möllendorff once again left Korea, leaving his family behind. At this juncture the Tsungli Yamen, apparently pressured by the British and German ministers in Peking, asked von Möllendorff to return to China. Thus, he had no choice but to leave Korea. His plan was to return to Tientsin and stay there for about two weeks and wait for the king's invitation by telegraph. Arriving at Tientsin via Chefoo on July 12, he gave a detailed report concerning the Korean situation to Li. Meanwhile, his trip to and from Korea became widely known, and there arose massive campaigns against his reappointment. The British were opposed to it. German minister von Brandt in Peking again urged Li and the Tsungli Yamen not to send him back to Korea. Neither Viceroy Li nor the Tsungli Yamen was about to defy the wishes of important foreign governments by sending him back to Korea. Under the circumstances von Möllendorff had to postpone his dream and withdraw his family from Korea.

Feeling terribly hurt and insulted by von Brandt's actions against him and also feeling abandoned by the German Foreign Office, of which he was still technically a member, von Möllendorff decided to resign formally from it and enter into the service of the Chinese government.[52] Although the German Foreign Office never revoked his passport or demanded his withdrawal from China, as von Brandt had apparently recommended, von Möllendorff believed that it had grossly mistreated him by siding with von Brandt.

Actually, his unhappy experiences with the German Foreign Office and von Brandt date back to the 1870s and the early 1880s. In the 1870s he was demoted from the position of second secretary to third secretary at the German consulate in Shanghai.[53] While later serving as German vice-consul in Tientsin between 1879 and 1881, he ran into many obstacles with Minister von Brandt. The German minister considered von Möllendorff arrogant, unruly, haughty, and irresponsible; at the same time von Möllendorff believed that the minister always unwarrantedly blocked his promotions. Then in 1881 when von Möllendorff resigned from the position of vice-consul at Tientsin after his failure to be promoted to consul general and joined the staff of Viceroy Li Hung-chang, von Brandt concluded that this talented but impertinent diplomat was his mortal enemy, irrespective of their common nationality and profession. Throughout von Möllendorff's career, when he disagreed with others over a political or some other issue and even when he disliked them personally, he did not allow himself any deep ill-feeling toward them, however strongly influenced by his own subjectivity. On the other hand, when his adversaries disliked him or disapproved of his policies or actions, they showed an enmity toward him that was intense. This was the situation with von Brandt, with the British Hart and O'Conor, and with the Americans Foote and Foulk. The one exception was Denny, with whom the rule was contrary: von Möllendorff hated the American much more assiduously than the latter hated the German. There seems to be a good explanation for this one-sided hatred between von Möllendorff and his adversaries: von Möllendorff was so superior intellectually and in other facets of his life that he was likely to show his contempt when disagreeing with others to the point where they were hurt and perturbed; at the same time he himself was not bothered by what they did or said to him, because deep down he was convinced that he was much superior to them anyway. Needless to say, this kind of superiority complex might not be detrimental to those in a scholarly profession, but this attitude proved to be a disaster to von Möllendorff's diplomatic career. Even so, his inclination not to hate his enemies—for whatever reasons—as much as they hated him is indeed an admirable quality in and of itself.

In view of the fact that Minister von Brandt strongly resisted von Möllendorff's reappointment in Korea and that the German Foreign Office did not interfere in favor of von Möllendorff's cause but rather sustained the minister's position and even connived to support it, Hart's concern that the German diplomat's reappointment in Korea might lead to the furtherance of the interests of the German government in Korea is both misplaced and illogical. Whatever justifications or reasons Hart used for opposing von Möllendorff's reappointment in Korea, his real reason was as much personal as nationalistic. Hart, despite what he had been doing for the modernization of China, was opposed to von Möllendorff's idea of making Korea prosperous and independent of China, a policy Resident Yüan, Viceroy Li, and other Chinese leaders were also equally opposed to.

Back in Tientsin once again, von Möllendorff was hired as Viceroy Li's "personal secretary," in which position he worked until 1889. In 1889, Hart, out of sympathy and from a desire to appear magnanimous, made him deputy commissioner at Shanghai and later statistical secretary (1897) and then commissioner at Ningpo, technically under his direction. The hidden but real reason why Hart provided von Möllendorff with a few insignificant jobs was—as he confessed—"to take a man from the enemy."[54] Thus, Hart wanted to keep von Möllendorff closely under his control lest this German of stubborn personality be sent to Seoul and hired back by the Korean government.

In view of his excellent professional qualifications and experiences (in addition to his scholarship), one cannot help wondering why von Möllendorff endured all these experiences that must have been humiliating to him—rejection from his own minister in Peking and from his own Foreign Office and work under Hart, whom he knew to be his enemy. Rosalie von Möllendorff, who apparently not only loved but deeply admired and adored her husband for what he was, recalled later on that her man had endured all these humiliations principally because he felt obligated to take care of the welfare of his family. One may then ask why von Möllendorff under such undesirable circumstances in China did not give up whatever dreams he might have had in the Orient and return, with his family, to his native land, where he most likely would have earned a respectable living. Since neither Paul nor Rosalie left any clear-cut answer to that question, one is compelled to speculate on it: a convert tends to become a strong believer, whether it is in religious conversion, or political conviction, or acculturation to a foreign civilization. Once von Möllendorff became "orientalized"—that is, came to love the Oriental culture and way of living—he wished to live, to die, and to be buried there. Neither nationalism nor national boundary meant that much to him. More than anything else, this kind of philosophy of life was responsible for his remaining in China until his death in 1901. His strong desire to return to Korea played an important part in his decision to stay in China, but that was not the determining reason. What was central was his philosophy of life, which had become increasingly Oriental.

Even though von Möllendorff's income was meager in comparison with what he had earned in the service of Korea, or with that of Hart or other important Western employees in China, he and his family lived in peace and happiness, relatively speaking to be sure, in the eastern port cities to which he was assigned throughout the decade of the 1890s. During this period he even served as vice president of the China branch of the Royal Asiatic Society and proved to be a productive scholar. Von Möllendorff was no doubt aware of Hart's real motive in keeping him under his jurisdiction by offering him insignificant but better-than-nothing positions. Yet, as explained, he bore the unfortunate circumstances rather magnanimously, because he felt that he had no choice but to accept them if he wanted to remain in China. Fortunately, his family liked the eastern port cities, as he himself did.

During all this time, he kept up a storng interest in the fate of Korea and a hope that sometime soon he would be invited back as an adviser. In December 1896, he recommended that Russian finance minister Sergei Witte form a Russo-American syndicate for the construction of railroads in Korea. Witte, however, rejected his idea for fear of losing money in the tiny peninsula kingdom.[55] When his wife and three children left China for Germany in 1899 mainly to see to the educational needs of the youngsters, von Möllendorff decided to stay in China and finish his massive project of compiling two dictionaries—one volume German-Chinese and the other Chinese-German. Although he had promised his family that he would return to Germany sometime the following year (1900) upon completion of his project, he in fact never returned to his birthplace but instead kept up his hope of returning to Korea.

Throughout the late 1880s and the 1890s King Kojong dispatched many messages to von Möllendorff, in which he asked him to return to Korea. In undertaking these requests Kojong utilized Min Yŏng-ik, who lived in China most of the time in this period, as well as other available persons as intermediaries.[56] As late as April 1900, Emperor Kojong, being well aware of Hart's power over the German scholar-diplomat and the Chinese government, officially asked him to "send back von Möllendorff to take the place of the deceased Legendre [Charles W. LeGendre]," who had been serving in an advisory capacity to the Korean government.[57] While Hart felt that "I am a bit puzzled how to say no!" he decided not to relieve von Möllendorff from his position as commissioner at Ningpo and send him back to Korea.[58] It should be emphasized that one way or another Hart controlled not only Merrill, who had succeeded von Möllendorff as head of the Korean Customs Service in 1886, but also J. F. Schoenicke, McLeavy Brown, and others who later occupied this controversial post. For his part Hart had no intention of letting von Möllendorff take over the post of heading the Korean Customs Service again or of allowing him to assume any other new position in Korea.

Even after 1900 the emperor made it known to von Möllendorff that he wanted him back in Korea. But owing to opposition from the British, and especially Hart, and from the Japanese and even from the Russians, at least in the late 1890s, the emperor was frustrated in his efforts to rehire him as an adviser. Without ever fulfilling his dream of returning to Korea, von Möllendorff died at Ningpo on April 20, 1901, ironically the same year that Viceroy Li passed away —a coincidence also symbolizing the tragic fate of Emperor Kojong himself. Two years after the premature death of this talented German scholar-diplomat, whose career Hart had helped to destroy and whom Hart now referred to as "poor von Möllendorff," two of von Möllendorff's children, Margaret and Dora, visited their place of birth in China. Hart, who heard these two "charming girls" play music together commented that Margaret was "a splendid pianist" and that Dora was "an even finer violinist."[59] One can only speculate if the children or grandchildren of these two von Möllendorffs might still be living somewhere in Germany.

Following the Sino-Japanese War the Chinese were finally forced out of Korea in 1895, which they should have left voluntarily in the early 1880s, giving the Koreans the opportunity to develop their country and to strengthen its independence on their own terms. Following the Russo-Japanese War the Russians were expelled from Korea and Japan forcefully made Korea its protectorate in August

1905. Emperor Kojong, naively believing that the United States might intervene in favor of Korea on the basis of the good offices clause of the Korean-American Treaty of 1882, repeatedly urged President Theodore Roosevelt to take action on behalf of his kingdom against the Japanese aggression.[60] Roosevelt refused to help Korea, telling his secretary of state, John Hay, that "We cannot possibly interfere for the Koreans against Japan. They could not strike one blow in their own defense."[61]

It should be noted that the British policy of treating Korea as an appendage of China (despite the Anglo-Korean Treaty of 1883) continued until 1895, after which time Japan attempted to dominate Korea in competition with Imperial Russia. Favorably disposed to Japanese control of Korea vis-à-vis Russia, the London government in 1902 finally recognized Japan's special rights in Korea by concluding the Anglo-Japanese Alliance of 1902, thereby making the recognition of Japan's paramount interests in Korea much easier for the already pro-Japanese President Theodore Roosevelt. In 1907, the extremely unhappy Kojong tried to appeal his case in secret to the Second International Peace Conference held at The Hague in the Netherlands. The furious Japanese retaliated by deposing him on July 24, 1907, and they finally annexed Korea as a part of their empire in 1910.

# Conclusion

Within the framework of Confucian and traditional East Asian concepts of world order, Korea was the most important of China's dependencies, owing to its geographical propinquity to the Middle Kingdom and also due to the thorough Confucianization (sinicization) of its own civilization. As such, Korea maintained formal relations only with China (based on suzerain-dependency relations) and with other nations within the East Asian world order, such as Japan (based on more-or-less equal relationships). Good or bad, such a system of world order functioned "satisfactorily" for its members, so long as East Asian nations were not challenged and forced to enter into modern (Western) treaty relations with Western nations based on entirely different concepts of international order.

After coercing China and Japan to enter into treaty relations with them in the 1840s and the 1850s, the expansionistic-minded Western powers began to bother the Koreans. Though ignorant and misinformed as to Western intentions and capabilites, the Korean authorities under the anachronistic regent, the Taewŏn'gun, successfully, but with quite a bit of bloodshed, resisted Western attempts in the 1860s and early 1870s. In the 1860s and early 1870s even Japan, which succeeded in establishing new relations with China on the basis of modern international rules in 1871, tried to negotiate and conclude a treaty with Korea, its closest neighbor. But the Koreans rejected the Japanese overtures, thereby intensifying *Sei-Kan ron* (Conquer Korea) sentiments within Japan.

By 1873 and 1874, two important events had taken place in

Korea: (1) in 1873 the more flexible and pragmatic King Kojong took over the government; and (2) in 1874 the Chinese emperor finally advised the Korean government to negotiate with Japan first and then with Western nations, lest they ally themselves and invade the Korean peninsula—the kind of advice that the Chinese government should have given some twenty, or at least ten, years earlier. The result was the conclusion of the Korean-Japanese Treaty in 1876 and Korean-American Treaty in 1882. Once Korea was opened to Japan and the West, King Kojong became eager to "modernize" his ancient kingdom in imitation of Japan, which had in turn been successfully modernizing itself in imitation of Western nations. Japanese leaders strongly urged Korean leaders not only to imitate what they had been doing but also to make Korea truly independent of China, which by this time the islanders had begun to "despise," owing to China's "inability" and unwillingness to make their once-great but now degenerate empire strong and respectable. Moreover, by the early 1880s King Kojong himself had come to realize that China, which had proved unable to take care of itself vis-à-vis Western powers, was in no position to be of much benefit to his kingdom, although he was not yet ready to renounce all traditional ties with China, which were deeply rooted in the Confucian concept of *li*.

It was under these circumstances that Viceroy Li Hung-chang, concerned and worried about Japan's increasing activities in Korea, manipulated the Korean government to request that he send a foreign adviser to Korea, which in the early 1880s, Korea badly needed. Thus, in December 1882, Viceroy Li sent Paul Georg von Möllendorff to Korea. For good or for ill, he served the Korean government during a very stormy period, and the role that he played seems to have been both complicated and controversial. To be sure, he was sent to Korea by Viceroy Li to guide the Korean government through the vagaries of modern diplomatic practice in such a way as to promote and strengthen Chinese interests and influences in the country. Once in Korea, however, von Möllendorff decided to promote Korean rather than Chinese interests.

Von Möllendorff arrived in Seoul before the consummation and implementation of the Korean-American Treaty of 1882. For the first year or so, he was busily involved in Korea's domestic matters and negotiation and conclusion of the Korean-Japanese Trade Regulations and Tariff Agreement. Among other things, his most urgent task was to establish a customs service to collect the customs duties provided for by the Korean-American Treaty, by the Korean-Japanese Trade Regulations and Tariff Agreement of 1883, and by treaties soon to be concluded with European nations. In order to establish a customs service, he needed huge sums of money that the Korean government did not have. For the purpose of securing a prearranged loan and hiring experienced customs officials, von Möllendorff made a trip to China, which turned out to be successful. Although he soon came to believe that some country other than China should become Korea's new elder brother, he shared Kojong's idea that Korea should maintain loose ties with China and receive whatever aid it could provide for Korea.

Von Möllendorff swiftly set up and ran the Korean Customs Service, although he did it in an informal and disorganized manner—which invited a great deal of criticism from his successor, Merrill, and British and French diplomats later on. In addition, he initiated a great many innovative reforms for the modernization of Korea. If his programs had been continued and expanded after his dismissal in 1885, the result would have been good for Korea.

His concrete accomplishments in foreign affairs did not occur until the summer of 1883, when he and Minister Takezoe successfully concluded the Korean-Japanese Trade Regulations and Tariff Agreement. The next summer he and Karl Waeber were able to conclude the Russo-Korean Treaty, which provided that warships of either country could visit any port of the other, an arrangement that Korea did not grant to other signatory powers. This action reveals the fact that even before the *Kapsin* Coup of 1884, von Möllendorff was a Russophile. Even so, if the Korea of his time had been more resourceful and stronger than its neighbors, no doubt his advice would have indicated, among other things, how the interests of Korea might be advanced even at the sacrifice of those of its neighbors—as did, for example, the advice given to the Japanese government at about the same time by such Western advisers as Gustave E. Boissonade, Charles W. LeGendre, and others. But the Korea of the 1880s was unlike Japan, a newly rising and aggressive power; China, declining yet still mighty in the eyes of the Koreans; or Russia, a mysterious but expanding country, the largest in the world, which had shared a common border with the Korean peninsula since 1860.

Moreover, if China after 1882 had recognized Korea as a truly sovereign and independent nation and had treated it as such, leaving it alone in its efforts toward modernization and independency, and also if Japan had treated Korea with more respect and concern for their mutual rather than its unilateral interest, then von Möllendorff would not have advised Kojong to seek a protective alliance with Russia. The important point here is that von Möllendorff's pro-Russian posture and efforts to make Russia a senior ally of Korea had a pluralistic base, whose focus was not only on Korea's traditional political heritage but, more importantly, on considerations of geopolitical factors and of the imperialism registered against Korea by China and supposedly by Japan. Understanding the limited resources that Korea could offer to Russia and familiar with the history of Korea's (younger brother's) tributary relations with China (elder brother), von Möllendorff conceived the prospective relations between Korea and Russia in terms of a protectorate (junior ally) and protector (senior ally).

Von Möllendorff reasoned that, of all the powers, Russia was the best country to help Korea. He therefore considered that the right course for Korean foreign policy should be to seek aid from Russia. He believed that Russia would be willing to aid Korea if its interest could be deeply aroused in something that Korea had to offer. His idea was to induce Russia to become the protector of Korea and to train the Korean army in exchange for Port Lazareff. Even before the *Kapsin* Coup, but especially after seeing and experiencing how easily Japanese foreign minister Inoue was able to impose such harsh terms on Korea (the Treaty of Seoul of 1884), von Möllendorff concluded that the salvation of Korea lay in aligning itself with Russia in a bilateral alliance. Although he was flexible about the details of the alliance and left them to later negotiations, he was interested in making Russia not only the protector of Korean independence but also the supplier of its military needs.

So far as King Kojong was concerned, after the conclusion of the treaties, he wanted to modernize his kingdom and make it more independent of China. But the problem he encountered was that the more he tried to distance Korea from China, the more China attempted to control Korea—in the name of suzerain-dependency relations but actually in a new imperialistic and unprecedented way. Kojong wanted to escape from China's domination, preferably with American aid but even with Japanese or Russian aid, if necessary.

Since assistance from America was not forthcoming and since the Japanese failed in the *Kapsin* Coup of 1884, Kojong unofficially and secretly decided to give active support to von Möllendorff's idea of inducing Russia to come into Korea in return for a lease on Port Lazareff.

There were, however, two important areas in which Kojong and von Möllendorff disagreed. First, influenced by Viceroy Li's distorted perception of the United States and also by American diplomats in Korea, Kojong, even after being disappointed with America's lukewarm attitude toward his country, still clung to his strong and undue faith in the United States—until 1907, when he was finally deposed by the Japanese. Von Möllendorff, however, from the beginning of his career in Korea, correctly reasoned that the United States, thousands of miles away, would never become actively involved in Korean affairs during the nineteenth century. Second, prior to the *Kapsin* Coup, Kojong, influenced by the Progressives, came to believe in the ability and willingness of the Japanese to help Korea in its modernization and independence vis-à-vis China, even trusting in the "goodness" of their motivation. Von Möllendorff, on the contrary, never liked or trusted the Japanese and refused to cooperate with the pro-Japanese Korean Progressives. History later proved that von Möllendorff was more right than Kojong on both of these issues.

On another important issue, that of involving Russia in Korean affairs, both of them wholeheartedly agreed to the point of action. But later events showed that both were wrong this time. Be that as it may, in the mid-1880s, after feeling rejected by the Americans as well as by the Japanese, Kojong was ready and willing to accept as a new elder brother even Russia—a country much less known to the Koreans than China or Japan. Cognizant of the long history of Korea's tributary relations with China and easily intimidated by bigger and more powerful neighbors such as China and Japan, Kojong was attracted to von Möllendorff's concept of making Russia a senior and protective ally to his deeply troubled kingdom.

It should be emphasized that, to the extent that Kojong—even after realizing that his kingdom had become independent of China —was still looking for a new elder brother, there was historical continuity in his outlook toward the world. After all, he was striving to solve Korea's new foreign policy problems in a traditional Korean way. In that sense, Korea vacillated among the various prospects of overlordship of its neighbors.[1] To be objective about the whole issue, however, two other factors should be proffered: First, if China, after 1882, had treated Korea as a completely independent nation, as the United States and even Japan had done, the Koreans, with their Western advisers' help, would have acted more like an independent people, instead of seeking a new senior ally. Second, if Korea had been stronger than its neighbors, then it would have become independent faster, despite its historical ties with China. In the absence of those two factors, and constantly intimidated by the Chinese and rejected by the Americans and the Japanese, Kojong naturally responded to von Möllendorff's idea of collaborating with the Russians. In the final analysis, therefore, it can be argued that Kojong's search for a new elder brother, even after his kingdom had become independent, was principally due to his keen perception of Korea's circumscribed position geopolitically and not only due to his belief in the country's political tradition.

So far as Russia was concerned, Czar Alexander III and Foreign Minister Giers were definitely interested in sending Russian military instructors to Korea and in gaining equal and due treaty rights in Korea in the mid-1880s. On the subject of Russia's becoming Korea's protector, Alexander III felt complimented and flattered with King Kojong's request. But for two reasons—that such a move might provoke China and Japan and that Russia in the 1880s was not in a position to play such an aggressive role in the peninsula kingdom—the Russian government adopted a posture of noncommitment. Thus, it neither rejected the Korean proposal nor seized upon it wholeheartedly. With regard to the Korean proposal that Russia lease Port Lazareff, the Russian government was not interested in occupying it except under one eventuality: namely, if the British fleet were to stay at Port Hamilton permanently or for a prolonged period of time. Of particular importance is the fact that, because the Russian leadership intentionally kept alive Korean hopes on the issue of a Russian protectorship over Korea even after von Möllendorff had left Korea for China and even after Russia had established its legation in Seoul in 1885, King Kojong and his pro-Russian advisers made several more attempts to win Russian protection, vis-à-vis China in 1886 and Japan in 1896.

It is interesting to compare Russian policy toward Korea with that of other treaty powers during the mid- and late-1880s. In the case of Russia, the real policy toward Korea was to let the king and his independent-minded advisers cling to an undue faith in it, while officially appearing to be noncommittal. In the case of the United States, on the other hand, the official and unofficial policy between 1882 and 1905 was not to encourage the Korean king and his advisers to have unwarranted faith in it, while the American diplomats stationed in Seoul skillfully helped the Korean king and his pro-American advisers to do just the opposite—to develop and sustain a strong faith in their government.[2] As for the British government, it treated Korea as if it were a province or a colony of China, despite the conclusion of the Anglo-Korean Treaty on the basis of sovereign equality. The Japanese government, which had been officially dealing with Korea on the basis of sovereign equality ever since 1876, treated its small neighbor, in reality, on a basis even more unequal than the treatment that Western powers had extended to the island nation. Moreover, after the failure of the pro-Japanese *Kapsin* Coup of 1884, the Japanese government mercilessly imposed harsh terms on Korea, as if it, not China, were the main enemy of Japan. The Chinese government, although it was utterly incapable of taking care of even itself vis-à-vis Japan and the Western powers, treated Korea as if it were a colony. So among all of the treaty powers in 1885 following the failure of the *Kapsin* Coup, the Imperial Russian government, as noncommittal and lukewarm as it had been toward the issue of the territorial and administrative integrity of Korea, still appeared (to von Möllendorff and King Kojong) to be the most viable and promising power on the horizon for keeping the overbearing China and Japan away from Korea. However, so far as the official policy of Alexander III and Giers was concerned, as of 1885 they showed only a limited interest in the affairs of Korea.

To be sure, there were some Russian officials who wanted their country to play a more expansionistic and aggressive role in Korea. Especially in the case of the young and aggressive Alexis de Speyer, whole-hearted support was lent to von Möllendorff's attempt to involve Russia more closely and intimately than the Russian Czar and Foreign Office cared to do. However, the so-called secret Russo-Korean Agreement of 1885, supposedly signed by von Möllendorff and Russian legation officials in Tokyo, provided only for the Russian dispatch of military instructors to Korea. The agreement, reflecting the policies of Alexander III and his government, was quiet about Russian protection of Korea or Russian occupation of Port Lazareff.

Meanwhile, Great Britain, on account of the Afghan crisis and before learning anything about the Russo-Korean intrigue, occupied Port Hamilton in order to be in a position to attack Russian bases in Vladivostok in case of an Anglo-Russian war. Although the British tried to justify their occupation on the grounds that the Russians might have seized the islands if they had not done so themselves, their action was in fact nothing but a naked violation of international law and of their treaty with Korea. It should also be noted that the London goverment undertook the occupation without a clearly defined policy, leaving the detailed negotiations to its representatives in Peking and Seoul.

The Korean Foreign Office, guided and advised by von Möllendorff, vigorously protested the seizure of Port Hamilton, but to no avail. Since the British remained in the islands even after the Afghan crisis had supposedly subsided, the Koreans threatened the British with mediation by the other treaty powers. It is interesting to note that the British were extremely uneasy about the other treaty powers and reluctant to submit to their mediation on the matter and that, whenever the Korean government attempted to involve the other powers, the British promised an amicable solution to the crisis. What the British government proposed first to the Chinese government and then later to the Korean government was that it lease the islands with appropriate payments. In truth, however, they merely wanted to retain the islands, using the idea of negotiation for rent as a diplomatic trick.

The Chinese government supported the British action with the naive hope that the British might in return support China's policy of controlling Korea and might guarantee the territorial integrity of Korea against any future aggression by Russia or Japan. The Japanese government, which had adopted a policy of nonintervention in Korea after the failure of the *Kapsin* Coup of 1884, disapproved of the British action. The Russian government was understandably upset and threatened that it would indeed take similar action if the British should remain in the islands. Deeply worried by the Russian threat, the Chinese government now worked for a British evacuation from Port Hamilton.

Then in May–June 1885, the representatives of the governments of Japan, China, Great Britain, and the United States learned of the alleged Russo-Korean intrigue and of the vital role of von Möllendorff in it. They all campaigned for von Möllendorff's removal from Korea, which they succeeded in effecting in the end. It should be noted, however, that in the final analysis, the pressures exerted on Viceroy Li by the British and Japanese governments were mostly responsible for his dismissal.

In the meantime, in view of the alleged Russian intrigue in Korea, the Chinese government reversed itself and once again decided to support the British occupation of Port Hamilton. As for Japan, it preferred Chinese domination of Korea to a Russian presence. The British imperialists, for their part, made maximum use of the alleged Russian aggression in the peninsula, winning propaganda points from it; they loudly justified their illegal seizure of Port Hamilton on the basis of the secret agreement, in spite of the fact that, in truth, their occupation of it preceded the alleged intrigue by two months. So far as the U.S. Department of State was concerned, it consistently clung to a policy of indifference, noninterference, and neutrality toward Korea not only during the Port Hamilton crisis but also during the Russo-Korean intrigue. However, American chargé Foulk, who sympathized with the British, turned against von Möllendorff's pro-Russian posture.

In any case, the obvious consequences of von Möllendorff's unofficial attempt to involve Russia in Korean affairs turned out to be fourfold: (1) the destruction of his own diplomatic career; (2) an intensification of the Chinese control of Korea; (3) the seemingly reluctant consent of Japan to the Chinese policy of domination of Korea, at least, for the time being; and (4) a probable prolongation of the British occupation of Port Hamilton (until February 1887). Contrary to what he had originally anticipated, von Möllendorff's pro-Russian policy turned out to be more negative than constructive in its impact on Kojong's policy of fostering a "free Korea," independent of China. Moreover, von Möllendorff was almost universally criticized or condemned by contemporary foreign diplomats in Korea. American minister Foote, who had dealt with von Möllendorff prior to the Port Hamilton incident, charged that he had been acting as if he had owned the Korean Foreign Office. Dr. Allen accused him of being not only antimissionary but also anti-American. Chinese commissioner Ch'en was very hostile toward von Möllendorff, because of the latter's devotion to the welfare of Korea in disrespect of Chinese interests. Foulk, one of his rivals, condemned von Möllendorff with the charge that "the conduct of this man would seem to be without a parallel in history" and urged the Korean government to dismiss him for abusing the power he held in the name of the Korean government.[3] Japanese foreign minister Inoue recommended that Viceroy Li should persuade Kojong to replace von Möllendorff with a more reliable American adviser. Particularly notable were the strong condemnation of von Möllendorff by the British diplomats. British chargé O'Conor, who accused him of being an "unscrupulous agent," advised Li to remove the German from Korea, and British consul general Aston charged that he had "acted treacherously against Korea and for Russia." Robert Hart, a British Germanophobe who assisted in and contributed to undermining von Möllendorff's diplomatic career, charged that he had overstaffed the Korean Customs Service with too many German nationals.[4] Henry H. Merrill, Hart's American protege and von Möllendorff's successor, essentially agreed with his patron that the Korean Customs Service had been needlessly overstaffed prior to his assumption of the office.[5] The French minister in Japan, Joseph A. Sienkiewicz, insisted that although von Möllendorff was an intelligent person, he was not a good diplomat and could even be viewed as a money-grabbing crook.[6]

Not only Sienkiewicz but O'Conor charged that von Möllendorff was too much concerned with his own financial gain in running the Korean Customs Service.[7] Actually, such accusations were made partly because of the disorganized way he ran the customs service (especially compared with Merrill)[8] and only partly because of his having hired or invited many German nationals to positions he had something to do with. There is no impeachable evidence that indicates he was financially corrupt. Since Kojong allowed him to run the customs service the way he saw fit, he probably could have grabbed great sums of money if he had wanted to, but he did not.

To be sure, during his tenure in Korea he was paid reasonably well, as were most Western employees who did governmental work in China and Japan in those early pioneering days. Even so, his monthly salary of 300 taels was much less than what his successor, Denny, received (1,000 taels per month). In point of fact, however, von Möllendorff was provided with a big, attractive house and with many domestic servants and guards for him and for his family. He was also made a Korean noble—*ch'amp'an* (vice minister). In view of his status, he had all the rights and privileges that a Korean of his noble rank would have, plus those additional perquisites extended him at the king's discretion. And throughout most of his tenure in Korea he was the only "official Western adviser" to the monarch and decidedly one of his favorites.

Von Möllendorff, in turn, paid good salaries to the German and other Western employees who were hired by him and worked for him. Understandably, these personnel were paid somewhat better than other Westerners, such as Dr. Allen, who were not under the charge of the German diplomat-scholar. When the Korean government proposed that von Möllendorff replace his more highly paid European employees with less expensive Japanese workers, he rejected the suggestion partly because of his loyalty to them, partly because of their proven efficiency, and partly because he was comfortable working with them rather than with the Japanese, whom he did not care about anyhow.

All these circumstances still do not reveal that von Möllendorff was a "money-grabber" or a "crook," as those who were either hostile toward his policies or jealous of his official position in Korea contended. The fact that he and his family lived modestly, if not penuriously, in China after returning from Korea in late 1885 indicates that he did not accumulate a massive amount of personal wealth while in Korea—something he could have done if he had wanted to in view of the complete authority given him by the king in running the Korean Customs Service and many other projects.

With regard to his philosophy, character, and personality, he was a cosmopolitan, cross-culturally oriented, universalistic-minded individual. His extensive and intensive studies of the languages, cultures, and histories of many different countries made him that kind of international-minded, interculturally tolerant, and racially open-minded scholar-diplomat. In many ways he was "a genuine citizen of world" both intellectually and culturally. He certainly was not a narrow-minded Prussian "patriot." The last project he undertook, despite ill health, was the awesome and massive task of compiling German-Chinese and Chinese-German dictionaries, not for economic profit but as a reflection of his deep commitment to cross-cultural scholarship, which generally does and should transcend narrow nationalism or national boundaries. It is little wonder that von Möllendorff was buried in Shanghai, according to his own wishes. If the quality of a man is to be judged not so much by how well he serves his own national government or how much money he makes but by universally (interracially or internationally) valued services such as medical research, or educational works that can benefit all mankind, then von Möllendorff was a lofty and highly principled man. After all, anybody could become a nationalist or patriot, while not many people could become a genuine universalist or internationalist.

Despite his admirable philosophy of life, it must be conceded that he did not possess the personality and character ideal for a good diplomat. He was not a cautious, warm, or prudent diplomat. Rather, he was a stern, haughty, proud, overbearing, presumptuous, and daring person. His exceptionally brilliant mind and multilingual ability made him behave in a superior manner in dealing with foreign diplomats in Korea and China. That led, in part, to conflict with his colleagues from the United States, Japan, China, Great Britain, France, and even Germany, his own country, who resented his behavior and manner of conducting business for the Korean government. Even so, some of the conflicts would have been inevitable, even if his personality had been conciliatory and low-keyed. As the vice minister of the Korean Foreign Office, he insisted that diplomats from other countries do business with the Foreign Office through him, and diplomats like Foote and Foulk refused to comply. As "unofficial advisers" to Kojong, who held a strong confidence in them, these American diplomats insisted on dealing with the Korean government directly. Furthermore, conflicts between von Möllendorff and the British, Chinese, and Japanese representatives were also unavoidable, because he tried to serve the interests of Korea while the others strove to serve the interests of their own governments. Even if von Möllendorff had possessed the most charming and pleasant personality and had had impeccable integrity, which he certainly did not, he still would have had difficulties with his colleagues from other nations, because each had differing interests to pursue. Since a majority of his colleagues portrayed him as intrigue-minded, egotistical, and money-grabbing, he was branded and known as such.

Historians are generally critical toward von Möllendorff for the role he played in Korea.[9] Some go so far as to conclude that he "turned out to be an unscrupulous bully who betrayed the Viceroy as well as the Koreans"[10]—which is only partly accurate, inasmuch as he might have betrayed Viceroy Li, but not the Koreans; or, at least, betraying the Koreans was not his original intention. Actually, there seems to have been grossly unfair criticism of von Möllendorff both by his contemporaries and by today's historians, and particularly by the British diplomats. While there was definitely plenty of room for criticism of von Möllendorff, the major problem with all these condemnations was that they were directed against him for the wrong reasons. If von Möllendorff had worked for the interests of the British at the expense of Korea, in the same way that Durham White Stevens, an American adviser to the Korean government in the mid-1900s, worked for Japanese interests at the expense of Korea, then the British might have liked the German diplomat; but from the standpoint of Korea, he would have been a traitor, as Stevens was.[11]

From strictly legal and moralistic viewpoints, it was actually the British, not von Möllendorff, who had "acted treacherously against Korea." In spite of the fact that the British government had concluded a modern treaty with Korea and entered into diplomatic relations on the basis of sovereign equality, it seized Port Hamilton illegally; treated Korea as if it were a province or dependency of China; tried to negotiate a lease of the port mainly with the Chinese behind the back of the Seoul goverment; and, finally, evacuated the islands after making an arrangement with the Chinese, not with the Korean, government.

Moreover, in comparison with the "crimes" that Yüan Shih-k'ai committed against King Kojong, who had been "invested" by his own emperor, von Möllendorff's "wrongdoings" were marginal. In fact, everything that von Möllendorff did or tried to do was perfectly in accordance with international law and practice. For the vice foreign minister of a sovereign nation to try to conclude a secret alliance with another sovereign nation with the full (though tacit and secret) authorization of the head of that country is no crime at all, even if the act turned out to be politically unwise and disastrous, as in the case of von Möllendorff in 1885. He committed no legal or moral crime, however, while Yüan violated not only traditional Chinese and Korean legal statutes and moral norms but also modern

international law. Even the Tsungli Yamen recognized these of-
fenses and recommended that Viceroy Li recall Yüan from Korea;
but, for political and personal reasons, Li continued to support
Yüan.

There was plenty of occasion for criticism against British consul
general Baber. He was apparently deeply involved in Yüan's plot for
the dethronement of Kojong, although he does seem not to have
been the author of the so-called "forged" document, as some historians claim. Even if he had not been involved in the plot, however, he
could have exposed it at an early stage, since he had been apprised of
it by Yüan himself. Above all, Baber should have joined all of the
other foreign diplomats in Seoul in denouncing Yüan's plot as a matter of principle and the rule of law, but he did not. Yet no British diplomats criticized Baber for whatever corrupt role he played in this
bizarre incident. Instead, they all joined in attacking von Möllendorff, who had committed only a political blunder, not an illegal or
immoral act.

Regardless of how the British public servants felt, von Möllendorff, as an adviser to the Korean government, was supposed to
serve the interests of the Korean government, not those of the British, just as the British diplomats were to serve the interests of the
British government, not of the Korean or Chinese governments.
Von Möllendorff genuinely believed that bringing Russia into Korea
would be in the interest of Korea; and he was therefore doing what
he perceived to be beneficial to Korea, certainly not against Korea.
Like Foulk, one of his rivals, and like Owen N. Denny, one of his
successors in Korea, von Möllendorff was sincerely and genuinely
concerned with the destiny of Korea. In many ways, he was much
better qualified to serve the interests of Korea than Foulk or Denny.
As for Foulk, despite his sincere interest in the welfare and independence of Korea, he was still an American diplomatic agent. As such,
what he could advise or do for the Korean government was limited.
Denny, too, was genuinely concerned with the economic progress
and political independence of Korea. However, Denny was handi-
capped by the fact that he knew neither the Chinese nor the Korean
language.[12] Von Möllendorff, on the contrary, knew both languages
and virtually adopted a Korean style of living. These accommodations to the culture gave him a tremendous advantage in whatever
projects he was to carry out. During his tenure in Korea, he not only

organized and ran the customs service independently of China but also proved to be an innovative reformer and imaginative modernizer. But the problem was that Korea then needed many more von Möllendorffs to carry out these multifarious works. Moreover, unfortunately for the future of Korea, many, if not all of his modernization projects were discontinued after his dismissal, mainly for lack of support from the government leaders.

Whereas von Möllendorff's concern for Korea was genuine, his perception of the realities of international politics in the Far East was probably defective. To be sure, his assumptions that China was in no position to help Korea; that Japan was too ambitious toward Korea; that France, Germany, and the United States were too far away and indifferent toward Korea's fate; and that Great Britain was too selfish and pro-Japanese were largely accurate. However, his argument that Russia would be in a position to help Korea, if properly induced to do so, though reasonable from the standpoint of geopolitics, was but a fantasy in view of the dismal realities of Russian capability and military readiness. Despite the tremendous magnitudes of its territory, population, and armed forces, Russia in the 1880s was a paper tiger. Notwithstanding de Speyer's unwarranted aggression and despite the worries indulged in by the Chinese, Japanese, and British, the Russian government then had neither the intention nor the readiness to pursue such an active policy toward Korea. Therefore, even if von Möllendorff had been able to force Foreign Minister Kim to sign the draft agreement that he and de Speyer had written, the implementation of such a controversial agreement would certainly have been impossible. Consequently, the assertion that, without Kim, the Russian advance into Korea would most likely have been successful is a gross misjudgment, misunderstanding, and misperception of Russian Far Eastern policy in the 1880s and of the international politics surrounding the Korean peninsula at that time.

Von Möllendorff's notion that Russia was in a position to help Korea, like his assumption that he and King Kojong would be able to execute the pro-Russian plot, even in the face of strong opposition, was a miscalculation. In the initial stage of his pro-Russian plot, von Möllendorff apparently believed that, so long as he had the tacit support of the king, he would somehow be able to implement his secret scheme. And he further believed that he and Kojong might be able to implement it, even if their plot were discovered and regardless of how the governments of China and Japan felt about it. As events proved, however, he and Kojong learned how grossly they had overestimated what they could do, and there was no way for them to carry out their plot in the face of opposition from several forces, both outside and inside Korea (the Chinese, Japanese, British, Americans like Foulk, and the pro-Chinese foreign minister Kim Yun-sik). Thus, it seems that von Möllendorff's initial perception of his own power (and the king's) had been seriously defective.

Another important defect in von Möllendorff was his strategy for achieving his objectives. One of the most important tactics for a diplomat in implementing his instructions, whether for the benefit of his own government or for the government he happens to serve, is to make as many friends and as few enemies as possible among the diplomats and governments involved. Von Möllendorff, it seems, violated this cardinal rule.

Since the objectives of Minister Foote and Chargé Foulk with regard to Korea were identical with his own—modernization and greater independence of Korea from China—von Möllendorff should have tried to work closely with these American diplomats, but he did not; in fact, he made them his enemies. For that, he should be held responsible, at least partly. Again, since the aims of the Korean Progressives were similar to his own—the political independence of Korea from China and Korea's economic and educational development—von Möllendorff could have tried to have friendly working relations with them, but he did not, mainly because of his strong disagreement with the Progressives' pro-Japanese orientation. His mistrust of Japan's motives in Korea was so strong that he kept only minimum contact with the Japanese diplomats and nationals in and outside Korea. Even though history eventually proved that von Möllendorff's suspicion of Japanese ambitions in Korea was more correct than not, still, in the 1880s, he could have developed more flexible and open-minded relations with the Japanese and pro-Japanese elements in Korea, especially in view of the fact that in the 1880s Japan had no grand designs to seize Korea. Certainly, making enemies of the Japanese in and outside Korea was diplomatically unsound.

With regard to von Möllendorff's notion that, since the old and decadent China was no longer in a position to do much good for

Korea, the latter should not rely on it, not much criticism can be raised, because it was essentially correct. It is important to note, however, that despite his strong belief that China's influence should be kept out of Korea, he also believed in retaining cordial working relations with Viceroy Li and other Chinese officials in Korea. That certainly was the diplomatically and politically wise thing to do. Even in dealing with Americans, Japanese, and other foreign diplomats in Korea, he should have done the same thing.

Again, von Möllendorff's view that the British interest in the peninsula was entirely too selfish and one-sided, and exclusively economic and strategic, was largely accurate. Consequently, his anti-British attitude seemed perfectly justifiable. On the other hand, it must be conceded that, according to the standard of nineteenth-century European imperialism, British imperialism toward and in Korea was not unusually harsh. Even the British policy of treating Korea as an appendage of China after the conclusion of the Anglo-Korean Treaty of 1883, on the basis of the equality of sovereignty, though contradictory and illogical, was not wrong. For example, the British government continued to recognize Burma as a vassal of China and permitted it to send tributary missions to China even after Britain had made the country one of its colonies in 1884 and 1885. Although two wrongs do not make a right and even though British policy toward Korea appeared to be contradictory, in comparison with America's consistent treatment of Korea as a full-fledged sovereign and independent nation, von Möllendorff could have made an effort to develop less hostile relations with British diplomats in Korea and China, but he did not.

All in all, von Möllendorff could have tried to cultivate better working relations with numerous diplomats in Korea, but he failed to do so, letting his emotions and personal prejudices interfere with the performance of his diplomatic duties and influence him to implement the scheme he had plotted with King Kojong. He should have attempted to minimize the opposition from his adversaries, or to at least neutralize them. But the evidence indicates that von Möllendorff did not try hard enough to develop and cultivate amicable relations with foreign diplomats stationed in Korea, and he was too easily disappointed by their lack of support for whatever projects he had developed for Korea. As brilliant and energetic as he was, von Möllendorff was simply not a model or good diplomat.

On the other hand, to be objective about the issues and especially to see them from the complex point of view of von Möllendorff, it is necessary to understand that he was convinced that Japan, China, and the United States, Great Britain, France, and Germany had been either too aggressive in Korea or indifferent to its fate; it was therefore logical that he decided not to count on their support or cooperation in implementing his ideas for the salvation of Korea. That was logically sound, yet diplomatically and politically unsound.

Whatever von Möllendorff's personality and ideological defects and whatever misguided diplomatic strategy and tactics he applied for implementation of his ideas in Korea, they were not the main reason for his ultimate failure to make Russia the protector of Korea. The most important causes lay mainly in Peking and Tientsin and partly in Tokyo, London, St. Petersburg, and even in Seoul itself—all beyond his influence.

Von Möllendorff's willingness to be "used" by Viceroy Li in succeeding or checkmating Judge Denny in Korea should be considered an aberration from his usual behavior and pattern of thinking, because he did so out of desperation and despair, into which he had fallen upon his removal from Korea and from which he sought to escape. If things had worked out well and von Möllendorff had been reappointed as adviser to the Korean king and government, as Kojong desired so strongly (despite strong opposition by the British government and officials), it is doubtful that he would have served as nothing but a puppet of Viceroy Li in Korea. Given a second opportunity to serve the Korean government, he would likely have worked for the welfare and interest of Korea in a more cautious and diplomatic manner.

More importantly, however, it should be pointed out that, in view of the strong certainty that both the British and Japanese governments, and even German minister von Brandt, would have vigorously campaigned against von Möllendorff if he had been reappointed and that the Chinese government would have been unable to resist such opposition, Li's "back door" attempt to reinstall the supposedly "reformed" German diplomat into such a sensitive post in Korea in 1888 shows, once again, the extreme naivete of Li and his government in matters of international relations. Equally important is the fact that von Möllendorff himself, like King Kojong, was artless in power politics, thinking that somehow he could again become adviser to the Korean government despite massive opposition on the part of the British and Japanese governments. He apparently failed to realize that, even though two years had elapsed since his exit from Korea, neither China (Viceroy Li) nor Korea (King Kojong) was in a position to regain for him his lost position in the face of opposition from the mighty British empire and the newly rising Japanese empire. In the opinions of the British and Japanese, the "mistakes" he had made in connection with the Russian government in 1885 were simply too serious to be forgotten and forgiven.

These hindsight interpretations of von Möllendorff's accomplishments, objectives, ideology, personality, and even of his "empty" reentry into Korea in 1888 completed, a careful analysis directed toward what he should have done in trying to achieve his ultimate goal of strengthening and maintaining the political independence and integrity of Korea is in order. In retrospect, there are two actions that von Möllendorff should have attempted. First he should have tried to establish direct contact with Czar Alexander III. Since he was vice minister of the Korean Foreign Office as well as a trusted adviser to King Kojong and thus occupied what he himself described as "the most powerful position in East Asia," and since he enjoyed the tacit approval of the king, he should have visited St. Petersburg and tried to negotiate with the Czar or with the Czar's Foreign Minister directly rather than intriguing with Russian diplomats in Tokyo. However, his mission would still have failed for the reasons explained in this study. On the other hand, even had the mission succeeded, the implementation of such a thorny agreement would have met with too much opposition both from within and without Korea. If the pro-Kojong and pro-Möllendorff forces had been able to put the agreement into practice, Korea would not have benefited appreciably from Russian aid, simply because Russia was at that time incapable of providing what Korea needed. By negotiating with Czar directly, however, von Möllendorff could have at least added some dignity and importance to his and the king's position.

Second and most important of all, in view of the numerous proposals, made by people in responsible positions, for the internationalization of Korea, and also in view of the Tientsin Convention of 1885 providing an equal footing to both Japan and China, von Möllendorff would have had a feasible opportunity for working out some kind of neutralization for the status of Korea. After all, the neutralization of Korea was one of his earlier choices, and he had talked about it to the British representative in Korea. Rather than secretly pursuing a course that neither China, Japan, the United States, nor England would consent to, he should have attempted openly and with dignity to persuade the Korean king and his leaders to search for a policy effecting the neutralization of Korea. Most likely, China would not have readily agreed to the neutralization of Korea, inasmuch as its strategy in the mid-1880s was preponderantly one of dominating Korea in the name of suzerain-dependency relations. Yet the idea of Korean neutralization would have been notable and worthwhile enough to be tried by himself and by Kojong. Moreover, by diplomatically pursuing a course aimed at the neutralization of Korea in cooperation with the other treaty powers, von Möllendorff would have left an inspiring imprint upon the minds of the Korean king and leaders both then and thereafter. Inspired by von Möllendorff's precedent, the Korean leaders might, therefore, have vigorously sought and pursued the neutralization of Korea at a later time.

In fact, in the 1890s and early 1900s, several interesting proposals were made by various powers for the neutralization or joint guarantee—or even the territorial division—of Korea. Unfortunately, however, the powers, in proposing such ideas, were doing so in order to check the influence of their rivals rather than as a means for maintaining peace and tranquility in the peninsula. Therefore, as soon as the balance of power would shift in their favor, they would simply drop the idea. As for the influential Korean leaders in the 1880s and 1890s, they were not particularly interested in the idea of neutralizing their country and so never cared to learn how to play a dynamic, vigorous, and constructive role in its neutralization. To be sure, a few leaders—such as Ŏ Yun-jung, Kim Hong-jip, and Yu Kil-chun —did advocate or propose the neutralization of their country; but they were not influential enough to have any positive and significant effect on the course of foreign policy. As for the king, as this study shows, he was eager to form an alliance with a senior partner (a traditional elder brother) who would protect his kingdom and aid in modernizaing it. Thus, he was interested in a bilateral alliance with the United States, Japan, or Russia rather than in the neutralization of his country by the great powers.

Both Korea's conclusion of a bilateral alliance with another powerful nation and Korea's neutralization guaranteed by international arrangement in the 1880s would have been difficult tasks to undertake in view of the conflicting interests of the powers. Nonetheless, between these two possibilities the idea of neutralization of his kingdom might have served Kojong better. And probably that was the approach King Kojong and his advisers should have pursued rather than striving to obtain a new elder brother. But unfortunately for his kindom and people, Kojong failed to seek the neutralization idea in the 1880s and 1890s.

After 1900 and especially on the eve of the Russo-Japanese War of 1904 and 1905, the Korean government became belatedly interested in neutralizing its country and publicly declared neutrality; but by then it was too late, since two of the most important powers—first Great Britain and then the United States—had already consented to the Japanese domination of Korea. Of course, von Möllendorff should not be held responsible for all of these consequences. But the significant point is this: in the 1880s, when Korea became a member of the international community and was trying to learn modern international rules and power politics, von Möllendorff could have played a more positive and enlightening role in Korean politics, thereby inspiring and influencing Korean leaders to generate constructive, practical, feasible, and appealing ideas for the solution of the foreign policy problems of their country.

In hindsight, it could be argued that three foreigners—Li, Foote, and von Möllendorff, who were probably the most influential foreigners affecting King Kojong in the early 1880s—all gave misguided or misdirected advice to the monarch. Li demanded that Korea behave like a good old tributary to China—in fact, more like a modern day colony—despite (and contrary to) the spirit and letter of the treaties that Korea had concluded with Japan and the United States, which he himself not only initiated but negotiated for Korea. Foote delighted Kojong with the misperception that the United States was a benevolent and moralistic country that usually took sides with weak nations against the strong, regardless of American national interests or any security issues involved. Von Möllendorff advised King Kojong to have his government conclude a secret treaty with Russia, first engaging Russian military instructors, and only afterwards to worry about the repercussions and consequences of such a treaty. All three suggestions eventually proved less than beneficial for the interests of Korea.

After von Möllendorff had left Korea in 1885, Li continued his imperialistic policy toward Korea, which plunged China into a war with Japan in 1894. Eventually compelled to sign the humiliating Treaty of Shimonoseki of 1895 following the Sino-Japanese War, Li only then bitterly realized how China's aggressive and imperialistic policy toward Korea in the 1880s and early 1890s was responsible for its disastrous defeat in 1895. Because he was, in part, identified with and held responsible for China's defeat at the hands of the Japanese, Li was not permitted to play a prominent role after 1895. Ironically, he died the same year that von Möllendorff died, 1901. To be sure, there was no guarantee that Korea would have become a strong and prosperous buffer state if China, after 1882, had let it alone or treated it as a sovereign and independent nation. Nonetheless, in view of the fact that China's policy of tight control of Korea contributed significantly to its retardation and led to the Sino-Japanese War, and in light of the possibility that a noninterventionist policy in the peninsula on the part of China might have helped the kingdom become stable—and therefore would have prevented the tragic war (for China as well as Korea)—China's new imperialism in and toward Korea in the 1880s and early 1890s cannot escape condemnation.

As for Kojong's pro-Russian posture, even after the fiasco of the 1886 pro-Russian plot, he held firm to his faith in Russia and kept close relations with Russian minister Waeber, although he did not make, because of the presence and watchful eyes of Resident Yüan, another request to Imperial Russia to become the protective ally of his kingdom vis-à-vis China. After the elimination of China from Korea following the Sino-Japanese War of 1894 and 1895, Japan became the most influential power in the peninsula, but not all by itself. The Russian government began to struggle for supremacy in Korea vis-à-vis Japan. Frustrated and threatened by Japanese aggression and misconduct, worse than that of the Chinese, Kojong sought Russian protection in 1896 and thereafter. But the Russians were unable to compete against the Japanese and, by 1905, were finally driven out of Korea by the Japanese. In the case of Foote's American government, before, during, and after the Russo-Japanese War of 1904 and 1905, President Theodore Roosevelt not only supported the Japanese but actually encouraged them to take over Korea, to the bitter disappointment of Emperor Kojong and his people.

Ultimately, Korea, beset by a host of both domestic and foreign crises, became no more than a pawn in the game of power politics. That game would only end in 1910 with Japan's complete absorption of the once-proud peninsula kingdom.

# ABBREVIATIONS USED IN NOTES

| | |
|---|---|
| Allen Papers | Horace N. Allen Papers |
| *BFSP* | Great Britain. *British and Foreign State Papers* |
| *CJCC* | Wang Chung-chi. *Chung-Jih chang-cheng* [Sino-Japanese war] |
| *CKS* | Itō Hirobumi. *Chōsen koshō shiryō* [Materials on Korean intercourse] |
| *CKYJP* | Wang Yun-sheng. *Liu-shih nien lai Chung-kuo yu Jih-pen* [Sino-Japanese relations for the past sixty years] |
| *CSS* | Japan. *Chōsen shi* [History of Korea] |
| *CSSL* | China. *Ch'ing Kuang-hsü ch'ao Chung-Jih chiao-she shih-liao* [Documents on Sino-Japanese relations during the Kuang-hsü reign] |
| *CT* | China. Tsungli Yamen. *Chao-hsien tang* [Korean archives] |
| *CWS* | Korea. *Chosŏn Wangjo sillok* [Annals of the Yi dynasty] |
| *CWS, CS* | Korea. *Ch'ŏljong sillok* [Annals of King Ch'ŏljong] in *Chosŏn Wangjo sillok* |
| *CWS, HS* | Korea. *Hŏnjong sillok* [Annals of King Hŏnjong] in *Chosŏn Wangjo sillok* |
| *CWS, SS* | Korea. *Sunjo sillok* [Annals of King Sunjo] in *Chosŏn Wangjo sillok* |
| Denny Papers | Owen Nickerson Denny Papers |
| Dip. Desp., China | United States. Despatches from the United States Ministers to China |
| Dip. Desp., Japan | United States. Despatches from the United States Ministers to Japan |
| Dip. Desp., Korea | United States. Despatches from the United States Ministers to Korea |
| Dip. Inst., China | United States. Instructions of the U.S. Department of State: China |

| | |
|---|---|
| Dip. Inst., Japan | United States. Instructions of the U.S. Department of State: Japan |
| Dip. Inst., Korea | United States. Instructions of the U.S. Department of State: Korea |
| FO | Great Britain. Foreign Office, England |
| Foulk Papers, LC | George C. Foulk Papers, U.S. Library of Congress |
| Foulk Papers, NYPL | George C. Foulk Papers, New York Public Library |
| FR | United States. *Papers Relating to the Foreign Relations of the United States* |
| Hart Papers | Robert Hart Papers |
| HGSC | Yi Sŏn-gŭn. *Han'guksa, Ch'oegŭnse p'yŏn* [History of Korea: recent era] |
| HGSH | Yi Sŏn-gŭn. *Han'guksa, Hyŏndae p'yŏn* [History of Korea: modern era] |
| HH | Li Hung-chang. *Li Wen-chung-kung ch'üan-shu: Hai-chün han-kao* [Complete works of Li Hung-chang: Letters to Navy Office] |
| HTSL | China. *Ta-Ch'ing hui-tien shih-li* [Annals of the Ch'ing dynasty] |
| ISHK | Li Hung-chang. *Li Wen-chung-kung ch'üan-shu: I-shu han-kao* [Complete works of Li Hung-chang: Letters to the Tsungli Yamen] |
| ISN | Korea. *Ilsŏngnok* [Royal diary of the Yi dynasty] |
| IWSM, TC | China. *Ch'ou-pan i-wu shih-mo: T'ung-chih ch'ao* [The complete account of the management of barbarian affairs: the Tung-chih reign] |
| IWSM, TK | China. *Ch'ou-pan i-wu shih-mo: Tao-kuang ch'ao* [The complete account of the management of barbarian affairs: the Tao-kuang reign] |
| Japanese Archives | Japan. Japanese Ministry of Foreign Affairs, Archives. U.S. Library of Congress microfilm. SP 5. |
| KAR.I | McCune and Harrison. *Korean-American Relations* |
| KAR.II | Palmer. *Korean-American Relations* |
| KHCH | Korea. *Ku Hanmal choyak hwich'an* [Treaties of the late Yi dynasty] |
| KHSL | China. *Ch'ing-chi Chung-Jih-Han kuan-hsi shih-liao* [Documents on Sino-Japanese–Korean relations during the late Ch'ing period] |
| KHOM:Aan | Korea. *Ku Han'guk oegyo munsŏ: Aan* [Diplomatic documents of the late Yi dynasty: Russian archives] |
| KHOM:Ch'ŏngan | Korea. *Ku Han'guk oegyo munsŏ: Ch'ŏngan* [Diplomatic documents of the late Yi dynasty: Chinese archives] |
| KHOM:Ilan | Korea. *Ku Han'guk oegyo munsŏ: Ilan* [Diplomatic documents of the late Yi dynasty: Japanese archives] |
| KHOM:Mian | Korea. *Ku Han'guk oegyo munsŏ: Mian* [Diplomatic documents of the later Yi dynasty: American archives] |

| | |
|---|---|
| *KHOM: Tōgan* | Korea. *Ku Han'guk oegyo munsŏ: Tōgan* [Diplomatic documents of the late Yi dynasty: German archives] |
| *KHOM: Yŏngan* | Korea. *Ku Han'guk oegyo munsŏ: Yŏngan* [Diplomatic documents of the late Yi dynasty: British archives] |
| *KHOM:MKGY* | Korea. *Ku Hanmal oegyo munsŏ: Miguk kwang'gye p'yŏn* [Diplomatic documents of the late Yi dynasty: Relations with the United States] |
| *KNK* | Tabohashi Kiyoshi. *Kindai Nissen kankei no kenkyū* [A study of modern Japanese-Korean relations] |
| *KSDS* | Korea. *Kojong sidaesa* [History of the Kojong era] |
| *KS* | Korea. *Kojong sillok* [Annals of King Kojong] |
| *MCYR* | Hwang Hyŏn. *Maech'ŏn yarok* [Unofficial records of Korean history] |
| Merrill Papers | Henry F. Merrill Papers |
| Möllendorff's Diary | Ko Pyŏng-ik, "Mok In-dŏk ŭi sugi" |
| *NGB* | Japan. *Nihon gaikō bunsho* [Japanese diplomatic documents] |
| *NGSS* | Kim Chŏng-myŏng. *Nikkan gaikō shiryō shūsei* [Collection of sources of diplomatic relations between Japan and Korea] |
| *PLHK* | Li Hung-chang. *Li Wen-chung-kung ch'üan-shu: Peng-liao han-kao* [Complete works of Li Hung-chang: Letters to friends and colleagues] |
| *PT* | Korea. *Pibyŏnsa tŭngrok* [Records of the defense council] |
| Shufeldt Papers | Robert W. Shufeldt Papers |
| *SI* | Korea. *Sŭngjŏngwŏn ilgi* [Diary of the royal secretariat] |
| *Tien-kao* | Li Hung-chang. *Li Wen-chung-kung ch'üan-shu: Tien-kao* [Complete works of Li Hung-chang: Telegrams] |
| *TK* | Li Hung-chang. *Li Wen-chung-kung ch'üan-shu: Tsou-kao* [Complete works of Li Hung-chang: Memorials] |
| *TKC* | Chōsen sōtōkufu. *T'ongmun kwan chi* [Records of the Bureau of Interpreters] |
| *T'ongni* | Korea. *T'ongni kyosŏp t'ongsang samu amun ilgi* [Records of the Office of Foreign Affairs] |
| *WCSL* | Wang Yen-wei. *Ch'ing-chi wai-chiao shih-liao* [Sources of the diplomatic history toward the end of the Ch'ing dynasty] |

# NOTES

## Introduction

1. Rosalie von Möllendorff, who had been with her husband in China and also in Korea, wrote an interesting book about him—*P. G. von Möllendorff: Ein Lebensbild*—published thirty years after his death based upon her husband's diary and letters and also upon her recollections and memories of his activities. Understandably, she exhibited a highly subjective admiration for her husband and for his accomplishments in both China and Korea. Nevertheless, if the book is used in conjunction with other reliable sources, it becomes a very important resource. Professor Ko Pyŏng-ik translated a portion of Mrs. von Möllendorff's book into Korean; see his "Mok In-dŏk ŭi sugi" [Möllendorff's diary], *Chindan Hakpo* 24 (August 1963): 149–196. Ko's translation covers most of the parts dealing with the activities of von Möllendorff in and for Korea.

2. The following studies deal with the role von Möllendorff played in Korea: *KNK*, 2:1–18; *HGSC*, pp. 775–800; Pak Il-gŭn, *Kŭndae Han-Mi oegyosa* [A modern diplomatic history of America and Korea], pp. 378–389; Lo Key-hyŏn, *Han'guk oegyosa yŏn'gu* [Studies on Korean diplomatic history], pp. 18–31, 248–267; Ch'oe T'ae-ho, *Kaehang chŏn'gi ŭi Han'guk kwanse chedo* [The Korean tariff system in the early period of opening ports], pp. 227–232; Sin Ki-sŏk, *Hanmal oegyosa yŏn'gu* [Studies on diplomatic history of the late Yi dynasty], pp. 167–180; Ko Pyŏng-ik, *Tonga kyosŏpsa ŭi yŏn'gu* [Studies on the history of East Asian interrelations], pp. 436–463; Homer B. Hulbert, "Baron von Möllendorff," *Korean Review* 1 (1901): 245–252; Hosea B. Morse, *The International Relations of the Chinese Empire*, 3:10–13; Dalchoong Kim, "Korea's Quest for Reform and Diplomacy in the 1880's: With Special Reference to Chinese Intervention and Controls," pp. 263–270; Martina Deuchler, *Confucian Gentlemen and Barbarian Envoys: The Opening of Korea, 1875–1885*, pp. 158–176; Philip M. Woo, "The Historical Development of Korean Tariff and Customs Administration, 1875–1958," pp. 35–55; Walter Leifer, "Paul-Georg von Möllendorff—Scholar and

Statesman," *Transactions of the Royal Asiatic Society, Korea Branch* 57 (1982): 41–52; Seung Kwon Synn, "The Russo-Korean Relations in the 1880s," *Korea Journal* 20, no. 9 (September 1980): 28–33; Seung Kwon Synn, *The Russo-Japanese Rivalry over Korea, 1876–1904,* pp. 36–48; Frederick Foo Chien, *The Opening of Korea: A Study of Chinese Diplomacy, 1876–1885,* pp. 176–181; and George Alexander Lensen, *Balance of Intrigue: International Rivalry in Korea and Manchuria, 1884–1899,* 1:31–86. For the circumstances and background of the Korean employment of von Möllendorff, see Kim, "Korea's Quest," pp. 235–243; Ko Pyŏng-ik, "Mok In-dŏk ŭi kobingwa kŭ paegyŏng" [Background of von Möllendorff's employment], *Chindan Hakpo* 25/27 (December 1964): 225–244.

3. Lensen's coverage on von Möllendorff in *Balance of Intrigue* is more thorough than others. Unfortunately, however, his sections on von Möllendorff and on the Port Hamilton affair suffer from serious loopholes and flaws, because—except for a few insignificant Japanese-language materials—he used none of the Korean, Chinese, and Japanese sources and thereby failed to present the perspectives and viewpoints of those countries toward von Möllendorff's pro-Russian policy and toward British imperialism in Korea. In spite of the fact that his main concern is, as he states on page xvi, not only with the international diplomacy and intrigues of Russia and other Western powers but also with those of China, Korea, and Japan in the Korean peninsula and in Manchuria, and in spite of the fact that he did list some Korean and Japanese Archives in the bibliography, Lensen's study is based mainly on American, British, Russian, French, and Belgium sources. Consequently, for example, he was less than successful in analyzing the important roles played by the governments of Korea, Japan, and China in coping with the von Möllendorff-de Speyer intrigue and with the British seizure of Port Hamilton. Nonetheless, Lensen's two-volume work as a whole is a fine analysis of Russian policy toward Korea and Manchuria in the 1880s and 1890s and constitutes an important contribution to the studies of Russian-Asian relations.

4. For example, see Pak, *Kŭndae,* pp. 378–388; Yi Kwang-rin, "The Role of Foreign Military Instructors in the Later Period of the Yi Dynasty," p. 243; Hugh Seton-Watson, *The Decline of Imperial Russia, 1855–1914,* p. 198; Tyler Dennett, *Americans in Eastern Asia,* p. 48: A. L. Narochnitsky, *Kolonial Nai Politika Kapitalisticheskikh Derzh na Dalnem Vostoke, 1860–1895* [Colonial policy of capitalistic countries in the Far East, 1860–1895], p. 371.

5. John K. Fairbank, *The United States and China,* p. xiii.

6. In 1955, following the Communist victory in China and the end of the Korean War but before American involvement in the Vietnam War, Reischauer warned that there was "an urgent need for us in America to develop a sound and comprehensive Asian policy." He then outlined what ought to be done by American leaders and the public to give reality to such a policy. See Edwin O. Reischauer, *Wanted: An Asian Policy.*

7. While arguing that the Japanese takeover of Korea in 1910 was not the result of a long-planned plot, Conroy clearly suggests that a more modernized nation (Japan) might have had the mission of civilizing a less stable and less developed country (Korea) for the good of both, at least, during the age of

imperialism. See Hilary Conroy, *The Japanese Seizure of Korea, 1868–1910: A Study of Realism and Idealism in International Relations.*

## Chapter 1

1. The word *li* has several characters: *li* means the right principles, which govern everything in the universe; *li* in another character means proper ceremonies or property; *li* in still another character means material gains; and *li* in a yet different character is used as the family name of many Chinese, for example, Li Hung-chang. In this study *li* is used as "right principles." For the explanations of the different characters of *li*, see John K. Fairbank, "A Preliminary Framework," in *The Chinese World Order: Traditional China's Foreign Relations*, p. 6; see also Key-Hiuk Kim, *The Last Phase of the East Asian World Order: Korea, Japan, and the Chinese Empire, 1860–1882*, pp. 2–3; M. Frederick Nelson, *Korea and the Old Orders in Eastern Asia*, pp. 6, 13–14. Nelson is confused about the several different characters of *li;* see p. 6, especially, n. 6.

2. Neo-Confucianism is the reinterpretation and redefinition of Confucianism by the School of Chu Hsi of the late Sung dynasty (A.D. 907–1126). After Confucianism was eclipsed by Buddhism during the T'ang dynasty (618–905), it was reinvigorated in the late Sung and especially during the Ming dynasty (1368–1644). For the study of suzerain-dependency relations between Ming China and Yi Korea, see Sin Sŏk-ho, "Chosŏn wangjo kaeguk tangsi ŭi tae-Myŏng kwan'ge" [Relations with the Ming at the time of founding the Yi dynasty], *Kuksasang ŭi chemunje* 1 (1959): 93–134; Hugh D. Walker, "The Yi-Ming Rapprochment"; Kim Yong-gi, "Chosŏn ch'ogi ŭi tae-Myŏng chogong kwan'gye ko" [A study of tributary relations with the Ming in the early Yi period], *Pusandae nonmunjip* 14 (1972): 131–182; Chŏn Hae-jong, *Han-Chung kwan'gyesa yŏn'gu* [Study of the Sino-Korean relations], pp. 50–54; Tieh-min Ch'en, "The Sino-Japanese War, 1894–1895: Its Origin, Development, and Diplomatic Background," pp. 11–12.

3. For the stormy relations between Yi Korea and the Manchus during the early seventeenth century, see Chŏn, *Han-Chung*, pp. 50–54; Yi Pyŏng-do, "Kwanghaegun ŭi tae-Hugŭm chŏngch'aek" [Prince Kwanghae's policy toward the Manchus], *Kuksasang ŭi chemunje* 1 (1959): 135–175; Inaba Iwakichi, *Kōkaikun jidai no Man-Sen kankei* [Manchu-Korean relations during Prince Kwanghae's reign]; Chang Ts'un-wu, "Ch'ing-Han kuan-hsi, 1636–1644" [Ch'ing-Korean relations, 1636–1644], *Ku-kung wen-hsien* 4, no. 1 (December 1972): 15–37; 4, no. 2 (March 1973): 15–35; Na Man-gap, *Pyŏngja rok* [Record on Manchu invasion of 1636]; Edward Harper Parker, "The Manchu Relations with Corea," *Transactions of the Royal Asiatic Society, Japan Branch* 15 (1887): 93–95.

4. Chun Hae-jong (Chŏn Hae-jong), "Sino-Korean Tributary Relations during the Ch'ing Period," pp. 90–96; Kim Sŏng-ch'il, "Yŏnhaeng sogo: Cho-Chung kyosŏp ŭi ilgu" [A short study of missions to Peking: an aspect of Korean-Chinese relations], *Yŏksa Hakpo* 12 (May 1960): 7–13.

5. Kim, "Yŏnhaeng sogo," 27–46; Chun, "Sino-Korean Tributary Relations," pp. 107–109; George M. McCune, "Korean Relations with China and Japan, 1800–1864," pp. 96–123; Chu Djang, "Chinese Suzerainty: A Study of Diplomatic Relations Between China and her Vassal States, 1870–1895," pp. 31–37.

6. *ISN,* 1858.2.15; *CSS,* pt. 6, 3:517, 543.

7. *HGSC,* pp. 151–163. For studies on the Taewŏn'gun period, see Paek Chong-gi, *Han'guk Kŭndaesa yŏn'gu* [Studies on Korean recent history], pp. 17–58. See also Ching Young Choe, *The Rule of the Taewŏn'gun, 1864–1873: Restoration in Yi Korea;* James B. Palais, *Politics and Policy in Traditional Korea,* pp. 1–201; Lee Sun-keun (Yi Sŏn-gŭn), "Some Lesser-Known Facts about Taewongun and His Foreign Policy," *Transactions of the Royal Asiatic Society, Korea Branch* 39 (1962): 23–46; Soo Bock Choi, "Political Dynamics in Hermit Korea: The Rise of Royal Power in the Decade of the Taewongun, 1864–1873"; Gergory Henderson, *Korea: The Politics of the Vortex,* pp. 60–65. For an interesting analysis of the various interpretations on the contributions made by the Taewŏn'gun, see Palais, *Politics and Policy,* pp. 2–4.

8. For the Taewŏn'gun's anti-Western and anti-Japanese attitude and policy, see Kim, *Last Phase,* 46–47, 118–119, 247–248; Palais, *Politics and Policy,* pp. 177–179, 262–263, 270–271; Choe, *Rule of the Taewŏn'gun,* pp. 106–108, 139–150; Kikuchi Kenjō, *Taiinkun den, fu: Ōhi no isshō* [Life of the Taewŏn'gun, with supplement: life of the queen]; *HGSC,* pp. 208–340; Han Woo-keun, *The History of Korea,* pp. 361–370.

9. *PT,* 1855.6.2, 1866.5.23; *ISN,* 1866.5.17/22; *IWSM, TC,* 12:24b–25; *FR,* 1867.1:414–416, 1871.133–135; Kim Wŏn-mo, *Kŭndae Han-Mi kyosŏpsa* [The recent history of Korean-American relations], pp. 88–97, 101–109; Pak Il-gŭn, *Mi'guk ŭi kae'guk chŏngch'aek kwa Han-Mi oegyo kwan'gye* [American open door policy and Korean-American diplomatic relations], pp. 16–19; Earl Swisher, "The Adventure of Four Americans in Korea and Peking in 1855," *Pacific Historical Review* 21 (August 1952): 239–241; Earl Swisher, ed., *China's Management of the American Barbarians: A Study of Sino-American Relations, 1841–1861, with Documents,* pp. 308–309; Kim Wŏn-mo, "Ch'ogi Han-Mi kyosŏp ŭi chŏn'gye, 1852–66" [American contacts with Korea: early Korean-American relations, 1852–66], *Tan'guk taehakkyo nonmunjip* 10 (December 1977): 18–20. On another similar incident that took place in March 1866, see *ISN* and *KS,* 1866.2.25.

10. *CWS, SS,* 32:27b–30b; see also Pak Il-gŭn, *Kŭndae Han-Mi oegyosa* [A modern diplomatic history of America and Korea], pp. 12–14.

11. *CWS, SS,* 12:5a–b.

12. *IWSM, TC,* 47:25b–26b. For Korean immigration into Siberia before and after 1860, see Choe, *Rule of the Taewŏn'gun,* pp. 83–90, and Kim, *Last Phase,* pp. 44–45. Kim Tong-jin, "Chae-Ro tongp'o ŭi kwakŏ hyŏnjae" [The past and the present of our compatriots in Russia], *Shin tong-a* no. 9 (September 1932): 21–29.

13. For Korean persecution of native converts and French priests during the eighteenth and nineteenth centuries, see Yamaguchi Masayuki, *Chōsen Seikyō shi: Chōsen Kirisutokyō no bunkashiteki kenkyū* [A history of Christianity in Korea: a cultural historical study of Korean Christianity]; Yu Hong-nyŏl, *Kojong ch'iha ŭi*

*Sŏhak sunan ŭi yŏn'gu* [A study of Christian ordeals under the rule of King Kojong]; Ch'oe Sŏg-u, "Pyŏng'in yang'yo sogo" [A short study of the 1866 Western invasion], *Yŏksa Hakpo* 30 (April 1966): 108–112; W. J. Kang, "Early Korean Contact with Christianity and Korean Response," pp. 44–46; Yi Sangbaek, *Han'guksa: Kŭnse hugi p'yŏn* [History of Korea: late modern period], pp. 380–392; and Charles Dallet, *Histoire de l'église de Corée.*

14. For instance, see *IWSM, TC,* 42–54b–55a.

15. Ibid. 42:54b–55a, 44–12b–14a; *ISN* and *KS,* 1866.7.8.

16. Mary C. Wright, "The Adaptability of Ch'ing Diplomacy: The Case of Korea," *Journal of Asian Studies* 17 (May 1958): 363–366, 368–369, 381.

17. For Bellonet's letter to Prince Kung, see *IWSM, TC,* 43:54a–b; *FR,* 1867, pt. 1, p. 420. Prince Kung's letter to Bellonet is in *IWSM, TC,* 42:54b–55a; *FR* 1867, pt. 1, p. 421.

18. For a detailed military account of this war between the French and the Koreans, see *HGSC,* 246–274; Yur-Bok Lee, *Diplomatic Relations between the United States and Korea, 1866–1887,* pp. 23–25; Choe, *Rule of the Taewŏn'gun,* pp. 91–108; Soo Bock Choi, "Korea's Response to America and France in the Decade of the Taewŏn'gun, 1864–1873," pp. 111–116; Choi, "Political Dynamics in Hermit Korea," pp. 154–168.

19. For the Korean account of the incident, see *ISN,* 1866.7.27; *KS,* 1866.7.27. For the American account, see *FR,* 1867, pt. 1, pp. 427–430, and 1871, pp. 130–145. See also U.S. *Congressional Records,* 45th Cong., 2nd sess., April 17, 1878, pp. 2600–2605; E. M. Cable, "The United States–Korean Relations, 1866–1871," *Transactions of the Royal Asiatic Society, Korea Branch* 28 (1938): 11–62.

20. *IWSM, TC,* 57:25–28; *FR,* 1867, pt. 1, pp. 426, 545–546; Cable, "The United States–Korean Relations," p. 34.

21. *ISN,* 1866.11.5; *IWSM, TC.,* 45:10b–13b, 47:3.

22. Wright, "Adaptability of Ch'ing Diplomacy," pp. 363–366, 368–369, 381. The sources Wright used in her study (such as *IWSM, TC*) show no evidence to support her thesis that in the 1860s China "advised" or "suggested" that Korea enter into treaty relations with Western powers by accepting modern international relations. Beginning in 1874, however, China not only advised but also urged Korea to come to terms with Japan and Western nations; see *IWSM, TC,* 94:47a–b.

23. *FR,* 1867, pt. 1, p. 428.

24. Choe, *Rule of the Taewŏn'gun,* p. 115; Tyler Dennett, *Americans in Eastern Asia,* pp. 148–149.

25. A. L. Narochnitsky, *Kolonial Nai Politika Kapitalisticheskikh Derzh na Dalnem Vostoke,* p. 152; B. D. Pak, *Rossia i Korea* [Russia and Korea], p. 46.

26. For the French difficulties in Vietnam in the 1860s, see Henry McAleavy, *Black Flags in Vietnam: The Story of a Chinese Intervention,* pp. 75–81; John F. Cady, *Southeast Asia: Its Historical Development,* pp. 419–423; Lloyd E. Eastman, *Throne and Mandarins: China's Search for a Policy During the Sino-French Controversy, 1880–1885,* pp. 31–34.

27. *FR,* 1870, pp. 334–335. The Board of Rites forwarded Low's letter to Korea with a supplementary letter of its own explaining that Korea was "free to

make whatever decision it deemed appropriate." See *IWSM, TC,* 80:12a–13b. The Low-Rodgers squadron consisted of five ships and 1,200 men.

28. Lee, *Diplomatic Relations,* pp. 26–30; Choe, *Rule of the Taewŏn'gun,* pp. 127–133; Kim, *Last Phase,* pp. 51–62; Choi, "Korea's Response," pp. 117–126.

29. Choe, *Rule of the Taewŏn'gun,* p. 132.

30. Low to Fish, June 20, 1871, No. 35, Dip. Desp., China.

31. *ISN,* 1871.4.20 and 25.

32. *IWSM, TC,* 82:31b.

33. *NGB,* 10:316–318; *IWSM, TC,* 98:16a–17b.

34. *HGSC,* pp. 342–358; Choe, *Rule of the Taewŏn'gun,* pp. 166–176; Palais, *Politics and Policy,* pp. 176–202; Kim, *Last Phase,* pp. 207–209. Some historians characterize the Mins (relatives of Queen Min) as "the open-minded faction" and credit them with opening Korea to Japan in 1876. See Hō Takushu, *Meiji shoki Nis-sen kankei no kenkyū* [Japanese-Korean relations in the early Meiji period], pp. 58–59; and Han, *History of Korea,* pp. 372–375. In actuality, however, in the 1870s the Mins and their allies—Confucian literati—were as isolationistic as the Taewŏn'gun. They were opposed to the Taewŏn'gun in domestic policies, not in foreign policy.

35. *ISN,* 1872.12.26.

36. *IWSM, TC,* 94:37a–b.

37. The secret memorandum was drafted by the Tsungli Yamen and sent to Korea by the Board of Rites. It reached Seoul on August 6, 1874. It read in part: "After the Japanese soldiers withdraw from Formosa they probably will encroach upon Korea with the remaining forces in Nagasaki. . . . If France and the United States join in a Japanese expedition, it is obvious that Korea will not be able to resist them." See *KS* and *ISN,* 1874.6.25; *CSS,* pt. 6, 4:333–334.

38. For various Japanese missions to Korea in the 1860s and early 1870s, see Choe, *Rule of the Taewŏn'gun,* pp. 139–165; Kim, *Last Phase,* pp. 110–116; Palais, *Politics and Policy,* pp. 21–22.

39. For the discussion of the reasons for Korea's rejection of the Japanese overture, see *ISN,* 1870.5.12; *KHSL,* 2:126; Kim Yun-sik, *Ŭmch'ongsa* [Diary of Kim Yun-sik], pp. 79–80; *KNK,* 1:156–160; Kim, *Last Phase,* pp. 122–123. The Korean authority argues that if the Japanese wished to do business with Korea continuously, then they had to obey the Korean law. If the Japanese did things against the law, "they must be contained." See *NGB,* 6:252, 256–258, 280–283.

40. *NGB,* 9:690–697; *KNK,* 1:133–197.

41. Ōkubo Toshimichi, ed., *Ōkubo Toshimichi bunshō* [Ōkubo Toshimich documents], 5:53–63; Hilary Conroy, *Japanese Seizure of Korea, 1868–1910,* pp. 75–77.

42. See *KS,* 1876.1.13; *CSS,* pt. 6, 4:389–390; *KNK,* 1:516–518. Mori told Li that if Korea was not to receive a Japanese mission with courtesy, "Korea would bring incalculable calamity upon itself" (*CSSL,* 1:1–6). Li warned Mori that any Japanese aggression against Korea might be considered an affront to China. See *ISHK,* 4:34.

43. Two important Japanese specialists on Korea played a significant role in Ōkubo's gunboat diplomacy toward Korea. First, Moriyama Shigeru, who had been in Korea, recommended that since Korean leaders were frightened after learning of the Japanese victory in the Taiwan adventure, Japan should show "military strength to the Koreans" in order to change their traditional attitude toward Japan; see *KNK*, 1:393–395. Second, Hirotsu Koshin of the Japanese Foreign Office, who had also been in Korea on a fact-finding mission, proposed the dispatch of several warships to Korean waters under the pretext of a water survey; see *NGB*, 8:71–72.

44. For the vital role Kojong played for the conclusion of the treaty, see *KS*, 1876.1.25, and *ISN*, 1876.1.25. For the analysis of Kojong's role in behalf of the treaty, see Robert R. Swartout, Jr., *Mandarins, Gunboats, and Power Politics: Owen Nickerson Denny and the International Rivalries in Korea*, pp. 30–35; Martina Deuchler, *Confucian Gentlemen and Barbarian Envoys: The Opening of Korea, 1875–1885*, pp. 38–44. Some historians insist that Kojong proved to be weak and ineffective during this time; see Kim, *Last Phase*, pp. 243, 249, 289; Palais, *Politics and Policy*, pp. 4, 260, 252–271. The Taewŏn'gun might have felt free to oppose the treaty because he was in semiretirement and out of government at the time. Had he been in power, it would have been most difficult for him not to take China's strong advice.

45. The originals were signed in both Japanese and Chinese; see *KHCH*, 18:12–16. For the Japanese text, see *NGB*, 9:114–119; for the Chinese (and Korean) text, see *KS*, 1876.2.3; *PT*, 1876.2.3. For the English text, see *BFSP*, 67:530–533. Some historians attach no significance to the treaty; see Nelson, *Korea and the Old Orders*, p. 134; John W. Foster, *American Diplomacy in the Orient*, p. 321. For examinations of the historical significance of the treaty, see Conroy, *Japanese Seizure*, pp. 66–67; Chien, *Opening of Korea*, p. 195; Jae Schick Pae, "The Historical Background of the Development of International Law in Korea," p. 2; Palais, *Politics and Policy*, p. 284; Deuchler, *Confucian Gentlemen*, pp. 48–49; Tingfu Tsiang, "Sino-Japanese Diplomatic Relations, 1870–1894," *Chinese Social and Political Science Review* 17, no. 1 (April 1933): 60–61; T. C. Lin, "Li Hung-chang: His Korea Politics," *Chinese Social and Political Science Review* 19 (July 1935): 217; Shū-hsi Hsü, *China and Her Political Entity*, p. 109; Yŏng-ho Ch'oe, "Sino-Korean Relations, 1866–1876, Tributary Relationship to China," *Journal of Asiatic Studies* 9, no. 1 (March 1966): 178–181; Kim, *Last Phase*, pp. 252–255; *KNK*, 1:515–519.

46. *NGB*, 9:97–99; *KNK*, 1:472–491; Ch'oe T'ae-ho, *Kaehang Chŏn'gi ŭi Han'guk kwanse chedo* [The Korean tariff system in the early period of opening of ports], p. 15.

47. Frederick V. Dickens and Stanley Lane Poole, *The Life of Sir Harry Parkes*, 2:204. For similar comments on the treaty made by two prominent Korean historians, see Cho Ki-jun, "Kaehwagi Ilje ŭi kyŏngje ch'imnyak" [Economic aggression of Japanese imperialism during the period of enlightenment], pp. 2–3; and Ch'oe Jun, "Myŏng'chi chogi ŭi Ilbon Ŏlnon" [Japan's public debate at the beginning of the Meiji era], pp. 61–62.

48. Hatada Takashi, *A History of Korea*, p. 93. Shinobu Seisaburō insists that

the treaty "denied Korea's tributary status to China"; see his *Kindai Nihon gaikō shi* [Diplomatic history of modern Japan], p. 52.

49. Lin, "Li Hung-chang," pp. 278-279.

50. Yur-Bok Lee, *Establishment of a Korean Legation in the United States, 1887-1890: A Study of Conflict between Confucian World Order and Modern International Relations*, pp. 4, 27-28; Kim, *Last Phase*, p. 253.

51. Ŏ Yun-jung, *Chongjŏng yŏnp'yo* [Diary of Ŏ Yun-jung], pp. 122-127; Kim, *Ŭmch'ongsa*, p. 131.

52. Some Chinese leaders were in favor of war with Japan over the Ryūkyūs. Li argued, however, that in view of China's unpreparedness for a war against Japan, China should pursue "a cautious" policy in dealing with the Ryūkyūs, which he considered "insignificant" in any case. With regard to Korea, he strongly urged the Ch'ing court to devise and take necessary "ways and means for the security" of it. See *ISHK*, 8:1-5, 9:34.

53. Ibid., the Tsungli Yamen Letters, 1:49a.

54. Ying-shih Yu, *Trade and Expansion in Han China: A Study of Sino-Barbarian Economic Relations*, pp. 14-16. In June 1879 Ting Jih-ch'ang, the governor of Fukien, advocated that Korea enter into treaty relations with Western powers as a means of checking Japanese ambition; see *CSSL*, 1:31-32; Pao Tsun-peng, Li Ting-i, and Wu Hsiang-hsiang, eds. *Chungo-kuo chin-tai-shih lun-tsung* [A collection of writings on modern Chinese history], 6:163. British minister Wade gave a similar suggestion to China; see *CSSL*, 1:31-32.

55. Michael H. Hunt, *The Making of a Special Relationship: The United States and China to 1914*, chaps. 3 and 4.

56. By early 1880 many Chinese leaders considered the Board of Rites too ignorant of foreign affairs and too tradition-bound and felt that Li should be placed in charge of Korean affairs. From 1881 Viceroy Li was the official to whom the Chinese commissioner in Korea referred all matters concerning Korea. See the Tsungli Yamen's memorial in *CSSL*, 1:31b-32b; *WCSL*, 25:1-3; Tsiang, "Sino-Japanese Diplomatic Relations," p. 64.

57. *WCSL*, 16:14-17; *KHSL*, 2:366-369; *ISHK*, 11:42-45. Li presented the same kind of argument to Kim Yun-sik; see *ISHK*, 23:7b.

58. For the content of the booklet, see Kuksa p'yŏnch'an wiwŏnhoe, ed., *Susinsa kirok* [Records of envoys], pp. 160-171; *NGB*, 12:389-396; *CSS*, pt. 6, 4:538-542. For an analysis of the impact of the booklet on Kojong and his government, see Yi Sŏn-gŭn, "Kyŏngjin susinsa Kim Hong-jip kwa Hwang Chun-hŏn jŏ Chosŏn ch'aeknyak e kwanhan chae-kŏmt'o" [Re-evaluation of Susinsa Kim Hong-jip and Hwang Chu-hŏn's "A Policy for Korea"], *Tonga nonch'ong* 1 (1963): 254-259; Kim Si-t'ae, "Hwang Chun-hŏn ŭi Chosŏn ch'aeknyak i Hanmal Chŏngguk-e kkich'in yŏnghyang" [The impact of Hwang Chun-hŏn's "A Policy for Korea" on the Korean political situation], *Sach'ong* 8 (November 1963): 81-87; Cho Hang-nae, "Hwang Chun-hŏn ŭi Chosŏn ch'aeknyak e taehan kŏmt'o" [Evaluation of Hwang Chun-hŏn's "A Policy for Korea"], *Taegu-dae nonmun-jip* 3 (1963): 244-246; Cho Hang-nae, *Kaehanggi tae-il kwan'gyesa yŏn'gu* [A study of Korean-Japanese relations in the opening of Korea], pp. 81-102; Hō, *Meiji*, p. 361; Kim Yŏng-jak, *Kan-matsu*

*nashonarizumu no kenkyū* [A study of nationalism of the late Yi Korea], pp. 95–98. The conservative Korean Confucian scholars considered Huang's booklet as heresy; see *CSS*, pt. 6, 4:538–540.

59. *CSS*, pt. 6, 4:533; Deuchler, *Confucian Gentlemen*, pp. 90–92; Kim, *Last Phase*, pp. 308–309; Chien, *Opening of Korea*, pp. 74–75; William E. Griffis, *Corea: The Hermit Nation*, p. 431.

60. Viceroy Li and the Chinese emperor concurred that an imperial edict ordering the Korean king to conclude a treaty with the United States might be opposed and become a source of complaint by the American plenipotentiary; see *TK*, 42:37a–39a; Imperial edict to Li, January 23, 1882, *CSSL*, 2:45a.

61. Han U-gŭn, "Shufeldt chedok ŭi Han-Mi suho choyak kyosŏp ch'ujin yŏnyu e taehayŏ" [A study on the reasons for sending Commodore Shufeldt to open negotiations with Korea in 1880], *Chindan Hakpo* 24 (August 1963): 7–22; Robert W. Shufeldt, "The Opening of Korea: Admiral Shufeldt's Account of It," *Korean Repository* 1 (February 1892): 57–62; Frederick C. Drake, *The Empire of the Seas: A Biography of Rear Admiral Robert Wilson Shufeldt, USN*, pp. 108–109, 251–252.

62. American chargé Holcombe assisted Shufeldt, while Ma Chien-chung and Chou Fu, two of China's experts on international rules, helped Li. For the vitally important role that Li played in the negotiation of the Korean-American Treaty, see Chien, *Opening of Korea*, pp. 56–93; Lee, *Diplomatic Relations*, pp. 36–42; Deuchler, *Confucian Gentlemen*, pp. 113–122; Nelson, *Korea and the Old Orders*, pp. 135–151.

63. For the Chinese (Korean) and English text, see *KHCH*, 26:294–305. For the Chinese version, see *WCSL*, 27:13b–18b; *KHSL*, 2:611–616. For an American document, see *United States Statutes at Large*, 33:720–725.

64. Wagner writes that "the question of equal trade rights, for American citizens, an issue inseparable from that of Korea's independence, must have been the dominant factor in determining U.S. foreign policy goals at that point of time." See Edward W. Wagner, "The First Century," pp. 17–18; see also John Chay, "The First Three Decades of American-Korean Relations, 1882–1910: Reassessment and Reflections," pp. 20–21.

65. See *KHCH*, 26:295. Viceroy Li included this article in the treaty provision to use it as a check against Japanese and Russian ambitions in Korea. However, the Korean leaders felt that the article meant that the United States became an official ally to Korea against any aggressive power, including Japan, Russia, England, and even China; see also Wayne Patterson and Hilary Conroy, "Duality and Dominance: A Century of Korean-American Relations," pp. 2–3.

66. Robert R. Swartout, Jr., *Mandarins, Gunboats, and Power Politics: Owen Nickerson Denny and the International Rivalries in Korea*, pp. 34–35; Henry Chung, *The Oriental Policy of the United States*, p. 31; George A. McGrane, *Korea's Tragic Hours: The Closing Years of the Yi Dynasty*, p. 64; Kim Wŏn-mo, "American 'Good Offices' in Korea," *Journal of Social Sciences and Humanities* 41 (June 1975): 93–139; Young-ick Lew, "The Shufeldt Treaty and Early Korean-American Interaction, 1882–1905," p. 11.

67. For the Chinese text of the king's letter to President Arthur, see *CSSL,* 3:10–13. For the English text, see *FR,* 1888, pt. 2, pp. 255–256. For a somewhat different English translation, see Holcombe to Frelinghuysen, enc. 1, June 26, 1882, no. 133, Dip. Desp., China; China, Imperial Maritime Customs, *Treaties, Regulations, Etc. Between Corea and Other Powers, 1876–1889,* p. 52. Li and Shufeldt agreed that the letter would be dated and sent after the conclusion of the treaty, but Ma Chien-chung and Shufeldt later agreed to date the letter earlier; see Pae, "Historical Background," pp. 3–4; Chien, *Opening of Korea,* pp. 85–87; Dennett, *Americans in Eastern Asia,* pp. 46–64; Payson J. Treat, *Diplomatic Relations between the United States and Japan, 1853–1895,* 2:160.

68. Kim, *Ŭmch'ongsa,* pp. 106–197; *ISHK,* 12:8–9; *CSS,* pt. 6, 4:608; Ma Chien-chung, *Tung-hsing san-lu* [Records of three trips to Korea], p. 17.

69. *ISHK,* 15:19–20. Historians disagree on the importance of the Korean king's letter to the American president. Nelson attaches a great significance to the spirit and letter of this controversial letter; see his *Korea and the Old Orders,* pp. 145–149. Others claim that the letter was practically meaningless; see Dennett, *Americans in Eastern Asia,* pp. 459–464; Chien, *Opening of Korea,* pp. 92–93; Deuchler, *Confucian Gentlemen,* p. 127; Pak, *Mi'guk,* pp. 224–229. Actually, such a letter from the Korean king to President Arthur could constitute a reservation to the treaty to which it was attached; see Charles G. Fenwick, *International Law,* pp. 437–438. See also my *Establishment of a Korean Legation,* pp. 11–12, 38n. 82.

70. See Lee, *Diplomatic Relations,* pp. 163–172, and Lee, *Establishment of a Korean Legation,* pp. 5–20.

71. Bingham to Frelinghuysen, June 19, 1882, no. 1515, Dip. Desp., Japan. This dispatch included a newspaper clipping from the *Japan Daily Herald* expressing Japanese feelings against the treaty.

72. Japanese Archives, SP 5, 31–32.

73. Okudaira Takehiko, *Chōsen kaikoku kōshō shimatsu* [A complete account of the negotiations leading to the opening of Korea], pp. 145–148; Moo-Soo Kwon, "British Policy towards Korea, 1882–1910," pp. 76–81; Yung-Chung Kim, "Great Britain and Korea, 1883–1887," pp. 50–53. The text of the British-Korean Treaty is in *CSSL,* 3:20–23b; China, *Treaties, Regulations, Etc.,* pp. 53–61.

74. Okudaira, *Chōsen,* pp. 150–152.

75. *ISN,* 1882.4.12, 1882.4.22, 1882.5.7, 1882.5.10, 1882.5.15; *KHSL,* no. 434, p. 686, no. 435, p. 687; *CSSL,* 3:19b, 24b–30b; Ma, *Tung-hsing,* 1:23–32, 2:41–45, 50–52; Kim, *Ŭmch'ongsa,* pp. 137, 148–149, 159–161, 165–167; *CSS,* pt. 6, 4:613–619; *FO,* 17/897, Wade, (conf.), July 6, 1882, no. 51; *FO,* 17/915, Willes Report to the Secretary to the Admiralty, Nagasaki, June 9, 1882; Lee, *Diplomatic Relations,* pp. 56–57; Kwon, "British Policy," pp. 83–92; Kim, "Great Britain," pp. 59–80.

76. Foulk to Secretary of the Navy, enc., to Foote to Frelinghuysen, December 17, 1884, no. 128, Dip. Desp., Korea; *KAR,* 1:105. Yun Ch'i-ho, Foote's interpreter, cultivated close and amicable relations between Foote and King Kojong; see Yun Ch'i-ho, *Yun Ch'i-ho ilgi* [Diary of Yun Ch'i-ho], vol. 1, *passim;* Yi Kwang-rin (Lee Kwang-rin), "Early Relations: Conflicting Images," p. 68.

77. William F. Sands, "Korea and the Korean Emperior," *Century* 69 (1905): 582.

78. See Yur-Bok Lee, "Korean-American Diplomatic Relations, 1882–1902," pp. 15–20.

79. *KAR,* 1:3; Fred Harvey Harrington, *God, Mammon and the Japanese: Dr. Horace N. Allen and Korean-American Relations, 1884–1905,* p. 211. See also Lee, "Korean-American Diplomatic Relations," pp. 12–45.

80. Chun, "Sino-Korean Tributary Relations," pp. 90–111.

81. See Lee, *Establishment of a Korean Legation,* pp. 15–17.

82. The historians in the school of sinocentricism (with regard to Sino-Korean relations) insist that even after the conclusion of the Korean-Japanese Treaty of 1876 and the Korean-American Treaty of 1882 Korea remained a full-fledged vassal to China and that Korean relations with Japan and the United States must be interpreted only from the standpoint of sinocentricism.

83. Kim, *Last Phase,* p. 348.

84. *FR,* 1888, p. 437.

85. Ibid., 1887, pp. 222–223.

86. See Lloyd E. Eastman, "Ch'ing-i and Chinese Policy Formation during the Nineteenth Century," *Journal of Asian Studies* 24, no. 4 (August 1965): 604–608; Hao Yen-p'ing, "A Study of the Ch'ing-liu Tang: The 'Disinterested' Scholar-official Groups (1875–1884)," *Papers on China* 16 (December 1962): 40–43; Chang P'ei-lun, *Chien-yü ch'üan-chi* [Collected works of Chang P'ei-lun], 2:59–66.

87. Immanuel C. Y. Hsü, *The Ili Crisis: A Study of Sino-Russo Diplomacy, 1871–1881,* pp. 189–195.

88. At the time of Japanese annexation of the Ryūkyūs, Chang argued that if China would not defend the integrity of the islands against Japan, eventually the French would push into Annam, the British into Burma, and Russia into Korea and Manchuria. See *WCSL,* 24:1–3; *CSSL,* 2:11–12; Chang Chih-tung, *Chang Wen-hsiang-kung ch'üan-chi* [Complete Works of Chang Chih-tung], 3:22a–24b; Chang, *Chien-yü,* 1:68.

89. Wang Yun-sheng, ed., *Liu-shih nien lai Chung-kuo yu Jih-pen* [Sino-Japanese relations for the past sixty years], 1:207; *KNK,* 1:861–862; Samuel C. Chu, *Reformer in Modern China: Chang Chien, 1853–1926,* p. 15.

90. For some competent examinations of the causes and reasons for the riot, see Sin Kuk-chu, *Kŭndae Chosŏn oegyosa yŏn'gu* [Studies on modern diplomatic history of Korea], pp. 139–140; Kim, "Korea's Quest," pp. 136–137; Kwŏn Sŏk-pong, "Imo gunbyŏn," [The 1882 soldiers' revolt], 16:392–441; *SI,* 1882.6.9; *CSS,* pt. 6, 4:622; *KNK,* 1:770–771; *NGB,* 15:153.

91. *ISN,* 1882.6.10/11/12/13/14/15. Some Mins, including Min Kyŏm-ho, were murdered.

92. *HGSC,* pp. 479–487; *ISN,* 1882.6.9/10/11/12; *KHSL,* 2:734–735.

93. The role the Taewŏn'gun played in the revolt has been controversial. Some insist that he instigated it; see Wang Hsin-chung, *Chung-Jih chia-wu chang-cheng chih wai-chiao pei-ching* [Diplomatic background of the Sino-Japanese War], pp. 30–32. Actually, he did not initiate the riot. When the rioters appealed to

him, he was hesitant at first to take over the government; however, soon he decided to lead them and take advantage of the situation by persuading his terribly frightened son, Kojong, to consent to his own return to power in order to subdue the riot. See *ISN,* 1882.6.10/11; *KNK,* 1:773; Sin Kuk-chu, *Kindai Chōsen gaikō shi kenkyū* [Studies in diplomatic history of modern Korea], pp. 121–122; Yi Pyŏng-do, *Han'guksa taekwan* [A general history of Korea], pp. 484–485.

94. *KNK,* 1:773; *NGB,* 15:216–221; *CJCC,* 2:452–457. Before Hanabusa decided to abandon the legation building, he set it afire along with some secret papers; see ibid.

95. *NGB,* 15:226–227; *KNK,* 1:803–805. The Japanese forces consisted of one infantry battalion, four warships, and three transports. The dispatch of the Japanese troops and warships was "only to protect residents and not to open fire." See *NGB,* 15:160–162, 229–230.

96. Hanabusa was instructed in writing to make the following demands: (1) an apology from the Korean government; (2) punishment of the criminals; (3) pensions for the victims; (4) indemnity; (5) the stationing of a guard in the Japanese legation for five years; and (6) an increase in the number of open ports. He was given three oral instructions: (1) cession of either Kŏje Island or Ullŭng Island, if Hanabusa discovered that the Korean government should bear a responsibility for the riot; (2) punishment of government officials involved if the rebels had been protected by them; and (3) compulsory compensation as Hanabusa saw fit; see *NGB,* 15:228–229; *CSS,* pt. 6, 4:627–628; *CJCC,* 2:424–425; Wang, *Chung-Jih chia-wu,* pp. 35–36. For the Taewon'gun's rejection of these demands, see *ISHK,* 12:34b–35b; Wang, *Chung-Jih chia-wu,* p. 46.

97. Some Korean officials such as Kim Yun-sik and Ŏ Yun-jung, who were in Tientsin at the time, proposed that China send troops and warships to Korea to suppress the mutiny, to prevent the Japanese government from taking advantage of the situation, and also to have the Taewŏn'gun condemned to death by an order from Queen Dowager Cho. See *KHSL,* 2:769–772; Kim, *Ŭmch'ongsa,* pp. 180–183; Hsüeh Fu-ch'eng, *Hsüeh Fu-ch'eng ch'üan-chi* [Complete works of Hsüeh Fu-ch'eng], 1:2, 33a–35b; *CJCC,* 2:225–227; Ma, *Tung-hsing,* pp. 56–57; *KHSL,* 3:798–804.

98. Governor Chang proposed the dispatch of Chinese warships and troops to Korea on the basis of the recommendation made by Chinese minister Li Shuchang in Tokyo. Ting and Ma arrived in Korea on August 10, a day after the arrival of the Japanese forces. On August 17, China sent six battalions under Wu Chang-ch'ing and Yüan Shih-k'ai, Wu's aide. See *KHSL,* 2:748–750; *CJCC,* 2:215–216; Wang, *Chung-Jih chia-wu,* pp. 39–40.

99. *KSDS,* 2:389, 402; Lin Ming-te, *Yüan Shih-k'ai yü Chao-hsien* [Yüan Shih-k'ai and Korea], pp. 30–33, 42; Sin Ki-sŏk, *Hanmal oegyosa yŏn'gu* [Studies on diplomatic history of the late Yi dynasty], pp. 100–101.

100. Dong Jae Yim (Dong-jae Yim), "The Abduction of the Taewŏn'gun: 1882," *Papers on China* 21 (February 1968): 99–130; Wang, *Chung-Jih chia-wu,* pp. 32–45.

101. *CSSL,* 3:44–45; *NGB,* 15–245.

102. *ISN,* 1882.7.15.

103. *ISN* and *SI,* 1882.7.14; *CSS,* pp. 641–642; *CJCC,* 2:205–206.

104. *CJCC,* 2:205.

105. For the provisions of the treaty and Additional Convention, see *NGB,* 15:200–202; *KHOM: Ilan,* no. 95, pp. 68–69; *CSS,* pt. 6, 4:641–642; Carnegie Endowment for International Peace, Division of International Law, *Korea: Treaties and Agreements,* pp. 1–6.

106. For a different comment on the treaty, see Treat, *Diplomatic Relations,* 2:165.

107. *WCSL,* 29:8–9; *CSSL,* 4:5–6; *KNK,* 1:858; *CSS,* pp. 663–664.

108. *CSSL,* 6:18–20; *WCSL,* 41:3.

109. *ISHK,* 13:38–39.

110. Ibid. 13:39–41.

111. Chou Fu, *Chou Ch'iao-shen-kung ch'üan-chi* [Complete works of Chou Fu], 2:1–2. For the Chinese text of the regulations, see *CSSL,* 5:9b–11b. For the English text, see *FR,* 1884, pp. 173–176; China, Imperial Maritime Customs, ed., *Treaties, Conventions, Etc., Between China and Foreign States,* 2:1521–1527.

112. In November 1883 the Korean government dispatched Kim Sŏn-gŭn, the minister of the Board of Works, to Tientsin as a Korean trade commissioner to supervise the activities of Korean merchants and traders there. In February 1884, Kim was replaced by Nam Chŏng-ch'ŏl. See *ISN* and *SI,* 1883.10.3, 1884.1.27.

113. Foote to Frelinghuysen, July 13, 1883, no. 14, Dip. Desp., Korea.

114. Unfortunately, there is no official record of the conversation on the subject of American advisers that took place between the Korean delegates and Frelinghuysen. But the subject was retrospectively discussed by Ensign George C. Foulk, the Korean mission's official escort. See Foote to Frelinghuysen, Sept. 10, 1884, no. 109, Dip. Desp., Korea; Foulk to Bayard, Dec. 1, 1885, no. 257, Dip. Desp., Korea; Foulk to Shufeldt, Oct. 4, 1886, Shufeldt Papers. See also Harold J. Noble, "The Korean Mission to the United States in 1883, the First Embassy sent by Korea to an Occidental Nation," *Transactions of the Royal Asiatic Society, Korea Branch* 18 (1929): 14; Gary Dean Walter, "The Korean Special Mission to the United States," *Journal of Korean Studies* 1, no. 1 (1960): 106. According to Tyler Dennett, however, as far as Frelinghuysen was concerned, most of the oral exchanges concerning the advisers "appear to have been intended merely as pleasant conversation . . . and he appears to have assured the Koreans that the Americans could be only too happy to oblige" without meaning to make any kind of formal commitment. See Tyler Dennett, "Early American Policy in Korea, 1883–7," *Political Science Quarterly* 38 (March 1923): 87. But the Koreans apparently took the conversation much more seriously than the Americans.

115. Foulk to Bayard, December 1, 1885, no. 257, Dip. Desp., Korea.

116. Foote to Frelinghuysen, October 19, 1883, (conf.), no. 32, September 3, 1884., no. 105, September 10, 1884, no. 109, September 17, 1884, no. 117, Dip. Desp., Korea.

117. Frelinghuysen to Foote, November 6, 1884, no. 14, Dip. Inst., Korea.
118. Ibid.
119. United States Congress, *House Executive Documents,* 163, 48th Cong., 2nd Sess., pp. 1884–1885; Lee, *Diplomatic Relations,* p. 69. Actually, the proposed measure was brought before the Senate and was referred to the Committee on Military Affairs. It was designated a Senate Resolution and read twice by title, but no action was taken. See Frelinghuysen to the President, January 19, 1885, in *Congressional Record,* 48th Cong., 2nd Sess., pp. 1106, 1142, 2175; *Congressional Record,* 49th Cong., 1st Sess., p. 1721; Bayard to Foulk, June 18, 1885, no. 184, Dip. Inst., Korea.
120. *KHOM; MKGY,* p. 89; Foote to Frelinghuysen, September 3, 1884, no. 105, September 17, 1884, no. 110, Dip. Desp., Korea; Frelinghuysen to Foote, March 9, 1883, no. 3, Dip. Inst., Korea; *FR,* 1885, p. 366; Percival Lowell to Shufeldt, January 24, 1884, and Foulk to Shufeldt, October 4, 1886, Shufeldt Papers.
121. Foote to Frelinghuysen, November 15, 1884, no. 124, Dip. Desp., Korea.
122. *KAR,* 1:14; Fred Harvey Harrington, "An American View of Korean-American Relations, 1882–1905," pp. 55–56.


## Chapter 2

1. *CSSL,* 4:35; *ISHK,* 13:37; *WCSL,* 30:10–11; Kim Yun-sik, *Ŭmch'ongsa,* pp. 142–182, 202, 206; Choe T'ae-ho, *Kaehang chŏn'gi ŭi Han'guk kwanse chedo,* pp. 147–149; Ko Pyŏng-ik, "Mok In-dŏk ŭi kobinggwa kŭ paegyŏng," pp. 227–232; Ko Pyŏng-ik, *Tonga kyosŏpsa ŭi yŏn'gu,* p. 443.
2. *WCSL,* 30:10–11; Kim, *Ŭmch'ongsa,* p. 206.
3. Rosalie von Möllendorff, *P. G. von Möllendorff: Ein Lebensbild,* p. 3.
4. Ibid., p. 4.
5. More important scholarly works by von Möllendorff are: *Manual of Chinese Bibliography: Being a List of Works and Essays relating to China,* coauthored with his brother, O. F. von Möllendorff, a comprehensive bibliography on the languages, literatures, histories, geographies, governments, religions, and foreign relations of China, Manchuria, Mongolia, Tibet, Korea, and the Ryūkyūs in German, English, French, and other languages; *Ningpo Colloquial Handbook,* edited by Rev. G. W. Sheppard, an extensive study of Wu dialects of the Chinese language spoken in the Ningpo area, edited by Rev. G. W. Sheppard in English nine years after the death of the author; *Catalogue of P. G. von Möllendorff's Library,* a catalogue of a philological collection compiled by Rosalie von Möllendorff in several different languages; *A Manchu Grammar with Analysed Texts,* a concise grammar book of the Manchu language in English "intended for the practical purpose of guiding the students in learning to read Manchu works"; *Catalogue of Manchu Library,* a list with brief explanation on studies of Manchuria (language, philosophy, history, religion, and etc.) in the Manchurian, Chinese and Mongolian languages; *The Family Law of the Chinese,* a study

of traditional marriage and family law of the Chinese compared with that of the Jews and the Romans in English explanation; "Essay on Manchu Literature," *Journal of the China Branch of the Royal Asiatic Society* 24 (1889-1890): 1-45, a brief summary of Manchu literature in English since 1599; "The Ghilyak Language," *The Chinese Review* 21 (1894): 141-146, a study of the language of the Ghilyaks, a Siberian Altaic tribe living between the Amur River and the Sakhalin Island, in which von Möllendorff concluded that "the Ghilyak languages possesses the characteristics of the Ural-Altaic language"; "A Reply to Mr. O. N. Denny's Pamphlet Entitled: 'China and Korea',"; and an English translation of Ernest Faber's *A Systematical Digest of the Doctrines of Confucius,* a German-language monograph on the three principal books of Confucianism (Analects, Great Learning, and Doctrine of the Mean). For a complete list of von Möllendorff's publications, see American Library Association, *The National Union Catalog: Pre-1956 Imprints,* 389:60-61.

Whether or not von Möllendorff was a genius would be an intriguing question. The very fact that such question would be posed respecting him suggests that he was of an extremely brilliant mind and of a scholarly talent, whose ramifications were of awesome proportion. In a way the answer depends, of course, on the definition of genius. If one were to define the term as a person possessing "exceptional natural capacity for creative and original conceptions," von Möllendorff was not a genius, because, original as his researches were, they were not of so creative conceptualizations. One wonders, however, if he had chosen the life of a full-time scholar (philologist and linguist) rather than that of a diplomat, as he did, and if he had lived much longer than he did, then it is likely that he would have produced such extensive original findings in his research that he would have been classifiable as a near-genius, at the least. While still young, he exhibited qualities that would have warranted such classification.

6. Ko, "Mok In-dŏk," pp. 233-234; "Möllendorff's Diary," p. 155; Ko, *Tonga,* p. 450; Stanley F. Wright, *Hart and the Chinese Customs,* pp. 501-502; Henry F. Merrill, "Note on Mr. P. G. von Möllendorff's Proceedings in Corea," in Letters to Sir Robert Hart and Others in the Chinese Customs Service, 1884-1913, pp. 2-3, Merrill Papers.

7. Ko, "Mok In-dŏk," pp. 233-234; Harold F. Cook, "Möllendorff: First Western Official," *Korea Times,* April 11, 1971, p. 3.

8. For the high opinion Viceroy Li had toward von Möllendorff, see Kim, *Ŭmch'ongsa,* pp. 205-211.

9. *ISN,* 1882.9.7/26, 1882.10.12, 1883.1.28, 1883.4.4/19, 1883.10.4; *CSS,* pp. 692-693; Ŏ Yun-jung, *Chongjŏng* yŏnp'yo, pp. 142-144.

10. Hart to Campbell, October 30, 1882, in Letters to Various Westerners in the Chinese Customs Service, 1865-1910, Hart Papers. See also John K. Fairbank, Katherine Frost Bruner, and Elizabeth MacLeod Matheson, eds., *The I. G. in Peking: Letters of Robert Hart, China Maritime Customs, 1868-1907,* 1:437-438, Hart to Campbell, December 17, 1882; ibid., 1:496-497, Hart to Campbell, November 6, 1883; Wright, *Hart and the Chinese Customs,* p. 194; "Möllendorff's Diary," p. 155.

11. Ibid.

12. Hart to Campbell, December 7, 1883, Hart Papers.

13. *KS,* 1882.9.17/24; Kim, *Ŭmch'ongsa,* pp. 195-197, 200-211.

14. For the text of the contract, see *CT,* 1882.10.13; Chŏng Kyo, *Taehan kyenyŏnsa* [History of the last years of the Yi dynasty], p. 17; Von Möllendorff, *Von Möllendorff,* p. 39; Kim, *Ŭmch'ongsa,* pp. 200-202; Ko, *Tonga,* pp. 452-454.

15. "Möllendorff's Diary," pp. 157-159.

16. Von Möllendorff, *von Möllendorff,* p. 51.

17. *PT, SI,* and *ISN,* 1882.11.16/17.

18. Von Möllendorff, *von Möllendorff,* p. 68.

19. *SI,* 1882.11.16/17, and 12.6; *ISN,* 1882.11.16/17, and 12/6; *PT,* 1882.11.16/17, and 12.6; *MCYB,* p. 66; Von Möllendorff, *von Möllendorff,* pp. 44-49.

20. *ISN,* 1883.2.17, 1883.5.20, 1883.10.28.

21. Lo Kye-hyŏn, *Han'guk oegyosa yŏn'gu,* pp. 263-264.

22. *HGSC,* p. 544; Okudaira Takehiko, *Chōsen kaikoku kōshō shimatsu,* pp. 169-170; Dalchoong Kim, "Korea's Quest for Reform and Diplomacy in the 1880's," p. 241; Hosea B. Morse, *The International Relations of the Chinese Empire,* 3:10.

23. Ch'oe, *Kaehang,* pp. 148-149; Lo, *Han'guk,* pp. 18-19; Ko, "Mok Indŏk," pp. 235-244.

24. Kim, "Korea's Quest," p. 242.

25. Kim, *Ŭmch'ongsa,* p. 206.

26. *WCSL,* 3:5-10b.

27. For the list of the names of von Möllendorff's appointees, see Ch'oe, *Kaehang,* p. 153; Horace N. Allen, *Korea: Fact and Fancy,* p. 162.

28. "Möllendorff's Diary," pp. 163-165.

29. *KHOM: Mian,* pp. 239-240; *CSS,* pt. 6, 4:661.

30. Ch'oe, *Kaehang,* p. 152-156.

31. Von Möllendorff, *von Möllendorff,* pp. 51, 54-55.

32. Later the salaries of the port superintendents were paid by the Ministry of Foreign Affairs, then by the Ministry of Finance, and then again by the customs service.

33. *T'ongni,* 1884.5.4.

34. *ISN* and *SI,* 1883.6.22.

35. *ISN* and *SI,* 1883.6.22.

36. Ch'oe, *Kaehang,* p. 156.

37. *ISN* and *SI,* 1883.12.22/24.

38. *KS,* 1884.5.22; *T'ongni,* 1884.5.16, 1884.7.4; Von Möllendorff, *von Möllendorff,* pp. 60, 67-69.

39. Hart to Campbell, November 6, 1883, Hart Papers.

40. Foote complained to Secretary of State Bayard that von Möllendorff had been acting as if he had owned the Korean government. See Foote to Bayard, October 1885, no. 34, Dip. Desp., Korea. For the difficulties Foote and Foulk had with von Möllendorff, see Yur-Bok Lee, *Diplomatic Relations between the United States and Korea, 1866-1887,* pp. 103-106; Fred Harvey Harrington, *God, Mammon, and the Japanese,* pp. 17, 48; and chap. 4 and 6 of this book.

41. Chŏng, *Taehan,* p. 18; Von Möllendorff, *von Möllendorff,* pp. 56-59.

42. Von Möllendorff, *von Möllendorff,* p. 54; Chŏng, *Taehan,* p. 25; *T'ongni,* 1883.8.4, 1883.9.16/17/18, 1883.10.10/18, 1884.5.4.

43. For English text, see U.S. House of Representatives, *Miscelleanous Documents,* vol. 6. 48th Cong., 1st sess., 1883–1884, pp. 334–335.

44. See Foote to Frelinghuysen, October 23, 1884, no. 34, Dip. Desp., Korea.

45. See *KHOM: Ilan,* 1:37–40; *NGB,* 15:219.

46. Kim Hong-jip, *Susinsa ilgi* [Diary of Kim Hong-jip mission to Japan], pp. 173–174; Kim Hong-jip, *Kim Hong-jip yugo* [Writings of Kim Hong-jip], p. 261.

47. Kim, *Susinsa ilgi,* pp. 175–176.

48. *ISN,* 1880.6.25; Inoue kō denki hensankai, *Seiai Inouekō den* [Biography of Marquis Inoue Kaoru], 3:439–442.

49. *KHOM: Ilan,* 1:58–60; *NGB,* 14:317–326; *KNK,* 1:643–645.

50. *KHOM: Ilan,* 1:61–63; *NGB,* 15:178–195.

51. *KHOM: Ilan,* 1:61–63; *NGB,* 15:177–195.

52. Inoue, *Inouekō den,* 3:496.

53. Andrew C. Nahm, "Durham White Stevens and the Japanese Annexation of Korea," p. 119.

54. Ibid., pp. 110–136.

55. *KNK,* 1:666.

56. "Möllendorff's Diary," p. 164; *KNK,* 1:669; Ch'oe, *Kaehang,* pp. 75, 153–154.

57. *KHOM: Ilan,* 1:96; *ISN* and *SI,* 1883.6.22/23; *NGB,* 11:283–289.

58. Von Möllendorff, *von Möllendorff,* pp. 57–59, 103.

59. *ISN,* 1882.7.5/13, 1884.2.17, 1884.3.29; *KHOM: Tōgan,* 3; Won Youhan (Wŏn Yu-han), "Chŏnhwan'guk ko" [A Study on the first modern Korean government mint], *Yŏksa Hakpo* 37 (June 1968): 56–58, 74–76; Von Möllendorff, *von Möllendorff,* p. 57–58.

60. *ISN,* 1883.5.11/23/24/25, 1884.3.28, 1884.10.2; *KS,* 1883.5.11, 1884. 1.23; Kim, *Ŭmch'ongsa,* pp. 168–171, 201–213.

61. Kim Yŏng-ho, "Hanmal sŏyang ki sul ŭi suyong" [The acculturation of Western techniques in the late period of the Yi dynasty], *Asea Yŏn'gu* 31 (September 1968): 325.

62. Yi Kwang-rin, *Han'guk kaehwasa yŏn'gu* [A study on the history of enlightenment in Korea with reference to the 1880s], pp. 95, 126–127; Von Möllendorff, *von Möllendorff,* p. 58.

63. Tai-jin Kim, ed. and trans., *A Bibliographical Guide to Traditional Korean Sources,* pp. 512–513. *T'onggi* is also called *T'ongsŏ Ilgi,* which is an official diary of the Office of International Trade and Diplomatic Affairs [T'ongni kyosŏp t'ongsang samu amun] and is used in this study as *T'ongni* [Records of the Office of Foreign Affairs].

64. *KHOM: Tōgan,* 3: 1885.10.21, 1885.11.3, 1885.11.10; *North China Herald,* May 8, 1885.

65. *CSS,* pt. 6, 4:705; Hō Takushu, *Meiji shoki Ni-sen kankei no kenkyū,* pp. 376–377.

66. Yi, *Han'guk kaehwasa,* pp. 94–95, 102, 126, 151, 154, 208; Ch'oe,

*Kaehang,* pp. 151–156; Martina Deuchler, *Confucian Gentlemen and Barbarian Envoys,* p. 164; Morse, *International Relations,* 3:10–11; C. I. Eugene Kim and Han-kyo Kim, *Korea and the Politics of Imperialism, 1876–1910,* pp. 61–62.

67. Von Möllendorff, *von Möllendorff,* pp. 102–105.

68. Homer B. Hulbert, "Baron von Möllendorff," *Korean Review* 1 (1901): 247.

69. "Möllendorff's Diary," pp. 166–167.

70. *KS,* 1883.4.10; *T'ongni,* 1883.9.24/25/26/27; *ISHK,* 15:4–7.

71. Von Möllendorff, *von Möllendorff,* p. 66.

72. *KS,* 1883.10.27; *CSS,* 4:700–701; Moo-Soo Kwon, "British Policy towards Korea, 1882–1910," pp. 83–92; Yung-Chung Kim, "Great Britain and Korea, 1883–1887," pp. 59–80; Lee, *Diplomatic Relations,* pp. 56–57; Deuchler, *Confucian Gentlemen,* pp. 167–170. For the English text of the new treaties, see Henry Chung, *Korean Treaties,* pp. 157–163; *BFSP,* 75:510–517.

73. *KHOM: Ilan,* 1:128; *T'ongni,* 1884.5.4/23/25/27.

74. *KHOM: Ilan,* 1:128, 144–147; *T'ongni,* 1884.6.25/26/27, 1884.7.6.

75. *T'ongni,* 1884.6.27.

76. *KHOM: Ilan,* 1:146; *T'ongni,* 1884.6.30.

77. *KHOM: Ilan,* 1:161; Ch'oe, *Kaehang,* pp. 86–87.

78. *T'ongni,* 1884.10.4.

79. *SI,* 1884.5.15, 1885.9,7; *KS,* 1884.5.15; *ISN,* 1885.9.7; *T'ongni,* 1884.5.4/6, 1884.5.15; B. D. Pak, *Rossia i Korea,* p. 8.

## Chapter 3

1. For some interesting studies on the Progressives, see Andrew Chang-woo Nahm, "Kim Ok-kyun and the Korean Progressive Movement, 1882–1884"; Harold F. Cook, *Korea's 1884 Incident: Its Background and Kim Ok-kyun's Elusive Dream;* Sin Kuk-chu, *Han'guk Kŭndae chŏngch'i oegyosa* [Recent political and diplomatic history of Korea], pp. 237–325.

2. For a competent analysis on Fukuzawa's influence on the Korean Progressives, see In K. Hwang, *The Korean Reform Movement of the 1880s: A Study of Transition in Intra-Asian Relations,* pp. 97–111; see also Ishikawa Mikiakira, *Fukuzawa Yukichi den* [A biography of Fukuzawa Yukichi], 3:289–290; Hilary Conroy, *The Japanese Seizure of Korea,* pp. 133–139; Hilary Conroy "Chōsen Mondai: The Korean Problem in Meiji Japan," *Proceedings of the American Philosophical Society* 5 (1956): 445–446. Cook writes that although Kim Ok-kyun was inspired and supported by Fukuzawa, Kim's goal was reform, modernization, and independence for Korea, while Fukuzawa's objective was the extension of Japan's national power and prestige into Korea. As a result, Fukuzawa "took advantage of Kim and used him as his tool"; see Cook, *Korea's 1884 Incident,* p. 223.

3. *KNK,* 1:965–966; *CSS,* p. 5. 6, 4:681; Kokin Kinenkai, *Kin Kyoku-kin den* [Biography of Kim Ok-kyun], pp. 366–367; Gordon Haddo, "The Rise and Fall of the Progressive Party of Korea," *Chautauquan* 16 (1892–1893): 46–49;

Pak Yŏng-hyo, "Kaehwa e taehan sangso" [Memorial on enlightenment], *Sindonga* (January 1966): 12-23; "Kim Ok-kyun's Memorial on Modernization," App. B. and "Program of the Reform Government as Described in Kim Ok-kyun's Journal of 1884," App. D. in Cook, *Korea's 1884 Incident*, pp. 238-247.

4. B. D. Pak, *Rossia i Korea*, pp. 70-78.

5. In the Korean language the Conservatives were called *Sadaedang* (the Party serving Great Power—China). Leaders of this Conservative party comprised Queen Min and her relatives and their close associates. Among other things, they wanted to preserve traditional close relations with China and adopt gradual reforms in imitation of China's so-called self-strengthening movement. Their pro-China mentality and posture were, however, mainly motivated by selfish interest, political expediency, and partisan animosity rather than by any philosophical or intellectual convictions. In the mid- and late-1880s when China tightened its control over Korea, these misguided souls became pro-Russia and anti-China. See Yi Ki-ha, *Han'guk Chŏngdang paldalsa* [Historical development of Korean political parties], pp. 6-7; Andrew C. Nahm, "Reaction and the Response to the Opening of Korea, 1876-1884," p. 146. On Queen Min's dominant personality, see Annie Ellers Bunker, "My First Visit to Her Majesty the Queen," *Korean Repository* 2 (1895): 374; Lillias H. Underwood, *Underwood of Korea*, pp. 87-89; Mary V. T. Lawrence, *A Diplomat's Helpmate: How Rose F. Foote, Wife of the First United States Minister and Envoy Extraordinary to Korea, Served Her Country in the Far East*, pp. 12-25; Hong So-min, *Yŏgŏl Minbi* [A great woman Queen Min]; Yi T'ae-yŏng, "Minbi" [Queen Min].

6. Pak Yŏng-hyo, *Sahwakiryak* [Diary of Pak Yŏng-hyo Mission to Japan], pp. 213-214, 250.

7. See *CSSL*, 5:14; see also Memorandum from Aston to Parkes in Parkes to For. Off. no. 91, May 31, 1883, *FO*, 46/300.

8. This "gradual reform group" advocated maintaining good relations with both China and Japan as well as adopting new Western civilization through Japan; see Yi, *Han'guk Chŏngdang*, pp. 8-9; Kokin Kinenkai, *Kin Kyoku-kin den*, pp. 275-276; Kikuchi Kenjō, *Kindai Chōsen shi* [History of modern Korea], 1:649-654; Nahm, "Reaction and Response," pp. 149-150.

9. Conroy, *Japanese Seizure*, p. 135; Hilary Conroy, *The Japanese Frontier in Hawaii, 1868-1889*, pp. 52-53; *KNK*, 1:924-925; *KS*, 1884.9.15; *T'ongni*, 1884.9.22; *NGB*, 15:252-253.

10. *CJCC*, 2:458-507; *KNK*, 1:928-929; Kim Ok-kyun, *Kapsin illok* [Diary of Kim Ok-kyun], 1884.11.4/25/28. Cook states that Takezoe "gave them [the Progressives] his qualified endorsement. His ultimate purpose, however, was more akin to that of Fukuzawa than to that of Kim and his friends"; see Cook, *Korea's 1884 Incident*, p. 225. However, Conroy insists that Takezoe was "dragged" into the plot rather than led it; see his *Japanese Seizure*, p. 153; see also Kuzū Yoshihisa, *Tōa senkaku shishi kiden* [Records of pioneer East Asian adventurers], 1:115, 118.

11. For some competent studies on the subject, see Lloyd E. Eastman, *Throne and Mandarins*; Henry McAleavy, *Black Flags in Vietnam*; Ella S. Laffey, "Relations between Chinese Provincial Officials and the Black Flag Army,

1883-1885"; Lewis M. Chere, "The Diplomacy of the Sino-French War, 1883-1885: Finding a Way Out of an Unwanted, Undeclared War."

12. Yüan to Li, November 12, 1884, *ISHK,* 16:10a-b; Kim, *Kapsin illok,* 1884.9.23; *CKS,* 1:431-432; Foote to Frelinghuysen, September 2, 1884, Dip. Desp., Korea. It should be emphasized that official Japanese policy was to prevent "French-Liberal party cooperation" in favor of the Korean Progressives and against the Chinese. See Conroy, *Japanese Seizure,* pp. 142-144.

13. Takezoe to Inoue, November 2, 1882, *CKS,* 1:255-264. See Cook, *Korea's 1884 Incident,* pp. 118-119.

14. Foote to Frelinghuysen, September 2, 1884, no. 104 (conf.), Dip. Desp., Korea.

15. Ōmachi Keigetsu, *Hakushaku Gotō Shōjirō den* [Biography of Count Gotō Shōjirō], pp. 544-552.

16. *CT,* Li's letter to the Tsungli Yamen, 1884.5.11; *KNK,* 1:891-892; Yüan to Li, November 12, 1884, *ISHK,* 16:10a-b. On November 29, Kojong supposedly told Kim that "we have no better opportunity than now to win our independence"; see Kim, *Kapsin illok,* 1884.11.29.

17. Foote, Foulk, and British consul general Aston, all three diplomats, had a fairly good knowledge about the impending coup. Both Foote and Foulk tried to discourage the plot and advised the plotters not to rely on the Japanese too much. Aston thought that China would intervene if the Progressives attempted a coup, despite its involvement in Vietnam; see Foote to Frelinghuysen, December 17, 1884, no. 128, enc. Foulk's Report, December 4-7, 1884, Dip. Desp., Korea; *KAR,* 1:101-111; Aston's Report, enc. Parkes, December 12, 1884, no. 38, *FO,* 17/953; Cook, *Korea's 1884 Incident,* pp. 101-134.

18. *KS,* 1884.9.15; *T'ongni,* 1884.9.22; *KNK,* 1:924-925.

19. *T'ongni,* 1884.9.23/24; Alfred Stead, ed., *Japan by the Japanese: A Survey by Its Highest Authorities,* pp. 190-191.

20. *HGSC,* pp. 619-630; *KNK,* 1:955-962; Woongsang Choi, *The Fall of the Hermit Kingdom,* p. 21.

21. Six were ordered to come to the king. As they came, they were beheaded. In addition to elder Min, the other five included Min Yŏng-mok, Cho Yŏng-ha, Yi Cho-yŏn, Yun T'ae-jun, and Han Kyu-jik. See *TKC,* 12:7; Cook, *Korea's 1884 Incident,* pp. 204-220. For some eyewitness accounts, see Foote to Frelinghuysen, December 5, 1884, no. 127, Dip. Desp., Korea; Rosalie von Möllendorff, *P. G. von Möllendorff: Ein Lebensbild,* pp. 71-74; Aston's Report, enc. Parkes, January 24, 1885, no. 27, *FO,* 17/977. Naval Attaché Foulk was out of Seoul at the time of the coup but later prepared a report for the Navy Department; see Foulk to the Secretary of Navy, December 20, 1884, Foulk Papers, NYPL.

22. Fred Harvey Harrington, *God, Mammon, and the Japanese,* pp. 22-24.

23. *KNK,* 1:947.

24. *HGSC,* pp. 637-639; *KNK,* 1:965-966; Cook, *Korea's 1884 Incident,* App. D., p. 247; Kim, *Kapsin illok,* 1884.12.5. Nahm writes that "Thus, began 'Kim Ok-kyun's *Samil ch'ŏn ha'* (Three Days Mastery of the World)"; see his "Reaction and Response," p. 152.

25. Von Möllendorff, *von Möllendorff,* pp. 72-76.

26. Foote to Frelinghuysen, December 17, 1884, no. 128, Dip. Desp., Korea.

27. Yüan was the chief military aide to Admiral Wu Chao-yu in Korea. See Lin Ming-te, *Yüan Shih-k'ai yü Chao-hsien,* p. 42; Yüan's Report, *CSSL,* 6:16-20.

28. The Japanese later charged that the Chinese had fired first, whereas the Chinese claimed that the Japanese had initiated the battle; see *NGB,* 18:321-323; *CSSL,* 6:13-15.

29. Yüan's Report, *CSSL,* 6:16-20; *KNK,* 1:973-982; *HGSC,* pp. 642-655; Kokin Kinenkai, *Kin Kyoku-kin den,* pp. 420-421. Only nine Progressive leaders survived and went to Japan. Altogether forty-three of the Progressives died while only six pro-China Conservatives were killed, and forty Japanese were killed.

30. *ISN,* 1884.10.19/20/21/22/23; *CSSL,* 5:24, 28, 30, 35, 6:14-21, 22-26; *WCSL,* 50:31-33; *KNK,* 1:978; Chŏng Kyo, *Taehan kyenyŏnsa,* 1:32; *T'ongni,* 1884.10.19.

31. Von Möllendorff, *von Möllendorff,* pp. 76-77; Aston's Report enc. Parkes, December 12, 1884, no. 38, *FO,* 17/953. Even Foulk's Japanese cook was killed while trying to save his papers; see Foulk to family, December 20, 1884, Foulk Papers, LC.

32. *HGSC,* pp. 655-658; *KNK,* 1:981-986.

33. *ISN,* 1884.10.21; *T'ongni,* 1884.10.20; *CSS,* pt. 6, 4:739; *HGSC,* pp. 658-660; *KNK,* 1:987-988.

34. *ISN* and *SI,* 1884.10.21/22/23.

35. Von Möllendorff, *von Möllendorff,* pp. 55-57.

36. Watanabe Shūjirō, *Tōhō kankei* [Korean-Japanese relations], pp. 187-188; Ōmachi, *Hakushaku,* pp. 555-556; Wang Hsin-chung, *Chung-Jih, chia-wu chang-cheng chih wai-chiao pei-ching,* pp. 72-73.

37. Japanese Archives, SP 5, 48-49; *KNK,* 1:1015-1018; *NGB,* 17:337-338; *CKS,* 1:336-337.

38. *KNK,* 1:1015-1019; *CKS,* 1:336-337.

39. *NGSS,* 3:93, 106-113; Watanabe, *Tōhō,* pp. 185-188; Stead, *Japan by the Japanese,* p. 195; *Tien-kao,* 4:30; Komatsu Midori, ed., *Itō Hirobumi den* [Biography of Itō Hirobumi], 2:399; Genyōsha, ed., *Genyōsha shashi* [History of Genyōsha], p. 239.

40. *NGSS,* 3:114; *NGB,* 17:344-346, 348-350.

41. *NGB,* 5:25a-26a; *WCSL,* 49:15b-16b, 50:32-33.

42. *CT,* Wu's memorial, 1885.1.3; *T'ongni,* 1884.10.23/24/25/26; *CSS,* pp. 744-745; *CKYJP,* 1:226-229; *WCSL,* 51:17-23.

43. *WCSL,* 51:17-23.

44. *CSK,* 1:318-319; *KNK,* 1:1004-1005.

45. *ISN* and *SI,* 1884.10.27; *T'ongni,* 1884.10.27.

46. Foote to Frelinghuysen, December 25, 1884, no. 133, Dip., Desp., Korea.

47. Foote to Frelinghuysen, December 29, 1884, no. 135, December 31, 1883, no. 136, Dip. Desp., Korea.

48. Foote to Frelinghuysen, December 19, 1884, no. 131, Dip. Desp., Korea.

49. Foote to Frelinghuysen, December 29, 1884, no. 135, Dip. Desp., Korea.

50. Foote to Frelinghuysen, December 31, 1884, no. 136, January 1, 1885, no. 137, Dip. Desp., Korea.

51. Foote to Frelinghuysen, January 1, 1885, no. 137, January 4, 1885, no. 139, Dip. Desp., Korea.

52. *CKS,* 1:356–357; *T'ongni,* 1884.11.20/21.

53. For the Japanese text of the treaty, see *NGB,* 28:348–350. For the Korean (Chinese) text of the treaty, see *SI,* 1884.11.24; *T'ongni,* 1884.11.24/25.

54. Foote to Frelinghuysen, January 9, 1885, no. 140, enc., Dip. Desp., Korea. Chien, Conroy, and Treat essentially agree with Foote's assessment of the treaty; see Frederick Foo Chien, *The Opening of Korea: A Study of Chinese Diplomacy, 1876–1885,* p. 162; Conroy, *Japanese Seizure,* p. 161; and Payson J. Treat, *Diplomatic Relations between the United States and Japan,* 2:215–216. See also Japanese Archives, SP 5, 50–53. However, others such as Vinacke insist that the treaty was too harsh in view of Japan's involvement in the coup; see Harold M. Vinacke, *A History of the Far East in Modern Times,* p. 133. Learning of the contents of the treaty, Minister Parkes commented that Takezoe should not have been "so closely connected with the conspirators and the criminal proceedings." See E. V. G. Kiernan, *British Diplomacy in China, 1880–1885,* p. 165.

55. Li to the Tsungli Yamen, January 18, 1885, *CSSL,* 6:37a. After the failure of the coup, Takezoe supposedly told Kim Ok-kyun that Japan would use force against China; see *CKS,* 1:466, 2:126–132.

56. *NGB,* 18:206–210.

57. For the Japanese text of the treaty, see *NGB,* 18:306–309. For the Chinese (Korean) text, see *CSSL,* 8:6b–7a. For the English text, see *BFSP,* 76:297–298.

58. As for Foote, having previously arranged a leave with the objective in mind of resigning his Korean station, he left Korea in February 1885. The main reason for his resignation was the reduction of his rank from envoy extraordinary and minister plenipotentiary to minister resident and consul general. See Frelinghuysen to Foote, July 14, 1884, no. 58, Dip. Inst., Korea; Foote to Frelinghuysen, September 17, 1884, no. 122, Dip. Desp., Korea; *KAR,* 1:9.

59. Foulk to Bayard, May 9, 1885, no. 152, May 14, 1885, (tel.) no. 171, Dip. Desp., Korea.

60. Foulk to Bayard, April 18, 1885, no. 166, Dip. Desp., Korea; *KAR,* 1:10.

61. Foulk to Bayard, March 1, 1885, no. 149, March 13, 1885, no. 153, Dip. Desp., Korea.

62. Bayard to Foulk, August 19, 1885, (conf.) no. 63, Dip. Inst., Korea. The Commanding General of the Army, Philip Sheridan, was also far from enthusiastic about the idea of sending American officers "to be detailed to duty in some foreign country" without benefit to the United States military service. See Richard P. Weinert, "The Original KAMG," *Military Review,* (June 1965): 95.

63. *KAR*, 1:14. It was not until 1886 that an American diplomat, O. N. Denny, was hired and not until 1888 that four American military advisers were hired by the Korean government. For Denny's works in Korea, see Robert R. Swartout, Jr., *Mandarins, Gunboats, and Power Politics*. As for the American military advisers, it was W. W. Rockhill, chargé d'affaires of the American legation in Seoul, who successfully arranged for them to come to Korea by recommending to the secretary of state that the constitutional provision causing the delay could be avoided if the officers sent to Korea were chosen either from men who had resigned from the armed forces or who had not received commissions in the army after having graduated from the military academy. See Rockhill to Bayard, February 13, 1887, no. 63, Dip. Desp., Korea.

64. M. Frederick Nelson, *Korea and the Old Orders in Eastern Asia*, p. 294.

## Chapter 4

1. Rosalie von Möllendorff, *P. G. von Möllendorff: Ein Lebensbild*, pp. 61–62.

2. Foote to Frelinghuysen, July 13, 1883, no. 14, Dip. Desp., Korea; Von Möllendorff, *von Möllendorff*, pp. 61–62.

3. George W. Woods Diary, March 25, 1884, in *Naval Surgeon in Yi Korea: The Journal of George W. Woods*, edited by Fred C. Bohm and Robert R. Swartout, Jr., p. 31.

4. Foote to Frelinghuysen, October 23, 1883, no. 34, Dip. Desp., Korea.

5. Allen to Ellinwood, October 8, 1884, Allen Papers; see also Fred Harvey Harrington, *God, Mammon, and the Japanese*, pp. 17, 22–24, 48.

6. For Foulk's view on missionary activities in Korea, see Yur-Bok Lee, *Diplomatic Relations between the United States and Korea, 1866–1887*, p. 115; also Foulk to Bayard, June 3, 1886, no. 308, Dip. Desp., Korea.

7. *NGB*, 18:315–316, *HGSC*, pp. 790–791; Lee, *Diplomatic Relations*, p. 88; *KAR*, 1:12.

8. *CSSL*, 7:8; *ISHK*, 16:4.

9. Andrew Malozemoff, *Russian Far Eastern Policy, 1881–1904: With Special Emphasis on the Causes of the Russo-Japanese War*, p. 27; Sin Ki-sŏk, *Hanmal oegyosa yŏn'gu*, p. 168.

10. "Möllendorff's Diary," pp. 156.

11. Lo Kye-hyŏn, *Han'guk oegyoso yŏn'gu*, pp. 25–26; Seung Kwon Synn, "The Russo-Korean Relations in the 1880s," *Korea Journal* 20, no. 9 (Sept. 1980): 28.

12. "Möllendorff's Diary," pp. 166–167; Yi Ki-baek (Lee Ki-baek), *A New History of Korea*, pp. 279–280.

13. "Möllendorff's Diary," p. 178; Sin, *Hanmal*, p. 168; Synn, "Russo-Korean Relations," pp. 28–29; Lo, *Han'guk*, pp. 252–253.

14. A. L. Narochnitsky, *Kolonial Nai Politika Kapitalisticheskikh Derzh na Dalnem Vostoke, 1860–1895*, pp. 370–371.

15. Aston to O'Conor, May 4, 1885, *FO*, 17/996.

16. Von Möllendorff, *von Möllendorff*, p. 78.

17. "Möllendorff's Diary," pp. 176–178.

18. *ISN,* 1884.11.13; *PT,* 1884.11.12; *CT,* Li's letter to the Tsungli Yamen, 1885.6.8; *KNK,* 2:6–7; Synn, "Russo-Korean Relations," p. 28.

19. James William Morley, "The Dynamics of the Korean Connection," pp. 274–275. See also Bong-youn Choy, *A History of the Korean Unification: Its Issues and Prospects,* pp. 1–2; A. Doak Barnett, *Communist China and Asia: Challenge to American Policy,* p. 287; Richard C. Allen, *Korea's Syngman Rhee,* p. 17.

20. "Möllendorff's Diary," pp. 167, 178.

21. *HGSC,* pp. 791–792; Sin, *Hanmal,* pp. 167–170; Lo, *Han'guk,* pp. 16–17; "Möllendorff's Diary," p. 188.

22. Narochnitsky, *Kolonial Nai Politika,* pp. 370–373; Seung Kwon Synn, "The Russo-Japanese Struggle for Control of Korea, 1894–1904," p. 15.

23. Von Möllendorff insisted that de Speyer came to Korea at his invitation; see Von Möllendorff, *Von Möllendorff,* p. 77. See also Narochnitsky, *Kolonial Nai Politika,* p. 371. Yi Sŏn-gŭn asserts incorrectly that de Speyer's mission to Korea was to help the ratification process of the Russo-Korean Treaty that Waeber had signed and also to study the general situation in Korea after the *Kapsin* Coup, not necessarily to comply with von Möllendorff's telegram request for the Russian protection of Korea. Yi doubts that von Möllendorff had even sent such a telegram to the Russian Embassy in Tokyo. See *HGSC,* pp. 795–797.

24. Narochnitsky, *Kolonial Nai Politika,* pp. 370–371; Synn, "Russo-Japanese Struggle," p. 15.

25. Narochnitsky, *Kolonial Nai Politika,* pp. 372–373; B. D. Pak, *Rossia i Korea,* p. 85.

26. Pak, *Rossia i Korea,* pp. 86–87; Narochnitsky, *Kolonial Nai Politika,* pp. 372–373.

27. Watanabe Shūjirō, *Tōhō kankei,* pp. 341–342. Lo writes that von Möllendorff knew of this mission; see his *Han'guk,* pp. 255–256. However, both Yi Sŏn-gŭn and Sin Ki-sŏk say that von Möllendorff was unaware of the mission. See *HGSC,* pp. 791–793, and Sin, *Hanmal,* p. 169.

28. Pak, *Rossia i Korea,* p. 86.

29. *SI,* 1885.5.25; *CSS,* 6:773; *CSSL,* 8:28–31; Pak, *Rossia i Korea,* p. 86.

30. M. N. Pak (with Wayne Patterson), "Russian Policy toward Korea before and during the Sino-Japanese War of 1894–1895," *The Journal of Korean Studies* 5 (1984): 115.

31. Narochnitsky, *Kolonial Nai Politika,* pp. 372–373; Pak, *Rossia i Korea,* pp. 85–86.

32. *CT,* Li's letter to the Yamen, 1885.3.23; *ISHK,* Li to the Korean king, July 16, 1885, 17:33–34; *KNK,* 2:5–7; Sin, *Hanmal,* pp. 160–170; Lo, *Han'guk,* pp. 255–256; *CKS,* 2:124–130. Yi Sŏn-gŭn doubts the conclusion of such an agreement; see his *HGSC,* pp. 795–796.

33. *CJCC,* 2:347–357; *ISHK,* 11:35–36; *TK,* 38:24–27, 46–52; George Alexander Lensen, *Balance of Intrigue,* p. 8; Kuo Ting-i, "Chung-kuo yu ti-i-chih Mei-Han t'iao-yüeh" [China and the first United States–Korean Treaty], pp. 15–16; E. V. G. Kiernan, *British Diplomacy in China, 1880–1885,* p. 75.

34. Seung Kwon Synn, *The Russo-Japanese Rivalry over Korea, 1876–1904,* p. 4; Pak, *Rossia i Korea,* pp. 33–35; George Alexander Lensen, *Russia's Japan*

*Expedition of 1852 to 1855*, pp. 70–71; *PT*, 1854.4.27; *CWS*, *CS*, 1854.5.4; *ISN*, 1854.4.26; *SI*, 1854.4.27; Watanabe Katsumi, *Chōsen kaikoku gaikō shi kenkyū* [A study on the diplomatic history of the opening of Korea], p. 57; Lo, *Han'guk*, p. 6; Horace H. Allen, *Korea: Fact and Fancy*, p. 152; Yi Yong-hŭi, "Kŏmundo chŏmryŏng oegyo chonggo" [Diplomacy respecting the occupation of Kŏmundo], p. 462.

35. Donald Ross Hazelton Macdonald, "Russian Interest in Korea to 1895: The Pattern of Russia's Emerging Interest in the Peninsula from the Late Seventeenth Century to the Sino-Japanese War," pp. 80–81.

36. Narochnitsky, *Kolonial Nai Politika*, p. 119; Synn, *Russo-Japanese Rivalry*, pp. 4–5.

37. Narochnitsky, *Kolonial Nai Politika*, pp. 119–120.

38. Pak, *Rossia i Korea*, p. 46; Narochnitsky, *Kolonial Nai Politika*, p. 152.

39. Narochnitsky, *Kolonial Nai Politika*, pp. 280–281.

40. Allen, *Korea*, p. 153; Charles Dallet, *Histoire de l'église de Corée*, 1:520; Soo Bok Choi, "Political Dynamics in Hermit Korea," p. 138; Francis Jones, "Foreign Diplomacy in Korea, 1866–1894," p. 22; Macdonald, "Russian Interest," pp. 112–114.

41. *NGB*, 12:127–129.

42. Pak, *Rossia i Korea*, pp. 28–30, 39.

43. For discussions of the reasons for Korean emigration into Siberia and of the policy of the Korean and Russian authority toward it, see Yi Nŭng-hwa, *Chosŏn Kidokkyo kŭp oegyo sa* [A history of Christianity and foreign relations in Korea], 2:169–171; Ching Young Choe, *The Rule of the Taewŏn'gun, 1864–1873*, pp. 84–90; Walter Kolarz, *The Peoples of the Soviet Far East*, pp. 32–42; George Ginsburg, "The Citizenship Status of Koreans in Pre-Revolutionary Russia and the Early Years of the Soviet Regime," *Journal of Korean Affairs* 5, no. 2 (1975): 1–19; John J. Stephan, "The Korean Minority in the Soviet Union," *Mizan* 13, no. 3 (1971): 138–139; Hyŏn Kyu-hwan, *Han'guk yuimin sa* [A history of Korean wanderers and emigrants], 2:776–778.

44. For examples, see *ISN* and *KS*, 1867.4.20/21, 1867.6.7, 1871.5.28.

45. Pak, *Rossia i Korea*, pp. 28–30.

46. *IWSM, TC*, 47:25b–26b.

47. Pak, *Rossia i Korea*, pp. 40–41.

48. Narochnitsky, *Kolonial Nai Politika*, p. 152.

49. *HGSC*, pp. 763–764; Pak, *Rossia i Korea*, pp. 38, 43.

50. Pak, *Rossia i Korea*, p. 49.

51. Ibid., p. 50; Narochnitsky, *Kolonial Nai Politika*, pp. 28, 257.

52. Pak, *Rossia i Korea*, pp. 51–53, 56.

53. *ISN*, 1882.2.7/17; Kim, *Ŭmch'ongsa*, pp. 148, 152, 162–163, 170; *CSS*, pt. 6, pp. 521, 619–621; *HGSC*, pp. 763–766; Lo, *Han'guk*, pp. 6–17; Lensen, *Balance of Intrigue*, pp. 6–11.

54. "The Ports and Trades of Corea," *Edinburg Review* 162 (July 1885): 280; Yi, "Kŏmundo," pp. 463–464; B. D. Pak insists that the British and the Japanese "exaggerated" Russian ambitions toward Korea; see his *Rossia i Korea*, pp. 21–60.

55. In the West (Great Britain and the United States) historians disagree on

the origin and intensity of Russia's interest in the Korean peninsula. Some insist that Russia showed its aggressive interest in Korea before 1860; see William E. Griffis, *Corea: The Hermit Nation,* pp. 205, 212, 373, 528. Others claim that it was only in 1860 and thereafter that Russia became interested in expanding into the Far Eastern region, including Korea; see David J. Dallin, *The Rise of Russia in Asia,* pp. 28–29; William Leonard Langer, *The Diplomacy of Imperialism,* pp. 168–169; Hugh Seton-Watson, *The Decline of Imperial Russia,* p. 198. Still others hold that it was not until 1884 that the Russian government became actively interested in Korea, although some Russian leaders had shown some interest in Korea before then or had even actively engaged in "intrigues"; see Donald W. Treadgold, "Russia and the Far East," p. 542; Malozemoff, *Russian Far Eastern Policy,* pp. 14–27.

56. For Kondō's report, see *CKS,* 2:124–126, and *KNK,* 2:5–6. For Ch'en's report, see *CSSL,* 8:21–23. Although the Kwŏn and Kim Mission may have brought some kind of understanding concerning Russian aid to Korea, there must have been no concrete and written agreement between the two parties. In June Kondō's successor, Takahira Kogorō, reported to Tokyo that the secret Kwŏn and Kim Mission was without bona fide credentials from the king, and so got the passage to Russian territory on the pretext of purchasing arms, and that there appeared to be no concrete agreement between the mission and Korf concerning the Russian protectorate of Korea. See *CKS,* 2:129–131.

57. "Möllendorff's Diary," pp. 179–180; Lo, *Han'guk,* pp. 7–8, 25; *CSSL,* 8:31–32; *T'ongni,* 1884.12.12/13.

58. Von Möllendorff, *von Möllendorff,* p. 78.

59. Lo, *Han'guk,* pp. 257–258, *CSSL,* 8:31–32; O'Conor to Aston, June 4, 1885, *FO,* 17/981; Narochnitsky, *Kolonial Nai Politika,* p. 372; Sin, *Hanmal,* p. 170.

60. Narochnitsky, *Kolonial Nai Politika,* pp. 372–373.

61. Ibid., p. 383; Malozemoff, *Russian Far Eastern Policy,* p. 30.

62. Pak, *Rossia i Korea,* p. 85.

63. Pak, "Russian Policy toward Korea," p. 114.

## Chapter 5

1. For the Russian interest and penetration into Central Asia during the nineteenth century, see Seymour Becker, *Russia's Protectorates in Central Asia: Bukhara and Khiva, 1865–1924,* pp. 3–147; Firuz Kazemzadeh, "Russia and the Middle East," pp. 492–514; Henry S. Bradsher, *Afghanistan and the Soviet Union,* pp. 9–11. For Foreign Minister Gorchakov's rationale and explanation for Russian expansionism into Central Asia, see Alfred Erich Senn, *Readings in Russian Political and Diplomatic History; Vol. 1, The Tsarist Period;* and Vol. 2, *The Soviet Period,* 1:139–142; W. Kerr Fraser-Tyler, *Afghanistan: A Study of Political Development in Central and Southern Asia,* pp. 129–130, 319–323; *BFSP,* 58:635–639. For the British interest and advancement in Afghanistan during the nine-

teenth century, see R. C. Majumdar, H. C. Raychaundhuri, and Kalikinkar Datta, *An Advanced History of India,* pp. 754–760; William Habberton, *Anglo-Russian Relations Concerning Afghanistan, 1837–1907,* pp. 9–57; Fraser-Tyler, *Afghanistan,* pp. 82–173.

2. Habberton, *Anglo-Russian Relations,* pp. 54–55; Andrew Malozemoff, *Russian Far Eastern Policy, 1881–1904,* p. 29. Granville to Tseng, April 16, 1885, *BFSP,* 78: 143; Dowell to Admiralty, April 15, 1885, and memo, in *FO,* 17/1000; Agatha Ramm, ed., *The Political Correspondence of Mr. Gladstone and Lord Granville, 1876–1886,* 2:363; Moo-Soo Kwon, "British Policy towards Korea, 1882–1910," pp. 113–114.

3. For instance, see "Port Hamilton," *The Spectator* 59 (January 1886): 108–109; Kwon, "British Policy," p. 112.

4. Bingham to Bayard, August 11, 1886, no. 427, Dip. Desp., Japan; Frederick Foo Chien, *The Opening of Korea,* pp. 169–170; George Alexander Lensen, *Balance of Intrigue,* p. 54.

5. Young to Frelinghuysen, December 14, 1882, no. 63, Dip. Desp., China; Kim Yun-sik, *Ŭmch'ongsa,* pp. 142–143; Yi Yong-hŭi, "Kŏmundo chŏmryong oegyo chonggo," pp. 466–467; Kwon, "British Policy," pp. 80–81.

6. Foreign Office to Admiralty, March 20, 1885, (conf.), *FO,* 17/969; Admiralty to Foreign Office, April 14, 1885, (conf.), *FO,* 17/1001; memo in *FO,* 17/1000.

7. Parkes to Granville, Dec. 15, 1883, (conf.), no. 4, *FO,* 17/927; Kwon, "British Policy," pp. 108–109.

8. Tyler Dennett, "Early American Policy in Korea, 1883–7," *Political Science Quarterly* 38 (March 1923): 94; William Leonard Langer, *The Diplomacy of Imperialism,* 1:169; Hugh Seton-Watson, *The Decline of Imperial Russia,* p. 198; Hosea B. Morse, *The International Relations of the Chinese Empire,* 3:12; Shu-hsi Hsü, *China and Her Political Entity,* p. 126; Sin Ki-sŏk, *Hanmal oegyosa yŏn'gu,* p. 171; Mun Il-p'yŏng, *Han-Mi osipnyŏnsa* [Fifty-year history of Korean-American relations], p. 163; Yi Ki-baek (Lee Ki-baek), *A New History of Korea,* pp. 280–281.

9. O'Conor to Aston, June 4, 1885, *FO,* 17/981.

10. B. D. Pak, *Rossia i Korea,* pp. 86–87.

11. Rose L. Greaves, *Persia and the Defense of India, 1884–1892,* p. 228.

12. Ramm, *Political Correspondence of Gladstone,* 1:xviii–xxx; William Leonard Langer, *European Alliance and Alignments, 1871–1890,* p. 300; William Osgood Aydelotte, *Bismarck and British Colonial Policy: The Problems of South West Africa, 1883–1885,* pp. 130, 163.

13. Sin, *Hanmal,* p. 171; Langer, *Diplomacy of Imperialism,* p. 169.

14. *NGB,* 18:373, 599–602; Plunkett to Granville, April 23, 1885, *BFSP,* 78:144; May 20, 1885, *BFSP,* 78:152–153; Foulk to Bayard, August 16, 1885, no. 214, Dip. Desp., Korea; Yi, "Kŏmundo," pp. 482–483.

15. *WCSL,* 56:24–27; *CT,* Li's letter to the Tsungli Yamen, 1885.2.29; *CSSL,* 8:1; *ISHK,* 16:38; *HGSC,* pp. 699–703; Yi Pyŏng-do, *Han'guksa taekwan,* p. 489.

16. *NGSS,* 7:583; *NGB,* 18:324; Korea (Republic of), *Thus Neutralization is*

*Impossible for Korea*, p. 11; In K. Hwang, *The Neutralized Unification of Korea*, p. 141.

17. Young to Frelinghuysen, January 28, 1883, no. 112, Dip. Desp., China; *FR*, 1883, p. 177; Payson J. Treat, *Diplomatic Relations between the United States and Japan*, 2:164–165; Hilary Conroy, *The Japanese Seizure of Korea, 1868–1910*, pp. 117–119.

18. Kikuchi Kenjō, *Kindai Chōsen shi*, 1:649–654; Kokin Kinenkai, *Kin Kyoku-kin den*, pp. 275–276.

19. Foulk to Bayard, July 5, 1885, no. 192, Dip. Desp., Korea.

20. Lin Ming-te, *Yüan Shih-k'ai yü Chao-hsien*, p. 95.

21. Ibid., pp. 95–96.

22. For Yu's interesting idea for the neutralization of Korea, see Yu Kil-chun, *Yu Kil-chun chŏnsŏ* [Complete works of Yu Kil-chun], 4:319–328. For an English translation of Yu's text on *On Neutrality*, see In Kwan Hwang, "A Translation and Critical Review of Yu Kil-chun's *On Neutrality*," *Korean Studies* 9 (1985): 1–13.

23. *NGB*, 1:359–360; *CSSL*, 8:24–26; Tingfu Tsiang, "Sino-Japanese Diplomatic Relations, 1870–1894," *Chinese Social and Political Review* 17, no. 1 (April 1933): 89–90.

24. *BFSP*, 78:160–161.

25. *NGB*, 1:357–369; Wang Hsin-chung, *Chung-Jih chia-wu chang-ching chih wai-chiao pei-ching*, pp. 107–108.

26. Lin, *Yüan*, p. 95.

27. Ibid.

28. Ibid.

29. Yi, *Han'guksa taekwan*, p. 489.

30. See chapter 7 of this book; also Yur-Bok Lee, *Establishment of a Korean Legation in the United States, 1887–1890*, pp. 163–186; Pak, *Kŭndae Han-Mi oegyo-sa*, pp. 396–418; Mun, *Han-Mi*, pp. 169–174.

31. Some historians insist that the best time for an international guarantee for the neutralization of Korea was in the early 1880s rather than in the mid-1880s. For instance, Tyler Dennett states that "nothing could have saved Korea but an international guarantee. Such a guarantee should have been secured before the peninsula was opened by the treaty of Commodore Shufeldt"; see his "Early American Policy in Korea," p. 102.

32. The Chinese minister to London, Tseng Ch'i-tse, telegraphed to the Tsungli Yamen on the British move. But Tseng mistook Port Hamilton for Quelpart Island (Chejudo), and so did Viceroy Li at the beginning. (See Li En-han, *Tseng Ch'i-tse ti wai-chiao* [Diplomacy of Tseng Ch'i-tse], p. 261; Tseng Ch'i-tse to the Tsungli Yamen, April 5, 1885, *WCSL*, 55:24–25. For Li's conversation with O'Conor, see O'Conor to Granville, June 2, 1885, no. 259, *FO*, 17/981.

33. *Tien-kao*, 5:28–30.

34. Foreign Office to O'Conor, July 6, 1885, no. 157, *FO*, 17/976.

35. *Tien-kao*, 6:12b.

36. Granville to O'Conor, May 29, 1885, *BFSP*, 78:148. Tseng to Granville, April 27, 1885, *BFSP*, 78:145. Granville to Tseng, April 28, 1885, *BFSP*,

78:145-146; O'Conor to Granville, May 9, 1885, (very conf.), no. 218, *FO,* 17/980.

37. *Tien-kao,* 5:37.

38. Granville to Tseng, April 16, 1885; Tseng to Granville, April 27, 1885; draft agreement, enc. in Granville to Tseng, April 28, 1885, *BFSP,* 78:143, 145-146.

39. A. L. Narochnitsky, *Kolonial Nai Politika Kapitalisticheskikh Derzh na Dalnem Vostoke, 1860-1895,* pp. 383-384.

40. Li to the Korean King, May 4, 1885, *CSSL,* 8:18a-b; Li to the Tsungli Yamen, May 1 and 3, 1885, (tel.), *Tien-kao,* 5:38; *BFSP,* 78:147; Stanley F. Wright, *Hart and the Chinese Customs,* p. 505.

41. Malozemoff, *Russian Far Eastern Policy,* pp. 30, 266; *The Times* (London), April 18, 22, and May 1, 1885.

42. Pak, *Rossia i Korea,* pp. 85-86.

43. Malozemoff, *Russian Far Eastern Policy,* pp. 30-31, 266.

44. *ISHK,* 17:19-20; Sin, *Hanmal,* p. 171.

45. *ISHK,* 17:19-20; Granville to O'Conor, April 23, 1885, *BFSP,* 78:144-145; Kwon, "British Policy," p. 116; Yi, "Kŏmundo," p. 471.

46. O'Conor to Granville, May 9, 1885, (very conf.), no. 218, *FO,* 17/980.

47. Wright, *Hart,* p. 504.

48. Yi, "Kŏmundo," pp. 468-469.

49. For the northern boundaries fixed in 1885, see Lewis M. Alexander, *International Boundary Study, No. 26: Afghanistan-USSR Boundary,* p. 3. Neither Russia nor Britain wanted war in Afghanistan. So both the Russian and British governments agreed to submit their claim to arbitration in May 1885. In September they signed a protocol. See S. Laing, "Peace With Russia," *Fortnightly Review* 43 (June 1885): 869-878.

50. Li to the Tsungli Yamen, May 5, 1885, *ISHK,* 17:9-10; Yi, "Kŏmundo," p. 486.

51. *ISHK,* 17:23-24; Captain Maclean to Admiral Dowell, May 16, 1885, *BFSP,* 78:150-151.

52. Dowell to Secretary of Admiralty, May 19, 1885, *BFSP,* 78:149-150; Conversation between Korean officials and Admiral Dowell in Nagasaki, May 18, 1885, *ISHK,* 17:24-25; Yi, "Kŏmundo," p. 487.

53. Kim to Carles, May 20, 1885, *BFSP,* 78:152.

54. Foulk to Bayard, May 19, 1885, no. 172, Dep. Desp., Korea.

55. Carles to O'Conor, June 2, 1885, *FO,* 17/980. Chargé O'Conor had a joint appointment both in Peking and Seoul. Consul General Aston was on vacation in Japan at that time.

56. Kim to foreign representatives in Seoul, May 20, 1885, *ISHK,* 17:21; Foulk to Bayard, May 21, 1885, no. 173, and May 19, 1885, no. 172, Dip. Desp., Korea; Yi, "Kŏmundo," pp. 483-484.

57. Replies from Ch'en, Kondō, Zembsch, and Foulk to Kim, May 21, 1885, *ISHK,* 17:21-23; Yi, "Kŏmundo," pp. 483-486.

58. Memo of conversation with Foulk, May 22, 1885, *FO,* 17/996; O'Conor to Granville, June 17, 1885, (secret), no. 298, *FO,* 17/982.

59. Granville to O'Conor, May 27, 1885, (conf.), no. 120, *FO,* 17/975; May 29, 1885, (secret), no. 124, *FO,* 17/975; Yi, "Kŏmundo," pp. 488–489.

60. O'Conor to Granville, June 2, 1885, (conf.), no. 255, *FO,* 17/981.

## Chapter 6

1. For Ch'en's report, see *CSSL,* 8:21-23, 31b-33b. For Kondō's report, see *CKS,* 2:124-126, and *KNK,* 2:5-7. It should be noted that Takahira Kogorō, Kondō's successor, doubted the existence of any written agreement between Governor General Korf and the Kwŏn and Kim Mission; see *CKS,* 2:129-131; *HGSC,* p. 796.

2. O'Conor to Aston, June 4, 1885, *FO,* 17/981.

3. *CSSL,* 8:21-24, 31b-33b.

4. *CT,* Li's letter to the Tsungli Yamen, 1885.5.11, 1886.6.19; *CSSL,* 8:30; *WCSL,* 59:10.

5. *ISHK,* 17:9-12, 18-19; Yi Yong-hŭi, "Kŏmundo chŏmryong oegyo chonggo," pp. 471-473.

6. Great Britain, *Foreign Office Archives,* June 7, 1885, no. 269, 17/981.

7. Aston to O'Conor, July 10, 1885, no. 81, *FO,* 17/986; O'Conor to Salisbury, July 16, 1885, (tel.), no. 54, *FO,* 17/987.

8. *NGB,* 1:356-359.

9. *CSSL,* 8:21-23, 26.

10. "Möllendorff's Diary," p. 180.

11. Aston to O'Conor, June 22, 1885, *FO,* 17/983; O'Conor to Salisbury, June 27, 1885, *FO,* 17/982; see also *North China Herald,* May 8, 1885.

12. O'Conor to Granville, May 20, 1885, (conf.), no. 235, *FO,* 17/981; July 4, 1885, (conf.), no. 338, *FO,* 17/982; Yung-chung Kim, "The Kŏmundo Incident, 1885-1887: An Early Phase in British-Korean Relations," *Korean Observer, a Quarterly Journal* 15, no. 3 (Autumn 1984): 311.

13. George Alexander Lensen, *Balance of Intrigue,* p. 166.

14. *KNK,* 2:11, *CSSL,* 8:31-32; Sin Ki-sŏk, *Hanmal oegyosa yŏn'gu,* p. 172; Lo Kye-hyŏn, *Han'guk oegyosa yŏn'gu,* pp. 258-259; Lensen, *Balance of Intrigue,* p. 37; Seung Kwon Synn, "The Russo-Japanese Struggle for Control of Korea, 1894-1904," p. 30; A. L. Narochnitsky, *Kolonial Nai Politika Kapitalisticheskikh Derzh na Dalnem Vostoke, 1860-1895,* p. 384.

15. B. D. Pak, *Rossia i Korea,* p. 89.

16. Narochnitsky, *Kolonial Nai Politika,* p. 384.

17. Foulk to Bayard, June 16, 1885, no. 180, Dip. Desp., Korea; *KAR,* 1:77-78; Yi, "Kŏmundo," pp. 491-492. It seems likely that this kind of blustering statement on the part of de Speyer was a false or empty diplomatic threat. In a private conversation with French Bishop Msgr. Blanc in Seoul, de Speyer told that his government had no intention of acquiring Korean territory or establishing a protectorate over Korea. See Lensen, *Balance of Intrigue,* p. 47.

18. Pak, *Rossia i Korea,* pp. 81-84.

19. Narochnitsky, *Kolonial Nai Politika,* pp. 359, 362; Synn, "Russo-Korean Struggle," pp. 26-28.

20. Narochnitsky, *Kolonial Nai Politika,* p. 257; Thornton to Granville, April 8, 1885, *BFSP,* 77:246; Andrew Malozemoff, *Russian Far Eastern Policy, 1881–1904,* p. 24; George Nathaniel Curzon, *Problems of the Far East, Japan-Korea-China,* p. 225.

21. Narochnitsky, *Kolonial Nai Politika,* pp. 384–385.

22. *SI,* 1885.5.25.

23. *CSSL,* 8:21–23; *CKS,* 2:124–126; *KNK,* 2:6–7; Lo, *Han'guk,* pp. 258–259.

24. Frederick Foo Chien, *The Opening of Korea,* p. 181.

25. *CSSL,* 8:32–36; Lensen, *Balance of Intrigue,* pp. 38–39.

26. *CSSL,* 8:32–36.

27. *ISHK,* 18:2–4.

28. *SI,* 1885.5.25.

29. Pak, *Rossia i Korea,* p. 90.

30. Allen Diary, July 19, 1885, Allen Papers; see also Fred Harvey Harrington, *God, Mammon, and the Japanese,* p. 83.

31. *NGB,* 1:359–360, 380–381; *CSSL,* 8:24–26.

32. *NGB,* 1:382–384, 386; *ISHK,* 17:27–28.

33. Seung Kwon Synn, *The Russo-Japanese Rivalry over Korea,* p. 64.

34. O'Conor to Salisbury, July 17, 1885, no. 356, July 22, 1885, no. 383, *FO,* 17/983.

35. *CSSL,* 27–31; *CT,* Li's letter to the Tsungli Yamen, 1885.6.7; *ISHK,* 17:30–36.

36. *SI,* 1885.2.25; *KNK,* 2:14; *WCSL,* 59:10; *CSSL,* 8:30 and 9:8.

37. Conversation between Kim and de Speyer, June 20, 1885, *CSSL,* 8:31–32.

38. Lensen, *Balance of Intrigue,* p. 47.

39. Conversation between Ch'en and de Speyer, June 23, 1885, *CSSL,* 8:33. De Speyer was not fooled by Ch'en's seemingly neutral attitude and doubted his sincerity; see Lensen, *Balance of Intrigue,* pp. 47–48.

40. See conversation between Kim and de Speyer, June 20, 1885, *CSSL,* 8:31–32; Foulk to Bayard, June 18, 1885, no. 184, and June 23, 1885, no. 186. Dip. Desp., Korea; Narochnitsky, *Kolonial Nai Politika,* pp. 384–385.

41. Conversation between Kim and de Speyer, July 2, 1885, *CSSL,* 8:35.

42. Conversation between Kim and Yüan Shih-k'ai, October 8, 1885, *ISHK,* 18:2–4.

43. Pak, *Rossia i Korea,* p. 90.

44. Conversation between Kim and de Speyer, July 2, 1885, *CSSL,* 8:31–35; see also Lensen, *Balance of Intrigue,* pp. 45–46.

45. Foulk to Bayard, July 15, 1885, no. 192, Dip. Desp., Korea.

46. Lensen, *Balance of Intrigue,* pp. 48–49.

47. Pak, *Rossia i Korea,* p. 91.

48. For example, see Pak Il-gŭn, *Kŭndae Han-Mi oegyosa,* pp. 387–388; Yi Kwang-rin, "The Role of Foreign Military Instructors in the Later Period of the Yi Dynasty," p. 243.

49. "Möllendorff's Diary," p. 188.

50. Foulk to Bayard, July 5, 1885, no. 192, Dip. Desp., Korea.

51. Foulk to Bayard, June 26, 1885, no. 187, Dip. Desp., Korea.

52. Lester B. Shippee, "Thomas Francis Bayard," 8:85.

53. Foulk to Bayard, June 18, 1885, no. 184, Dip. Desp., Korea.

54. Bayard to Foulk, August 19, 1885, no. 63, Dip. Inst., Korea; Charles Callan Tansill, *The Foreign Policy of Thomas F. Bayard, 1885–1897*, p. 428. There was another reason why Bayard sent such an instruction to Foulk. In view of the existing Anglo-Russian tension, Foulk advised the Japanese and Chinese representatives in Seoul to postpone their scheduled withdrawal of troops from Korea. Although Foulk's advice had not been accepted, Bayard thought that Foulk was playing too aggressive a role in Korea. See Yur-Bok Lee, *Diplomatic Relations between the United States and Korea, 1866–1887*, p. 102; Tansill, *Foreign Policy*, p. 427.

55. For the sad end of Foulk's professional career in Korea, see Lee, *Diplomatic Relations*, pp. 172–186; Bishop, "Policy and Personality," pp. 51–55; Robert E. Reordan, "The Role of George Clayton Foulk in United States-Korean Relations, 1884–1887," pp. 205–252.

56. Lo, *Han'guk*, p. 264.

57. "Möllendorff's Diary," p. 167. Yi states that it was quite proper for the Korean government to put the blame on von Möllendorff, since he had indeed abused the power. See *HGSC*, p. 797.

58. Rosalie von Möllendorff, *P. G. von Möllendorff: Ein Lebensbild*, pp. 100–101.

59. See James B. Palais, "Political Leadership in the Yi Dynasty," p. 13; James B. Palais, *Politics and Policy in Traditional Korea*, pp. 260–261; Harrington, *God, Mammon, and the Japanese*, pp. 42–43; Tyler Dennett, *Roosevelt and the Russo-Japanese War*, pp. 305–306; Tyler Dennett, "American Choices in the Far East in 1882," *American Historical Review* 30 (Oct. 1924): 88n. 9; Wayne Patterson, *The Korean Frontier in America: Immigration to Hawaii, 1896–1910*, Conclusion; and Wayne Patterson, "Japanese Imperialism in Korea: A Study of Immigration and Foreign Policy"; Key-Hiuk Kim, *The Last Phase of the East Asian World Order*, pp. 249, 298. See also a negative view on Kojong by one of his American advisers, William F. Sands, "Korea and the Korean Emperor," 69; William F. Sands, *Undiplomatic Memories: The Far East, 1896–1904*, pp. 54–56.

60. Robert Swartout, Jr., *Mandarins, Gunboats, and Power Politics*, pp. 58–60; Dalchoong Kim, "Korea's Quest for Reform and Diplomacy in the 1880s," pp. 502–504; Martina Deuchler, *Confucian Gentlemen and Barbarian Envoys*, pp. 49, 92–104. Unlike Sands, Denny, another American adviser, held a very positive opinion of Kojong; see Owen N. Denny, *China and Korea*, pp. 45–46; see also Foulk to family, July 2, 1884, Foulk Papers, LC; G. H. Jones, "His Majesty the King of Korea," pp. 427–429. For some reserved but still moderately favorable views on Kojong, see Count Vay de Vaya and Luskod, *Empires and Emperors of Russia, China, Korea, and Japan*, pp. 270–273; Donald M. Bishop, "Policy and Personality in Early Korean-American Relations: The Case of George Clayton Foulk," p. 33; Yur-Bok Lee, "Korean-American Diplomatic Relations, 1882–1905," p. 44.

61. Palais, *Politics and Policy*, pp. 247–251.

62. *SI,* 1885.5.25; *CSSL,* 8:28–31; *CSS,* 6:773. While in Tientsin, Nam and Pak also reported to Viceroy Li the rumor that the exiled Kim Ok-kyun in Japan sought an alliance with Russia for Korean independence; see *ISHK,* 17:35–37.

63. Foulk to Bayard, August 4, 1885, no. 211, Dip. Desp., Korea; Aston to O'Conor, June 22, 1885, (conf.), no. 72, *FO,* 17/983. See also Harrington, *God, Mammon, and the Japanese,* p. 210 n. 9.

64. Foulk to Bayard, August 4, 1885, no. 211, Dip. Desp., Korea.

65. *SI,* 1885.6.16 and 7.27; *CSSL,* 9:25–26; Foulk to Bayard, August 16, 1885, no. 214, Dip. Desp., Korea; *ISN,* 1885.6.16.

66. Ch'oe T'ae-ho, *Kaehang chŏn'gi ŭi Han'guk kwanse chedo,* p. 262.

67. Von Möllendorff, *Von Möllendorff,* p. 66; Foulk to Bayard, August 14, 1885, no. 238, Dip. Desp., Korea; Sin, *Hanmal,* pp. 168–169; Lo, *Han'guk,* p. 254.

68. Lo, *Han'guk,* p. 262; Pak, *Rossia i Korea,* p. 95; Narochnitsky, *Kolonial Nai Politika,* p. 390.

69. Foulk to Bayard, August 14, 1885, no. 238, Dip. Desp., Korea.

70. Harrington, *God, Mammon, and the Japanese,* p. 296; see also Allen to Wilson, October 11, 1897, Allen to Morse, November 17, 1896, Allen Papers.

71. Allen to Sherman, December 21, 1897, no. 49, Dip. Desp., Korea.

72. Baron Rosen, *Forty Years of Diplomacy,* 1:142.

73. *The Independent,* September 1, 1896.

74. *WCSL,* 61:15; *ISHK,* 17:33, 53–54; Von Möllendorff, *Von Möllendorff,* pp. 83–84.

75. See chap. 4; *WCSL,* 59:20–26; *CSSL,* 8:38–40; *ISHK,* 17:59–60.

76. *SI,* 1885.9.7; *ISN,* 1885.9.9; Hart to Merrill, September 25, 1885, Hart Papers; see also Hart to Campbell, September 5, 1885, in John K. Fairbank, Katherine Frost Bruner, and Elizabeth MacLeod Matheson eds., *The I. G. in Peking: Letters of Robert Hart,* 1:605–606.

77. *CT,* 1886.4.4. At the time when Li offered Denny the position of adviser to the Korean government, Denny thought that Li was acting merely as a liaison between himself and the Korean king; see Denny to the Editor of *Chinese Times,* October 12, 1888, Denny Papers.

78. Swartout, *Mandarins, Gunboats, and Power Politics,* pp. 42–44; M. Frederick Nelson, *Korea and the Old Orders in Eastern Asia,* p. 180; Hosea B. Morse, *The International Relations of the Chinese Empire,* 3:14.

## Chapter 7

1. *CSSL,* 9:13; *WCSL,* 61:18–19.

2. *ISHK,* 7:28, 42; *CSSL,* 9:13–14; *WCSL,* 61:18–20.

3. *CSSL,* 9:13; *WCSL,* 61:18–19.

4. *ISHK,* 18:5–6.

5. Foulk to Bayard, November 25, 1885, (conf.), no. 255, Dip. Desp., Korea.

6. Shen Tsu-hsien and Wu K'ai-sheng, *Jung-an ti-tzu-chi* [Records kept by the disciples of Jung-an (Yüan)], pp. 9–11; Young-ick Lew, "Yüan Shih-k'ai's Residency and the Korean Enlightenment Movement, 1885–94," *Journal of Korean Studies* 5 (1984): 72.

7. *KS* and *ISN*, 1888.8.9/16; Ŏ Yun-jung, *Chongjŏng yŏnp'yo*, p. 139.

8. Lin Ming-te, *Yüan Shih-k'ai yü Chao-hsien*, p. 42; Sin Ki-sŏk, *Hanmal oegyo-sa yŏn'gu*, pp. 100–101; Shen and Wu, *Jung-an*, pp. 15–16.

9. *CSSL*, 9:5; *ISHK*, 18:5.

10. *KHSL*, 11:36.

11. *WCSL*, 50:31–33; *CSSL*, 5:24, 28, 30, 35, 6:14–21.

12. *KHSL*, 4:2145–2150; 5:2564–2568.

13. Foulk to Bayard, May 27, 1887, no. 20, Dip. Desp., Korea; George Alexander Lensen, *Balance of Intrigue*, pp. 88–91.

14. *CSSL*, 9:25–26; Lin, *Yüan*, p. 46.

15. *ISN* and *SI*, 1885.8.27/28; *CSSL*, 9:5.

16. *CSSL*, 10:5–7.

17. Lew, "Yüan Shih-K'ai's Residency," p. 75.

18. *HH*, 2:5–6.

19. O'Conor to Salisbury, Korea, October 25, 1885, no. 3, *FO*, 17/983.

20. B. D. Pak, *Rossia i Korea*, pp. 93–95; A. L. Narochnitsky, *Kolonial Nai Politika Kapitalisticheskikh Derzh na Dalem Vostoke, 1860–1895*, p. 390.

21. *T'ongni*, 1885.8.25 and 1885.9.15; *ISN* and *SI*, 1885.9.7.

22. The Russo-Korean Trade Agreement of 1888 was signed by Cho Pyŏng-sik and Waeber, respectively. For the Korean text of the agreement, see *KSDS*, 3:30–39; *ISN*, *KS*, and *SI*, 1888.7.13. For an evaluation of the agreement, see Robert R. Swartout, Jr., *Mandarins, Gunboats, and Power Politics*, pp. 130–131. For the "advice" Foulk offered to the Korean officials on this Russo-Korean negotiation, see Yur-Bok Lee, *Diplomatic Relations between the United States and Korea, 1866–1887*, pp. 146–150.

23. *ISHK*, 18:28; Foulk to Bayard, November 25, 1885, no. 255, Dip. Desp., Korea.

24. *T'ongni*, 1886.3.24, and 1886.6.18; *ISN* and *SI*, 1886.4.18.

25. *T'ongni*, 1886.7.18/19; *ISN* and *SI*, 1886.7.17/25; *Tien-kao*, 7:45. *CSSL*, 10:14; *KNK*, 2:36.

26. Aston to O'Conor, July 30, 1885, nos. 84 and 85, *FO*, 17/996.

27. Aston to O'Conor, September 30, 1885, O'Conor to Salisbury, October 4, 1885, no. 61, *FO*, 17/987.

28. O'Conor to Kim, June 30, 1885, July 22, 1885, *FO*, 17/982; Moo-Soo Kwon, "British Policy towards Korea, 1882–1910," pp. 121–122.

29. The best account on Merrill's contribution in Korea is Ko Pyŏng-ik, "Chosŏn hae'gwan kwa Ch'ŏngguk hae'gwan kwa ŭi kwan'gye—Merrill kwa Hart rŭl chungsim ŭro" [The relationship between the Korean and Chinese customs service: Merrill and Hart], *Tonga Munhwa* 4 (October 1965): 1–30.

30. Hart repeatedly urged Merrill to support China's (Li's and Yüan's) policy of control of Korea; see, for example, Hart to Merrill, December 4, 1886, Hart Papers.

31. For examples, see Merrill to Hart, October 8, 1885, October 25, 1885, Merrill Papers; *KS* and *ISN,* 1885.9.7; *CT,* 1885.10.23.

32. Hart to Merrill, September 25, 1885, Hart Papers.

33. Hart to Merrill, September 25, 1885, November 30, 1885, Hart Papers.

34. Hart to Merrill, May 29, 1885, Hart Papers.

35. *HH,* 2:13; Merrill to Detring, August 28, 1886, Merrill Papers; Shen Yün-lung, ed. *Hsien-tai cheng-chih jen-wu shu-p'ing* [A critical account of some political personalities of recent times], 6:30.

36. Owen N. Denny, *China and Korea,* p. 34.

37. *HH,* 2:13; Merrill to Detring, August 28, 1886, Merrill Papers; Shen Yün-lung, ed., *Hsiangch'eng Yüan-shih chia-chi* [Family collections of the Yüan clan of Hsiangch'eng] 6:30–31.

38. Denby to Bayard, January 27, 1885, no. 635, Dip. Desp., China.

39. Bayard to Denby, October 12, 1885, no. 12, Dip. Inst., China.

40. *KAR,* 1:59, 64–65; see Yur-Bok Lee, "Korean-American Diplomatic Relations, 1882–1905," pp. 27–34.

41. Parker to Bayard, June 13, 1886, no. 7, Foulk to Bayard, October 6, 1886, no. 10, Dip. Desp., Korea.

42. Foulk to Bayard, September 7, 1886, no. 2, September 8, 1886, no. 3, Dip. Desp., Korea; *KAR.* I:59.

43. Denny to Frazar, November 14, 1886, Denny Papers; Foulk to Bayard, November 23, 1886, no. 23, Dip. Desp., Korea; Fred Harvey Harrington, *God, Mammon, and the Japanese,* pp. 219–220.

44. Frederick C. Drake, *Empire of the Seas,* pp. 319–320.

45. Rockhill to Bayard, December 13, 1886, no. 27, Dip. Desp., Korea.

46. Rockhill passed away in Honolulu on the way to China to take up the post.

47. Dinsmore to Bayard, May 3, 1887, no. 14, Dip. Desp., Korea.

48. Dinsmore to Bayard, May 27, 1887, no. 20, Dip. Desp., Korea.

49. Pak Il-gŭn, *Kŭndae Han-Mi oegyosa,* pp. 404, 408.

50. *ISN* and *SI,* 1886.4.16, 1886.7.23/26/27. Swartout, *Mandarins, Gunboats, and Power Politics,* p. 62.

51. *CSSL,* 10:14; *Tien-kao,* 7:45; *KNK,* 2:36.

52. *CSSL,* 10:14; *Tien-kao,* 7:45.

53. *CSSL,* 10:14; *Tien-kao,* 7:45; *KNK,* 2:36.

54. Lew, "Yüan Shih-K'ai's Residency," pp. 83–84.

55. *HH,* 2:5–6.

56. Ibid., 2:14.

57. *KHOM: Aan,* I:11–12.

58. Foulk and Denny believed that Yüan forged the document; see Foulk to Bayard, September 8, 1886, no. 3, October 14, 1886, no. 13, Dip. Desp., Korea; Denny to Detring, August 12, 1886, Denny Papers; Denny, *China and Korea,* p. 33. See also Swartout, *Mandarins, Gunboats, and Power Politics,* pp. 83–84; Tyler Dennett, *Americans in Eastern Asia,* p. 483. Pak Il-gŭn states that the document was forged by Yüan and Min Yŏng-ik; see his *Kŭndae,* pp. 409–410.

59. Jerome Ch'en, *Yuan Shih-K'ai,* p. 37; Seung Kwon Synn, *The Russo-Jap-*

*anese Rivalry over Korea,* p. 67; Kwon, "British Policy," pp. 59, 61–62. Lensen insists that the part of the document showing the Korean request for Russian warships is genuine, but that showing the Korean request for Russian protectorship is "forgery," probably authored by Min Yŏng-ik, or Baber, or Yüan himself; see his *Balance of Intrigue,* p. 75.

60. *Krasny Archiv.* "First Steps of Russian Imperialism in Far East, 1888–1903: Proceedings of the Meeting of the Special Committee, Held May 8 (April 26), 1888," *Chinese Social and Political Science Review* 18, no. 2 (1934–35): 240. See also Pak, *Rossia i Korea,* pp. 95–96; and Narochnitsky, *Kolonial Nai Politika,* pp. 389–390.

61. Pak, *Rossia i Korea,* p. 95.

62. Narochnitsky, *Kolonial Nai Politika,* p. 390; Lensen, *Balance of Intrigue,* p. 75; Pak, *Rossia i Korea,* pp. 95–96.

63. *ISHK,* 1:5–6; *HH,* 2:7, 12; Pak, *Kŭndae,* pp. 405–406.

64. *Tien-kao,* 7:31.

65. *HH,* 2:3–12.

66. *CSSL,* 10:6; *HH,* 2:9–12.

67. *T'ongni,* 1886.7.26/27; Wang Hsin-chung, *Chung-Jih chia-wu chang–cheng chih wai-chiao pei-ching,* p. 103.

68. *ISN,* 1886.7.17/22; Foulk to Bayard, September 8, 1885, no. 3, Dip. Desp., Korea; Harrington, *God, Mammon, and the Japanese,* p. 216; Lensen, *Balance of Intrigue,* p. 74.

69. *KHOM: Aan,* 1:12–13.

70. *HH,* 2:9–12; *KNK,* 2:42–43.

71. *ISHK,* 1:3–5; *Tien-kao,* 7:32–34; *HH,* 2:12–13; Narochnitsky, *Kolonial Nai Politika,* p. 395; Pak, *Kŭndae,* p. 409; *HGSC,* p. 829.

72. *HH,* 2:12–13; *Tien-kao,* 7:32–34; *CSSL,* 10:6–7.

73. *HH,* 2:5, 14–15; *Tien-kao,* 7:34–35; *CSSL,* 10:7.

74. Lensen, *Balance of Intrigue,* pp. 76–77.

75. Denny, *China and Korea,* p. 35.

76. Ibid., p. 37.

77. Later they were finally pardoned.

78. *T'ongni,* 1886.7.28.

79. *T'ongni,* 1886.8.6/7.

80. *CSSL,* 10:12–13; *ISHK,* 18:35–39; *T'ongni,* 1886.8.15.

81. *CT,* Li's Letter to the Tsungli Yamen, 1886.9.25; *CSSL,* 10:14.

82. See Hilary Conroy, *The Japanese Seizure of Korea, 1868–1910,* pp. 492–507.

83. *CT,* Li's Letter to the Tsungli Yamen, 1886.9.26.

84. *CSSL,* 10:14.

85. See notes of 91, 92, and 93 of this chapter.

86. *HH,* 2:13–14.

87. Shen, *Hsiangch'eng,* 6:30; *HH,* 2:13; Merrill to Hart, August 20, 1886, Merrill to Detring, August 28, 1886, Merrill to Hart, September 13, 1886, Merrill Papers; Hart to Merrill, December 4, 1886, Hart Papers.

88. Denny to Frazar, November 14, 1886, Denny Papers.

89. *CT,* the Korean king's memorandum to the Tsungli Yamen, 1886.9.27.

90. *WCSL,* 82:9–16; *ISHK,* 19:49–53; *CT,* the Korean king's memorandum to the Tsungli Yamen, 1886.12.1.

91. *ISHK,* 19:24–26; *Tien-kao,* 13:30.

92. For examples, see Parker to Bayard, June 13, 1887, no. 7, and Foulk to Bayard, October 6, 1886, no. 10, Dip. Desp., Korea.

93. See Lee, *Diplomatic Relations,* pp. 150–151; Donald M. Bishop, "Policy and Personality in Early Korean-American Relations," pp. 51.

94. *FR,* 1885, pp. 335–343.

95. *The North China Daily News,* November 15, 16, 17, 1886.

96. *CT,* Correspondences between Korean Foreign Minister and American Representative, 1886.12.6; Kim to Rockhill, December 30, 1886, enc., Rockhill to Bayard, January 3, 1887, no. 46, Dip. Desp., Korea.

97. *CT,* 1886.12.21; Rockhill to Kim, January 11, 1887, enc., Rockhill to Bayard, January 24, 1887, no. 52, Dip. Desp., Korea.

98. Bayard to Rockhill, March 3, 1887, no. 55, Dip. Inst., Korea.

99. *CT,* 1887.4.9, 1887.5.8/26; Dinsmore to Bayard, May 3, 1887, no. 14, Dip. Desp., Korea.

100. *CT,* 1887.5.26, 1887. 9.10; Dinsmore to Bayard, May 9, 1887, no. 16, June 20, 1887, no. 29, Dip. Desp., Korea.

101. Harrington, *God, Mammon, and the Japanese,* p. 224.

102. Dinsmore to Bayard, May 24, 1887, no. 19, Dip. Desp., Korea; Harrington, *God, Mammon, and the Japanese,* p. 223.

103. Dinsmore to Bayard, May 30, 1887, no. 23, Dip. Desp., Korea.

104. *ISHK,* 1887.4.12.

105. Bayard to Dinsmore, June 17, 1887, no. 21, Dip. Inst., Korea.

106. Bayard to Dinsmore, June 17, 1887, no. 21, Dip. Inst., Korea.

107. For example, see Yur-Bok Lee, *Establishment of a Korean Legation in the United States, 1887–1890,* pp. 7–9.

108. Denny, *China and Korea,* p. 38. Even Jerome Ch'en, a sympathetic biographer of Yüan, admits that Yüan generally sought his goals by means of "threat, bribes, and murder"; see his *Yuan Shih-k'ai,* p. 197.

109. Ch'en insists that even without Yüan's "obstructionism," the constitutional monarchism in China might have not succeeded for a variety of reasons, but admits that "Yuan's most single legacy was the creation of a large number of warlords," and that all in all he "can command our respect neither as a statesman nor as a man of integrity"; see his *Yuan Shih-k'ai,* pp. 211–215. For condemnations of Yüan by Dr. Sun Yat-sen and others, see Pai Chiao, ed., *Yüan Shih-k'ai yü Chung-hua min-kuo* [Yüan Shih-k'ai and the Republic of China], pp. 372–373; Chang Ch'i-yün, *Chung-hua min-kuo shih-kang* [An outline history of the Republic of China], 1:204–205.

110. Ch'en, *Yuan Shih-k'ai,* p. 206.

111. *CSSL,* 11:120; *Tien-kao,* 10:27; *WCSL,* 81:96–97.

112. For examples, see *CSSL,* 12:29–30; *Tien-kao,* 12:19; *NGB,* 24:443–449; *SI, KS,* and *PT,* 1888.5.10; *T'ongni,* 1885.5.5.

113. *NGB,* 21:209–210.

114. Lew, "Yüan Shih-k'ai's Residency," p. 78.

115. Ch'en states that "no other Han Chinese so lacking in academic distinction had reached such a high position under the Ch'ing dynasty"; see his *Yuan Shih-k'ai*, p. 208; and also Lin, *Yüan*, pp. 6, 10–12, 17.

## Chapter 8

1. Yi Yŏng-hui, "Kŏmundo chŏmryŏng oegyo chonggo," pp. 496–498; O'Conor to Salisbury, November 17, 1885, no. 457, *FO*, 17/986; January 7, 1886, *BFSP*, 78:157–158.

2. O'Conor to Salisbury, November 17, 1885, no. 457, *FO*, 17/986; Salisbury to O'Conor, December 12, 1885, and O'Conor to Salisbury, January 7, 1886, *BFSP*, 78:157–158; Yung-Chung Kim, "Great Britain and Korea, 1883–1887," pp. 175–176.

3. *BFSP*, 78:157–159; Moo Soo Kwon, "British Policy towards Korea, 1882–1910," p. 123; Yi, "Kŏmundo," pp. 498–499.

4. *BFSP*, 78:160–161; Kwon, "British Policy," p. 123.

5. Walsham to Kim, July 28, 1886, no. 2, *FO*, 228/1013.

6. Walsham to Rosebery, July 31, 1886, Iddesleigh to Walsham, August 12, 1886, *BFSP*, 78:161; Kwon, "British Policy," p. 124.

7. Russian Official (Waeber) to Denny, June 12, 1886, Denny Papers.

8. Denny to Li, June 29, 1886, Denny Papers. See also Robert R. Swartout, Jr., ed., *An American Adviser in Late Yi Korea: The Letters of Owen Nickerson Denny*, p. 8.

9. A. L. Narochnitsky, *Kolonial Nai Politika Kapitalisticheskikh Derzh na Dalem Vostoke, 1860–1895*, pp. 394–395.

10. B. D. Pak, *Rossia i Korea*, pp. 98–99; Kwon, "British Policy," pp. 175–176; Tingfu Tsiang, "Sino-Japanese Diplomatic Relations, 1870–1894," pp. 98–99; Seung Kwon Synn, "Russo-Korean Relations in the 1880s," *Korea Journal* 20, no. 9 (Sept. 1980): 35–36; Krasny Archiv., "First Steps of Russian Imperialism in Far East," *Chinese Social and Political Science Review* 18, no. 2 (1934–1935): 240.

11. *ISHK*, 18:39, 46–47.

12. Walsham to Iddesleigh, December 25, 1886, *BFSP*, 78:166.

13. Ibid., 78:167–169; Kwon, "British Policy," pp. 125–126.

14. Pak, *Rossia i Korea*, p. 99.

15. Paul King, *In the Chinese Customs Service*, pp. 88–89.

16. Denny to Mitchell, February 6, 1888, Denny Papers.

17. Bayard to Dinsmore, March 21, 1888, no. 67, Dip. Inst., Korea.

18. Dinsmore to Bayard, May 16, 1888, no. 109, Dip. Desp., Korea.

19. Denny to Detring, August 8, 1888, Denny Papers; Dinsmore to Bayard, May 16, 1888, no. 109, Dip. Desp., Korea.

20. Denny to Lo, October 16, 1877, Denny to McCracken, January 7, 1888, Denny Papers; Dinsmore to Bayard, February 7, 1888, no. 91, April 3, 1888, no. 99, Dip. Desp., Korea.

21. Dinsmore to Bayard, May 10, 1888, no. 166, Dip. Desp., Korea.

22. Rosalie von Möllendorff, *P. G. von Möllendorff: Ein Lebensbild,* pp. 85–86.

23. Robert Swartout, Jr., *Mandarins, Gunboats, and Power Politics,* pp. 43–44, 64–65.

24. Von Möllendorff, *Von Möllendorff,* pp. 85–86.

25. See *SI* and *ISN,* 1886.1.7/29; *CSSL,* 9:25–26.

26. Denny to Wetmore, July 13, 1886, Denny Papers.

27. Denny completed the final version of his manuscript entitled *China and Korea* in the spring of 1888. Kelly and Walsh in Shanghai, China, published the manuscript (47 pages) in the summer of 1888. Swartout's edited book, *An American Adviser in Late Yi Korea,* contains the complete text of Denny's *China and Korea* at pages 139–161. A shorter and earlier but identical version (in terms of thesis) was printed in the *Congressional Record.* 50th Cong., 1st sess., vol. 19, pt. 9, August 31, 1888.

28. Owen N. Denny, *China and Korea,* p. 38.

29. For Denny's influence on Kojong, see *Tien-kao,* 8:31; *CSSL,* 10:29; Denny to Detring, July 21, 1888, Denny Papers; Merrill to Hart, October 4, 1889, Merrill Papers; Swartout, *Mandarins, Gunboats, and Power Politics,* pp. 89–95. For Allen's influence on Kojong, see Allen to Ellenwood, June 11, 1888, August 2, 1888, Allen to Foulk, July, 1887, Allen to Everett, July 2, 1887, Allen Papers; *FR,* 1888, p. 433; Fred Harvey Harrington, *God, Mammon, and the Japanese,* p. 226. For Min's influence on Kojong, see *Tien-kao,* 8:31; *CSSL,* 10:29.

30. *ISN,* 1887.6.29; *KHOM: Aan,* 1:43.

31. For Yüan's threat, see *CSSL,* 10:30, 34–35; *Tien-kao,* 8:32; *CT,* Li's Letter to the Tsungli Yamen, 1887.7.27. For the official position taken by the Chinese government on this matter, see *Tien-kao,* 8:32; *KHOM: Ch'öngan,* 1:374.

32. See Yur-Bok Lee, *Establishment of a Korean Legation in the United States, 1887–1890,* pp. 17–20.

33. Paul Georg von Möllendorff, "A Reply to Mr. O. N. Denny's Pamphlet Entitled: 'China and Korea'" in von Möllendorff, *Von Möllendorff,* pp. 125–136.

34. Ibid., pp. 132–133.

35. Ibid., p. 133.

36. Ibid., pp. 133–134.

37. Ibid., p. 135.

38. For examples, see *CSSL,* 5:24, 28, 30, 35, 6:14–21, 22–26; *WCSL,* 50:31–33; *ISN,* 1884.10.19/20/21/23/24; *HH,* 2:5–14.

39. Von Möllendorff, "A Reply to Mr. Denny's Pamphlet," p. 131.

40. Ibid., p. 136.

41. For some analysis and evaluation of Denny's *China and Korea,* see my *Establishment of a Korean Legation,* pp. 22–23; Swartout, *Mandarins, Gunboats, and Power Politics,* pp. 108–118; M. Frederick Nelson, *Korea and the Old Orders in Eastern Asia,* pp. 194–198.

42. See my *Establishment of a Korean Legation,* pp. 27–28; Key-Hiuk Kim, *The Last Phase of the East Asian World Order,* pp. 253–254; Hilary Conroy, *The Japanese Seizure of Korea,* pp. 66–67.

43. See von Möllendorff, "A Reply to Mr. Denny's Pamphlet," pp. 125–

136; Ch'oe Sŏg-u, "Han-Pul choyak kwa sin'gyo chayu" [The Korean-French Treaty and religious freedom], *Sahak yŏn'gu* 21 (September 1969): 210–211.

44. Von Möllendorff, *Von Möllendorff,* p. 85.

45. Ibid., pp. 85–86.

46. *The Chinese Times,* June 30, 1888, p. 44.

47. Hart to Campbell, June 3, 1888, Hart Papers.

48. Hart to Campbell, June 16, 1888, July 1, 1888, Hart Papers.

49. Von Möllendorff, *Von Möllendorff,* p. 92.

50. For Denny's relations with some influential leaders of Republican Party in the United States, see Swartout, *Mandarins, Gunboats, and Power Politics,* pp. 5–7, 106–107.

51. Von Möllendorff, *Von Möllendorff,* pp. 87–88.

52. Ibid., pp. 92–93.

53. Ko Pyŏng-ik, "Mok In-dŏk ŭi kobbingwa kŭ paegyŏng," *Chindan Hakpo* 25/27 (December 1964): 233.

54. Hart to Campbell, October 6, 1889, Hart Papers.

55. Andrew Malozemoff, *Russian Far Eastern Policy, 1881–1904,* pp. 90–91.

56. Von Möllendorff, *Von Möllendorff,* pp. 109–114.

57. In 1890, General Charles W. LeGendre succeeded Denny. A military adventurer of French extraction and a naturalized American citizen, he had been an adviser to the Japanese Foreign Office between 1872 and 1875. His performance as an adviser to the Korean government and king was rather poor. See Yur-Bok Lee, "Korean-American Diplomatic Relations, 1882–1905," pp. 32–33.

58. Hart to Campbell, April 1, 1900, Hart Papers.

59. Hart to Campbell, October 11, 1903, Hart Papers.

60. Between September 1904 and December 1905 the Korean government made six different appeals to the Roosevelt Administration, but all in vain. For examples, see Allen to Hay, September 30, 1904, Morgan to Root, September 30, October 19, 1905, Dip. Desp., Korea; *FR,* 1905, pp. 629–630.

61. Roosevelt to Hay, January 28, 1905, in Etling E. Morrison, John M. Blum, and Alfred D. Chandler, Jr., eds., *The Letters of Theodore Roosevelt,* 2:1394.

## Conclusion

1. M. Frederick Nelson, *Korea and the Old Orders in Eastern Asia,* p. 294.

2. See my chapter, "Korean-American Diplomatic Relations, 1882–1905," and Fred Harvey Harrington's "An American View of Korean-American Relations," in *One Hundred Years of Korean-American Relations,* edited by Yur-Bok Lee and Wayne Patterson, pp. 12–45, 46–67.

3. Foulk to Bayard, August 4, 1885, no. 211, Dip. Desp., Korea.

4. Hart to Merrill, November 30, 1885, Hart Papers.

5. Merrill to Hart, October 26, 1885, Merrill to Detring, October 26, 1885, Merrill Papers.

6. George Alexander Lensen, *Balance of Intrigue,* pp. 31–32.

7. O'Conor to Salisbury, June 27, 1885, *FO,* 17/982; O'Conor to Granville, May 20, 1885, (conf.), no. 235, *FO,* 17/981; July 4, 1885, (conf.), no. 338, *FO,* 17/982; Rosalie von Möllendorff, *P. G. von Möllendorff: Ein Lebensbild,* pp. 91–92.

8. Ch'oe T'ae-ho, *Kaehang chŏn'gi ŭi Han'guk kwanse chedo,* pp. 151–202; Ko Pyŏng-ik, "Chosŏn hae'gwan kwa Ch'ŏngguk hae'gwan kwa ŭi kwan'gye," 1–29; Dalchoong Kim, "Korea's Quest for Reform and Diplomacy in the 1880's," pp. 429–449; Philip Woo, "The Historical Development of Korean Tariff and Customs Administration, 1875–1958," 33–86.

9. For some moderate criticism of von Möllendorff, see Lo Kye-hyŏn, *Han'guk oegyosa yŏn'gu,* pp. 263–264; Martina Deuchler, *Confucian Gentlemen and Barbarian Envoys,* p. 164.

10. Tyler Dennett, "Early American Policy in Korea, 1883–7," p. 90.

11. Andrew C. Nahm, "Durham White Stevens and the Japanese Annexation of Korea," pp. 110–136.

12. For an interesting evaluation of Denny's educational and professional qualifications, see Robert R. Swartout, Jr., *Mandarins, Gunboats, and Power Politics,* pp. 1–3.

# BIBLIOGRAPHY

## Manuscript and Archival Collections

Horace N. Allen Papers. New York Public Library, New York.

China. Tsungli Yamen. *Chao-hsien tang* [Korean archives]. The Institute of Modern History, Academia Sinica, Taipei, Taiwan.

Owen Nickerson Denny Papers. Special Collections. University of Oregon, Eugene.

George C. Foulk Papers. New York Public Library, New York; Library of Congress, Washington, D.C.

Great Britain. Foreign Office Archives, London.

Great Britain. Public Record Office. Foreign Office, General Correspondence, China: *FO.* 17; *FO.* 228; Foreign Office, General Correspondence, Japan: *FO.* 46.

Robert Hart. Letters to Various Westerners in the Chinese Customs Service, 1865–1910. Typed transcripts. Houghton Library, Harvard University, Cambridge, Mass.

Japan. Ministry of Foreign Affairs, Archives. History of Japanese-Korean Relations. U.S. Library of Congress Microfilm. SP–5.

Korea. *T'ongni kyosŏp t'ongsang samu amun ilgi* [Records of the Office of Foreign Affairs]. 44 vols. The Royal Kyujanggak Collection. Central Library, Seoul National University, Seoul.

Henry F. Merrill Papers. Letters to Sir Robert Hart and Others in the Chinese Customs Service, 1884–1913. Houghton Library, Harvard University, Cambridge, Mass.

Robert Wilson Shufeldt Papers. U.S. Library of Congress, Washington, D.C.

United States. Department of State. Despatches from United States Ministers to China, 1855–1906, file microcopy no. 92. Despatches from United States Ministers to Japan, 1855–1906, file microcopy no. 133. Despatches from United States Ministers to Korea, 1883–1905, file microcopy no. 134. National Archives, Washington D.C.

United States. Department of State. Diplomatic Instructions of the Department of State, 1801–1906, China, Japan, Korea; file microcopy no. 77. National Archives, Washington, D.C.

United States. Department of State. Notes to Foreign Legations in the United States from the Department of State, 1883–1906, file microcopy no. 166. National Archives, Washington, D.C.

United States. Department of State. Notes to Foreign Legations in the United States from the Department of State: Korea, Persia, and Siam, file microcopy no. 99. National Archives, Washington, D.C.


## Newspapers

*Chinese Times* (Tientsin)
*Independence (Tongnip Shinmun)* (Seoul)
*Korea Times*
*Japan Daily Herald*
*North China Daily News*
*North China Herald*
*San Francisco Chronicle*
*Times* (London)


## Other Sources

Alexander, Lewis M. *International Boundary Study, No. 26: Afghanistan–USSR Boundary.* Washington, D.C.: Office of Research in Economics and Science, 1963.

Allen, Horace N. *Things Korean: A Collection of Sketches and Anecdotes, Missionary and Diplomat.* New York: Fleming H. Revell, 1908.

―――. *Korea: Fact and Fancy.* Seoul: Methodist Publishing House, 1904.

Allen, Richard C. *Korea's Syngman Rhee.* Rutland, Vt.: Charles E. Tuttle Co., 1960.

American Library Association. *The National Union Catalog: Pre-1956 Imprints.* 685 vols. London: Mansell Publishing, 1968–1980.

Aydelotte, William Osgood. *Bismarck and British Colonial Policy: The Problems of South West Africa, 1883–1885.* Philadelphia: University of Pennsylvania Press, 1937.

Barnett, A. Doak. *Communist China and Asia: Challenge to American Policy.* New York: Vintage Books, 1960.

Becker, Seymour. *Russia's Protectorates in Central Asia: Bukhara and Khiva, 1865–1924.* Cambridge: Harvard University Press, 1968.

Bishop, Donald M. "Policy and Personality in Early Korean-American Relations: The Case of George Clayton Foulk." In *The United States and Korea: American-Korean Relations, 1866–1976,* edited by Andrew C. Nahm, pp. 27–63. Kalamazoo, Mich.: The Center for Korean Studies, Western Michigan University, 1979.

Bohm, Fred C., and Robert R. Swartout, Jr., eds., *Naval Surgeon in Yi Korea: The Journal of George W. Woods*. Berkeley: Institute of East Asian Studies, University of California, 1984.

Bradsher, Henry S. *Afghanistan and Soviet Union*. Durham, N.C.: Duke University Press, 1983.

Bunker, Annie Ellers. "My First Visit to Her Majesty the Queen." *Korean Repository* 2 (1895): 373–375.

Cable, E. M. "The United States–Korean Relations, 1866–1871." *Transactions of the Royal Asiatic Society, Korea Branch* 28 (1938): 1–299.

Cady, John F. *Southeast Asia: Its Historical Development*. New York: McGraw-Hill Book Company, 1964.

———. *The Roots of French Imperialism in Eastern Asia*. Ithaca, N.Y.: Cornell University Press, 1954.

Carnegie Endowment for International Peace, Division of International Law. *Korea: Treaties and Agreements*. Washington, D.C.: Gibson Brothers, 1921.

Chang Ch'i-yün. *Chung-hua min-kuo shih-kang* [An outline history of the Republic of China]. 2 vols. Taipei: Chung-Hua wen-hua, 1954.

Chang Chih-tung. *Chang Wen-hsiang-kung ch'üan-chi* [Complete works of Chang Chih-tung]. 6 vols. Edited by Wang Shu-nan. Reprint. Taipei: Wen-hai, 1963.

Chang P'ei-lun. *Chien-yü ch'üan-chi* [Collected works of Chang P'ei-lun]. 20 vols. Shanghai: Chung-hua Shu-chü, 1924.

Chang Ts'un-wu. *Ch'ing-Han tsung-fan mou-i, 1637–1894* [Sino-Korean tributary trade, 1637–1894]. Taipei: The Institute of Modern History, Academia Sinica, 1978.

———. "Ch'ing-Han kuan-hsi, 1636–1644" [Ch'ing-Korean relations, 1636–1644]. *Ku-kung wen-hsien* 4, no. 1 (December 1972): 15–37; 4, no. 2 (March 1973): 15–35.

———. "Ch'ing-tai Chung-kuo tui Chao-hsien wen-hua chih ying-hsiang" [Chinese cultural influence on Korea during the Ch'ing period]. *Bulletin of the Institute of Modern History, Academia Sinica* 4, no. 2 (December 1972): 551–599.

Chay, John. "The First Three Decades of American-Korean Relations, 1882–1910: Reassessments and Reflections." In *U.S.-Korean Relations, 1882–1982*, edited by Tae-Hwan Kwak, John Chay, Soon Sung Cho, and Shannon McCune, pp. 15–33. Seoul: Kyungnam University Press, 1982.

Ch'en, Jerome. *Yuan Shih-k'ai*. Stanford: Stanford University Press, 1961.

Ch'en, Tieh-min. "The Sino-Japanese War, 1894–1895: Its Origin, Development, and Diplomatic Background." Ph.D. diss., University of California, Berkeley, 1944.

Chere, Lewis M. "Great Britain and the Sino-French War: The Problems of an Involved Neutral, 1883–1885." *Selected Papers in Asian Studies* New Series Paper No. 7. Western Conference of the Association for Asian Studies.

———. "The Diplomacy of the Sino-French War, 1883–1885: Finding a Way Out of an Unwanted, Undeclared War." Ph.D. diss., Washington State University, 1978.

Chien, Frederick Foo. *The Opening of Korea: A Study of Chinese Diplomacy,* 1876–1885. Hamden, Conn.: The Shoe String Press, 1967.

China (Ch'ing dynasty). *Ta Ch'ing li-ch'ao shih-lu: Teh-tsung-ch'ao* [Annals of the Ch'ing dynasty: Kuang-hsü reign]. Taipei: Hua-wen shu-chü, 1964.

China. Imperial Maritime Customs. *Treaties, Conventions, Etc., Between China and Foreign States.* 2 vols. Shanghai: Statistical Department of the Inspectorate General of Customs, 1917.

———. *Treaties, Regulations, Etc., Between Corea and Other Powers, 1876–1889.* Shanghai: Statistical Department of the Inspectorate General of Customs, 1891.

China. National Palace Museum. *Ch'ing Kuang-hsü ch'ao Chung-Jih chiao-she shih-liao* [Documents on Sino-Japanese relations during the Kuang-hsü reign]. 44 vols. Peking: National Palace Museum, 1932.

———. *Ch'ou-pan i-wu shih-mo: Tao-kuang ch'ao* [The complete account of the management of barbarian affairs: the Tao-kuang reign]. 80 vols. Peking: National Palace Museum, 1930.

———. *Ch'ou-pan i-wu shih-mo: T'ung-chih ch'ao* [The complete account of the management of barbarian affairs: the T'ung-chih reign]. 100 vols. Peking: National Palace Museum, 1930.

China. The Institute of Modern History, Academia Sinica. *Ch'ing-chi Chung-Jih-Han kuan-hsi shih-liao* [Documents on Sino-Japanese–Korean relations during the late Ch'ing period]. 3 vols. Taipei: The Institute of Modern History, Academia Sinica, 1970.

Cho Hang-nae. *Kaehanggi tae-Il kwan'gyesa yŏn'gu* [A study of Korean-Japanese relations in the opening of Korea]. Taegu: Hyŏngsŏl ch'ulp'ansa, 1973.

———. "Hwang Chun-hŏn ŭi Chosŏn ch'aeknyak e taehan kŏmt'o" [Evaluation of Hwang Chun-hŏn's "A Policy for Korea"]. *Taegu-dae nonmun-jip* 3 (1963): 244–246.

Cho Ki-jun. "Kaehwagi Ilje ŭi kyŏngje ch'imnyak" [Economic aggression of the Japanese imperialism during the period of enlightenment]. In *Ilbon ŭi ch'imnyak chŏng chaek sa yŏn'gu* [A study on history of Japan's aggressive policy], edited by Yŏksa hakhoe. Seoul: Ilchogak, 1984.

Choe, Ching Young. *The Rule of the Taewŏn'gun, 1864–1873: Restoration in Yi Korea.* Cambridge: East Asian Research Center, Harvard University, 1972.

Ch'oe Jun. "Myŏng'chi chogi ŭi Ilbon Ŏlnon" [Japan's public debate at the beginning of the Meiji era]. In *Ilbon ŭi ch'imnyak chŏng chaek sa yŏn'gu* [A study on history of Japan's Aggressive Policy], edited by Yŏksa hakhoe. Seoul: Ilchogak, 1984.

Ch'oe Sŏg-u, "Han-Pul choyak kwa sin'gyo chayu" [The Korean-French Treaty and religious freedom], *Sahak yŏn'gu* 21 (September 1969): 209–229.

———. "Pyŏng'in yang'yo sogo" [A short study of the 1866 Western invasion]. *Yŏksa Hakpo* 30 (April 1966): 108–124.

Ch'oe T'ae-ho. *Kaehang chŏn'gi ŭi Han'guk kwanse chedo* [The Korean tariff system in the early period of opening ports]. Seoul: Han'guk yŏn'guwŏn, 1976.

Ch'oe, Yŏng-ho. "The Kapsin Coup of 1884: A Reassessment." *Korean Studies* 6 (1982): 105–124.

———. "Sino-Korean Relations, 1866–1876, Tributary Relationship to China." *The Journal of Asiatic Studies* 9, no. 1 (March 1966): 131–184.

Choi, Soo Bock. "Korea's Response to America and France in the Decade of the Taewongun [Taewŏn'gun], 1864–1873." In *Korea's Response to the West,* edited by Yung-Hwan Jo, pp. 109–140. Kalamazoo, Mich.: The Korean Research and Publications, 1971.

———. "Political Dynamics in Hermit Korea: The Rise of Royal Power in the Decade of the Taewonkun [Taewŏn'gun], 1864–1873." Ph.D. diss., University of Maryland, 1963.

Choi, Woonsang. *The Fall of the Hermit Kingdom.* Dobbs Ferry, N.Y.: Oceana Publications, 1967.

Chŏng Kyo. *Taehan kyenyŏnsa* [History of the last years of the Yi dynasty]. Seoul: Kuksa p'yŏnch'an wiwŏnhoe, 1957.

Chŏng Yon-sŏk. *Miguk ŭi taeHan chŏngch'aek, 1845–1980* [American policy toward Korea, 1845–1980]. Seoul: Ilchogak, 1979.

Chōsen sōtokufu [Government General of Korea]. *T'ongmun kwanji* [Records of Bureau of Interpreters]. Keijō (Seoul): Chōsen sōtokufu, 1944.

Chou Fu. *Chou Ch'iao-shen-kung ch'üan-chi* [Complete works of Chou Fu]. 36 vols. Chinfu, 1922.

Choy, Bong-youn. *A History of the Korean Unification: Its Issues and Prospects.* Peoria, Ill.: Research Committee on Korean Unification, Institute of International Studies, Bradley University, 1984.

Chu, Samuel C. *Reformer in Modern China: Chang Chien, 1853–1926.* New York: Columbia University Press, 1965.

Chun Hae-jong (Chŏn Hae-jong). "Sino-Korean Tributary Relations during the Ch'ing Period." In *The Chinese World Order,* edited by John K. Fairbank, pp. 90–111. Cambridge: East Asian Research Center, Harvard University, 1972.

———. *Han-Chung kwan'gyesa yŏn'gu* [Study of the Sino-Korean relations]. Seoul: Ilchogak, 1970.

———. "Ch'ŏngdae Han-Chung chogong kwan'gye chonggo" [A study on the Sino-Korean tributary relations]. *Chindan Hakpo* no. 29/30 (1967): 239–284.

———. *Han'guk kŭnse taeoe kwan'gye munhŏn piyo* [Manual of recent Korean foreign relations, 1870–1910]. Studies on the Kyujanggak Archives, no. 1. Seoul: Institute of Asian Studies, Seoul National University, 1966.

———. "Han-Chung chogong kwan'gye ko—Han-Chung kwan'gyesa ŭi chogam ŭl wihan toron" [A historical survey of Sino-Korean tributary relations]. *Tongyang sahak yŏn'gu* 1 (October 1966): 10–41.

Chung, Henry. *The Oriental Policy of the United States.* New York: Fleming H. Revell Co., 1919.

———, ed. *Korean Treaties.* New York: H. S. Nichols, 1919.

Conroy, Hilary. *The Japanese Seizure of Korea, 1868–1910: A Study of Realism and Idealism in International Relations.* Philadelphia: University of Pennsylvania Press, 1960.

————. "Chōsen Mondai: The Korean Problem in Meiji Japan." *Proceedings of the American Philosophical Society* 5 (1956): 443–454.

————. *The Japanese Frontier in Hawaii, 1868–1898.* Berkeley: University of California Press, 1953.

Conroy, Hilary, Sandra T. W. Davis, and Wayne Patterson, eds. *Japan in Transition: Thought and Action in the Meiji Era, 1868–1912.* Madison, N.J.: Fairleigh Dickenson University Press, 1984.

"Conversations on the U.S.-Korean Treaty in 1882 between the Korean Delegates and the Chinese Envoys." *Yŏksa Hakpo* 22 (January 1964): 121–132.

Cook, Harold F. *Korea's 1884 Incident: Its Background and Kim Ok-kyun's Elusive Dream.* Seoul: Royal Asiatic Society, Korea Branch, 1972.

————. "Möllendorff: First Western Official." *Korea Times,* April 11, 1971.

"Corea." *The Edinburg Review* 136 (October 1872): 155–173.

Curzon, George Nathaniel. *Problems of the Far East, Japan–Korea–China.* London: Longmans and Green, 1894.

Dallet, Charles. *Histoire de l'église de Corée.* 2 vols. Paris: V. Palmé, 1874.

Dallin, David J. *The Rise of Russia in Asia.* New Haven: Yale University Press, 1949.

Dennett, Tyler. *Americans in Eastern Asia: A Critical Study of the Policy of the United States with Reference to China, Japan and Korea in the 19th Century.* Reprint. New York: Barnes & Noble, 1963.

————. *Roosevelt and the Russo-Japanese War: A Critical Study of American Policy in Eastern Asia in 1920–5, Based Primarily upon the Private Papers of Theodore Roosevelt.* Garden City, N.Y.: Doubleday and Co., 1925.

————. "American Choices in the Far East in 1882." *American Historical Review* 30 (October 1924): 84–108.

————. "Early American Policy in Korea, 1883–7." *Political Science Quarterly* 38 (March 1923): 82–103.

Denny, Owen N. *China and Korea.* Shanghai: Kelley and Walsh, 1888.

Deuchler, Martina. *Confucian Gentlemen and Barbarian Envoys: The Opening of Korea, 1875–1885.* Seattle: University of Washington Press, 1977.

Dickens, Frederick V., and Stanley Lane Poole. *The Life of Sir Harry Parkes.* 2 vols. London: Macmillan Co., 1894.

Djang, Chu. "Chinese Suzerainty: A Study of Diplomatic Relations between China and her Vassal States, 1870–1895." Ph.D. diss., Johns Hopkins University, 1935.

Drake, Frederick C. *The Empire of the Seas: A Biography of Rear Admiral Robert Wilson Shufeldt, USN.* Honolulu: University of Hawaii Press, 1984.

Eastman, Lloyd E. *Throne and Mandarins: China's Search for a Policy during the Sino-French Controversy, 1880–1885.* Cambridge: Harvard University Press, 1967.

————. "Ch'ing-i and Chinese Policy Formation during the Nineteenth Century." *Journal of Asian Studies* 24, no. 4 (August 1965): 595–611.

Fairbank, John K. *The United States and China.* 4th ed. Cambridge: Harvard University Press, 1983.

————, ed. *The Chinese World Order: Traditional China's Foreign Relations.* Harvard East Asian Series, no. 32. Cambridge: Harvard University, 1968.

Fairbank, John K., Katherine Frost Bruner, and Elizabeth MacLeod Matheson, eds. *The I. G. in Peking: Letters of Robert Hart, China Maritime Customs 1868-1907.* 2 vols. Cambridge: The Belknap Press of Harvard University Press, 1975.

Fenwick, Charles G. *International Law.* 3rd ed. New York: Appleton–Century-Crofts, 1962.

Foster, John W. *American Diplomacy in the Orient.* Boston: Houghton Mifflin Co., 1900.

Fraser-Tyler, W. Kerr. *Afghanistan: A Study of Political Development in Central and Southern Asia.* Reprint. London and New York: Oxford University Press, 1962.

Fukuzawa Yukichi. *Fukuzawa Yukichi zenshū* [Complete works of Fukuzawa Yukichi]. 17 vols. Tokyo: Iwanami shoten, 1958–1960.

Genyōsha, ed. *Genyōsha shashi* [History of Genyōsha]. Tokyo: Genyōsha, 1917.

Ginsburg, George. "The Citizenship Status of Koreans in Pre-Revolutionary Russia and the Early Years of the Soviet Regime." *Journal of Korean Affairs* 5, no. 2 (1975): 1–19.

Great Britain. Foreign Office. *British and Foreign State Papers.* Vols. 75–78. London: His Majesty's Printing Office, 1876–1894.

————. *Hansard's Parliamentary Debates,* 3rd series. Vol. 276 (1883). Vol. 297 (1885). Vol. 308 (1886). Vol. 310 (1887). Vol. 311 (1887).

————. *House of Commons Sessional Papers* (Parliamentary Papers). Vol. 91 (1887).

Greaves, Rose L. *Persia and the Defense of India, 1884-1892.* London: University of London, Athlone Press, 1959.

Griffis, William E. *Corea: The Hermit Nation.* New York: Charles Scribner's Sons, 1907.

Habberton, William. *Anglo-Russian Relations Concerning Afghanistan, 1837-1907.* Illinois Studies in the Social Sciences, vol. 21, no. 4. Urbana: University of Illinois Press, 1937.

Haddo, Gordon. "The Rise and Fall of the Progressive Party of Korea." *Chautauquan* 16 (1892–1893): 46–49.

Han Woo-keun (Han U-gŭn). *The History of Korea.* Seoul: Eul-Yoo Publishing Co., 1970.

————. "Shufeldt chedok ŭi Han-Mi suho choyak kyosŏp ch'ujin yŏnyu e taehayŏ" [A study on the reasons for sending Commodore Shufeldt to open negotiations with Korea in 1880]. *Chindan Hakpo* 24 (August 1963): 7–22.

Hao, Yen-p'ing. "A Study of the Ch'ing-liu Tang: The 'Disinterested' Scholar-official Groups (1875–1884)." *Papers on China* (Cambridge, Mass,: East Asian Research Center, Harvard University), no. 16 (December 1962): 40–65.

Harrington, Fred Harvey. "An American View of Korean-American Relations, 1882-1905." In *One Hundred Years of Korean-American Relations,*

*1882–1982*, edited by Yur-Bok Lee and Wayne Patterson, pp. 46–67. University, Alabama: University of Alabama Press, 1986.

———. *God, Mammon, and the Japanese: Dr. Horace N. Allen and Korean-American Relations, 1884–1905*. Madison: University of Wisconsin Press, 1944.

Hatada Takashi. *A History of Korea*. Translated and edited by Warren W. Smith, Jr., and Benjamin H. Hazard. Santa Barbara, Calif.: American Bibliographical Center, Clio Press, 1969.

Henderson, Gregory. *Korea: The Politics of the Vortex*. Cambridge: Harvard University Press, 1968.

Hō Takushu. *Meiji shoki Nis-sen kankei no kenkyū* [Japanese-Korean relations in the early Meiji period]. Tokyo: Hanawa Shobō, 1969.

Hong So-min. *Yŏgŏl Minbi* [A great woman Queen Min]. Seoul: Samjungdang, 1958.

Hsü, Immanuel C. Y. *The Ili Crisis: A Study of Sino-Russian Diplomacy, 1871–1881*. Oxford: Oxford Universtiy Press, 1965.

Hsü, Shu-hsi. *China and Her Political Entity: A Study of China's Foreign Policy with Reference to Korea, Manchuria, and Mongolia*. New York and London: Oxford University Press, 1926.

Hsüeh Fu-ch'eng. *Hsüeh Fu-ch'eng ch'üan-chi* [Complete works of Hsüeh Fu-ch'eng]. 3 vols. Reprint. Taipei: Kwang-wen, 1963.

Hulbert, Homer B. "Baron von Möllendorff." *Korean Review* 1 (1901): 245–252.

Hunt, Michael H. *The Making of a Special Relationship: The United States and China to 1914*. New York: Columbia University Press, 1983.

Hwang Hyŏn. *Maech'ŏn yarok* [Unofficial records of Korean history, 1864–1910]. Han'guk saryo ch'ongsŏ, no. 1. Seoul: Kuksa p'yŏnch'an wiwŏnhoe, 1955.

Hwang, In Kwan. "A Translation and Critical Review of Yu Kil-chun's *On Neutrality*." *Korean Studies* 9 (1985): 1–13.

———. *The Neutralized Unification of Korea*. Cambridge: Schenkman Publishing Co., 1980.

———. *The Korean Reform Movement of the 1880s: A Study of Transition in Intra-Asian Relations*. Cambridge: Schenkman Publishing Co., 1978.

Hyŏn Kyu-hwan. *Han'guk yuimin sa* [A history of Korean wanderers and emigrants]. 2 vols. Seoul: Ŏmungak, 1967.

Inaba Iwakichi. *Kōkaikun jidai no Man-Sen kankei* [Manchu-Korean relations during Prince Kwanghae's reign]. Keijō: Osakayago shoten, 1933.

Inoue kō denki hensankai. *Seiai Inouekō den* [Biography of Marquis Inoue Kaoru]. 5 vols. Tokyo: Naigai shoseki kabushiki kaisha, 1934.

Ishikawa Mikiakira. *Fukuzawa Yukichi den* [A biography of Fukuzawa Yukichi]. 4 vols. Tokyo: Iwanami shōten, 1932.

Itō Hirobumi, ed. *Chōsen koshō shiryō* [Materials on Korean intercourse]. 3 vols. Tokyo: Hisho ruisan kankōkai, 1936.

Japan. Chōsen Sōtokufu [Government general in Korea]. *Chōsen shi* [History of Korea]. 37 vols. Edited by *Chōsen shi henshukai*. Keijō: Chōsen Sōtokufu, 1932–40.

Japan. Ministry of Foreign Affairs (Gaimushō). *Nihon gaikō bunsho* [Japanese diplomatic documents]. 33 vols. Tokyo: Japanese Association for the League of Nations, 1936–1956.

Jones, Francis. "Foreign Diplomacy in Korea, 1886–1894." Ph.D. diss., Harvard University, 1935.

Jones, G. H. "His Majesty the King of Korea." *Korean Repository* 3 (November 1896): 423–430.

Kang, W. J. "Early Korean Contact with Christianity and Korean Response." In *Korea's Response to the West*, edited by Yung-hwan Jo, pp. 43–56. Kalamazoo, Mich.: The Korean Research and Publications, 1971.

Kazemzadeh, Firuz. "Russia and the Middle East." In *Russian Foreign Policy: Essays in Historical Perspective*, edited by Ivo J. Lederer, pp. 492–514. New Haven: Yale University Press, 1962.

Kiernan, E. V. G. *British Diplomacy in China, 1880–1885*. Cambridge: The University Press, 1939.

Kikuchi Kenjō. *Kindai Chōsen shi* [History of modern Korea]. 2 vols. Tokyo: Tairiku kenkyūsho, 1940.

————. *Taiinkun den, fu: Ōhi no isshō* [Life of the Taewŏn'gun, with supplement: life of the queen]. Keijō: Nikkan shobō, 1910.

Kim, C. I. Eugene, and Han-kyo Kim. *Korea and the Politics of Imperialism. 1876–1910*. Berkeley: University of California Press, 1967.

Kim Chŏng-myŏng, ed. *Nikkan gaikō shiryō shūsei* [Collection of sources of diplomatic relations between Japan and Korea]. 7 vols. Tokyo: Gannandō, 1962–1966.

Kim, Dalchoong. "Korea's Quest for Reform and Diplomacy in the 1880's: With Special Reference to Chinese Intervention and Controls." Ph.D. diss., Fletcher School of Law and Diplomacy, 1972.

Kim Hong-jip. *Susinsa ilgi* [Diary of Kim Hong-jip mission to Japan]. In *Susinsa Kirok* [Records of envoys]. Seoul: Kuksa p'yŏnch'an wiwŏnhoe, 1958.

————. *Kim Hong-jip yugo* [Writings of Kim Hong-jip]. Edited by Koryŏ taehakkyo chung'ang tosŏgwan. Seoul: Koryŏ University Press, 1976.

Kim, Key-Hiuk. *The Last Phase of the East Asian World Order: Korea, Japan, and the Chinese Empire, 1860–1882*. Berkeley and Los Angeles: University of California Press, 1980.

Kim Ok-kyun. *Kapsin illok* [Diary of Kim Ok-kyun]. Edited by Cho Il-mun. Reprint ed. Seoul: Kŏn'guk University Press, 1977.

Kim Si-t'ae. "Hwang Chun-hŏn ŭi Chosŏn ch'aeknyak i Hammal Chŏngguk-e kkich'in yŏnghyang" [The impact of Hwang Chun-hŏn's "A Policy for Korea" on the Korean political situation]. *Sach'ong* 8 (November 1963): 81–89.

Kim Sŏk-hyŏng, et al., *Kim Ok-kyun*. Edited by the Institute of History, Academy of Social Sciences, the Democratic People's Republic of Korea. P'yŏngyang: Sahoe kwahakwŏn ch'ulpansa, 1964.

Kim Sŏng-ch'il. "Yŏnhaeng sogo: Cho-Chung kyosŏp ŭi ilgu" [A short study of missions to Peking: an aspect of Korean-Chinese relations]. *Yŏksa Hakpo* 12 (May 1960): 1–79.

Kim, Tai-jin, ed. and trans. *A Bibliographical Guide to Traditional Korean Sources.* Seoul: Asiatic Research Center, Korea University, 1976.

Kim Tong-jin. "Chae-Ro tongp'o ŭi kwakŏ hyŏnjae" [The past and the present of our compatriots in Russia]. *Shin tong-a,* no. 9 (September 1932): 21–29.

Kim Wŏn-mo. *Kŭndae Han-Mi kyosŏpsa* [The recent history of Korean-American relations]. Seoul: Hongsŏngsa, 1979.

———. "Ch'ogi Han-Mi kyosŏp ŭi chŏn'gye, 1852–66" [American contacts with Korea: early Korean-American relations, 1852–66]. *Tang'guk taehakgyo nonmunjip* 10 (December 1977): 93–121.

———. "American 'Good Offices' in Korea." *Journal of Social Sciences and Humanities* 41 (June 1975): 93–139.

Kim Yong-gi. "Chosŏn ch'ogi ŭi tae-Myŏng chogong kwan'gye ko" [A study of tributary relations with the Ming in the early Yi period]. *Pusandae nonmunjip* 14 (1972): 131–182.

Kim Yŏng-ho. "Hanmal sŏyang ki sul ŭi suyong" [The acculturation of Western techniques in the late period of the Yi dynasty]. *Asea Yŏn'gu* 31 (September 1968): 295–343.

———. "Yu Kil-chun ŭi kaehwa sasang" [The enlightened thought of Yu Kil-chun]. *Ch'angjak kwa pip'yŏng* 11 (Fall 1968): 476–492.

Kim Yŏng-jak. *Kan-matsu nashonarizumu no kenkyū* [A study of nationalism of the late Yi Korea]. Tokyo: Tokyo University Press, 1975.

Kim Yun-sik. *Ŭmch'ŏngsa* [Diary of Kim Yun-sik]. Seoul: Kuksa p'yŏnch'an wiwŏnhoe, 1958.

———. *Unyangjip* [Collected writings of Kim Yun-sik]. 8 vols. Edited by Hwang Pyŏng-uk, 1913.

Kim, Yung-Chung, "The Kŏmundo Incident, 1885–1887: An Early Phase in British Korean Relations." *Korean Observer, a Quarterly Journal* 15, no. 3 (Autumn 1984): 301–330.

———. "Anglo-Russian Crisis and Port Hamilton, 1885–1887." *Han'guk munhwa Yŏn'gusŏ nonch'ong* 18 (1971): 243–266.

———. "Great Britain and Korea, 1883–1887." Ph.D. diss., Indiana University, 1965.

King, Paul. *In the Chinese Customs Service.* Rev. ed. London: Heath Cranton, 1930.

Ko Pyŏng-ik. *Tonga kyosŏpsa ŭi yŏn'gu* [Studies on the history of East Asian interrelations]. Seoul: Seoul National University Press, 1970.

———. Chosŏn hae'gwan kwa Ch'ŏngguk hae'gwan kwa ŭi kwan'gye—Merrill kwa Hart rŭl chungsim ŭro" [The relationship between the Korean and Chinese Customs Service: Merrill and Hart]. *Tonga Munhwa* 4 (October 1965): 1–30.

———. "Mok In-dŏk ŭi kobinggwa kŭ paegyŏng" [Background of von Möllendorff's employment]. *Chindan Hakpo* 25/27 (December 1964): 225–244.

———. "Mok In-dŏk ŭi sugi" [Möllendorff's diary], *Chindan Hakpo* 24 (August 1963): 149–196.

Kokin Kinenkai. *Kin Kyoku-kin den* [Biography of Kim Ok-kyun]. Tokyo: Keiō Shuppan sha, 1944.

Kolarz, Walter. *The Peoples of the Soviet Far East.* New York: Praeger, 1954.

Komatsu Midori, ed. *Itō Hirobumi den* [Biography of Itō Hirobumi]. 3 vols. Tokyo: Shumpokō tsuishōkai, 1940.

Korea (Republic of). Minister of Public Information, ed. *Thus Neutralization Is Impossible for Korea.* Seoul: Ministry of Public Information, 1965.

Korea (Yi dynasty). *Ch'ŏljong sillok* [Annals of King Ch'ŏljong]. In *Chosŏn Wangjo sillok* [Annals of the Yi dynasty]. Seoul: Kuksa p'yŏnch'an wiwŏnhoe, 1955–1958.

————. *Chosŏn Wangjo sillok* [Annals of the Yi dynasty]. 48 vols. Seoul: Kuksa p'yŏnch'an wiwŏnhoe, 1955–1958; Index, 1963.

————. *Hŏnjong sillok* [Annals of King Hŏnjong]. In *Chosŏn Wangjo sillok.* Seoul: Kuksa p'yŏnch'an wiwŏnhoe, 1955–1958.

————. *Ilsŏngnok* [Royal diary of the Yi dynasty]. Seoul: Seoul National University Press, 1967–1972.

————. *Kojong sidaesa* [History of the Kojong era]. 6 vols. Seoul: Kuksa p'yŏnch'an wiwŏnhoe, 1970–1972.

————. *Kojong sillok* [Annals of King Kojong]. In *Chosŏn Wangjo sillok.* Seoul: Kuksa p'yŏnch'an wiwŏnhoe, 1955–58.

————. *Ku Han'guk oegyo munsŏ* [Diplomatic documents of the late Yi dynasty]. 22 vols. Compiled by Asiatic Research Center, Korea University. Seoul: Asiatic Research Center of Korea University, 1965–1970. Documents consulted: *Ku Han'guk oegyo munsŏ: Aan* [Diplomatic documents of the late Yi dynasty: Russian archives]; *Ku Han'guk oegyo munsŏ: Ch'ŏngan* [Diplomatic documents of the late Yi dynasty: Chinese archives]; *Ku Han'guk oegyo munsŏ: Ilan* [Diplomatic documents of the late Yi dynasty: Japanese archives]; *Ku Han'guk oegyo munsŏ: Mian* [Diplomatic documents of the late Yi dynasty: American archives]; *Ku Han'guk oegyo munsŏ: Tōgan* [Diplomatic documents of the late Yi dynasty: German archives]; and *Ku Han'guk oegyo munsŏ: Yŏngan* [Diplomatic documents of the late Yi dynasty: British archives].

————. *Ku Hanmal choyak hwich'an* [Treaties of the late Yi dynasty]. Seoul: Kukhoe tosŏgwan, 1965.

————. *Ku Hanmal oegyo munsŏ: Miguk kwan'gyep'yŏn* [Diplomatic documents of the late Yi dynasty: relations with the United States]. Edited by Ministry of Foreign Affairs, Republic of Korea. Seoul: Ministry of Foreign Affairs, 1960.

————. *Pibyŏngsa tŭngnok* [Records of the defense council]. Edited by Kuksa p'yŏnch'an wiwŏnhoe. Seoul: Tongguk munhwasa, 1959.

————. *Sŭngjŏngwŏn ilgi* [Diary of the royal secretariat]. Edited by Kuksa p'yŏnch'an wiwŏnhoe. Seoul: Kwangmyŏng insoegongsa, 1968.

————. *Sunjo sillok* [Annals of King Sunjo]. In *Chosŏn Wangjo sillok.* Seoul: Kuksa p'yŏnch'an wiwŏnhoe, 1955–1958.

Krasny Archiv. "First Steps of Russian Imperialism in Far East, 1888–1903: Proceedings of the Meeting of the Special Committee, Held May 8

(April 26), 1888." *Chinese Social and Political Science Review* 18, no. 2 (1934–1935): 236–281.

Kuksa p'yŏnch'an wiwŏnhoe, ed. *Susinsa kirok* [Records of envoys]. Seoul: Kuksa p'yŏnch'an wiwŏnhoe, 1958.

Kuo Ting-i. "Chung-kuo yu ti-i-chih Mei-Han t'iao-yüeh" [China and the first United States–Korean Treaty]. *Chung-kuo wai-chiao-shih lun-chi* [Symposium on Chinese diplomatic history], edited by Huang Tsen-ming, et al. Taipei: Chung-yang wen-wu kung-ying-she, 1975.

Kuzu Yoshihisa. *Tōa senkaku shishi kiden* [Records of pioneer East Asian adventurers]. 3 vols. Tokyo: Kokuryūkai, 1933–1936.

Kwak, Tae-Hwan, John Chay, Soon Sung Cho, and Shannon McCune. *U.S.–Korean Relations, 1882–1982*. Seoul: Kyungnam University Press, 1982.

Kwon, Moo-Soo. "British Policy towards Korea, 1882–1910." Ph.D. diss., University of Sheffield, 1979.

Kwŏn Sŏk-pong. "Imo gunbyŏn" [The 1882 soldiers' revolt]. In *Han'guksa* [History of Korea], edited by Ch'oe Yŏng'hŭi, et al., 16:392–441. Seoul: Kuksa p'yŏnch'an wiwŏnhoe, 1975.

———. "Yi Hong-chang ŭi tae-Chosŏn yŏlguk ibyak kwŏndoch'aek e tae-hayŏ" [On Li Hung-chang's policy of inducing Korea to sign treaties with powers]. *Yŏksa Hakpo* 21 (August 1963): 101–130.

*Kyujanggak tosŏ, Han'gukpon ch'ongmongnok* [Catalogue of Korean books and manuscripts in the Kyujanggak collection]. Seoul: Institute of Asian Studies, Seoul National University, 1965.

Laffey, Ella S. "Relations between Chinese Provincial Officials and the Black Flag Army, 1883–1885." Ph.D. diss., Cornell University, 1971.

Laing, S. "Peace with Russia." *Fortnightly Review* 43 (June 1885): 869–878.

Langer, William Leonard. *The Diplomacy of Imperialism*. New York: Alfred A. Knopf, 1935.

———. *European Alliance and Alignments, 1871–1890*. Reprint. New York: Alfred A. Knopf, 1966.

Lawrence, Mary V. T. *A Diplomat's Helpmate: How Rose F. Foote, Wife of the First United States Minister and Envoy Extraordinary to Korea, Served Her Country in the Far East*. San Francisco: H. S. Crocker Co., 1918.

Ledyard, Gari. *The Dutch Come to Korea: An Account of the Life of the First Westerners in Korea, 1653–1666*. Seoul: Royal Asiatic Society, Korea Branch, 1971.

Lee, Chong-sik. *The Politics of Korean Nationalism*. Berkeley and Los Angeles: University of California Press, 1963.

Lee, Yur-Bok. "Korean-American Diplomatic Relations, 1882–1905." In *One Hundred Years of Korean-American Relations, 1882–1982*, edited by Yur-Bok Lee and Wayne Patterson, pp. 12–45. University, Ala.: University of Alabama Press, 1986.

———. *Establishment of a Korean Legation in the United States, 1887–1890: A Study of Conflict between Confucian World Order and Modern International Relations*. Illinois Papers in Asian Studies, vol. 3. Urbana, Ill.: Center for Asian Studies, University of Illinois, 1983.

———. "P. G. Von Möllendorff and the First Secret Russo-Korean Agreement of 1885." In *Proceedings of the Southwest Conference for Asian Studies*, pp. 90–107. New Orleans, Louisiana, 1980.

———. *Diplomatic Relations between the United States and Korea, 1866–1887*. New York: Humanities Press, 1970.

Lee, Yur-Bok, and Wayne Patterson, eds. *One Hundred Years of Korean-American Relations, 1882–1982*. University, Ala.: University of Alabama Press, 1986.

Leifer, Walter. "Paul-Georg von Möllendorff–Scholar and Statesman." *Transactions of the Royal Asiatic Society, Korea Branch* 57 (1982): 41–52.

Lensen, George Alexander. *Balance of Intrigue: International Rivalry in Korea and Manchuria, 1884–1899*. 2 vols. Tallahassee: University Presses of Florida, 1982.

———. *Russia's Japan Expedition of 1852 to 1855*. Gainesville: University of Florida Press, 1955.

Lew, Young-ick. "Yüan Shih-k'ai's Residency and the Korean Enlightenment Movement, 1885–94." *Journal of Korean Studies* 5 (1984): 63–107.

———. "The Shufeldt Treaty and Early Korean-American Interaction, 1882–1905." In *After One Hundred Years: Continuity and Change in Korean-American Relations*, edited by Sung-joo Han, pp. 3–27. Seoul: Asiatic Research Center, Korea University, 1982.

———. "American Advisers in Korea, 1885–1894." In *The United States and Korea: American-Korean Relations, 1866–1976*, edited by Andrew C. Nahm, pp. 64–90. Kalamazoo, Mich.: Center for Korean Studies, Western Michigan University, 1979.

Li En-han. *Tseng Ch'i-tse ti wai-chiao* [Diplomacy of Tseng Ch'i-tse]. Taipei: Shang-wu, 1966.

Li Hung-chang. *Li Wen-chung-kung ch'üan-shu* [Complete works of Li Hung-chang]. Edited by Wu Ju-lun. 100 vols. Published by the Li family, Nanking, 1908. Documents consulted: *Li Wen-chung-kung ch'üan-shu: Hai-chün han-kao* [Complete works of Li Hung-chang: Letters to Navy Office]; *Li Wen-chung-kung ch'üan-shu: I-shu han-kao* [Complete works of Li Hung-chang: Letters to the Tsungli Yamen (Foreign Office)]; *Li Wen-chung-kung ch'üan-shu: Peng-liao han-kao* [Complete works of Li Hung-chang: Letters to friends and colleagues]; *Li Wen-chung-kung ch'üan-shu: Tien-kao* [Complete works of Li Hung-chang: Telegrams]; and *Li Wen-chung-kung ch'üan-shu: Tsou-kao* [Complete works of Li Hung-chang: Memorials].

Lin Ming-te. *Yüan Shih-k'ai yü Chao-hsien* [Yüan Shih-k'ai and Korea]. Taipei: Institute of Modern History, Academia Sinica, 1970.

Lin, T. C. "Li Hung-chang: His Korea Policies." *Chinese Social and Political Science Review* 19 (July 1935): 202–233.

Lo Kye-hyŏn. *Han'guk oegyosa yŏn'gu* [Studies on Korean diplomatic history]. Seoul: Haemunsa, 1967.

Ma Chien-chung. *Tung-hsing san-lu* [Records of three trips to Korea]. Reprint. Taipei: Kwang-wen, 1967.

McAleavy, Henry. *Black Flags in Vietnam: The Story of a Chinese Intervention.* New York: Macmillan, 1968.

McCune, George M. "Korean Relations with China and Japan, 1800–1864." Ph.D. diss., University of California, Berkeley, 1941.

McCune, George M. and John A. Harrison, eds. *Korean-American Relations, Documents Pertaining to the Far Eastern Diplomacy of the United States.* Vol. 1: *The Initial Period, 1883–1886.* Berkeley and Los Angeles: University of California Press, 1951.

Macdonald, Donald Ross Hazelton. "Russian Interest in Korea to 1895: The Pattern of Russia's Emerging Interest in the Peninsula from the Late Seventeenth Century to the Sino-Japanese War." Ph.D. diss., Harvard University, 1957.

Majumdar, R. C., H. C. Raychaundhuri, and Kalikinkar Datta. *An Advanced History of India.* 2nd ed. New York: St. Martins Press, 1960.

McGrane, George A. *Korea's Tragic Hours: The Closing Years of the Yi Dynasty.* Edited by Harold F. Cook and Alan M. MacDougall. Seoul: Taewon Publishing Co., 1973.

Malozemoff, Andrew. *Russian Far Eastern Policy, 1881–1904: With Special Emphasis on the Causes of the Russo-Japanese War.* Berkeley and Los Angeles: University of California Press, 1958.

Min T'ae-wŏn. *Kapsin chŏngbyŏn'gwa Kim Ok-kyun* [The *Kapsin* Coup and Kim Ok-kyun]. Seoul: Kukche munhwa hyŏphoe, 1947.

Möllendorff, Paul Georg von. "A Reply to Mr. O. N. Denny's Pamphlet Entitled: 'China and Korea'." In *P. G. von Mollendorff: Ein Lebensbild,* by Rosalie von Möllendorff, pp. 125–136. Leipzig: Otto Harrassowitz, 1930.

———. *Ningpo Colloquial Handbook.* Edited by Rev. G. W. Sheppard. Shanghai: American Presbyterian Mission Press, 1910.

———. *Catalogue of P. G. von Möllendorff's Library.* Shanghai: American Presbyterian Mission Press, 1905.

———. "Essay on Manchu Literature." *Journal of the China Branch of the Royal Asiatic Society* 24 (1889–1890): 1–45.

———. *The Family Law of the Chinese.* Shanghai: Kelly and Walsh, 1896.

———. "The Ghilyak Language." *The Chinese Review* 21 (1894): 141–146.

———. *A Manchu Grammar with Analysed Texts.* Shanghai: American Presbyterian Mission Press, 1892.

———. Trans. *A Systematical Digest of the Doctrines of Confucius,* by Ernest Faber. Hongkong: China Mail Office, 1875.

———. *Catalogue of Manchu Library.* N.p., n. d. Available at the Library of Congress, Washington, D.C.

Möllendorff, Paul Georg von, and O. F. von Möllendorff. *Manual of Chinese Bibliography: Being a List of Works and Essays Relating to China.* Shanghai: Kelly and Walsh; London: Trübner and Co., Ludgate Hill; and Görlitz, Germany: H. Tzschaschel, 1876.

Möllendorff, Rosalie von. *P. G. von Möllendorff: Ein Lebensbild.* Leipzig: Otto Harrassowitz, 1930.

Morrison, Elting E., John M. Blum, and Alfred D. Chandler, Jr., eds. *The Letters of Theodore Roosevelt.* 8 vols. Cambridge: Harvard University Press, 1951–1954.

Morley, James William. "The Dynamics of the Korean Connection." In *After One Hundred Years: Continuity and Change in Korean-American Relations,* edited by Sung-jo Han, pp. 271–292. Seoul: Asiatic Research Center, Korea University, 1982.

Morse, Hosea B. *The International Relations of the Chinese Empire.* 3 vols. London and New York: Longmans and Green, 1910–1918.

Mun Il-p'yŏng. *Han-Mi osipnyŏnsa* [Fifty-year history of Korean-American relations]. Seoul: Chogwangsa, 1945. Reprint, edited by Yi Kwang-rin. Seoul: T'amgudang, 1975.

Na Man-gap. *Pyŏngja rok* [Record on Manchu invasion of 1636]. Seoul: Chŏngŭmsa, 1947.

Nahm, Andrew Chang-woo. "American-Korean Relations, 1866–1876, An Overview." In *The United States and Korea: American-Korean Relations, 1866–1976,* edited by Andrew C. Nahm, pp. 9–26. Kalamazoo, Mich.: Center for Korean Studies, Western Michigan University, 1979.

————. "Durham White Stevens and the Japanese Annexation of Korea." In *The United States and Korea: American-Korean Relations, 1866–1976,* edited by Andrew C. Nahm, pp. 110–136. Kalamazoo, Mich.: Center for Korean Studies, Western Michigan University, 1979.

————. "Reaction and the Response to the Opening of Korea, 1876–1884." In *Korea's Reponse to the West,* edited by Yung-hwan Jo, pp. 141–162. Kalamazoo, Mich: Korean Research Publication, Inc., 1970.

————. "Kim Ok-kyun and the Korean Progressive Movement, 1882–1884." Ph.D. diss., Stanford University, 1961.

Narochnitsky, A. L. *Kolonial Nai Politika Kapitalisticheskikh Derzh na Dalnem Vostoke, 1860–1895* [Colonial policy of capitalistic countries in the Far East, 1860–1895]. Moscow: Academia Nauk S.S.S.R., Institute Vostokoviendieniya, 1956.

Nelson, M. Frederick. *Korea and the Old Orders in Eastern Asia.* Baton Rouge: Louisiana State University Press, 1945. Reprint. New York: Russell & Russell, 1967.

Noble, Harold J. "Korea and Her Relations with the United States before 1895." Ph.D. diss., University of California, Berkeley, 1931.

————. "The Korean Mission to the United States in 1883: The First Embassy sent by Korea to an Occidental Nation." *Transactions of the Royal Asiatic Society, Korean Branch* 18 (1929): 1–21.

Ŏ Yun-jung. *Chongjŏng yŏnp'yo* [Diary of Ŏ Yun-jung]. Han'guk saryŏ ch'ongsŏ, No. 6. Seoul: Kuksa p'yŏnch'an wiwŏnhoe, 1958.

Ōkubo Toshimichi, ed. *Ōkubo Toshimichi bunshō* [Ōkubo Toshimichi documents]. 10 vols. Tokyo: Nihon Shiseki kyōkai, 1927–1931.

————. *Ōkubo Toshimichi nikki* [Diary of Ōkubo Toshimichi]. 2 vols. Tokyo: Nihon Shiseki kyōkai, 1927.

Okudaira Takehiko. *Chōsen kaikoku kōshō shimatsu* [A complete account of the negotiations leading to the opening of Korea]. Reprint. Tokyo: Tōkō shoin, 1969.

Ōmachi Keigetsu. *Hakushaku Gotō Shōjirō den* [Biography of Count Gotō Shōjirō]. Tokyo: Fuzambo, 1914.

Pae, Jae Schick. "The Historical Background to the Development of International Law in Korea." In *Korean International Law,* edited by Jae Schick Pae, Nam Yearl Chai, and Choon-ho Park, pp. 1–4. Korean Research Monograph No. 4. Berkeley: Institute of East Asian Studies, University of California, 1981.

Pae, Jae Schick, Nam-Yearl Chai, and Choon-ho Park. *Korean International Law.* Korean Research Monograph No. 4. Berkeley: Institute of East Asian Studies, University of California, 1981.

Paek Chong-gi, *Han'guk Kŭndaesa yŏn'gu* [Studies on Korean recent history]. Seoul: Pakyŏngsa, 1981.

Pai Chiao, ed. *Yüan Shih-k'ai yü Chung-hua min-kuo* [Yüan Shih-k'ai and the Republic of China]. Reprint. Taipei: Wen-hai, 1966.

Paik, L. George. *The History of Protestant Mission in Korea, 1832–1910.* 2nd ed. Seoul: Yonsei University Press, 1971.

Pak, B. D. *Rossia i Korea* [Russia and Korea]. Moscow: Academia Nauk S.S.S.R., Institute Vostokoviedieniya, 1979.

Pak Chun-gyu. "Hanmal ŭi taeoe kwan'gye: 1880 nyŏndae ŭi yŏlguk ŭi taehan chŏngch'aek ŭl chungsim ŭro" [Foreign relations of the late Yi dynasty: with special reference to big powers' policies toward Korea]. *Kukche Chŏngch'i nonch'ong* 1 (1963): 5–47.

Pak Il-gŭn. *Mi'guk ŭi kae'guk chŏngch'aek kwa Han-Mi oegyo kwan'gye* [American open door policy and Korean-American relations]. Seoul: Ilchogak, 1981.

―――. *Kŭndae Han-Mi oegyosa* [A modern diplomatic history of America and Korea]. Seoul: Pakusa, 1968.

Pak, M. N. (with Wayne Patterson). "Russian Policy toward Korea before and during the Sino-Japanese War of 1894–1895." *Journal of Korean Studies* 5 (1984): 109–119.

Pak Yŏng-hyo. "Kaehwa e taehan sangso" [Memorial on enlightenment]. Supplement to *Sindonga* (January 1966): 12–23.

―――. *Sahwakiryak* [Diary of Pak Yŏng-hyo Mission to Japan]. In *Susinsa kirok* [Records of envoys], edited by Kuksa p'yŏnch'an wiwŏnhoe. Seoul: Kuksa p'yŏnch'an wiwŏnhoe, 1958.

Palais, James B. "Political Leadership in the Yi Dynasty." In *Political Leadership in Korea,* edited by Dae-sook Suh and Chae-jin Lee, pp. 3–38. Seattle: University of Washington Press, 1976.

―――. *Politics and Policy in Traditional Korea.* Cambridge: Harvard University Press, 1975.

Palmer, Spencer J., ed. *Korean-American Relations: Documents Pertaining to the Far Eastern Diplomacy of the United States.* Vol. 2, *The Period of Growing Influence, 1887–1895.* Berkeley and Los Angeles: University of California Press, 1963.

Pao Tsun-peng, Li Ting-i, and Wu Hsiang-hsiang, eds. *Chung-kuo chin-tai-shih lun-tsung* [A collection of writings on modern Chinese history]. Taipei: Chen-chung, 1956.

Parker, Edward Harper. "The Manchu Relations with Corea." *Transactions of the Royal Asiatic Society, Japan Branch* 15 (1887): 93–95.

Patterson, Wayne. *The Korean Frontier in America: Immigration to Hawaii, 1896–1910.* Honolulu: University of Hawaii Press, 1988.

———. "Japanese Imperialism in Korea: A Study of Immigration and Foreign Policy." In *Japan in Transition: Thought and Action in the Meiji Era, 1868–1912,* edited by Hilary Conroy, Sandra T. W. Davis, and Wayne Patterson. Madison, N.J.: Fairleigh Dickinson University Press, 1984.

Patterson, Wayne, and Hilary Conroy. "Duality and Dominance: A Century of Korean-American Relations." In *One Hundred Years of Korean-American Relations, 1882–1982,* edited by Yur-Bok Lee and Wayne Patterson, pp. 1–11. University, Ala.: University of Alabama Press, 1986.

"Port Hamilton." *The Spector* 59 (January 1886): 1088–1089.

"The Ports and Trades of Corea." *The Edinburg Review* 162 (July 1885): 265–285.

Ramm, Agatha, ed. *The Political Correspondence of Mr. Gladstone and Lord Granville, 1876–1886.* 2 vols. Oxford: Oxford University Press, 1962.

Reischauer, Edwin O. *Wanted: An Asian Policy.* New York: Alfred A. Knopf, 1955.

Reordan, Robert E. "The Role of George Clayton Foulk in United States–Korean Relations, 1884–1887." Ph.D. diss., Fordham University, 1955.

Rosen, Baron. *Forty Years of Diplomacy.* London: G. Allen and Unwin; New York: Alfred A. Knopf, 1922.

Sands, William F. *Undiplomatic Memories: The Far East, 1896–1904.* New York: Whittlesley House, 1930.

———. "Korea and the Korean Emperor." *Century* 69 (1905): 577–584.

Senn, Alfred Erich. *Readings in Russian Political and Diplomatic History.* Vol. 1, *The Tsarist Period.* Vol. 2, *The Soviet Period.* Homewood, Ill.: Dorsey Press, 1966.

Seton-Watson, Hugh. *The Decline of Imperial Russia, 1855–1914.* New York: Frederick A. Praeger, 1960.

Shen Tsu-hsien and Wu K'ai-sheng. *Jung-an ti-tzu-chi* [Records kept by the disciples of Jung-an (Yüan)]. Reprint. Taipei: Wen-hai, 1966.

Shen Yün-lung, ed. *Hsiangch'eng Yüan-shih chia-chi* [Family collections of the Yüan clan of Hsiangch'eng]. Taipei: Wen-hai, 1966.

———, ed. *Hsien-tai cheng-chih jen-wu shu-'p'ing* [A critical account of some political personalities of recent times]. Reprint. Taipei: Wen-hai, 1959.

Shinobu Seisaburō. *Kindai Nihon gaikō shi* [Diplomatic history of modern Japan]. Tokyo: Chūō Kōron sha, 1942.

Shippee, Lester B. "Thomas Francis Bayard." In *The American Secretaries of State and Their Diplomacy,* edited by Samuel Flagg Bemis, 8:47–106. 10 vols. New York: Pageant Book Co., 1958.

Shufeldt Robert W. "Opening of Korea: Admiral Shufeldt's Account of It."

Edited by Henry G. Appenzeller. *Korean Repository* 1 (February 1892): 57–62.

———. "Corea's Trouble." *San Francisco Chronicle.* October 30, 1887.

Sin Ki-sŏk. *Hanmal oegyosa yŏn'gu* [Studies on diplomatic history of the late Yi dynasty]. Seoul: Ilchogak, 1967.

Sin Kuk-chu. *Han'guk kŭndae chŏngch'i oegyosa* [Recent political and diplomatic history of Korea]. Seoul, T'amgudang, 1976.

———. *Kindai Chōsen gaikō shi kenkyū* [Studies on diplomatic history of modern Korea]. Tokyo: Yushindo Publishing Co., 1966.

———. *Kŭndae Chosŏn oegyosa yŏn'gu* [Studies on modern diplomatic history of Korea]. Seoul: T'amgudang, 1965.

Sin Sŏk-ho. "Chosŏn wangjo kaeguk tangsi ŭi tae-Myŏng kwan'ge" [Relations with the Ming at the time of the founding of the Yi dynasty]. *Kuksasang ŭi chemunje* 1 (1959): 93–134.

Stead, Alfred, ed. *Japan by the Japanese: A Study by Its Highest Authorities.* New York: Dodd and Mead, 1904.

Stephan, John J. "The Korean Minority in the Soviet Union." *Mizan* 13, no. 3 (1971): 139–150.

Swartout, Robert R., Jr., ed. *An American Adviser in Late Yi Korea: The Letters of Owen Nickerson Denny.* University, Ala.: University of Alabama Press, 1984.

———. "United States Ministers to Korea, 1882–1905: The Loss of American Innocence." *Transactions of the Royal Asiatic Society, Korea Branch* 57 (1982): 11–28.

———. *Mandarins, Gunboats, and Power Politics: Owen Nickerson Denny and the International Rivalries in Korea.* Asian Studies at Hawaii, No. 25. Honolulu: University Press of Hawaii, 1980.

———. "Cultural Conflict and Gunboat Diplomacy: The Development of the 1871 Korean-American Incident." *Journal of Social Sciences and Humanities* 43 (June 1976): 117–169.

Swisher, Earl. "The Adventures of Four Americans in Korea and Peking in 1855." *Pacific Historical Review* 21 (August 1952): 237–242.

———, ed. *China's Management of the American Barbarians: A Study of Sino-American Relations, 1841–1861, with Documents.* New Haven: Far Eastern Association, 1951.

Synn, Seung Kwon. *The Russo-Japanese Rivalry over Korea, 1876–1904.* Seoul: Yuk Phub Sa, 1981.

———. "The Russo-Korean Relations in the 1880s." *Korea Journal* 20, no. 9 (September 1980): 26–39.

———. "The Russo-Japanese Struggle for Control of Korea, 1894–1904." Ph.D. diss., Harvard University, 1967.

Tabohashi Kiyoshi. *Kindai Nissen kankei no kenkyū* [A study of modern Japanese-Korean relations]. 2 vols. Keijō: Chōsen sōtokufu chūsūin, 1940.

Tansill, Charles Callan. *The Foreign Policy of Thomas F. Bayard, 1885–1897.* New York: Fordham University Press, 1940.

Treadgold, Donald W. "Russia and the Far East." In *Russian Foreign Policy, Essays in Historical Perspectives,* edited by Ivo J. Lederer, pp. 531–574. New Haven: Yale University Press, 1962.

Treat, Payson J. *Diplomatic Relations between the United States and Japan, 1895–1905.* Stanford: Stanford University Press, 1938.

———. *Diplomatic Relations between the United States and Japan, 1853–1895.* 2 vols. Stanford: Stanford University Press, 1932.

Tsiang, Tingfu. "Sino-Japanese Diplomatic Relations, 1870–1894." *Chinese Social and Political Science Review* 17, no. 1 (April 1933): 1–106.

Underwood, Lillias H. *Underwood of Korea: Being an Intimate Record of the Life and Work of the Rev. H. G. Underwood.* New York: Fleming H. Revell Co., 1918.

United States. Congress. *Congressional Record.*

———. Department of State. *Papers Relating to the Foreign Relations of the United States.* Washington, D.C.: Government Printing Office, 1867–1888.

———. Historical Office. *A Historical Summary of United States–Korean Relations with a Chronology of Important Development, 1834–1962.* Washington, D.C.: Government Printing Office, 1962.

*United States Statutes at Large.* Washington, D.C.: Government Printing Office, 1850–1943.

Uyehara, Cecil H., comp. *Checklist of Archives in the Japanese Ministry of Foreign Affairs, Tokyo, Japan, 1868–1945.* Washington, D.C.: Library of Congress, 1954.

Varg, Paul A. *Open Door Diplomat: The Life of W. W. Rockhill.* Urbana: University of Illinois Press, 1952.

Vaya, Count Vay de and Luskod. *Empires and Emperors of Russia, China, Korea, and Japan.* New York: E. P. Dutton and Co., 1906.

Vinacke, Harold M. *A History of the Far East in Modern Times.* New York: Appleton-Century-Crofts, 1950.

Wagner, Edward W. "The First Century." In *Reflections on A Century of United States–Korean Relations, Conference Papers, June 1982,* pp. 17–27. Lanham, N.Y., and London: University Press of America for Academy of Korean Studies and the Wilson Center, 1983.

Walker, Hugh D. "The Yi-Ming Rapproachment: Sino-Korean Relations, 1392–1592." Ph.D. diss., University of California, Los Angeles, 1971.

Walter, Gary Dean. "1883 nyŏn Mihapchungguk e p'agyŏndoen tae Chosŏn'guk t'ukpyŏl sajŏltan e kwanhan yŏn'gu" [A study on the Korean special mission to the United States in 1883]. *Asea Hakpo* 6 (June 1969): 174–222.

———. "The Korean Special Mission to the United States of America in 1883." *Journal of Korean Studies* 1, no. 1 (1960): 89–142.

Wang Chung-chi. *Chung-Jih chang-cheng* [Sino-Japanese war]. Shanghai: Shangwu, 1929.

Wang Hsin-chung. *Chung-Jih chia-wu chang-cheng chih wai-chiao pei-ching* [Diplomatic background of the Sino-Japanese War]. Peking: National Tsing-hua University Press, 1937.

Wang Yen-wei, ed. *Ch'ing-chi wai-chiao shih-liao* [Sources of the diplomatic history toward the end of the Ch'ing dynasty: Kuang-hsü reign]. 111 vols. Peking: Wai-chiao shih-liao pien-ch'uan-shü, 1932–35.

Wang Yun-sheng, ed. *Liu-shih nien lai Chung-kuo yu Jih-pen* [Sino-Japanese relations for the past sixty years]. 7 vols. Tientsin: Ta-kung-pao, 1932.

Watanabe Ikujiro. *Meijishi Kenkyū* [A study of Meiji history]. Tokyo: Kyōritsu Shuppan, 1944.

Watanabe Katsumi. *Chōsen kaikoku gaikō shi kenkyū* [A study on the diplomatic history of the opening of Korea]. Keijō: Posŏng College, 1940.

Watanabe Shūjirō. *Tōhō kankei* [Korean-Japanese relations]. Tokyo: Nōkōtai, 1894.

Weinert, Richard P. "The Original KMAG." *Military Review* (June 1965): 93–99.

Won You-han (Wŏn Yu-han). "Chŏnhwan'guk ko" [A Study on the first modern Korean government mint]. *Yŏksa Hakpo* 37 (June 1968): 49–100.

Woo, Philip M. "The Historical Development of Korean Tariff and Customs Administration, 1875–1958." Ph.D. diss., New York University, 1963.

Woodside, Alexander B. *Vietnam and the Chinese Model: A Comparative Study of Nguyen and Ch'ing Civil Administration in the First Half of the Nineteenth Century.* Cambridge: Harvard University Press, 1971.

Wright, Mary C. "The Adaptability of Ch'ing Diplomacy: The Case of Korea." *Journal of Asian Studies* 17 (May 1958): 363–381.

Wright, Stanley F. *Hart and the Chinese Customs.* Belfast: William Mullen and Son, 1950.

Yamaguchi Masayuki. *Chōsen Seikyō shi: Chōsen Kirisutokyō no bunkashiteki kenkyū* [A history of Christianity in Korea: a cultural historical study of Korean Christianity]. Tokyo: Yūzankaku, 1967.

———. trans. and annot. "Yakuchū kō Shi-ei hankusho" [The letter of Hwang Sa-yŏng on silk cloth] *Chōsen gakuhō* 2 (1951): 121–145.

Yi Hyŏn-jong. "Ku Hanmal oegugin kobing ko" [A study on the invitation of foreign advisers during the late Yi dynasty]. *Han'guksa yŏn'gu* 8 (September 1972): 113–148.

Yi Ki-baek (Lee Ki-baek). *A New History of Korea.* Translated by Edward W. Wagner with Edward J. Shulta. Cambridge, Mass.: Harvard University Press, 1984.

———. *Han'guksa sillon* [New studies on Korean history]. Seoul: Ilchogak, 1967.

Yi Ki-ha. *Han'guk Chŏngdang paldalsa* [Historical development of Korean political parties]. Seoul: Ihoe Chŏngch'i Sa, 1960.

Yi Kwang-rin (Lee Kwang-rin). "Early Relations: Conflicting Images." In *Reflections on a Century of United States-Korean Relations, Conference Papers, June 1982.* Lanham, N.Y., and London: University Press of America for Academy of Korean Studies and the Wilson Center, 1983.

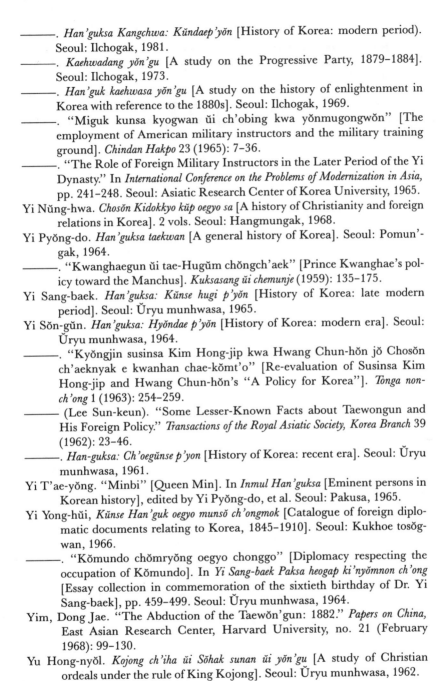

――――. *Han'guksa Kangchwa: Kŭndaep'yŏn* [History of Korea: modern period). Seoul: Ilchogak, 1981.

――――. *Kaehwadang yŏn'gu* [A study on the Progressive Party, 1879–1884]. Seoul: Ilchogak, 1973.

――――. *Han'guk kaehwasa yŏn'gu* [A study on the history of enlightenment in Korea with reference to the 1880s]. Seoul: Ilchogak, 1969.

――――. "Miguk kunsa kyogwan ŭi ch'obing kwa yŏnmugongwŏn" [The employment of American military instructors and the military training ground]. *Chindan Hakpo* 23 (1965): 7–36.

――――. "The Role of Foreign Military Instructors in the Later Period of the Yi Dynasty." In *International Conference on the Problems of Modernization in Asia*, pp. 241–248. Seoul: Asiatic Research Center of Korea University, 1965.

Yi Nŭng-hwa. *Chosŏn Kidokkyo kŭp oegyo sa* [A history of Christianity and foreign relations in Korea]. 2 vols. Seoul: Hangmungak, 1968.

Yi Pyŏng-do. *Han'guksa taekwan* [A general history of Korea]. Seoul: Pomun'-gak, 1964.

――――. "Kwanghaegun ŭi tae-Hugŭm chŏngch'aek" [Prince Kwanghae's policy toward the Manchus]. *Kuksasang ŭi chemunje* (1959): 135–175.

Yi Sang-baek. *Han'guksa: Kŭnse hugi p'yŏn* [History of Korea: late modern period]. Seoul: Ŭryu munhwasa, 1965.

Yi Sŏn-gŭn. *Han'guksa: Hyŏndae p'yŏn* [History of Korea: modern era]. Seoul: Ŭryu munhwasa, 1964.

――――. "Kyŏngjin susinsa Kim Hong-jip kwa Hwang Chun-hŏn jŏ Chosŏn ch'aeknyak e kwanhan chae-kŏmt'o" [Re-evaluation of Susinsa Kim Hong-jip and Hwang Chun-hŏn's "A Policy for Korea"]. *Tonga nonch'ong* 1 (1963): 254–259.

―――― (Lee Sun-keun). "Some Lesser-Known Facts about Taewongun and His Foreign Policy." *Transactions of the Royal Asiatic Society, Korea Branch* 39 (1962): 23–46.

――――. *Han-guksa: Ch'oegŭnse p'yon* [History of Korea: recent era]. Seoul: Ŭryu munhwasa, 1961.

Yi T'ae-yŏng. "Minbi" [Queen Min]. In *Inmul Han'guksa* [Eminent persons in Korean history], edited by Yi Pyŏng-do, et al. Seoul: Pakusa, 1965.

Yi Yong-hŭi, *Kŭnse Han'guk oegyo munsŏ ch'ongmok* [Catalogue of foreign diplomatic documents relating to Korea, 1845–1910]. Seoul: Kukhoe tosŏgwan, 1966.

――――. "Kŏmundo chŏmryŏng oegyo chonggo" [Diplomacy respecting the occupation of Kŏmundo]. In *Yi Sang-baek Paksa heogap ki'nyŏmnon ch'ong* [Essay collection in commemoration of the sixtieth birthday of Dr. Yi Sang-baek], pp. 459–499. Seoul: Ŭryu munhwasa, 1964.

Yim, Dong Jae. "The Abduction of the Taewŏn'gun: 1882." *Papers on China*, East Asian Research Center, Harvard University, no. 21 (February 1968): 99–130.

Yu Hong-nyŏl. *Kojong ch'iha ŭi Sŏhak sunan ŭi yŏn'gu* [A study of Christian ordeals under the rule of King Kojong]. Seoul: Ŭryu munhwasa, 1962.

————. *Han'guk Ch'ŏnjugyohoe sa* [A history of the Roman Catholic Church in Korea]. Seoul: K'atorik ch'ulpansa, 1962.

Yu Kil-chun. *Yu Kil-chun chŏnsŏ* [Complete works of Yu Kil-chun]. 5 vols. Seoul: Ilchogak, 1982.

Yü, Ying-shih. *Trade and Expansion in Han China: A Study of Sino-Barbarian Economic Relations.* Berkeley: University of California Press, 1967.

Yun Ch'i-ho. *Yun Ch'i-ho ilgi* [Diary of Yun Ch'i-ho]. 5 vols. Seoul: Kuksa P'yŏnch'an wiwŏnhoe, 1975.

# INDEX

# ABOUT THE AUTHOR

**Yur-Bok Lee** is professor of history at North Dakota State University, where he teaches modern East Asian and Russian history. He is the author of *Establishment of a Korean Legation in the United States, 1887–1890: A Study of Conflict between Confucian World Order and Modern International Relations* and *Diplomatic Relations between the United States and Korea, 1866–1887,* and editor (with Wayne Patterson) of and contributor to *One Hundred Years of Korea-American Relations, 1882–1982.*

**Production Notes**

This book was designed by Roger Eggers.
Composition and paging were done on the
Quadex Composing System and typesetting on
the Compugraphic 8400 by the design and
production staff of University of Hawaii Press.

The text and display typeface is Baskerville.

Offset presswork and binding were done by
Vail-Ballou Press, Inc. Text paper is Writers RR
Offset, basis 50.